The Figure of Knowledge

The Figure of Knowledge

Conditioning Architectural Theory, 1960s – 1990s

Edited by
Sebastiaan Loosen, Rajesh Heynickx,
and Hilde Heynen

Leuven University Press

Published with the support of the
KU Leuven Fund for Fair Open Access

Published in 2020 by Leuven University Press / Presses Universitaires de Louvain / Universitaire Pers Leuven. Minderbroedersstraat 4, B-3000 Leuven (Belgium).

Selection and editorial matter © Sebastiaan Loosen, Rajesh Heynickx, and Hilde Heynen, 2020
Individual chapters © The respective authors, 2020

This book is published under a Creative Commons Attribution Non-Commercial Non-Derivative 4.0 International Licence.

The license allows you to share, copy, distribute, and transmit the work for personal and non-commercial use providing author and publisher attribution is clearly stated. Attribution should include the following information:
Sebastiaan Loosen, Rajesh Heynickx, Hilde Heynen (eds.). *The Figure of Knowledge: Conditioning Architectural Theory, 1960s – 1990s*. Leuven, Leuven University Press. (CC BY-NC-ND 4.0)
Further details about Creative Commons licenses are available at http://creativecommons.org/licenses/

ISBN 978 94 6270 224 0 (Paperback)
ISBN 978 94 6166 322 1 (ePDF)
ISBN 978 94 6166 323 8 (ePUB)
https://doi.org/10.11116/9789461663221
D/2020/1869/31
NUR: 648

Layout: Crius Group
Cover design: Daniel Benneworth-Gray
Cover illustration: Superstudio, La moglie di Lot (Lot's Wife), Venice, 1978 © C Toraldo di Francia

Table of Contents

INTRODUCTION
The Shifting Contours of Postwar Architectural Theory   9
Sebastiaan Loosen, Rajesh Heynickx, and Hilde Heynen

SECTION 1
Modernism and its Discontents

CHAPTER 1
Meaning and Effect: Revisiting Semiotics in Architecture   31
André Loeckx and Hilde Heynen

CHAPTER 2
A Voice from the Margins: Robin Boyd and 1960s Architecture Culture   63
Philip Goad

CHAPTER 3
Contaminations: Art, Architecture, and the Critical Vision of Lara-Vinca Masini   81
Peter Lang

CHAPTER 4
Architecture Becomes Programming: Invisible Technicians, Printouts, and Situated Theories in the 1960s   101
Matthew Allen

CHAPTER 5
Troubled Dialogues: Intellectuality at a Crossroads at the *Carrefour de l'Europe* in Brussels   127
Sebastiaan Loosen

SECTION 2
Projects of Theory

CHAPTER 6
Institutionalized Critique? On the Re(birth) of Architectural Theory after
Modernism: ETH and MIT Compared 145
Ole W. Fischer

CHAPTER 7
Thinking Architecture, its Theory and History: A Case Study about
Melvin Charney 161
Louis Martin

CHAPTER 8
Dirtying the Real: Liane Lefaivre and the Architectural Stalemate
with Emerging Realities 181
Andrew Toland

CHAPTER 9
Between Making and Acting: The Inherent Ambivalence of Arendtian
Architectural Theory 195
Paul Holmquist

CHAPTER 10
Critical Regionalism: A not so Critical Theory 211
Carmen Popescu

SECTION 3
The Misuses of History

CHAPTER 11
The Historiographical Invention of the Soviet Avant-Garde:
Cultural Politics and the Return of the Lost Project   227
Ricardo Ruivo

CHAPTER 12
Effete, Effeminate, Feminist: Feminizing Architecture Theory   243
Sandra Kaji-O'Grady

CHAPTER 13
Anthologizing Post-Structuralism: Architecture Écriture, Gender,
and Subjectivity   255
Karen Burns

CHAPTER 14
Consequences of Pragmatism: A Retrospect on "The Pragmatist
Imagination"   269
Joan Ockman

CODA
A Discipline in the Making   299
Hilde Heynen

About the Authors   315

INTRODUCTION
The Shifting Contours of Postwar Architectural Theory

Sebastiaan Loosen, Rajesh Heynickx, and Hilde Heynen

"We do not play chess with eternal figures like the king and the bishop; the figures are what the successive configurations on the playing board make of them"
– Paul Veyne, *"Foucault révolutionne l'histoire,"* 1978.[1]

In recent international literature addressing the history of twentieth-century architectural theory, the year 1968 is often seen as a decisive moment, giving rise to a "new" architectural theory. From that moment onwards, less emphasis was placed on the aesthetics of architecture, and more on its critical potential. Increasingly, and also from that moment onwards, architectural theory became an academic discipline inhabited by full-time scholars rather than by practicing architects. Yet, according to some authors, this intensification and assumed relevance of theory was short-lived, leading to an unstable situation and resulting in an end-of-theory atmosphere around the turn of the millennium.[2] Different responses were formulated to deal with this crisis: some architects wanted to counter the dominant abstract reasoning by a pragmatic approach (New Dutch School), critics posited a "postcritical" stage,[3] others contradicted the end-of-theory thesis,[4] and a historiographical effort turned to mapping and historicizing the life course of architectural theory in the recent past.[5]

It is not a coincidence that the so-called "death" of architectural theory was accompanied by the upsurge of anthologies on architectural theory that collect and classify referential texts.[6] Whether or not these anthologies had the effect of "burying" theory, they certainly effectuated an institutionalization of the field.[7] They offered both closure to a past period and defined the locus of the next period of theorization, invoking a "historical turn". At the same time, architectural discourses, and especially architectural historiography, were engaging with new theoretical fields such as gender studies or postcolonial studies, giving rise to a continued production of theoretically informed books and articles.[8]

This historical gaze towards theory brings with it a set of methodological challenges that have not yet been sufficiently addressed. Undoubtedly, the history of architectural theory in the postwar period has been impacted by the coming and going of a series of theoretical frameworks, each with its fervent advocates: semiotics, critical theory, postmodernism, critical regionalism, deconstructivism, pragmatism, and so on. Considered this way, the evolution of architectural theory might be seen as a game of chess, where every actor is keen on launching a move that will be acknowledged as significant, responding to the existing field and anticipating future positions. For the historian studying architectural theories from the past, however, the metaphor of chess cannot be limited to questions regarding which moves were made by whom and to identifying the field's chess grandmasters (in figures such as Manfredo Tafuri or Peter Eisenman). It is indeed far more tantalizing to detect how the (implicit) rules of the game shifted throughout history. As historian Paul Veyne stated in his 1978 essay on Michel Foucault's historical method – quoted in the epigraph – the figures on the board do not remain stable: the rules of the game seem to be shifting as the configurations on the playing board generate new questions and new alliances. If in hindsight some moves mattered more than others, which processes then determine the relevance of particular moves? And how do these processes leave an imprint on the move itself?

Whereas chess players are familiar with specific piece movements, typical positions, and clear pawn structures, scholars who dissect the postwar history of architectural theory are deprived of easily detectable configurations. Architectural theory then, as now, continuously tried to reformulate itself. The knowledge paradigms undergirding it were not as self-contained as they are sometimes portrayed in historical accounts; in effect, they emerged from "a hybridized system involving the infrastructural or regional contexts in which they are set – the availability of funds, of people, epistemic currents, disciplinary audience, and so on."[9] Unraveling such hybrid histories asks for an exploration of multiple epistemic intersections and the dissection of (re)combined concepts. Though postcolonial studies introduced a solid awareness of dealing with cultural and epistemic hybridity when confronting postcolonial architecture and urbanism, this insight is much less prevalent in the historiography of architectural theory. The anthologies that appeared in the late 1990s – as valuable as they are – came at the price of categorizing and labeling neat streams of architectural theory, filtering out the background noise without acknowledging that messiness and confusion abounded.[10]

It is therefore relevant to address questions that go beyond the tendency to sanitize the hybrid histories of theory formation, thereby reducing them to the essence of knowledge paradigms. Hence, while anthologies inevitably narrate history with rough meshes, it is worth asking which aspects of theory formation have slipped through these nets of historiography. This inevitably raises questions about the nature of theory, evoking the question of what kind of texts count as "theory" and even whether it is only texts that do so.

The contributions in this volume focus on the concrete processes in which knowledge is produced and screen the unspoken rules of engagement that postwar architectural theory ascribed to, questioning dominant assumptions, biases, and absences that structure the field. In short, by thematizing "the figure of knowledge," they highlight aspects of a question fundamental to the field: how do you do historical research on something as intangible as theory?

Hence, this volume addresses a double question: what *kind* of knowledge has become important throughout the recent history of architectural theory and how did the resulting figure of knowledge set the conditions for the actual arguments made?

A double perspective

How to recover what the initial meshes of historiography left behind? Two main paths may be followed. Firstly, one can produce a broad map of burning issues that characterized the last decades and measure their impact on architecture's theoretical environment. That is what architectural historian and theoretician Anthony Vidler set out to do a few years ago. In a series of articles written for the *Architectural Review* between 2011 and 2014, he attempted to explain the roots of what he described as the "troubled" present condition of theory in the period between the 1950s and 1970.[11] His inquiry into theory's history was initially marked by the ambition of providing a chronological narrative: the first article was announced as the first installment of a trilogy consisting of a presentation of "the state of the art" covering the second half of the 20th century, a diagnosis of the phenomenon of "post-theory," and a prospective gaze identifying the budding "new critical paradigms" in "the global context."[12] Vidler's inquiry encompassed a couple of crucial decades during which new theoretical paths were explored by household names such as Robert Venturi, Denise Scott Brown, Colin Rowe, and Manfredo Tafuri. While developing the series, Vidler began to expand on specific issues or moments: the role of technology as well as of utopian thought, the rise of brutalism, and the social dimension of architecture. This attempt to account for past theoretical interventions in order to distil some kind of coherent narrative of the development of postwar theory thus resulted in a seemingly never-ending project of thematic essays, exposing the cracks in the initial chronological endeavor. If the initial ambitions of his diachronic gambit seemed to be tempered in the course of the series,

Vidler nonetheless presaged this outcome: "I will be unable to come to a definitive conclusion," he wrote in an "author's note" accompanying the inaugural article.[13]

As important as these attempts to construct singular, diachronic narratives are, some phenomena that they inevitably leave off the radar can only be grasped by tackling postwar architectural theory from a perspective unmarked by an encompassing historical arch. The late writer and media artist Svetlana Boym advocated just this second type of intellectual interrogation in her works *The Future of Nostalgia* and *Architecture of the Off-Modern*.[14] With the concept of the "off-modern," Boym argued, it becomes possible to recover unforeseen pasts and to venture into the side-alleys of modern history, untouched by the major philosophical, economic, and technological narratives of modernization and progress. Through exploring Russian architectural history and memory, she demonstrated that an off-modern reflection involves an exploration of the lateral potentialities of modernity: "the adverb *off* confuses our sense of direction; it makes us explore side shadows and back alleys rather than the straight road of progress; it allows us to take a detour from the deterministic narrative of twentieth-century history."[15] As such, the term can be understood as an intervention in the larger theoretical discussion surrounding modernity and postmodernity, disclosing "multiple modernities" that go against classical definitions of modernity based on rigid, univocal processes of modernization. The idea that classical views on modernity need to be supplemented by a notion of multiplicity encompasses a firm methodological statement. Following a nonlinear conception of cultural evolution, embodied by spirals and zigzags, Boym adopted an idea of the Russian literary critic and novelist Viktor Shklovsky, who famously proposed that the inner dynamic of cultural evolutions could best be compared to the L-shaped moves of the knight in the game of chess. The conclusion here must be that everyone who tries to make sense of culture has to follow the road of estrangement, wonder, and even dissent. Just as the knight's "L" move contrasts with the linear paths of rationality of the other figures on the chess board, such cultural interrogations add something unpredictable to the playing field.

An outline

In order to give space to both Vidler's and Boym's complementary strategies of disentangling the hybrid histories of theory, the current volume groups fourteen case studies into three sections, roughly following a historical arch delineated by the opening and closing chapters. These two lengthier chapters revisit the trajectories of two major paradigms that have left their mark on postwar architecture culture: semiotics and pragmatism. Directly or indirectly, the twelve other chapters can be easily linked to the aspirations, as well as problems or dilemmas, of these two influential architectural paradigms. The two bookending chapters span a historical arch that registers a shift from the big hope of semiotics during the 1960s and 1970s – that theory would offer the solution – to the attempt to recover the theoretical project through pragmatism at the turn of the millennium. In addition, they describe a geographic shift, from European semiotics to American pragmatism, from the intellectual scene in Paris to East Coast colleges in the United States, including the transformations resulting from this rising prominence of American academia.

The shifts one can detect when comparing Joan Ockman's [CHAPTER 14] and André Loeckx and Hilde Heynen's [CHAPTER 1] sweeping accounts of the intellectual fortunes of these two major paradigms shed light on the transformation of the contours of architectural theory during the second half of the 20th century, as it gradually became a more established discipline, developed its own customary practices, and perhaps for some even turned into a way of life. Similar transformations take center stage in a recent work by cultural historian Philipp Felsch, which offers a diachronic account of theory's history in *Der lange Sommer der Theorie: Geschichte einer Revolte, 1960-1990* ("The Long Summer of Theory: History of a Revolt").[16] By taking the perspective of a small independent Berlin publisher, Merve Verlag, Felsch interprets theory primarily as a cultural phenomenon, legible for instance in the contrast between sober and high-quality hardcover treatises found in university libraries and cheaply produced, pocket-sized paperbacks found in many young students' coats. Felsch makes the case for a "genre history" of theory, wherein theory's history includes the material culture and the intellectual practices that went along with it and where the ways in which texts were read and used are as important as their contents.[17] Reflecting on theory in the postwar period, he notes, "Theory was more than the result of mere mental activity; it was a claim to truth, an article of faith and a lifestyle accessory."[18]

In fact, Felsch demonstrates how, after the decline of the grand narratives, theory aspired to give room to a "conscience of the contemporary" by providing topical diagnoses about all facets of society.[19] This new intellectual fashion, resulting in myriad attempts to keep the finger on the pulse of the political and social questions of the day, led not to all-encompassing philosophies but rather to dispersed forms of thought. It is these ever-changing contours of theory that this volume aims to illuminate in the field of architecture. Though architectural theory is surely indebted to this wider vogue of "theory," it was not merely a side effect of the latter but was tied in with its own history of architectural thinking and responded to a set of topical challenges specific to the field of architecture.

In taking up the terms as offered by Vidler, Felsch, or as hinted at by the historical arch that connects the accounts of semiotics' and pragmatism's fortunes, the individual chapters collected in this volume contribute to reiterating and confirming a broader diachronic narrative, while simultaneously disrupting or ignoring it by unraveling detours and margins in the field of architectural theory. When asking which kind of knowledge was seen as desirable at a given moment, and which critical import it then had to provide, they pay tribute to Boym's dictum that architecture constantly mixes a conjuring of memories and an envisioning of possible futures. Grouped into three sections, the chapters dissect postwar intellectuality *through* a historical understanding of its conditions by zooming in on the challenges that architectural knowledge faced in a panoply of contexts.

Section 1: "Modernism and Its Discontents"

The first section covers a formative period when emerging forms of theory were heavily marked by the crisis of modernism. Arguing for the formative importance of these early years for the later course of architectural theory, these contributions offer a cross-section of the historical phase in which a growing critique of modernism became more and more ubiquitous. They analyze different aspects of the repercussions that the convulsions of modernism had on architectural knowledge during a time of a drastically changing architecture culture. As presented in the first contribution, the history of semiotics in architecture can be considered as paradigmatic: once invested with high hopes and hailed as being able to cope with modernism and its discontents, yet somehow in the course of history left behind without a murmur [LOECKX AND HEYNEN, CHAPTER 1].

Through the biographies of Australian Robin Boyd and Italian curator-critic Lara-Vinca Masini, the two subsequent contributions discern geographical and disciplinary mechanisms at play during these formative years on the level of historiography [GOAD, CHAPTER 2; LANG, CHAPTER 3]. The fourth contribution investigates how this waning faith in modernism went hand in hand with a more technically mediated discourse through the rising role of computer graphics, arguing that despite their purportedly more neutral stance, these technicians operated with a self-postulated claim of legitimacy [ALLEN, CHAPTER 4]. The same argument runs through the final contribution, where critics' clashing arguments over a vacant site in Brussels are extended to epistemological disagreements of a self-postulated nature [LOOSEN, CHAPTER 5].

Section 2: "Projects of Theory"

The second section focuses on a more mature period, one in which theory was more aware of its own status. While registering this intellectual move, the texts in this section discuss the stakes but also the limitations of a number of attempts to "go forward with theory." Together, they show that these specific "projects" of theory each can be considered to be articulated within a particular matrix – both in the sense of a structuring mold and referring to the particular conditions under which they were "born."

The first contribution discusses how this form of intellectuality was institutionalized in research programs at the ETH Zürich and at the Massachusetts Institute of Technology (MIT) [FISCHER, CHAPTER 6]. As a complement to this more pragmatic dimension of theory's place, the second contribution traces the thin line between what can be called theory's external and internal history, through a biography of Canadian artist and architect Melvin Charney, whose work in many ways grasped architecture's challenges throughout the second half of the 20th century [MARTIN, CHAPTER 7]. The subsequent two contributions bring to light the specific qualities and inherent limitations of what happens when theory consciously puts its eggs in one particular basket. The first case concerns, through the work of architectural critic Liane Lefaivre, the (very populated) basket of realism; the second that of Hannah Arendt's political philosophy, as appropriated in the works of Kenneth Frampton and George Baird [TOLAND, CHAPTER 8; HOLMQUIST, CHAPTER 9]. The final contribution questions the "critical" aspect of Critical Regionalism, as advocated by Lefaivre and Frampton, among others [POPESCU, CHAPTER 10].

Section 3: "The (Mis)Uses of History"

The contributions in the final section focus on the uses (and misuses) to which "history" has been put in these various theoretical efforts – not only in the sense of how history figured as inspiration for theory's own ambitions but also in the ways in which theory's history has been constructed.

The first contribution interprets the historiographic interest since the 1960s in the Soviet avant-garde as a way of redeeming an avant-garde position via historiography [RUIVO, CHAPTER 11]. The two subsequent contributions zoom in on the gendered aspects of theory's history, the first by critically interpreting the post-criticality turn, identifying the implicit gendering effects of its anti-intellectualist stance; the second by arguing how the legacy of post-structuralist writings in the field of architecture has been distorted by a gendered anthologisation process [KAJI-O'GRADY, CHAPTER 12; BURNS, CHAPTER 13]. Finally, the closing chapter on the fate of pragmatism recounts from a personal perspective the unanticipated outcomes of a deliberate attempt to revive an American philosophical tradition in order to critically revamp architectural theory and set architecture's future agenda [OCKMAN, CHAPTER 14].

Snapshots of theory's history

Taking note of Vidler's troubles in maintaining a seemingly straightforward chronology, and bearing in mind Boym's plea for the historical unforeseen, we end this introduction by offering a series of snapshots of four discrete, singular events in theory's history as a way of opening up some of the themes along this historical trajectory, in which many of the cases discussed in these contributions were implicated and which will be more systematically dealt with in Hilde Heynen's coda to this volume. Though the landscape of architectural theory is abundantly populated by individual "authors," as a discipline it was strongly consolidated by people coming together. With this in mind, the four events we discuss, which occurred roughly a decade apart from each other, have one formal trait in common: the genuine desire of a group of people to gather and reflect upon the status of architectural theory. With no particular intention of establishing a canon – the course of theory's history is full of such gatherings – we chose these four events because they offer us reference points that cross the globe as well as the course of history: Berlin 1967, Venice 1977, Delft 1990, and New York 2000. Why did people feel at that moment the need to gather? What was at stake? And what was actually *produced* during these occasions, which tended to be perceived and presented by their organizers as distinct turning points between epochs? In sketching the historical momentum of these moments, these brief vignettes are (yet another) attempt to catch history red-handedly in the act of theory – before it is caught by the nets of historiography.

1967 Berlin

In December 1967 Oswald Mathias Ungers, at the time dean of the architectural program at the Technische Universität Berlin, convened a five-day international congress in Berlin. It was quite significant that this gathering of architectural scholars was brought together under the banner of "architectural theory" (*Architekturtheorie*). Whereas architectural history already had a tradition of learned societies with annual gatherings (SAH, the Society of Architectural Historians, was established in the USA in 1940, its British counterpart SAHGB in 1956), this was not the case for architectural theory. The latter might figure in the heading of symposia alongside history and criticism, like in the Cranbrook seminar of 1964, but it was rare to see it taking the lead.[20] Ungers justified his choice of topic by arguing that the building boom of the 1960s required practitioners to take a step back and reflect on the theoretical foundations of architecture. More specifically, in his introduction to the meeting he mentioned four broad questions that warranted interrogation. There was first of all the societal relevance of architecture, which he saw as topical because of the concurrent phenomenon of so many groups – communes, interest groups, opposition forces – that asked critical and theoretical questions related to many spheres of life (and as chronicled, we might add, for instance by Philipp Felsch). Secondly, he referred to the challenges posed by technology – the introduction of computers in particular. The third theme to be addressed had to do with the experience of history and heritage, which might be brought to bear upon future architecture. A final question had to do with the possible autonomy of architecture: "Does something like an immanent appearance in the formal exist?" Ungers asked. Could one imagine a formal expression that would be independent from history, technology, or society?[21]

Responding to these broad challenges, the prestigious conference in Berlin brought together a plethora of well-known names, as well as emerging scholars from Europe and the USA – all men, and most of them publishing either in German or in English (Italy had apparently not yet registered as an important site of theory). Following up on Ungers's introduction, Peter Blake, editor of *Architectural Forum*, Ulrich Conrads, editor of *Bauwelt*, and Kenneth Frampton, still based in London at that time, addressed the social and societal relevance of architecture, picking up the atmosphere of critical questioning that pervaded the youth culture and students' movements of the time. Reyner Banham, still at the Bartlett in London, and Julius Posener, respected architect and critic in Berlin, discussed how architecture dealt with technology and with machines. Günther Feuerstein, an Austrian critic, Sigfried Giedion, long-time secretary of CIAM, and Adolf Max Vogt, from ETH Zürich, talked about historical themes and how they intertwined with current architectural problems. Ungers's last theme, architectural autonomy, was only reluctantly addressed. Antonio Hernandez, who taught in Basel, dealt with the theory of Jean-Nicolas-Louis Durand, relating this theory however to rationalism and functionalism rather than to formalism.[22] A surprisingly large number of contributors chose to deal with the status of architectural theory itself. André Corboz, at that time at the University of Geneva, advocated an open theory of architecture as an alternative to the functionalism of the Modern Movement. Colin Rowe, already at Cornell, saw theory's mission as debunking the myths on which modern architecture was built. Jürgen Joedicke, professor in Stuttgart, likewise spoke about the "functions of architectural theory," as did Eduard F. Sekler from Harvard University.

The Berlin event thus gathered a series of personalities only a few of which would later be unambiguously qualified as "theoreticians" (Feuerstein, Frampton, and Rowe might deserve the label most explicitly, with the others generally thought of instead as historians or critics). Nevertheless, Ungers's four themes lucidly prefigured a substantial portion of theory's future agenda: society, technology, history, and autonomy all remained central points of discussion in subsequent decades. The social and societal relevance the conference supposedly sought was for instance also the point of discussion in the troubled dialogues discussed in Sebastiaan Loosen's chapter in this book [CHAPTER 5]. Typically, however, this critical intention – so dear to the students who were embracing "theory" – tended to be somewhat muted by a multitude of other issues. The congress in Berlin also showed how difficult it was for these culturally informed intellectuals to think through the potential effects of the computer. As Matthew Allen argues [CHAPTER 4], new technologies, such as architectural computing, would develop according to their own logic, producing another figure of theory, which was totally invisible to this generation of scholars. As for Ungers's theme of history, Carmen Popescu's account of Critical Regionalism [CHAPTER 10] and Ricardo Ruivo's interpretation of the interest in the early Soviet avant-garde [CHAPTER 11] are only two of the more explicit ways history was solicited to play a role in the contemporary architecture scene.

The conference thus clearly put "theory" on the agenda and attempted to sketch the configuration of theory's chessboard. But there were important absences as well: the city and urbanity as central issues in architecture were not yet detectable in Berlin (though the event prefigured the connection between Ungers and Cornell through the figure of Rowe).[23] Other crucial influences such as (post)structuralism or semiotics – the latter's fortunes here being portrayed by Loeckx and Heynen [CHAPTER 1] – were absent too, just as neo-Marxist theory was largely absent (with the notable exception of Jörn Janssen).[24] This was to change in the years to come.

1977 Venice

Ten years later, things indeed had changed, as French philosophy and neo-Marxism had developed into major factors to reckon with. In 1977 the Istituto Universitario di Architettura di Venezia (IUAV) organized two events, a seminar and a conference, devoted specifically to historiography. As recently analyzed in depth by Mary Louise Lobsinger, at these events a select group of mainly Italian and French participants (among others Georges Teyssot, Manfredo Tafuri, Massimo Cacciari, Franco Rella, and Paolo Morachiello) gathered with the very specific intention of rethinking and rearticulating the tools of architecture historiography through the work of Michel Foucault, while simultaneously critiquing the philosopher's work from the perspective of architecture.[25] The best known outcome of these events is Georges Teyssot's architectural interpretation of Foucault's notion of "heterotopia" – as anthologized in K. Michael Hays' *Architecture Theory since 1968* – but they also captured Manfredo Tafuri in a moment of actively reflecting on and fine-tuning his own historical method.[26] His contemporaneous piece "The Historical 'Project'," written in 1977, is marked by the same preoccupations that led to these events, drawing attention to Foucault's genealogical method and its rejection of notions of linear causality.[27]

Seen within their historical context, the ambitions of these events were conditioned by the rising intellectual climates of research institutes like the IUAV. By the 1970s many American and European architectural institutes – such as the ETH Zürich's Institut für Geschichte und Theorie der Architektur (gta, Institute for the History and Theory of Architecture, founded in 1967) and MIT's History, Theory, and Criticism of Architecture and Art (HTC) program (founded in 1975), as recounted by Ole W. Fischer [CHAPTER 6] – provided the institutional, as well as intellectual, climate to engage with matters as specialized as historiography.[28] Likewise, the Venice events are testimony to the seminar culture of such fledgling research contexts: very specific questions, discussed by a limited group of people and strongly bearing the mark of those who advanced the specific theme at hand. Notably, the 1977 seminar and conference followed a restructuring of the institute: with Carlo Aymonino becoming dean of Tafuri's research institute, the latter was promoted into a full university department of analysis, criticism and history of architecture. With this restructuring, architectural history became more an aim in itself rather than being merely at the service of educating architects.[29] Thus, this institutional reconfiguration paved the way for more philological rigor and analytical accuracy. Issues such as "historical method," which were relatively distant from the more practical aspects of the architectural profession, became important. In this vein, Joan Ockman points out how much of the research climate at IUAV was characterized by "a deliberate challenge to the 'operative history' that writers on modern architecture had produced to date."[30]

As Ockman recalls, at the time of Tafuri's appointment in 1968 as director of the architectural history program at IUAV, the title of his first major book *Teorie e storia dell'architettura* (*Theories and History of Architecture*) seemed to oppose "theories" in plural to "history" in the singular – as if the first was a subjective affair, a matter of interpretation and hence prone to a multiplication of perspectives, and the second something objective and verifiable. Ten years later, a highly complex and thoroughly plural view of history was central to the methodological questions underlying the Foucault seminar. As Andrew Leach notes with regard to Tafuri's 1977 essay, "the terms of the argument evolve, as we might expect, to account for new thinking, theoretical refinement, and the changes that inevitably affect internal disciplinary 'languages'."[31] Anno 1977, the intellectual landscape takes on a different form when Tafuri's work is opened up towards a new field of referents, tying his argument to an emergent philosophical discipline (Jacques Derrida, Gilles Deleuze, and others). Since then, as Leach argues, Tafuri's work "lays claim to a seat at a table of broader theoretical debate, just as his *Dipartimento* calls for increasing academic authority (and accountability) within IUAV. There is little coincidence that this year sees Tafuri, Cacciari, Teyssot, and Rella welcome Foucault to Venice, even if the welcoming spirit is rapidly eroded by basic intellectual differences."[32]

The intellectual reservations that Tafuri and Teyssot expressed in regard to Foucault's methodology pertained to his overemphasis on text and neglect of the materiality of architecture and technology. The conference attempted to rebalance this neglect, by seeking alliance with a more material-based emerging French scholarship in the history of technology, as well as with urban history, via participants such as historians Jacques Guillerme and Jean-Claude Perrot. Hence, at heart, the events in Venice were shaped by the observation that apparently "theory" and architecture history could only take recourse to words and concepts for describing something with inherently material effects.[33] In short, the theoretical aspirations of the conveners were marked by an awareness of the limits of language, and hence, the search for theory at these gatherings is not only indicative of theory's rising status in academia but also of a decade that Jacques Lucan characterized as being traversed through an unease with regard to language.[34]

The mixed feelings with which Foucault's work was appropriated in Venice, at once heralded as employing an innovative method yet at the same time understood to be limited when mobilized for architecture, seem to relate to an inherent ambivalence that arises when one tries to fit a philosophical body of ideas to the aims of architecture – a theme extensively analyzed by Paul Holmquist in relation to Hannah Arendt's work [CHAPTER 9].

1990 Delft

When more than a decade later the Technische Universiteit Delft hosted an International Working Seminar on Critical Regionalism (June 12-15, 1990), the ideas of Derrida and Foucault were prominently present too. The seminar, with the catchy title "Context & Modernity," was organized by students, inspired and stimulated by Delft faculty member Alexander Tzonis, who, with Liane Lefaivre, had introduced the notion of "Critical Regionalism" in the early 1980s (see also the contribution of Carmen Popescu [CHAPTER 10]). Whereas one might have expected that the geopolitical events of 1989 (the dramatic fall of the Berlin Wall and its aftermath) would have inspired the question of "context," this was not really the case. It took a bit longer for this seismic shock to register on the architectural scale. The Delft students were instead wrestling with postmodernism and the postmodern condition and understood "context" as a stand-in for "difference" and for the importance of "region." Apart from Tzonis and Lefaivre, the main keynote speakers were Fredric Jameson, who would publish *Postmodernism, or, the Cultural Logic of Late Capitalism* one year later, and Marshall Berman, whose *All That is Solid Melts into Air: The Experience of Modernity* had appeared eight years before.

The Delft seminar was a way of taking stock of the issues that preoccupied architects and architectural scholars in 1990.³⁵ It was thus less focused on historiography than the events organized in Venice. The students formulated four main themes: society-structure; production-market; designing-methodology; and language-typology. These questions were not that far removed from the themes Ungers had put forward two decades earlier. The question of social relevance was now articulated as both "society-structure" and "production-market," whereas technology apparently was replaced by "designing-methodology." "Language-typology" was meant to also encompass questions of history and identity as the potential formal autonomy of architecture. Compared to the Berlin event, however, discussions were now much more informed by theories from other fields: Jameson was a cultural theoretician, Berman came from literary studies, and a third keynote speaker, Harry Kunneman, was a sociologist and philosopher of humanism. References to the philosophical debate between Jean-François Lyotard and Jürgen Habermas, about whether or not the "project of modernity" should be considered as "(un)finished," took center stage. Marshall Berman had a field day in denouncing the idea of "regionalism" as based on romanticized notions of community and authenticity.³⁶

Whereas philosophical debates thus dominated the exchanges in the plenary sessions, the Delft conference also broke down into several workshop strands, some of which addressed more specifically architectural themes. Local identities and the idea of "place" were central issues in workshops 3 and 4; the cultural-political potential of architecture and the role of participation came to the fore in workshops 5 and 6; the notions of the urban, of collective memory and of tradition were dealt with in workshops 7, 8, and 10. The discussions on the role of climate and topography with specific reference to Los Angeles, in workshop 9, drove Alexander Tzonis to infamously scratch four letters from the word "regionalism" in "critical regionalism," so that it now came to read as "critical realism" – an allusion to the concept of "dirty realism" that Liane Lefaivre was developing around this period, and whose genealogy is here uncovered by Andrew Toland [CHAPTER 8].³⁷

Whereas by then Derrida was a prominent figure in the US whose influence had spread to architectural practice, providing the intellectual ammunition for a "deconstructivist" paradigm in architecture – put on the agenda by a 1988 show at the Museum of Modern Art (MoMA) in New York – and even though his name appeared repeatedly in the discussions in Delft, the specifically *architectural* articulation of "deconstructivism" was barely mentioned. Thus, the Delft conference might be seen as indicative of the gap that somehow existed between the concerns of the East Coast American architectural elite and the European scene, which was much more focused on how architecture actually contributed to the construction of the city.

2000 New York

Again a decade later the MoMA played a significant, trendsetting role in the final event on our list. The event in question triggered journalist Sarah Boxer to herald a "budding architectural movement" after attending the conference "Things in the Making: Contemporary Architecture and the Pragmatist Imagination," organized in November 2000 by Joan Ockman [CHAPTER 14]. Boxer noted the appeal that pragmatism, the century-old American philosophy based on the work of Charles S. Peirce, John Dewey, and William James, had for many of the architects, philosophers, engineers, and critics gathered at the MoMA. This attempt to ground architecture in a philosophy that was all-American, known for considering thought in relation to its practical effects, appeared to be nothing less than a revelation. Many participants, Boxer argued, had become charmed by the idea that the domination of theory over practice should be countered.[38]

The idea that a responsive and agile architecture needed in the first place to act through buildings, not through theories, was indeed the conference's main pitch. But its eagerness to refocus on practice at the expense of theory linked the conference with the "postcritical" moment, fostering an anti-intellectual attitude contrary to Ockman's intention to revitalize architectural thought: it exposed the lingering schism between theory and practice and, most of all, gave an impetus to the so-called "projective turn" in the following years.[39] Yet, the pragmatist maxim that making had to be valued over thinking – less criticism, more actual work – was not shared by everyone in the auditorium of the MoMA. In the eyes of the theoretician K. Michael Hays, an advocate of critical theory, pragmatism's ambition to shun critical statements was seriously flawed, making way for an "ideological smoothing of architecture." By taking theory out of architecture – ignoring semiotics, deconstruction, and every other theoretical movement since 1968 – the only thing that would be left was a bunch of "structures to keep the rain out," he argued.[40]

Hays's objection to pragmatism, in the form of a defense of theory, highlights how much by the late 1990s the connection with continental philosophy seemed to have "exhausted" architectural theory.[41] Complicated philosophical readings were more and more disregarded, considered to be unmasterable, and hence not worth the effort. Yet the term "exhaustion" of theory does not do justice to the intellectual and institutional quarrels that accompanied this intellectual shift, as evidenced in the chapters of Karen Burns and Sandra Kaji-O'Grady [CHAPTER 12; CHAPTER 13]. In embracing a homegrown, analytic philosophical tradition that was thought to be an instrument for prediction, problem solving, and action, the MoMA conference undermined the idea that the ambition of thought is to describe, represent, or mirror reality – an ambition that arguably was characteristic of continental philosophy, especially structuralism and post-structuralism, imported into the United States in the decades before the MoMA conference.

Still, proposing the pragmatist maxim that building had to be placed above thinking did not put a stop to the reigning confusion; as critic Philip Nobel wrote after the conference: "Could pragmatism be that relief? It depends what you make of it. As a shortcut to a new style, it offers little; it will be a sad day when we see 'pragmatism' used to put a glamorous gloss on pipe rails or exposed steel. But as a method to reinforce skepticism, to erase credulity, to verify through action new ideas that work, it may be just what architecture needs."[42]

***

The chronological dissection executed above through the discussion of a couple of focal points – Berlin 1967, Venice 1977, Delft 1990, and New York 2000 – indicates how the "figure of knowledge" of architectural theory changed contours and how shifting intellectual norms and forms were formative in that process. In engaging with various fields of learning, architectural theory transmuted in multiple ways. Thinking along that line, all contributions in this volume try to get a grip on knowledge production in architecture, including an attempt at assessing the limits of that knowledge.

In that regard, the book cover of this volume, showing the installation "La moglie di Lot" (Lot's wife) of the Florentine architecture group Superstudio, displayed at the 1978 Venice Biennale of Art, is more than illustrative.[43] The piece consisted of an iron frame with a table, on which were placed five architectural models: a pyramid, an amphitheater, a cathedral, the Palace of Versailles, and Le Corbusier's *L'Esprit Nouveau* pavilion. The architectural forms were made out of salt; water dripped down on the architectural forms from plastic tubes attached to a high-rise armature above the table. The architectural mass slowly eroded into nothingness and the figures dissolved, revealing various elements initially covered by salt. Perhaps the installation can be read as a metaphor for the disappearance of Superstudio's careers and their fading hopes for radical change in culture and the architecture profession. But on a more general level, it suggests that every attempt to gather and group, shape and fix pieces of knowledge into relatively stable, seemingly "objective" configurations has its own lifespan and is inevitably for only a brief moment in sync with the demands of human existence.

As highlighted in this book's coda, all the authors herein probe, in many different ways, the contours of a discipline in the making. By taking the hybrid histories of theory formation as a vantage point, they promote a consciousness of the epistemology of architectural knowledge without occluding its unstable nature. Thus, the aim of this volume is not only to write and rewrite the history of architectural theory but also ultimately to reflect on what forms of intellectuality we appreciate and value enough to transmit via our historical accounts and theoretical considerations.

Acknowledgments

The present volume is one of the outcomes of the conference "Theory's History, 196X-199X: Challenges in the Historiography of Architectural Knowledge," convened in Brussels, February 6-8, 2017 and organized by the current volume's editors, together with Yves Schoonjans, Elke Couchez, Ricardo Agarez, and Maarten Delbeke.[44] The volume's introduction partly draws on the jointly drafted Call for Papers for this conference, while the majority of individual contributions are substantially revised versions of papers presented on the occasion itself. We are thankful to Andrew Leach and an anonymous reviewer for their constructive comments on an earlier draft of this introduction as well as the book's overall setup.

Notes

1. Paul Veyne, *Comment on écrit l'histoire : Suivi de Foucault révolutionne l'histoire* (Paris: Seuil, 1979), 236, authors' translation. Veyne's metaphor describes the relational aspect in Michel Foucault's philosophy: "Au lieu d'un monde fait de sujets ou bien d'objets ou de leur dialectique, d'un monde où la conscience connaît ses objets d'avance, les vise ou est elle-même ce que les objets font d'elle, nous avons un monde où la relation est première : ce sont les structures qui donnent leurs visages objectifs à la matière, dans ce monde on ne joue pas aux échecs avec des figures éternelles, le roi, le fou. Les figures sont ce que les configurations successives sur l'échiquier font d'elles."
2. Luigi Prestinenza Puglisi, ed., "Theoretical Meltdown," *Architectural Design* 79, no. 1 (January/February 2009); Harry Francis Mallgrave and David J. Goodman, *An Introduction to Architectural Theory: 1968 to the Present* (Chichester: Wiley-Blackwell, 2011).
3. George Baird, "'Criticality' and Its Discontents," *Harvard Design Magazine* no. 21, Rising Ambitions, Expanding Terrain: Realism and Utopianism (Fall/Winter 2004): 16-21.
4. Jane Rendell et al., eds., *Critical Architecture*, AHRA Critiques: Critical Studies in Architectural Humanities 1 (London: Routledge, 2007).
5. Hanno-Walter Kruft, *Geschichte der Architekturtheorie: Von der Antike bis zur Gegenwart* (Munich: C. H. Beck, 1985); English translation by Ronald Taylor, Elsie Callander, and Antony Wood: *A History of Architectural Theory: From Vitruvius to the Present* (London: Zwemmer, 1994); Paul-Alan Johnson, *The Theory of Architecture: Concepts, Themes and Practices* (New York: Van Nostrand Reinhold, 1993); Mark Gelernter, *Sources of*

Architectural Form: A Critical History of Western Design Theory (Manchester: Manchester University Press, 1995); Louis Martin, "The Search for a Theory in Architecture: Anglo-American Debates, 1957-1976" (PhD thesis, Princeton, 2002); Harry F. Mallgrave, ed., *Modern Architectural Theory: A Historical Survey 1673-1968* (Cambridge, UK: Cambridge University Press, 2005); Harry F. Mallgrave and David Goodman, *An Introduction to Architectural Theory: 1968 to the Present* (Sussex: Wiley-Blackwell, 2011).

6. Joan Ockman, ed., *Architecture Culture 1943-1968: A Documentary Anthology* (New York: Rizzoli, 1993); Kate Nesbitt, ed., *Theorizing a New Agenda for Architecture: An Anthology of Architectural Theory, 1965-1995* (New York: Princeton Architectural Press, 1996); Charles Jencks and Karl Kropf, eds., *Theories and Manifestoes of Contemporary Architecture* (Chichester: Academy Editions, 1997); K. Michael Hays, ed., *Architecture Theory since 1968* (Cambridge, MA: The MIT Press, 1998); Hilde Heynen et al., eds., *"Dat is architectuur": Sleutelteksten uit de twintigste eeuw* (Rotterdam: Uitgeverij 010, 2001); Fritz Neumeyer, ed., *Quellentexte zur Architekturtheorie: Bauen beim Wort genommen* (München: Prestel, 2002); Gerd De Bruyn and Stephan Trüby, eds., *Architektur_theorie. doc. Texte seit 1960* (Basel: Birkhäuser, 2003); Ákos Moravánszky, ed., *Architekturtheorie im 20. Jahrhundert: Eine kritische Anthologie* (Wien: Springer, 2003); Vittorio Magnago Lampugnani, ed., *Architekturtheorie 20. Jahrhundert: Positionen, Programme, Manifeste* (Ostfildern: Hatje Cantz, 2004); Andrew Ballantyne, ed., *Architecture Theory: A Reader in Philosophy and Culture* (London: Continuum, 2005); A. Krista Sykes, ed., *Constructing a New Agenda: Architectural Theory, 1993-2009* (New York: Princeton Architectural Press, 2010); Korydon Smith, ed., *Introducing Architectural Theory: Debating a Discipline* (New York: Routledge, 2012).

7. Sylvia Lavin, "Theory into History; Or, the Will to Anthology," *Journal of the Society of Architectural Historians* 58, no. 3, Architectural History 1999/2000 (September 1999): 494-99; Karen Burns, "A Girl's Own Adventure: Gender in the Contemporary Architectural Theory Anthology," *Journal of Architectural Education* 65, no. 2 (March 2012): 125-34.

8. Neil Leach, ed., *Rethinking Architecture: A Reader in Cultural Theory* (London: Routledge, 1997); Gülsüm Baydar Nalbantoğlu and Chong Thai Wong, *Postcolonial Space(s)* (New York: Princeton Architectural Press, 1997); Jane Rendell, Barbara Penner, and Iain Borden, eds., *Gender Space Architecture: An Interdisciplinary Introduction* (London: Routledge, 2000); C. Greig Crysler, Stephen Cairns, and Hilde Heynen, eds., *The SAGE Handbook of Architectural Theory* (London: SAGE, 2012).

9. Arindam Dutta, "Linguistics, Not Grammatology: Architecture's A Prioris and Architecture's Priorities," in *A Second Modernism: MIT, Architecture, and the "Techno-Social" Moment*, ed. Arindam Dutta (Cambridge, MA: SA+P Press/The MIT Press, 2013), 19.

10. Nesbitt, *Theorizing a New Agenda*; Jencks and Kropf, *Theories and Manifestoes*.

11. Anthony Vidler, "Troubles in Theory" (in 6 Parts), *The Architectural Review* 230-6, nos. 1376, 1379, 1386, 1394, 1404, 1412 (October 2011-October 2014).

12. Ibid., 230, no. 1376 (October 2011): 107.
13. Ibid., 102, "author's note."
14. Svetlana Boym, *The Future of Nostalgia* (New York: Basic Books, 2001); Svetlana Boym, *Architecture of the Off-Modern* (New York: Princeton Architectural Press, 2008).
15. Boym, *The Future of Nostalgia*, xvi-xvii.
16. Philipp Felsch, *Der lange Sommer der Theorie. Geschichte einer Revolte, 1960-1990* (Munich: C. H. Beck, 2015).
17. Philipp Felsch, "What Was Theory? Toward a Generic History," *New German Critique* 44, no. 132, Transatlantic Theory Transfer: Missed Encounters? (November 2017): 8.
18. Felsch, *Der lange Sommer der Theorie*, 12. "Theorie war mehr als eine Folge bloßer Kopfgedanken; sie war ein Wahrheitsanspruch, ein Glaubensartikel und ein Lifestyle-Accessoire."
19. Ibid., 58.
20. Marcus Whiffen, ed., *The History, Theory and Criticism of Architecture: Papers from the 1964 AIA-ACSA Teacher Seminar* (Cambridge, MA: The MIT Press, 1965).
21. Jörg Pampe, ed., *Architekturtheorie: Internationaler Kongress in der TU Berlin, 11. bis 15. Dezember 1967*, Veröffentlichungen zur Architektur 14 (Technische Universität Berlin, 1968), 6.
22. The lecture was later also published in English: Antonio Hernandez, "J. N. L. Durand's Architectural Theory: A Study in the History of Rational Building Design," *Perspecta*, no. 12 (1969): 153-60.
23. Lara Schrijver, "Transatlantic Crossings: New Forms of Meaning in the City of the 1970s," *Planning Perspectives* 31, no. 1 (2016): 103-13.
24. Angelika Schnell, "Von Jörn Janssen zu Aldo Rossi: Eine hochschulpolitische Affäre an der ETH Zürich," *ARCH+*, no. 215 (Spring 2014): 16-23.
25. This section is based on the ideas Mary Louise Lobsinger developed in the paper "Words, Concepts and Techniques, c. 1977," delivered at the conference "Theory's History, 196X-199X. Challenges in the Historiography of Architectural Knowledge," Brussels, February 6-8, 2017. The 1977 Venice events resulted in the publications of Franco Rella, ed., *Il dispositivo Foucault*, Materiali per la critica 1 (Venice: cluva, 1977); and Paolo Morachiello and Georges Teyssot, eds., *Le macchine imperfette: Architettura, programma, istituzioni, nel XIX secolo*, Collana di architettura 20 (Rome: Officina Edizioni, 1980).
26. Georges Teyssot, "Heterotopias and the History of Spaces," in *Architecture Theory since 1968*, ed. K. Michael Hays, trans. David Stewart (Cambridge, MA: The MIT Press, 1998), 296-305.
27. Manfredo Tafuri, *The Sphere and the Labyrinth: Avant-Gardes and Architecture from Piranesi to the 1970s*, trans. Pellegrino D'Acierno and Robert Connolly (Cambridge, MA: The MIT Press, 1987), 4.

28. Joan Ockman, "Venice and New York," *Casabella*, no. 619–620: The Historical Project of Manfredo Tafuri (February 1995): 57–71; Ruth Hanisch and Steven Spier, "'History Is Not the Past but Another Mightier Presence': The Founding of the Institute for the History and Theory of Architecture (gta) at the Eidgenössische Technische Hochschule (ETH) Zurich and Its Effects on Swiss Architecture," *The Journal of Architecture* 14, no. 6 (2009): 655-86; John Harwood, "How Useful? The Stakes of Architectural History, Theory and Criticism at MIT, 1945-1976," in *A Second Modernism: MIT, Architecture, and the "Techno-Social" Moment*, ed. Arindam Dutta (Cambridge, MA: SA+P Press/The MIT Press, 2013), 106-43.
29. Jean-Louis Cohen, *La coupure entre architectes et intellectuels, ou les enseignements de l'italophilie* (Brussels: Mardaga, 2015), 146-47; Andrew Leach, "Choosing History: A Study of Manfredo Tafuri's Theorisation of Architectural History and Architectural History Research" (PhD thesis, Ghent University, 2006), 39; cf. Andrew Leach, *Manfredo Tafuri: Choosing History* (Ghent: A&S/books, 2007), 45-53.
30. Joan Ockman, "Russia, Europe, America: The Venice School between the U.S.S.R. and the U.S.A.," in *Re-Framing Identities: Architecture's Turn to History, 1970-1990*, ed. Ákos Moravánszky and Torsten Lange, East West Central: Re-Building Europe, 1950-1990 (Basel: Birkhäuser, 2016), 122.
31. Leach, "Choosing History," 47.
32. Ibid.
33. Lobsinger, "Words, Concepts and Techniques, c. 1977."
34. Jacques Lucan, "Langage de la critique, critique du langage: La transition postmoderne," *Les Cahiers de la Recherche Architecturale et Urbaine*, no. 24/25: La critique en temps et lieux (2009): 113–20.
35. Richard Ingersoll, "Context and Modernity. Delft, June 12-15, 1990," *Journal of Architectural Education* 44, no. 2 (1991): 124-25, https://doi.org/10.2307/1425106.
36. These summaries are based on personal notes and on conference materials sent to Hilde Heynen at the time, since she was involved in this conference as a chairperson of one of its workshops.
37. Hans Van Dijk, "Het banier 'kritisch regionalisme' gestreken: Symposium Context and Modernity in Delft," *Archis*, no. 7 (July 1990): 3-4.
38. Sarah Boxer, "The New Face of Architecture," *The New York Times*, 25 November 2000, sec. Arts, B9.
39. Baird, "'Criticality' and Its Discontents."
40. Quoted in Boxer, "The New Face of Architecture."
41. Pauline Lefebvre, "What Difference Could Pragmatism Have Made? From Architectural Effects to Architecture's Consequences," *Footprint: Delft Architecture Theory Journal*, no. 20: Analytic Philosophy and Architecture: Approaching Things from the Other Side (Spring/Summer 2017): 23-36.
42. Philip Nobel, "What Pragmatism Ain't," *Metropolis*, July 2001.

43. The installation "La moglie di Lot" disappeared after 1978, but in 2014 a gallerist from Genova reconstructed it and built three of them for sale. It was on display during the 2014 Venice Biennale in the Moditalia Arsenale.
44. The other outcomes are: Ricardo Costa Agarez, Rajesh Heynickx, and Elke Couchez, eds., *Architecture Thinking across Boundaries* (London: Bloomsbury, 2020); Hilde Heynen and Sebastiaan Loosen, eds., "Marxism and Architectural Theory across the East-West Divide," Special Collection of *Architectural Histories* 6–7 (2018-2019). DOI: http://doi.org/10.5334/ah.401.

SECTION 1

Modernism and its Discontents

CHAPTER 1
Meaning and Effect: Revisiting Semiotics in Architecture

André Loeckx and Hilde Heynen

Semiotics 1960-1980: A new figure of knowledge for architectural theory

Semiotics did not originate in the mid-1960s. At the awakening of the 20th century, the development of a general "theory of signs" was announced almost simultaneously by the Swiss linguist Ferdinand de Saussure (1857-1913), who named it "sémiologie," and by the American philosopher and scientist Charles Sanders Peirce (1839-1914), who used the term "semiotic."[1] In Continental Europe Saussure's ideas matured slowly within language studies. In the Anglo-American context, Peirce's theory of signs survived under the wings of philosophical Pragmatism and behavioral sciences. These two semiotic strands differed from one another, in that Saussure's theory focused on the signification of signs, whereas Peirce's thinking gave preference to the working ("semiosis") and the effect of signs. Both strands developed rather independently from one another, although there were some crossovers, as we will see.

From the late fifties onwards, the widespread success of structuralism, which was informed by Saussurean structural linguistics, generated a spectacular resurrection of semiotics, not just in linguistics but also in social sciences and in the arts, which suddenly began to see their own object of study as structured just like languages. This "linguistic turn" also influenced the field of architecture. Indeed, many architectural scholars turned to semiotics in the 1960s and 1970s, in response not just to the overall surge of structuralism but also as a possible way out of the widely perceived crisis of legitimacy of modern architecture. Architectural historian and theorist Françoise Choay (1925) thought for example that investigating semiotics could help understand the process of "semantic reduction" that affected so many postwar housing estates, which displayed what she called a "hyposignifiance" of the daily life environment.[2] In such a process the "hypersignifiance," that is, the saturated meaning of other, more traditional environments (Choay referred to the Bororo village, the ancient Greek agora, and medieval Fribourg) was gradually replaced by one singular stratum of meaning in the modern city: the economic. Semiotics seemed to offer a way out of this impoverishment by providing an understanding of the conditions for contemporary signification in architecture and urbanism.

In hindsight, one can see that the turn to semiotics in architecture was remarkably short-lived, with virtually all the most relevant texts published between 1960 and 1980. It nevertheless included some attempts for a critical engagement with architecture that are worth revisiting. In this approach architecture is seen as a domain of general semiotics, or put more specifically, as a kind of language. Viewing architecture as language was not a new phenomenon: it had never been entirely absent in architectural thought. This is particularly true for the tradition of classical architecture, which tended to conceive of architecture as an autonomous visual language determined by an underlying system of rules.[3] Several architects and theorists of the Modern Movement, however, turned against the classical conception of architecture as a language that serves symbolic representation. The idea that architecture could represent something (status, majesty, power) outside its function was considered a fallacy. The "struggle of modern architecture," according to Mart Stam, was "a struggle against the representative, against excess."[4] Representation, in this view, was seen as corroding "the truth of the form" and encouraging the formal lie of style imitation and decoration.[5] Louis Sullivan's dictum "form follows function," Adolf Loos's famous tirade against the decadence of the ornament, and Le Corbusier's purism are all instances of modern architecture's advocacy of a mode of design that naturally emerges from an inner truth of logical objectives and functionality and that would thus comply with the rationality of nature, science, economics, and culture.[6] Form was seen as the outward figuration of that inner truth; furthermore, symbolic references to dubious external factors were suppressed.

In an important text from 1957, John Summerson considered the rupture with the classical language system an essential characteristic of a modern architecture that adopted the program as the source of the unity of a design. Nonetheless, "the conceptions which arise from a preoccupation with the programme have got, at some point, to crystallise into a final form," whereas "there is no common theoretical agreement as to what happens or should happen at that point. There is a hiatus. One may even be justified in speaking of *a 'missing architectural language'*[x] [our italics]."[7] According to Summerson, this generated a need for a more elaborate and self-reflective architectural theory.

Summerson's diagnosis was symptomatic of the confusion among architects as to how form and content, as well as aesthetics and utility, should relate to each other. They turned to semiotics because of its apparent promise to clarify the troubling relationship between form on the one hand and "content" or "meaning" on the other, a relationship considered similar to the semiotic definition of the sign.

Semiotics was expected to provide a scientifically operational definition of "the sign," which could be transferred to architecture. Unfortunately, all over the semiotic field, this definition generated some serious scholarly divergences. In fact, this field had become a dense "forest of symbols," characterized by controversial issues, fascinating crossovers, and meandering paradigms.[8]

Our aim in this chapter is to offer a mapping of this "forest of symbols" and of its effects on architectural theory. Unlike Louis Martin's earlier discussion of architectural semiotics, which deals with the Anglo-American discourse until 1976,[9] we do not limit ourselves to this brief period and this one paradigm. Our contribution also focuses on European semiology and includes the shift from structuralism to post-structuralism. Its aim is to critically reread a selection of relevant episodes, discussing both the paths taken as well as the opportunities missed with the ultimate intention of rethinking their merits and of reassessing whether some aspects of these semiotic adventures might not deserve to be redeemed rather than discredited.

Semiotic paradigms and passages to architecture

French semiology and the language of architecture

The contribution to structural linguistics by Ferdinand de Saussure situates itself at the level of *langue* (that is, the systematic or structural level of language), rather than dealing with *parole* (the use of language in context).[10] Within this system, Saussure's definition of the sign is based on two signifying operations that occur simultaneously and that activate two forms of relationality: a positive *association* and a negative *differentiation*. The sign is the *association* of "the signifier" *(le signifiant)*, which is usually an "acoustic image," and "the signified" *(le signifié)*, defined as a content or a concept, which does not necessarily refer to "something" out there in the world. According to Saussure, this association is arbitrary and unmotivated. It is, as it were, an alliance sealed by social convention. Within the signifier there is nothing specific that would refer to the signified: the acoustic images *"tree"* and *"arbre"* are totally different but refer to the same concept. So while the arbitrariness of the association affirms the difference between signifier and signified, the sealed character of the association negates that difference. Saussure however also understood language as a system held together by structural *differentiation*, which is connected to the sign's position within the overall system or, put otherwise, its "value" within a structure. In short, the sign acquires meaning in the simultaneous play of association and difference. Literary theorist Roland Barthes (1915-1980) clarified this twofold definition with a metaphor borrowed from Saussure himself: signs are like the snippets or shreds that are left after the cutting up of a piece of paper.[11] Every snippet has a recto and a verso (a signifier and a signified) and, at the same time, has its value fixed by its relative position in relation to the surrounding snippets.

From Saussure's twofold definition (association and differentiation) follows that the system of signs – language – does not merely serve to represent an outside reality or to display a number of preexisting meanings. Rather, meaning and language originate in the simultaneous articulation of what can be heard and what can be thought. In fact, this perspective asserts that the only cognizable, meaning-bearing reality is a linguistic reality. The thin materiality of the Saussurean sign, the arbitrary character of the association between signifier and signified and the absence of "a reality out there" to which the sign refers raised many objections but would also generate innovative amendments that later on would fuel post-structuralist thinking. These issues would also continue to differentiate Continental-European semiology from the Anglo-American semiotic paradigm.

Another important pair of notions in the Continental-European tradition is that of "syntagm" versus "paradigm," as explained by Barthes. "Syntagm" refers to the methodical stringing together of signifying elements on the basis of syntactic rules, and this process is related to metonymy (a figure of speech that replaces the name of a thing with the name of something else which is closely related). "Paradigm," on the other hand, refers to the selection of a signifying term from an associative series of similar terms and has to do with metaphor (a figure of speech that makes an implicit, implied, or hidden comparison between two things that are unrelated but which share some common characteristics). These notions make it possible, according to Barthes, to extend structural linguistics towards a structural semiology of fields such as fashion, food, furniture, or architecture, which can be seen as nonverbal and very material systems of signification.[12] Barthes thus corroborated Saussure's earlier statement that all domains of culture, science, and society in fact could be considered as various forms of language, and that hence his linguistics in the long run might become just another part of a more general science of semiology that would deal with all kinds of languages. Interestingly, Saussure himself explained syntagmatic stringing together and paradigmatic selecting by way of an architectural metaphor. He described how a column is "syntagmatically" connected with other parts of the construction (for example, the cornice), whereas the column itself is selected from a paradigmatic series of Doric, Ionic, or Corinthian versions. This was a very early indication that something like an architectural semiotics might be possible.[13]

Barthes's brilliant collection, *Mythologies* (1957), seemed to open a pathway towards a semiology of nonverbal languages. The book deals with a variety of topics, such as the Tour de France, publicity posters, catch-competitions, or even the avant-garde design of the Citroen DS, considering all of them as languages. Barthes analyzes their mythological effects as resulting from the interplay between "denotation" (a straightforward, literal meaning based on a simple and direct relation between a clear signifier and an obvious signified) and "connotation" (a more layered and implicit meaning beyond the literal one).[14] According to him, this interplay allows for the insertion of ideology in the language of sport, publicity, or design, because the apparently innocent denotation functions as a vehicle for ideologically charged connotations.

Whereas *Mythologies* offered a very promising start for a semiology of nonverbal systems, Barthes did not continue in the same vein. His *Système de la Mode* (1967), for instance, opts for a semiotic analysis of texts *about* fashion, rather than focusing on fashion itself. The issue of the nonverbal systems of signification, however, continued to intrigue Barthes. In an article that same year, "Sémiologie et Urbanisme," he claimed that urban spaces constitute in a certain way a discourse in themselves, because they always already act as signifiers. A really scientific semiotics of the city would imply, however, that one has to transition from the simplistic use of the metaphor of "the city as language" towards a much more methodical description and analysis of this "language of the city" (rather than analyzing the language about the city).[15]

Anglo-Saxon foundations of a semiotic pragmatism

Charles Sanders Peirce (1839-1914) and Charles W. Morris (1901-1979) are considered the foundational thinkers of a "semiotic" science, the Anglo-American counterpart to Saussure's semiology, both terms derived from the Greek "semeion" (sign). Peirce's definition of the sign is triadic: the sign consists of a "representamen" (an object, a characteristic, a thought, a pronouncement, an action…) that refers to an object (that can be a real one); it does so in such a way that this reference evokes a possible "interpretant," i.e., not an interpreter but an interpretative result, which could include information, a thought, an insight, a reaction, a new reference, or something else. Peirce's definition is quite different from the Saussurean one.[16] Whereas Saussure considers the sign as part of a language system irrespective of the world outside of that system, Peirce focuses on processes of signification (or "semiosis") that can refer to or have an effect in the physical world. Peirce's definition of the sign is moreover more inclusive than Saussure's, because it explicitly posits many different things, objects, gestures, concepts, or characteristics as potential representamens. This means that Peirce's conceptualization facilitates the application of his apparatus to architecture and its materiality.

A crucial contribution of Peirce's semiotics concerns his ideas about "the three modes of being." "Firstness" – the mode of being related to potentiality – pertains to what makes the representamen present (a color, a shape, a movement, a sound…). Based on this potentiality, "secondness" – the mode of being of the factual – can operate, whereby the representamen refers to an object that can be "out there" in the world. This referring process is conditioned by that of having a certain effect – "thirdness" – which is actualized or at least expected. Thirdness hence is the mode of being that has to do with a result, an effect, reaction, or interpretation that can be understood on the basis of a rule, a code, or a convention.[17] The three best-known classes of signs that Peirce discusses are presented in this context, when he deals with the impact of the three modes of being on the factual reference of the representamen to the object. When this reference mainly activates a potentiality (in cases where something resembles something else, like a roof resembling billowing sails), it has to do with an "icon." When the reference is based on a factual, functional, or causal relationship, the sign is an "index" (such as in the case of a shell roof construction). The "symbol," lastly, is the class of signs where the reference is understandable because a certain code or convention is applicable (the case of a well-known and much debated modern building).[18]

Peirce is one of the founding fathers of philosophical Pragmatism, which understands knowledge of the world as inseparable from agency within it.[19] This is also characteristic of the semiosis of the Peircean sign, which is motivated by the expectation of an effect (the interpretant or interpreting result).[20] Often the result or effect is provisional, evoking a new reference that in turn generates another reference. It is possible to compare Peirce's understanding of semiosis to the endless chain of signifiers that Derrida detects in any given text or reality (the "traces" that always lead to other traces without ever ending at the discovery of "truth").[21] For Peirce, however, "unlimited semiosis" does not have the same consequences as for Derrida, for whom meanings are always already provisional from the start, taking part in an endless chain, and thus negating the possibility of an ultimate, transcendental meaning (such as God). In contrast, Peirce's "pragmatic maxim" prevents unlimited or undetermined semiosis.[22] This means that the process of semiosis progresses until a point where "the significance" can be determined as the entirety of effects and interpreting thoughts evoked by the representamen.[23]

Equally pragmatic is Peirce's understanding that the dosage of three "modes of being" activated in the sign – firstness, secondness, and thirdness – is driven by the expected result or effect. Thus, the usage of signs relies on an anticipative, "what if" mode of reasoning that Peirce labels "abduction" – complementing the better known modes of induction and deduction.[24] Given the role of abduction in Peirce's theory of the sign, it is not difficult to see its appeal to architects, whose designerly way of thinking is equally based on an anticipative, "what if" reasoning.

Morris – also an important Pragmatist – likewise offered interesting ideas for an empirically relevant semiotics. In his early writings, Morris defined, just like Peirce, the sign as a triadic relation between a sign vehicle, an object, and an interpretant.[25] Later on, he complicated the definition of the sign by describing semiosis as a relation between five poles: a sign vehicle (A) evokes in an interpretor or addressee (B) a disposition (the interpretant, C) to react in a certain way to the object (D) and this under certain conditions (E). For Morris a phenomenon only qualifies as a sign when it works as a sign, i.e., when it evokes a certain behavior (disposition and reaction) that can be scientifically studied and empirically validated. This definition is interesting for the field of architecture, because it opens up the possibility of studying the way in which the built environment (as sign vehicle) evokes certain behaviors in people. His best-known contribution, however, has to do with how he subdivides semiotics into three subfields: syntactics (dealing with the relations between signs), semantics (dealing with the relation between sign vehicle and object), and pragmatics (dealing with the relation between sign vehicle and interpretant).[26] His followers tended to either interpret this as three aspects of the same process of semiosis or as three different domains of semiotic research. Morris himself clearly stressed the interrelation between the three fields.

The intimate ties of the Anglo-American strand of semiotics with Pragmatism are indicative of its empirical bias and its attention to sign users. John L. Austin's (1911-1960) theory of "Speech Acts" can be seen as closely connected to these aspects of semiotics.[27] This theory posits that many language utterances, such as wishes or promises, are not only communicating a certain informative content but also have a prerogative effect on the relation between speaker and listener. Language indeed can also *act*, in that it changes the reality outside of language. These ideas obviously have relevance for nonverbal languages as well, such as for body language or body movements. That is what Edward T. Hall investigated in his 1966 publication *The Hidden Dimension*, where he developed his theory of "proxemics," explaining how people determine the distance they keep from one another (differentiating between, for example, intimate distances, personal distances, social distances, and public distances).[28] Hall's insights into the wide variety of meanings associated with distance in different cultural contexts have had a certain impact on architectural thinking, which we will deal with later in this chapter.

Scenes of architectural semiotics: Freewheeling on paradigmatic tracks

Umberto Eco's redemption of functionalism

Italian philosopher and semiotician Umberto Eco (1932-2016) was responsible for turning Continental semiology towards a reappraisal of Peirce, Morris, and others, widening the scope of semiotics with his 1968 book *La struttura assente*.[29] In this book, he also presented a theoretical frame for dealing with nonverbal languages, with a special focus on architecture. Eco situates the sign within a twofold perspective of communication and signification, including codes and messages in the semiotic process. He steers away from endless epistemological polemics between Saussurean and Peircean semiotics by simply positioning all available bipolar and triadic definitions of the sign on a triangular scheme, with the signifier, the signified, and the referent (or equivalents such as sign vehicle, interpretant, object) occupying the three corners. Eco suggests that such a scheme defines a semiotic space that gathers all terminological disagreements in a coherent figure and simply situates his own semiotic concerns on the left side of that triangle, indicating his focus on the coded relation between signified and signified. He considers the debate regarding the "objective reality out there" as less relevant to a theory of signification and communication that focuses on meaning as a message to be transmitted, and not as an outside reality to be represented.[30] For him this is a matter of methodological choice, not epistemological truth. Moreover, this pragmatic maneuver gives him the opportunity to combine a Saussurean perspective with the much larger spectrum of phenomena, objects, and relations that Peirce handles, facilitating an interconnection between semiotics and architecture.

According to Eco, architectural signs consist of "sign vehicles" (signifiers) that have a pronounced, often complex materiality, and a range of meanings (signifieds). In light of certain codes (conventional systems linking specific signifiers to specific signifieds), architectural signifiers can "denote" precise functions as their meaning. The strictly functional meanings (Eco refers to "the primary functions") of these signifiers can be extended, with successive meanings ("secondary functions") obtained via "connotations" derived from other codes. Eco emphasizes that the primary, denotative functions are no less "symbolic" than the secondary ones and that the secondary connotative functions are no less "functional" than the primary ones.[31] For example, one does not automatically know, on the basis of its form, how to use a simple staircase; rather, one has to learn this use. Hence the relation between form and function is not intrinsic but symbolic. The symbolism of a majestic staircase, on the other hand, functions as an indication of power and prestige and is thus able to modify the perception and use of that staircase. Considering function as meaning is central to Eco's architectural semiotics. He quotes Barthes: –"every usage is converted into a sign of itself"[32] – and refers to Sullivan's "form follows function."[33] This means that the architectural form should make the function possible and at the same time communicate that function, that is, make the function obvious, necessary, and attractive. In this way, Eco's sign touches upon Austin's notion of a "speech act": in a certain way a form stimulates one to perform a function.

Eco's approach makes room for the complex temporality of architecture by pointing out that the three dimensions of the sign – the material sign vehicle, the denotative first functions, and the connotative second functions – have each their own life spans, durations and rhythms of change.[34] Built forms may undergo transformations; denotative primary functions may change, be disaffected, or reinstalled; connotative secondary functions may alter, become more prominent, or fade away. This results over time in a game of loss, recuperation, and substitution, and thus in a layering, densification, dilution, or shifting of forms, of denotative functions/meanings, and of connotative functions/meanings. In order to study a building's "history of signification," changes to its form, primary and secondary functions can be plotted along three separate timelines that together outline a complex semiotic narrative. The multiple time frames (immediacy, steady transformation, "longue durée") proper to the pace of construction, the histories of dwelling, and the life span of buildings bring in a kind of "timing of signification," an awareness of history, which offers an interesting amendment to the synchronic bias that often prevails in structural semiotics. At the same time, the separate timeline of form attributes a degree of autonomy to the architectural form. However, because of the semiotic association of sign vehicle and function, this autonomy is never an absolute one.

For Umberto Eco, signification is closely linked to communication, whereby architectural communication shows strong similarities to mass media, which work as "systems of rhetorical formulas" aimed at both convincing the mass of consumers and meeting their expectations.[35] Just like television or fashion, architecture is a part of everyday life. Hence people live with architecture without necessarily experiencing it on a conscious level. And yet, where mass media confirm and even reinforce existing social premises and prejudices, Eco is open for the possibility that architecture could succeed in distancing itself from social expectations and conventions in order to renew itself, to engage critically with social ideologies, and even to undermine them. In Eco's opinion, architecture functions according to the model of an "open language system" that relies upon both internal and external codes. He mentions technical and typological codes as examples of well-elaborated internal codes in architecture.[36] These codes can be denotative or connotative and can operate on both a syntactic and a semantic level. He grants these internal codes the capacity to innovate architecture in a technical, aesthetic, or functional sense. Achieving fundamental innovation, however, would only be possible by relying upon external codes that belong to the social or anthropological field outside architecture.

Eco refers to Hall's "proxemics" as an instance of such external cultural codes, which provide an underlying structure that conditions architecture.[37] This interpretation however evokes questions. Why does Eco refer to proxemics as an external code? Shouldn't one recognize that the logics of proxemics are intimately related to architectural settings and hence form a code internal to architecture? Hall refers after all to practices like "poking one's head in the door" in an office in Germany, or the table setting in a French restaurant. In his book *La struttura assente*, Eco criticizes many structuralists for mistakenly attaching an ontological reality to the structures they detect in their analysis of cultural practices. He argues that it makes more sense to consider these structures as "absent" or to rather characterize them as methodological choices. If we follow him in this respect, shouldn't we wonder whether he is making a similar mistake by considering proxemics as an underlying structure that ontologically exists outside of architecture? If this objection makes sense, it also makes sense to question Eco's assumption that fundamental innovation in architecture always comes from sources outside of architecture.

It might be that Eco himself also evolved in his opinion regarding this question. At the end of his chapter on the semiotics of architecture, there is a passage on the design of Brasilia, which suggests that the "failure" of Brasilia was less the responsibility of its designers than of the briefs they received, which did not adequately predict societal evolutions: since the architects expertly designed sign vehicles that closely responded to these external briefs, they were not at fault. He wonders however whether it would not have been a better option for the architects to design "forms and dispositions flexible enough to provide for different meanings as warranted in the course of events."[38] Here one can detect a suggestion that it might be possible for architecture to rely upon its own internal codes to develop, for example, innovative typologies that would be more open and that would allow for the accommodation of future societal contradictions, not yet taken into account in codes that are external to architecture.

Geoffrey Broadbent and the semiotics of design modes: Walking with Peirce

In the sixties and seventies architectural semiotics was not the only "nouvelle vague" in theory and criticism of architecture. Another wave, propelled by the hope of defining a design theory and methodology capable of dealing with the needs of society in full modernization, was articulated by, among others, Nigel Cross, Horst Rittel, Serge Chermayeff, Christopher Alexander, and Geoffrey Broadbent. Not surprisingly several scholars attempted to establish bridges between design theory and semiotics.

A case in point is British architect and educator Geoffrey Broadbent (b. 1955). In several texts Broadbent staked out four modes of design that he considered as fundamental.[39] In his view, "pragmatic design" is based on trial and error: the designer or builder experiments until a form is created that serves the intended purpose. Pragmatic design might be the oldest but still the most widespread design mode. Broadbent refers to the prehistoric shelter of mammoth hunters but also to today's experimentation with new materials and construction modes. If one includes ad hoc construction and self-help housing all over the world, pragmatic design is by far the predominant design mode. "Iconic design" relates to "fixed mental images," consolidated after a long process of pragmatic design and considered, by social convention and common knowledge, apt to specific briefs. Broadbent refers to vernacular forms such as "the Eskimo's igloo" but also to office buildings, "which become the contemporary fixed mental image for a generation of architects and clients."[40] In "analogic design," inspiration is sought in observable similarities with external images, forms, spatial arrangements, etc. Broadbent mentions Le Corbusier's comment on the "visual analogy" between the roof of his Ronchamp Chapel and a crab shell. He also points to the "structural analogy" between the plan of three Frank Lloyd Wright houses, all three based on an identical organogram but each elaborated with a different geometrical pattern.[41] Finally, "canonical or geometric design" uses an abstract system of relations based on geometric analogy with the human body, the cosmos, or mathematical figures.

Subsequently, Broadbent connects these four "fundamental" design modes with the three best-known sign types from Peirce's classification.[42] Peirce's "icon," in which the representamen (signifier/sign vehicle) refers to an object on the basis of potential visual or structural resemblance ("firstness"), is, according to Broadbent, especially relevant in the analogical and canonical design process. Peirce's "index," where that reference is based on a factual or causal link ("secondness"), would be active in pragmatic design, from ad hoc building to the experimental use of new materials and techniques. Peirce's "symbol," where the reference from the representamen towards the object is based on a rule or a convention, works in "iconic" designs based on "fixed mental images." Broadbent observes that his "iconic design," sustained by "fixed mental images," has less to do with Peirce's "iconicity" than with Peirce's "symbol," and changes the name from "iconic" into "typologic design." Finally, Broadbent makes a rather debatable move by ranking his four modes of design in terms of the degree of creativity they require. Pragmatic design (working with indexes) figures on top, followed by analogic design (working with icons of visual resemblance), typologic design (based on fixed mental images), and finally canonic design (involving icons of structural resemblance).

Broadbent's walk with Peirce makes an important move in the Anglo-American semiotics of architecture. The link Broadbent establishes between design methods and Peirce's semiotics opens the possibility of an interesting theoretical interplay between these two fields. Unfortunately, Broadbent limits his evocation of Peirce to the index-icon-symbol triplet that articulates the relationship between representamen (sign vehicle/signifier) and object, ignoring the fact that this triplet only deals with one of the three relationships at work in Peirce's triadic definition of the sign. Consequently, the impact of the "three modes of being" (firstness, secondness, and thirdness) at play in all three relationships that make the sign work as a sign, is, in Broadbent's writings, limited to their appearance as index, icon, or symbol. Equally absent are other concepts that could be of interest in the semiotics of design, such as "the unlimited semiosis" a sign is capable of generating and the "abductive" ("what if") mode of reasoning that prevails in Peirce's logic.

Nevertheless, Broadbent's move remains highly significant. By linking different design modes to different classes of signs in which different "modes of being" are at work, Broadbent implies that different "modes of signification" operate in design. This, in turn, can be connected to the idea of "modes of production," a concept that is mostly prevalent in (neo)Marxist theory and that refers to different systems of political economy (i.e., capitalism versus communism). Umberto Eco likewise uses the term *modes de production sémiotiques*, implying that the production of significations might follow some kind of logic that is reminiscent of the logic of political economy.[43] As we discuss later, this potential crossover between semiotics and neo-Marxism would become productive indeed in the hands of Jean Baudrillard.

Charles Jencks: "The Language of Postmodern Architecture." Reloading the metaphor

In accordance with Eco, British architectural historian Charles Jencks (1939-2019) posited the semiotic ideas that architecture is a medium for mass communication and signification, that it functions as a "language" that uses different sign types, and that it can be encoded and decoded in different ways. Similar to Broadbent, Jencks recycled the Peircean sign triplet of Index, icon, and symbol, but in his interpretation this classification is not a categoric one. On the contrary, in accordance with Peirce he sees all signs as compound signs: they all have indexical, iconic, and symbolic characteristics.[44] However, following Jencks, in architecture, signs are far more indexical and iconic than in linguistics: in the postwar period, the symbolic (conventional) aspects of architectural signs have been impoverished and the iconic dimension has lost its deeper metaphorical levels. In Jencks's opinion, modern architecture is therefore to be blamed "for its obsessive concentration on indexical meanings" that promotes "a banal and literalist life of simplified functionality."[45] Modern architecture has thus squandered architecture's ability to communicate in a meaningful and convincing way with the general public (a sentiment that echoes Choay's earlier complaint about "semantic reduction").

Jencks's agenda clearly takes aim at the failures of modernism. He grants the term "postmodern" to architects who regard architecture as a visual language to be renewed and who consciously do this by encoding it "in a double way." This "double-coding" allows on the one hand a small professional and cultural elite to enjoy "fine discriminations in a fast-changing language," while on the other hand it affords the general public or local residents who are interested in "beauty, a traditional ambience, and particular way of life" to identify themselves with the iconography of the postmodern building.[46]

In Jencks's discourse, the crucial importance of communication in all architecture, be it historical, modern, or postmodern, implies a "positive approach to metaphorical buildings." His semiotic method consists of identifying and describing as precisely as possible the metaphoric load of a building. Jencks thus inventorizes and interprets the metaphors used and points to their layering and interaction. The nature and intensity of the metaphors identified vary from explicit to hidden, from literal to suggestive, from ridiculous to intriguing. A good example is Le Corbusier's chapel in Ronchamp with its multiple references, subtle or caricatured — mother and child, ship, nun's hat … For Jencks this is a metaphorically highly suggestive building.[47] So too is the hotdog stall in the shape of a hotdog, which he sees as a building whose metaphors have been explicitly coded for the uploading of one intended meaning and for the efficient communication of that particular meaning.[48]

Jencks most convincingly manages to present the power of metaphor in the semiotic analysis of some historic pieces of architecture, such as Gaudi's Casa Batllo.[49] Here he succeeds in unraveling different layers of overt and covert meaning whereby the visual communication simultaneously deals with the exposure of commemorative emblems, the whispering of secret messages, and the framing of a forbidden ideology, all related to Catalunia's nationalist struggle. But even here Jencks limits his reading to the most outward appearance of the building: the roof and the street façade. No mention is made of the astonishing typology of its decorated interior, its noble floor, its lightwell, its atrium, its loft, its roof landscape, etc. In Jencks's semiotic understanding, the metaphor thus remains a somewhat superficial trope, closer to achieving a visual surprise and spectacular effect through the external shape and appearance of the building than to revealing less obvious and unnamed meanings that might reside in other architectural features.

No doubt Jencks's emphasis on metaphoric predication in architecture serves his purpose of promoting postmodern architecture and dismissing an exhausted modernism. This can be seen as a proactive form of semiotics that works somewhat like operative history, in that it legitimizes and supports a specific trend in contemporary architecture.[50] In refocusing on the role of metaphor in architectural thinking and practice, Jencks ventured into a potentially highly productive realm of cross-fertilization between architecture and semiotics. Though Jencks's own work allows only for a rather limited interpretation of the potentials of metaphorical semiosis, several authoritative voices from other fields engaging with semiotics suggest more intriguing perspectives on the possible role of metaphor in architecture.

In a fragment of *La Pensée Sauvage* (1962), anthropologist Claude Lévi-Strauss (1908-2009) narrates the story of Mr. Wemminck, a character from Charles Dickens's *Great Expectations*.[51] Mr. Wemminck is a dull cleric who meets his daily work obligations with "official sentiment" and who at home takes care of his elderly father. He takes genuine pleasure, however, in the reconversion of his suburban cottage in Walworth into a miniature castle, with a drawbridge, a cannon that fires one shot every day at dinner time, and a kitchen garden surrounding the cottage that would help the residents to survive a siege. This self-built castle is the result, according to Lévi-Strauss, of a metaphorical operation that realizes a complex transfer between the syntagmatic chain of the (absent) castle and the one of the (present) cottage: transfer of objects (drawbridge, cannon), transfer of typological features (the surrounding kitchen garden as a moat-like protection apparatus), and transfer of etiquette rules (announcing dinner time). This gives rise to a creative tension that generates a new spatial form (a cottage-castle or a castle-cottage) as well as a new sentiment: the Walworth feeling.

The metaphor also plays a crucial role in the anthropology of Victor Turner (1920–1983), which studies rituals addressing fundamental changes (such as the transition of power, curing illness, crime and punishment, etc.) needed in a condition of conflict or crisis.[52] Turner describes how in such rituals "multivocal symbols" (objects, creatures, costumes, rhythms, gestures …) are brought together and evoke a chain of associations and related meanings. These components play a role in choreographies or role-plays that perform a "root metaphor" confronting the structural crisis with its antistructural counterpart, alternately confirming and negating the conflict, and thus generating a condition of suspension or liminality. This metaphorical play allows for a complex transfer of meaning in which the crisis of the traditional symbolic order is consecutively presented, dissolved, and reformulated, which allows to amend or to repair the damaged order.

In addition to anthropologists such as Lévi-Strauss and Turner philosopher and psychiater Jacques Lacan (1901-1981) offers interesting insights into metaphors. For Lacan metaphors are crucial in the interaction between the psychiatrist and the individual patient, because they somehow shed light on the shaky borderline between the conscious and the unconscious. Lacan develops a semiotic interpretation of this process on the basis of a reading of Saussure. He posits that the line that Saussure draws between signifier and signified is analogous to the one between "the conscious" and "the unconscious." The conscious refers to the symbolic order with its syntagmatic or metonymic chain of signifiers, whereas the unconscious has to do with the domain of unreachable signifieds. The metaphor helps to bridge the line between both and to reach out to these hidden signifieds. The semantic gap in conscious reasoning might provoke a creative kindling of the metaphor, whereby a signified of the unconscious appears for a short while in conscious speech, as an unexpected signifier, creating a glimpse of new meaning.[53] This process helps the patient on his way to a *parole pleine* (full speaking), which is crucial for a healthy self-understanding of the subject.[54]

Semiotics in its full breadth thus offers quite some interesting discussions of the metaphor and its role in creative signification, far beyond Jencks's initial opening. The metaphor apparently can help in redeeming semantic gaps, in dealing with social conflicts, and in the becoming of the subject. These hints however have not necessarily been picked up by architectural theory in the last decades of the 20th century. Still one can assume that buildings such as the Unité d'Habitation in Marseille, or the Centre Pompidou in Paris, or the Teatro del Mondo in Venice, or Parc de la Villette in Paris, or the Jewish Museum in Berlin might be more fully understood when their metaphorical operations are analyzed aided by such semiotical sources. Surely such analyses would clarify how their "creative kindling" managed to produce new spatialities and new affects, if not the promise of a *parole pleine* in architecture.

From Rossi to Derrida: Semiosis without semiotics. The city as text

There is no official common name to cover the work of the Italian neorealist/neorationalist Tendenza, spearheaded by Aldo Rossi (1931-1997), Giorgio Grassi (b. 1935), and Carlo Aymonino (1926–2010); the French *analyse urbaine* or "morpho-typology" associated with figures like Philippe Panerai (b. 1940) and Jean Castex (b. 1942); the Belgian "Reconstruction de la ville Européenne" proclaimed by a group of scholars and architects linked to the magazine AAM (*Archives de l'Architecture Moderne*); and the team in charge of the preparation of IBA 1984, directed by Josef Kleihues (1933-2004) and Hardt Hämer (1922-2012). They can all be gathered under the heading "the Architecture of the City approach," in honor of Aldo Rossi's seminal book launched in 1966 and repeatedly reprinted, reedited, and translated in the 1970s and 1980s.

Rossi's *Architecture of the City* accords the city as a whole, as well as its various architectural elements, a level of relative autonomy vis-à-vis other domains, such as culture or politics.[55] The city is seen as "architecture," consisting of built forms that shape its functional and social life, rather than the outcome of social factors. In that sense, the city honors a "function follows form" adagium, reversing the "form follows function" principle. The architecture of the city is thus considered as an important domain of material culture. Accordingly, the architectural form has its own formal logic that can be objectively analyzed, consistently theorized, and managed by design. The *longue durée* of the city's built history allows for the slow development of spatial relations and types while at the same time the city's architecture is continuously adapted and transformed. Central to this approach is the idea of type – a category of buildings sharing common characteristics. The architecture of the city is made of types of buildings and open spaces. Hence typology, the identification and classification of types and variants, becomes central to analysis and design. This brings Rossi to posit the trope of "analogy," defined as the relationship between types, as central to the architecture of the city. Rossi calls the historical European city "the Analogous City" – with analogy understood as both a mode of analysis and of design. He explains this notion by referring to an eighteenth-century "capriccio" painted by Canaletto, which presents a fictional urban scene in Venice composed as a collage of buildings, (paradigmatically) selected out of various contexts but all linked by analogy. Rossi calls this painting "a project."

French urban analysis further invested in developing a consistent methodological frame for urban analysis. Revisiting various concepts of typology in history, typological analysis is brought together with morphology, the study of spatial relations and structures. The result is a coherent and workable method of "morpho-typology" that throughout the 1980s was taught in many schools in Europe. Urban analysis and urban history provided the typo-morphological principles that were also supposed to form the basis of design.[56]

At first glance, this "architecture of the city" approach would seem rather distant from semiotics. Nevertheless, various lines of congruence between them can be identified. In the introduction of his book, Rossi underlines the "very evident analogies" between the study of the city and "linguistic studies," mentioning how Saussure's contributions to the development of linguistics could serve as a program for the development of urban science.[57] Indeed, the concept of type shares several characteristics with that of the Saussurean sign. Both Rossi and the French scholars refer to Quatremère de Quincy's *Dictioinaire historique de l'Architecture* (1832) in order to define "type." Quatremère's concept of type is based on two complementary principles: on the one hand type stands for a set of heterogeneous, typological characteristics of an architectural object (form, style, plan, function, building components, construction mode, technology …); on the other, it is articulated by a series of variants which together constitute the type.[58] This indeed corresponds, to a certain extent, to the Saussurean sign, because the type as a signifier gathers and associates typological characteristics as signifieds and furthermore acquires "value" in the paradigmatic differentiation of variants and in the syntagmatic combination with other types into an urban fabric (remember Saussure's metaphor of the paper snippets). Secondly, typology and morphology can be compared to the two basic axes of language defined by Saussure, i.e., "selection" (of each sign from an associative or paradigmatic field of signs) and "combination" (of signs into a logic syntagma – remember the metaphor of the column).

The congruence between both fields highlights yet another aspect of the subject. Considering the morpho-typological method as an indirect, implicit form of architectural semiotics allows us to make a link with the shift from structuralism to post-structuralism. This shift took place under the influence of the work of, among others, Barthes, Lacan, Derrida, Althusser, Kristeva, Baudrillard, and Deleuze. In semiotics' main discipline, language studies, the object of interest shifted from structural linguistics to psychoanalytical conversation, written language ('*écriture*') and texts. The atomic aspect of the Saussurean sign, i.e., the association of a signifier and a signified, was no longer dominant. The signifier was liberated from its univalent association with a supposed signified and became the predominant element in the signification process (semiosis). This shift mobilized an understanding that presented an endless shifting of meaning, due to "a play of signifiers" that provoke a parade of signifieds, which in turn act as signifiers to highlight still other signifieds, in an endless chain of signification. In a post-structuralist understanding, signs and codes – but also analogies and metaphors – all work as different "modes of signification" or "modes of meaning production," eliciting temporary associations between signifiers and signifieds generating momentary meanings in different ways.

In language studies, complex or experimental writings by Dante, de Sade, Mallarmé, Balzac, Bataille, and others became privileged objects of semiotic research. Texts and text studies were seen as belonging to an intertextual field in which each text provided the potential material for new text production. For post-structural thinkers, reading – the production of a personal interpretation of a text – thus became a form of writing: reading/writing had to do with deciphering codes, tropes, and intertextual references, identifying the play of textual signifiers, pursuing the traces of these signifiers in their uncertain associations with (supposed) signifieds that disclose (provisional) meanings of the text. These signifieds turned out to be signifiers of yet other meanings, a process whereby ever new traces of meaning ensure that the finding of an ultimate meaning is endlessly postponed. Drawing on the verb *différer* ("to differ" but also "to postpone"), Jacques Derrida (1930-2004) called this process "*différance*" (instead of "*différence*").[59]

The post-structuralist fascination with texts and intertextuality is akin to the methodology of urban analysis that approaches the city as a text to be deciphered, to be read, to be written. The "city as text" is indeed one of the root metaphors of the architecture of the city approach. Jean Castex invoked Henri Lefebvre in this regard: "He decided to approach the city objectively by studying the physical form of the city, reading it as the text from which the context, that is to say the social reality behind the city, could come to the fore."[60] Likewise Panerai and Castex called the urban analysis they made of Versailles a "reading of a city."[61] Besides the metaphor of "the city as text," the metaphor of "the urban fabric" was called upon. This metaphor relies on the idea of the woven fabric, resulting from an interaction between warp and weft, generated by the double rhythm of the instant movement of the spool producing specific textures and colored motives interweaving the stable and robust warp. This "interweaving" is echoed in the interaction between the evervarying and diversifying types and the stable morphological frame outlining the public realm.[62] Both the text and the fabric metaphor point to the necessity of multiple readings of the city; as such, Panerai and Castex proposed a multitude of methods such as maps, measurements, graphical analysis, observations, conversations, texts, and walks in order to unlock the city's multiple codes and themes – that is, its modes of spatial articulation, inhabitation, and signification (i.e., the architecture of the city).[63]

Rossi also reused the metaphor of the city as "collective memory," caught in a never-ending dynamic of remembering and forgetting. As such, urban analysis became a form of "topo analysis," digging up motives and events out of the urban unconscious – the forgotten or repressed repository of the city's life and history.[64] Urban analysis allows us not only to understand the physical form of the city but also to take up this physical form in order to interpret the interplay with the social and historical context. This context is, so to speak, stored in the built memory of the city, sedimented and engraved in its architecture.

Finally, in the "architecture of the city" approach, there is no caesura between urban analysis (as reading the city) and urban design (as writing the city), which is comparable to the reading-as-writing concept in post-structuralist semiotics. According to Rossi and Castex, analysis rather forms an integral part of the design process.[65] The concept of "the analogous city" hence informs a double program of urban analysis *and* urban design.

Semiotics and ideology: The political economy of sign and design

Postsructuralism not only celebrated the predominance of texts as the ultimate semiotic objects but also excelled in the critique of ideology as one of its most important concerns. This aspect allows us to uncover the relevance of the semiotic figure of knowledge in terms of social and societal critique. The nonmotivated character of the Saussurean sign with its arbitrary association and imaginary identification of signifier and signified had already opened a window for ideological practices and critique of ideology. The same applies to the notions of denotation and connotation. Both Barthes and Eco understood the critique of ideology as the unveiling of connotative meanings or secondary functions that are carried along with the initial denotation or the primary functionality of the sign.

The French neo-Marxist philosopher Louis Althusser (1918-1990) distinguished between, on the one hand, ideology as the imaginary representation of the real conditions of life (this is in line with the orthodox Marxist understanding of the term, which implies that the relations of production are presented to the powerless in a distorted way) and, on the other, ideology as the imaginary narrative that people adhere to when explaining their conditions of life (which is more in line with the neo-Marxist use of the term).[66] In the second definition, ideology is always present and plays an important role in the formation of a person's or a group's identity.

This process of identification operates in a similar way as the mirror stage (Lacan) in the life of a young child: children develop a sense of identity by identifying with roles, names, and behaviors offered by the social environment (parents, relatives, teachers).[67] Through the work of Althusser and others, psychoanalysis thus joined forces with neo-Marxist thought, and both become aligned with post-structuralism, as practiced, for example, by the authors connected to *Tel Quel* magazine.[68] These alliances allowed such authors to operate on both the level of highly sophisticated analyses of avant-garde texts by Joyce, Bataille, Artaud, and others *and* the level of social and societal critique.

One of the *Tel Quel* authors venturing in this field was philosopher Julia Kristeva (b. 1944), who has identified several modes of meaning production active in texts and calls them "idéologèmes."[69] She searches in the "fenotext" (i.e., on the surface and performance level of the text) for traces of the idéologèmes that dominate meaning production on the level of the "genotext" (i.e., on the deep-structural and competence level of the text).[70] She sees the Saussurean sign as one of the most dominant idéologèmes, in that it is constituted as an arbitrary association of a signifier and a signified but also negates this arbitrariness by assuming an imaginary identification between signifier and signified.[71] For Kristeva, the meaning production in the text is not a process without a subject. It is an "*expèrience pratique*" (practical experience) through which the subject is able, in her writing/reading, to build critical awareness of the idéologèmes at work so as to increase *la parole pleine* and thus enhance the formation of her subjectivity.[72]

A very interesting text that presents a crossover between critical theory, neo-Marxism, and semiotics in the field of architectural theory was produced by social scientist and philosopher Jean Baudrillard (1929-2007).[73] Baudrillard posited that in capitalist production, "things" (utensils, tools, whose exchange value traditionally corresponds to their use value) are turned into "products" (commodities) by subjecting them to a separation of their exchange value and use value. This is followed by a manipulation of both entities (dictated by industrial production and by price setting on the basis of profit making) and then a reunification on the basis of an imaginary identification between manipulated price and use value (referring to the assumption that more expensively priced items indeed offer more use value – which clearly is not always the case). Baudrillard extended this Marxist analysis by arguing that in late capitalist consumer society the generalization of consumption objects corresponds to a generalization of the semiotic logic of the Saussurean sign. This sign is also based on an arbitrary (not intrinsically motivated) association and imaginary identification (of signifier and signified). The consumption product likewise becomes a sign-object with its own "exchange value/sign" as signifier and "use value/sign" as signified.

This mechanism underpinned what Baudrillard now labeled as "the political economy of the sign." It received an important theoretical and cultural impetus from "the Bauhaus" (Baudrillard clearly used the term as a *pars pro toto* for modernism). In Baudrillard's view, all possible values of an object, all its possible fulfillments of needs, requests, and desires, are reduced by the Bauhaus theory to two rationalized values: aesthetics and utility. Design artificially isolates these two values from each other in order to manipulate them and to reunite them after manipulation into one unsuspected and uncontested entity that is presented as rational, useful, natural, and true.[74] The Bauhaus in fact codified and promoted the denotative function of an object as that which is pure, beautiful, true, and desired, whereas any form of connotation was blamed and rejected as redundancy, uselessness, ugliness, falsification, kitsch, and fashion. In Baudrillard's view, the Bauhaus thus aimed at a synthesis between form and function, between the beautiful and the useful, between art and technology, between the superstructure of form and meaning and the social and technical infrastructure achieved by the industrial revolution, presenting itself "as a second revolution achieving the industrial revolution and solving the contradictions left behind by the latter."[75]

However, in Baudrillard's view, the Bauhaus saga does not end at this point. Two semiotic miscalculations break the power of the Bauhaus impetus. First, the distinction between denotation as "true" and connotation as "false" was an ideological construction, "a metaphysical fable,"[76] a "superior myth."[77] That fable or myth was not solid enough to continue to rule the game of consumption. Behind "the metaphysical fable" proliferated a general fetishism that marked continuous new domains of consumption: money, beauty care, pets, mass media, body culture, sex and nakedness, the celebration of holiday and sun, the cultivation of gender difference, the glorification of the accomplished subject, the appropriation of a domesticated unconscious, etc. The second semiotic miscalculation reinforced the first one: "The Bauhaus and design claimed to control the process by mastery of the signifieds (use value based on the 'objective' evaluation of functions), but in fact it is the play of signifiers (a play dictated by exchange value) that took the lead. But that play is unlimited and escapes all control."[78] As a consequence of both semiotic miscalculations, the Bauhaus functionalism, "the superior myth," collapsed for the sake of fashion, which does not care about denotative truth or beauty or correctness but is fully engaged in playing the game of connotation.[79] Having lost any substantive or intrinsic objective, fashion plays a game of change for the sake of change – a play of pure signifiers. The age of the signified and of "pure" functionalism in design and architecture is over.[80]

With this provocative analysis, Baudrillard attempted to disrupt the ideological veil that, in his view, was intrinsic to the Bauhaus (read modernism). Like Manfredo Tafuri, in his contemporary essay on *Architecture and Utopia*[81] Baudrillard pinpointed the structural and ideological analogies between modernist theories on the one hand and the functioning of capitalism on the other, in order to enhance architects' awareness of their embeddedness within socioeconomic structures that they were unlikely to escape. Neither Baudrillard nor Tafuri saw at that point any opportunities for architects to develop an architectural practice that might critically engage with this societal embeddedness and thus dismissed the relative autonomy that Rossi had granted to the architecture of the city and that Eco evoked with his call for an "open language system" capable of dealing with future social contradictions.[82] This critical engagement was nevertheless something that many architects in the 1970s aimed for; for some of them their interest in semiotics was generated precisely by that ambition.

From Chomsky, over Derrida to Deleuze: Peter Eisenman's restless quest

Around 1960 a new semiotic concept overwhelmed Anglo-American linguistics and semiotics. MIT professor and linguist Noam Chomsky (b. 1928) provoked, with his *Syntactic Structures* (1957) and his *Aspects of the Theory of Syntax* (1965), a paradigmatic revolution in American language studies, comparable to the structuralist awakening caused by Saussure and Levi-Strauss on the European continent.[83] Chomsky's hypothesis of inborn "deep structures" that provide each of us with a "competence" of language acquisition, and that via "transformational rules" generate "surface structures" with a "performance of generating an unlimited series of grammatically correct sentences," echoed far beyond the realm of linguistics. Chomsky's attempts to discover that so-called Transformational Generative Grammar inspired both great enthusiasm and deep skepticism but also activated animated debates among linguists and philosophers.

Chomsky's ideas greatly inspired architectural theory and semiotics and obtained a particular significance for New York–based architect Peter Eisenman (b. 1928).[84] Eisenman thought that a universal grammar of architecture would be a significant step in the necessary project of regenerating the moribund modernism. He therefore embarked on a series of designs for houses (labeled House I, House II, etc.) in which he searched for abstract elements of form and for syntactic operations that would be universally applicable. Such a design process would exclude all semantic interpretations in terms of architectural history and modes of inhabitation and would not generate any meaning at all. The design process unfolds, within a perfect Euclidian cubic void, an astonishing series of geometric transformations of lines, planes, and volumes, from (supposed) deep-structural to surface level.[85] Although Eisenman explicitly intended to avoid semantics, the emergence of meaning proved to be inevitable: indeed the very operations that Eisenman performed on the basis of a Chomskyan logic became famous and thus turned into cultural (hence meaningful) practices in themselves. Moreover, some of the houses were inhabited, which also implies that the interaction between house and residents generated processes of signification.[86] One could therefore hypothesize that Eisenman practices a splendid form of iconic design (in Broadbent's terms) by metaphorically transposing the linguistic idea of "universal grammar" to architecture and by morphing it into an architectural image in order to fill the semantic gap left by worn out modernism.

The Chomskyan wave however did not last long, as post-structuralism made its way across the Atlantic under the form of "French Theory."[87] In particular, Derrida's

"deconstruction," closely followed by Deleuze's "fold," hit the imagination of theorists and designers, including Peter Eisenman. One is left to wonder, however, how much effort was spent by architects on thoroughly understanding concepts such as "deconstruction" or "folding," and on thoughtfully interpreting these in terms of architecture. A lot of what came to be known as "deconstructivist" architecture, for example, seems to boil down to an almost literal rendering of the idea of deconstruction in an idiom of crooked corners, crumpled walls, and uneven floors that generate illusory suggestions of instability and vicissitude.[88] A similar straightforward "morphing" of epistemology into architecture led to an architecture of undulating walls and floors, pleated and continuous surfaces that supposedly evoked "the fold" theorized by Deleuze.[89] That the Derridean or Deleuzean inspiration sometimes resulted in remarkable and thus meaningful architecture such as Tschumi's Parc de la Villette, Libeskind's Jewish Museum, or Eisenman's Alteka Office Building has more to do with the design skills of these architects than with the semiotic soundness of the philosophy-aesthetic morphing that generated their architectural appearance.

Somewhere halfway in his astonishing series of paradigmatic evocations, Eisenman declared an absolute need for the radical rethinking of architecture itself and of its semiotics of representation.[90] His declaration echoed the post-structuralist semiotics of Baudrillard and Kristeva in putting forth the criticism that twentieth-century architecture was dominated by a classical conception of the sign, based on the "fictions" of representation, reason, and history. Eisenman rather advocated a "non-classical architecture," which would unmask itself as fiction by playing a game of "dissimulation" instead of "simulation." While "simulation" aims to eliminate the difference between reality and illusion so that the illusion can present itself as reality and hence replace it, "dissimulation" would leave the difference between reality and illusion unaffected (just like a mask does, because it does not deny that the wearer of the mask is not the being or the thing that the mask evokes). For Eisenman, this non-classical architecture is like a mask in that it "is no longer a certification of experience or a simulation of history, reason, or reality in the present. Instead, it may more appropriately be described as an *other* manifestation, an architecture *as is*, now as a fiction. It is a representation of itself, of its own values and internal experience."[91] If one includes Eisenman's own iconic representations of Chomsky, Derrida, or Deleuze in the history of representation, his move towards "dissimulation" might be seen as an interesting auto-critique. Unfortunately, however, it seems that non-semiotic dissimulation is not easily articulated into architecture. Maybe it is simply not possible to escape semiotics.

Eisenman's remarkable quest of paradigms illustrates both the paradigmatic volatility of late twentieth-century architectural theory and its eagerness to participate in the articulation of a relevant theoretical frame capable of dealing with the increasingly complex challenges of culture and society. It thus offers an interesting figure of knowledge, which operates as an architectural manifestation of different strands of semiotics, sometimes trying to outdo semioticians in a quest for radical moves[92] but ultimately bound by the social, economic, psychological, and technological limitations that delimit architecture's playing field. Nevertheless the simple suggestion that architecture *can* perform radical and critical gestures by concentrating on its own formal logic (i.e., its relative autonomy) represents a highly significant moment in late twentieth-century theory and practice – even when later critics wondered whether these consecutive experiments with different games of signifiers and modes of paradigmatic morphing indeed succeeded in performing the societal critique they were supposedly aiming at.[93]

Critical pragmatism, resetting semiotics

The two paradigmatic lines outlined above offer a certain coherence in the rhizomatic story of architectural semiotics from 1960 to 1980. In the Saussurean line, the arbitrary association and imaginary identification of the signifier and signified – together with the roles of denotation and connotation in the process of signification – made semiotics suitable for ideology critique and hence offered an anchorpoint for a sophisticated criticism that addressed architecture as a formal language *and* as a carrier of ideological functions (Tafuri, Baudrillard). The Saussurean line was also characterized by a development from structuralism to post-structuralism, from the semiotics of signs and syntax to the semiotics of signifiers and texts, from the identification of meaning to the tracing of multiple and provisional meanings, thus moving closer to urban analysis and urban design, a movement facilitated by the "city as text" metaphor, by the reading-writing / analysis-design nexus, and by the creative role of metaphor in language and design (Rossi, Panerai, Castex).

The Anglo-American line on the other hand started with the pragmatist semiotics of Peirce that opened up to a much wider field of sifnification. All objects and phenomena, all verbal and nonverbal languages, all elements of material and immaterial culture can figure in Peirce's complex definition of the sign and its process of semiosis. The purpose of signification is provoking an effect on the basis of "what if" hypotheses. Therefore each Peircean sign sets in motion an appropriate combination of three "modes of being" (potentiality, factuality, conventionality). Within this pragmatist set up, scholars in architecture such as Jencks and Broadbent made attempts to link "modes of design" to the Peircean modes of being presented by the sign classes: icon, index, and symbol. Starting from this Peircean frame, Jencks also unlocked the significance of metaphors in architecture, without however fully realizing the analytical and critical potentials that this approach might allow for.

A major conceptual move of interconnection between the Anglo-American and Saussurian lines was effectuated by Eco, who defined function as meaning. Eco attributed a relative autonomy to the architectural form defined as a complex sign vehicle that communicates and promotes denotative and connotative functions to which it is associated by cultural codes. For him, semiotics of communication involves performance of function and as such comes close to the pragmatist semiosis aiming at effect. We found another instance of interconnection between both lines in the work of Eisenman, who at first was deeply influenced by Chomsky's generative grammar and later became fascinated by post-structuralist authors such as Derrida.

Revisiting the brief but complex history of architectural semiotics brought us to a conclusion that is quite different from the one often reached by other observers. It seems to us that the "forest of symbols" that we explored was far too easily discredited as a kind of wasteland by authors eager to introduce fresh concepts or inspirations.[94] If the quick sequence of fascination, disappointment, dismissal, and replacement was particularly striking with respect to this specific episode of architectural theory, the phenomenon is not limited to semiotics. It rather reveals a modus operandi that persists within the discipline of architecture – that of borrowing paradigms from other fields (linguistics, cybernetics, philosophy, sociology, anthropology …) which are rapidly applied, consumed, and thrown away. The appropriation of each new paradigm is often limited to its most accessible text passages, to the most eloquent quotes, or to a collection of suggestive terms. Little intellectual energy seems to be spent on a careful translation of borrowed key concepts, which might lead to a truly creative metaphorical transfer rather than a fashionable gimmick.

Architectural semiotics is one of the paradigms that fell victim to the "postcriticality" wave that hit architecture around the turn of the century.[95] Postcriticality blamed postwar paradigms for charging architecture with an overdose of critical, epistemological, ideological, and social concerns that deviated the discipline from its core business of projecting and building. Semiotics was a prime target in the line of fire because of its emphasis on representation, its focus on deciphering and interpreting, its search for the ever-elusive meaning, its obsession with difference and contradiction, its hermetic jargon, and its lack of tangible results. In its war on theory and criticism the postcriticality paradigm advanced some interesting positions, including both a justified attempt to restore the balance between autonomy and heteronomy in architecture and a renewed focus on the importance of design and projects. On the other hand, postcritical positions often showed a reductive interpretation of the contributions of theory and criticism (including semiotics), and the postcritical "projective turn" often implied a problematic denial of the social and political implications of projects.

It is our contention therefore that rather than dismisssing successive paradigms out of hand – including both semiotics and postcriticality – architectural theory would do well to recognize, evaluate, and valorize its own recent history of thought and practice. In our opinion, our retrospective of semiotic paradigms and scenes did not unveil a collection of intellectual failures but rather a sequence of promising concepts, interrupted reasonings, unaccomplished adaptations, and semi-results. All this provides materials for critical evaluation, selective recycling, and further processing in the light of the actual condition of the discipline and its present challenges. For us, the two lines that we explored continue to offer valuable insights and the investigation of their potential interconnection remains a worthwhile intellectual challenge. Whereas we appreciate the ideology critique and political savviness that came out of the Continental line, we also value the common-sense logic and the potential social sensibility of Anglo-Saxon Pragmatism. For Umberto Eco, the different paradigmatic tracks do not really contradict each other but rather outline a common space of semiotic thinking and practice. Within such space reloading semiotics could be a meaningful program. "What if" crossovers and creative interplays between (post)structuralism and pragmatism, between the linguistic turn and the projective turn, between critical thinking and projective matters of concern,[96] could give form and content to something yet to be named ("'the semiotics of critical projectivism'"?, "design for critical pragmatism"?). A similar attitude seems to be shared by Joan Ockman, in her quest for theoretical support for contemporary architecture in American philosophical Pragmatism.[97] We think Ockman's seminal effort merits continuation. We indeed remain convinced that architectural practice, architectural history, and architectural education continue to be in need of the critical reflection provided by an architectural theory that recognizes, appreciates, and build upon its own intellectual legacies. The efforts to embrace a critical Pragmatism and to reset semiotics are dearly needed for an architectural practice that acknowledges its responsibilities in moving towards an ecologically sound and non-oppressive environment.

Notes

1. Following Umberto Eco's suggestion, we use the term "semiotics" as a general category that covers all contributions to "sémiologie" and semiotics. Occasionally the term "sémiologie" is used in its historical particularity. See: Umberto Eco, *La structure absente: Introduction à la recherche sémiotique* [1968] (Paris: Mercure de France, 1972), 11.
2. Françoise Choay, "Urbanism & Semiology," in *Meaning in Architecture*, eds. Charles Jencks and George Baird (London: Barrie & Rockliff, The Cresset Press, 1969), 27-39, 34.
3. Alexander Tzonis and Liane Lefaivre, *Classical Architecture. The Poetics of Order* (Cambridge, MA: MIT Press, 1986).
4. Mart Stam, "Das Mass, das richtige Mass, das Minimummass," [1929] in *Neues Bauen, neues Gestalten: Das Neue Frankfurt/die neue Stadt. Eine Zeitschrift zwischen 1926 und 1933*, ed. Heinz Hirdina (Berlin: Elefanten Press, 1984) 215-16, 216.
5. Adolf Loos, "Potemkin City" [1898], *Spoken into the Void: Collected Essays, 1897-1900* (Cambridge, MA: MIT Press, 1982), 95-96; Adolf Loos, "Ornament and Crime" [1908], in *Ornament and Crime: Selected Essays* (Riverside, CA: Ariadne Press, 1998) 167-76.
6. Louis Sullivan, "The Tall Office Building Artistically Considered," [1896], in *The Public Papers*, ed. Robert Twombly (Chicago: University of Chicago Press, 1988), 104-13; Loos, "Ornament and Crime"; Amédée Ozenfant and Charles-Edouard Jeanneret, "After Cubism," [1918], in *L'Esprit nouveau: Purism in Paris, 1918-1925*, ed. Carol S. Eliel (New York: Harry N. Abrams, 2001).
7. John Summerson, "The Case for a Theory of Modern Architecture," *RIBA Journal* (June 1957): 307-10, 310.
8. The forest metaphor is borrowed from: Victor Turner, *The Forest of Symbols: Aspects of Ndembu Ritual* (Ithaca: Cornell University Press, 1967).
9. Louis Martin, "The Search for a Theory in Architecture: Anglo-American Debates 1957-1976," (PhD diss., Princeton University, 2002); Louis Martin, "Semiotics and Architecture Revisited," in *The Architect and the Public: On George Baird's Contribution to Architecture*, ed. Roberto Damiani (Rome: Quodlibet, forthcoming).
10. Ferdinand de Saussure, *Cours de linguistique générale* [1916] (Paris: Payot, 2016), 85-88, 151-56.
11. Roland Barthes, "Éléments de sémiologie," *Communications* 4, no.1 (1964): 91-135; Saussure, *Cours*, 215-18.
12. Barthes, "Éléments de sémiologie." Barthes refers to Saussure's notions of "syntagm" and "association," redefined as "syntagm" and "paradigm" by the Russian linguist to the tropes of "metonymy" and "metaphor." Roman Jakobson, "Deux aspects du langage et deux types d'aphasie," in *Temps Modernes*, no. 188 (Jan 1962): 853 ff.

13. Saussure, *Cours,* 230-32; see also Umberto Eco, "A Componential Analysis of the Architectural Sign /Column/," in *Signs, Symbols and Architecture,* eds. Geoffrey Broadbent, Richard Bunt, and Charles Jencks (New York: Wiley, 1980), 213-32.
14. Roland Barthes, *Mythologies* [1957], trans. Annette Lavers (London: Paladin, 1972). Barthes refers, for the concepts of denotation and connotation, to Louis Hjelmslev, *Prolegomena to a Theory of Language* [1943] (Baltimore: Indiana University, 1953).
15. Roland Barthes, "Sémiologie et Urbanisme," *L'Architecture d'Aujourd'hui,* no. 153 (1971): 11-13.
16. Charles Sanders Peirce, *The Collected Papers of Charles Sanders Peirce,* eds. Charles Hartsthorne, Paul Weiss, and Arthur W. Burks (Cambridge, MA: Harvard University Press, 1931-1935, 1958), 2.227-228; 2.243; 5.475-476; 5.483; 5.488; 8.332; see also Eco, *La structure absente,* 22-23.
17. Peirce, *Collected Papers,* 1.23-26; 1.418-420; 8.328-331.
18. Ibid., 2.243-252.
19. Catherine Legg and Christopher Hookway, "Pragmatism," in *The Stanford Encyclopedia of Philosophy,* ed. Edward N. Zalta (Stanford University: Metaphysics Research Lab, Spring 2019), https://plato.stanford.edu/archives/spr2019/entries/pragmatism/.
20. This effect can be "emotional," "energetic," or "logical." Peirce, *Collected Papers,* 5.475-76; 8.338-39.
21. Jacques Derrida, *Positions* (Paris: Minuit, 1972), 35-41.
22. The pragmatic maxim states: "Consider what effects that might conceivably have practical bearings, we conceive the object of our conception to have. Then, our conception of these effects is the whole of our conception of the object." Peirce, *Collected Papers,* 5.402.
23. Peirce, *Collected Papers,* 4.536; 8.315. See also Umberto Eco, *Le Signe* [1972] (Brussels: Labor, 1988), 251-53; and Wilhelmus A. De Pater and Pierre Swiggers, *Taal en teken: Een historisch-systematische inleiding in de taalfilosofie* (Leuven: Leuven University Press, 2000), 125, 130.
24. Peirce, *Collected Papers,* 2.619-25; 2.632-44.
25. De Pater and Swiggers, *Taal en teken,* 137-51; Charles W. Morris, *Writings on the General Theory of Signs* (The Hague: Mouton, 1971), 17, 173-76, 224-27, 301-3, 340, 366, 401-5.
26. Morris, *Writings,* 21-22, 301-2.
27. John Langshaw Austin, *How to Do Things with Words: The William James Lectures Delivered in Harvard University in 1955,* eds. James Opie Urmson and Marina Sbisà (Cambridge, MA: Harvard University Press, 1975).
28. Edward T. Hall, *The Hidden Dimension* (Garden City: Doubleday, 1966).
29. Peter Bondanella, *Umberto Eco and the Open Text: Semiotics, Fiction, Popular Culture* (Cambridge, UK: Cambridge University Press, 1997). The history of Eco's relevant publications is rather complex. He first published *La Struttura Assente: Introduzione alla ricerca*

semiologica in Italian (Milan: Bompiani, 1968). Four years later this book appeared in a French translation as *La structure absente*. Section C of this book ("La function et le signe: Sémiotique de l'architecture") was translated in English as Umberto Eco, "Function and Sign: The Semiotics of Architecture," in *Signs, Symbols and Architecture*, 11-69. Another relevant book is Umberto Eco, *Segno* [1972] (Milan: Arnoldo Mondatore, 1980), translated in French as *Le Signe*.
30. Eco, *Le Signe*, 35-41.
31. Eco, "Function and Sign", 15-27.
32. Ibid., 13.
33. Sullivan, "The Tall Office Building".
34. Eco, "Function and Sign", 25-34.
35. Ibid., 41-42.
36. Ibid., 38-50.
37. Ibid., 50-57.
38. Ibid., 58-61.
39. Geoffrey Broadbent, "A Plain Man's Guide to the Theory of Signs in Architecture," *Architectural Design* no. 7-8, 1977; Geoffrey Broadbent, "The Deep Structures of Architecture" [1974], in *Signs, Symbols and Architecture*, 119-68; Geoffrey Broadbent, "Building Design as an Iconic Sign System" [1974], in *Signs, Symbols, and Architecture*, 311-31.
40. Broadbent, "The Deep Structures," 139.
41. Broadbent, "Building Design," 315.
42. Ibid., 314-30.
43. Eco, *Le Signe,* 165, 172-83.
44. Charles Jencks, "The Architectural Sign," in *Signs, Symbols and Architecture,* 71-118, especially 102-3.
45. Jencks, "The Architectural Sign," 107.
46. Charles Jencks, *The Language of Post-Modern Architecture* (London: Academy Editions, 1977), 8.
47. Jencks, *The Language,* 48.
48. Ibid., 40–52.
49. Jencks, "The Architectural Sign", 92-95.
50. Manfredo Tafuri, *Theories and History of Architecture* (London: Granada, 1980).
51. Claude Lévi-Strauss, *La Pensée Sauvage* (Paris: Plon, 1962), 26, 198-99.
52. Viktor Turner, *Dramas, Fields and Metaphors. Symbolic Action in Human Society* (London: Cornell University Press, 1974), 13-17, 25, 31, 33-52, 202, 248, 272-99.
53. Jacques Lacan, "L'instance de la lettre dans l'inconscient ou la raison depuis Freud," in Jacques Lacan, *Ecrits* (Paris: Seuil, 1966), 493-518.
54. Lacan, "Fonction et champs de la parole et du langage," in *Ecrits*, 247-59.

55. Aldo Rossi, *L'architettura della città* (Padua: Marsilio, 1966); English trans. *The Architecture of the City* (Cambridge, MA: MIT Press, 1982); French trans. *L'architecture de la ville* (Paris: L'Equerre, 1981).
56. Giorgio Grassi, "Architekturprobleme und Realismus," *Archithese* (19: Realismus in der Architektur), 1976, 18-24; Léon Krier, "The Blind Spot," *Architectural Design* no. 4, 1978, 219-21; Jean Castex, "Enjeu et nécessité," in *Eléments d'analyse urbaine,* ed. Philippe Panerai et al. (Brussels: AAM, 1980), 710; Philippe Panerai, "Typologies," in *Elements d'analyse urbaine,* 73-108; Christian Devillers, "Typologie de l'habitat & morphologie urbaine, " *L'Architecture d'Aujourd'hui* no. 174, July/August 1974, 18-22.
57. Rossi, *L'architecture de la ville,* 10.
58. Ibid., 25-27; Panerai, "Typologies."
59. Derrida, *Positions,* 35-41.
60. Castex, "Enjeu et nécessité," 7. Castex is referring to Henri Lefebvre, *Le droit à la ville* (Paris: Anthropos, 1968). A few years after Lefebvre, Greimas formulated a similar text-city metaphor. See A. J. Greimas, *Sémiotique et sciences sociales* (Paris: Seuil, 1976), 140-41.
61. Jean Castex, Patrick Céleste, and Philippe Panerai, *Lecture d'une ville*: *Versailles* (Paris: Moniteur, 1980).
62. The metaphor of the "urban fabric" is a common one. For the specific articulation into "warp" and "weft," see SAR-73, *Het methodisch formuleren van afspraken bij het ontwerpen van weefsels* (Eindhoven: Stichting Architecten Research, 1973); Castex et al., *Lecture d'une ville,* 9-10; Alain Borie, Pierre Micheloni, and Pierre Pinon, *Forme et déformation des objects architecturaux et urbains* (Paris: Centre d'études et de recherches architecturales, 1978), 27.
63. Panerai et al., *Eléments d'analyse urbaine.*
64. Rossi, *Architecture de la ville,* 171-73 (Rossi refers to Maurice Halbwachs, *La mémoire collective* [Paris: PUF, 1950]); Greimas, *Sémiotique,* 129-31 (Greimas discusses "une sémiotique topologique").
65. Rossi, *Architecture of the City,* 219-20; Castex, "Enjeu et nécessité," 8-9.
66. Louis Althusser, "Idéologie et appareils idéologiques d'état," in Louis Althusser, *Positions* (Paris: Editions Sociales, 1976), 67-125.
67. Jacques Lacan, "Le Stade du miroir comme formateur de la fonction du Je," in *Ecrits,* 93-100.
68. Julia Kristeva, "La sémiologie: Science critique et/ou critique de la science," in Tel Quel, *Théorie d'ensemble* (Paris: Seuil, 1968), 80-93.
69. Julia Kristeva, *Sémeiotikè: Recherches pour une sémanalyse* (Paris: Seuil, 1969), 60.
70. Julia Kristeva, "Sémanalyse et production de sens," in A. J. Greimas et al., *Essais de sémiotique poétique* (Paris: Larousse, 1972), 207-34.
71. Julia Kristeva, *Sémeiotikè,* 83-89.
72. Julia Kristeva, *La révolution du langage poétique* (Paris: Seuil, 1974), 176-85.

73. Jean Baudrillard, *Pour une critique de l'économie politique du signe* (Paris: Gallimard, 1972), 172-99; 229-48; an English version was published as "Design and Environment: Or, the Inflationary Curve of Political Economy," in *The Universitas Project,* ed. Emilio Ambasz (New York: Museum of Modern Art, 2006), 50-65; see also Matthew Holt, "Baudrillard and the Bauhaus: The Political Economy of Design," *Design Issues* 32, no. 3 (Summer 2016): 55-66, https://doi.org/10.1162/DESI_a_00399.
74. Baudrillard, *Pour une critique,* 235, 245.
75. Ibid., 231.
76. Ibid., 245.
77. Ibid., 196. The full citation reads: "Loin d'être le terme objectif auquel s'oppose la connotation comme terme idéologique, la denotation est donc, puisqu'elle naturalise ce process meme de l'idéologie, le terme le plus idéologique…le mythe supérieur dont parle Barthes." The reference is to Roland Barthes, *S/Z* (Paris: Seuil, 1970), 16.
78. Ibid., 247.
79. Ibid., 246.
80. Ibid., 248; Jean Baudrillard, "Modernité," in *La modernité ou l'esprit du temps* (Paris: L'Equerre, 1982), 28-31.
81. Manfredo Tafuri, *Architecture and Utopia: Design and Capitalist Development* [1973] (Cambridge, MA: MIT press, 1990).
82. Manfredo Tafuri, "Toward a Critique of Architectural Ideology" [1969], in *Architecture Theory Since 1968*, ed. Michael Hays (Cambridge, MA: MIT Press, 1998), 6-35 (this essay was further developed into the 1973 book *Architecture and Utopia*); Eco, "Function and Sign," 58-61.
83. Noam Chomsky, *Syntactic Structures* (The Hague: Mouton, 1957); Noam Chomsky, *Aspects of the Theory of Syntax* (Cambridge, MA: MIT Press, 1965).
84. Broadbent, "The Deep Structures"; Mario Gandelsonas and David Morton, "On Reading Architecture," in *Signs, Symbols and Architecture,* 243-74; Peter Eisenman, *Houses of Cards* (Oxford: Oxford University Press, 1987); Peter Eisenman, *Eisenman Inside Out. Selected Writings 1963-1988* (New Haven: Yale University Press, 2004).
85. Amir Djalali, "Eisenman beyond Eisenman: Language and Architecture Revisited," *The Journal of Architecture* 22, no. 8 (2017): 1287-98, https://doi.org/10.1080/13602365.2017.1394350.
86. Suzanne Frank, *Peter Eisenman's House VI: The Client's Response* (New York: Watson-Guptill, 1994).
87. François Cusset, *French Theory: Foucault, Derrida, Deleuze et cie et les mutations de la vie intellectuelle aux Etats-Unis* (Paris: La Découverte, 2003); François Cusset, *French Theory: How Foucault, Derrida, Deleuze & Co Transformed the Intellectual Life of the United States* (Minneapolis: University of Minneapolis press, 2008).
88. Philip Johnson and Mark Wigley, *Deconstructivist Architecture* (New York: Museum of Modern Art, 1988).

89. Douglas Spencer, "The New Phantasmagoria: Transcoding the Violence of Financial Capitalism," in ed. Nadir Lahiji, *The Missed Encounter of Radical Philosophy with Architecture* (London: Bloomsbury, 2014), 79-93.
90. Peter Eisenman, "The End of the Classical: The End of the Beginning, the End of the End," *Perspecta*, 21 (1984): 154-72.
91. Ibid., 167.
92. Céline Bodart analyses, in her PhD dissertation, the collaboration – or lack thereof – between Peter Eisenman and Jacques Derrida in their attempt to come up with a design for one garden in Parc de la Villette. See Céline Bodart, "Architecture et Déconstruction: Remises en jeu d'une rencontre: raconter, traduire, hériter" (doctoral dissertation presented at the Université 8 de Paris and the Université de Liège, 2018).
93. Mary McLeod, "'Other' Spaces and 'Others,'" in *The Sex of Architecture*, ed. Diana Agrest, Patricia Conway, and Leslie Kanes Weisman (New York: Harry N. Abrams, 1996), 15-28; Robert Somol and Sarah Whiting, "Notes around the Doppler Effect and Other Moods of Modernism," *Perspecta* 33 (2002): 72-77, https://doi.org/10.2307/1567298.
94. Deborah Hauptmann and Andrej Radman, "Asignifying Semiotics as Proto-Theory of Singularity: Drawing Is Not Writing and Architecture Does Not Speak," *Footprint* 8, no. 1 (2014): 1-12, https://doi.org/10.7480/footprint.8.1.794; Mark Foster Gage, "Deus Ex Machina: From Semiology to the Elegance of Aesthetics," *Architectural Design* 77, no. 1 (2007): 82–85, https://doi.org/10.1002/ad.401.
95. Ole W. Fischer, "Architecture, Capitalism, and Criticality," in *The SAGE Handbook of Architectural Theory*, eds. C. Greig Crysler, Stephen Cairns, and Hilde Heynen (London: SAGE, 2012), 56-70.
96. Bruno Latour, "Why Has Critique Run out of Steam? From Matters of Fact to Matters of Concern," *Critical Inquiry* 30, no. 2 (2004): 225-48, https://doi.org/10.1086/421123.
97. Joan Ockman, ed., *The Pragmatist Imagination. Thinking about «Things in the Making»* (New York: Princeton Architectural Press, 2000). See also Pauline Lefebvre, "Tracer des reprises du pragmatisme en architecture (1990-2010). Penser l'engagement des architectes avec le réel" (doctoral dissertation presented at the Université Libre de Bruxelles, 2016) as well as Ockman's own account of this endeavor elsewhere in this volume.

CHAPTER 2
A Voice from the Margins: Robin Boyd and 1960s Architecture Culture

Philip Goad

Internationally, the career of Australian architect and critic Robin Boyd (1919-1971), is today largely unacknowledged. But during his lifetime, and especially in the late 1950s and throughout the 1960s, Boyd wrote as a respected critic and theorist across a wide spectrum of architectural concerns, with his work appearing in a range of international publication venues, from *The Architectural Review* (UK) and *Architectural Forum* (US) to *Casabella* (Italy) and John Donat's series *World Architecture* (UK). He wrote two books on contemporary Japanese architecture, *Kenzo Tange* (1962) and *New Directions in Japanese Architecture* (1968), as well as important articles on what he termed "The Sad End of New Brutalism" (1967) and anti-architecture (1968). His 1960 book, *The Australian Ugliness*, predated Peter Blake's *God's Own Junkyard: The Planned Deterioration of America's Landscape* (1964). In 1965 he wrote *The Puzzle of Architecture*, a theoretical summary of the state of world architecture. Published a year before Robert Venturi's *Complexity and Contradiction in Architecture* (1966) and reviewed positively internationally, Boyd's book was an accurate depiction of the crisis of confidence in global architecture culture. But it has been overlooked in subsequent historiographical studies.

So why reexamine Boyd's writings now? Why do they deserve to be reintegrated into a broader reading of the late 1950s and 1960s architecture culture? One of the key reasons is that Boyd was at the cusp of a generational and career shift for architects who wrote about architecture for architects.[1] At one level, as an architect, his model for writing and practice paralleled that of older American architects like Eero Saarinen (1910-1961) and Philip Johnson (1906-2005), who wrote actively about the state of contemporary architecture in the professional journals and taught sporadically but never held continuing academic appointments throughout their lives. At another level, Boyd's writing career predates that of the slightly younger British architects turned critic-historian-academics – Alan

Colquhoun (1921-2012) and Robert Maxwell (b. 1922) – who served in World War II and shifted out of practice into the writing of scholarly history and theory from the late 1950s onward.[2] Boyd never did that – he remained a practicing architect throughout. Further, Boyd's professional allegiances and academic background differ from those of architectural historian/theorists Colin Rowe (1920-1999) and Reyner Banham (1922-1988), despite the fact that Boyd would often benchmark his own theoretical pronouncements against those of Banham.[3]

Furthermore, while Rowe studied under Rudolf Wittkower in London and then Henry-Russell Hitchcock at Yale and Banham's doctorate was supervised by Nikolaus Pevsner, Boyd had none of this pedigree. As an Australian and hence an outsider, he had the advantages and disadvantages of nonalignment. He was not steeped in the conventions of British, American, or European art historical traditions and was open to architectures of the East, namely Japan, and especially to the experimental architectures of the 1960s expositions. This gave Boyd a certain neutrality: he was able to comment objectively, frequently invoking a dialectic tradition of posing balanced commentary and asking critical questions of what he observed but not necessarily taking sides. At the same time, this critical relativity (often associated with the empirical strategies employed by British critics) also meant that his writings could not easily be identified as belonging to any specific aesthetic or ideological camp. If there was a weakness to Boyd's position it was this: in historiographic terms, his lack of an adversarial viewpoint or a clear theoretical and aesthetic allegiance – combined with an early death – consigned his legacy to near invisibility. His relativist position as a critic was arguably too balanced for a profession at an intellectual crossroad and in need of direction. Today, however, that neutrality, written from the margins, has the virtue, even the humility of accuracy.

Born at Armadale in Melbourne, Australia, in 1919, Robin Boyd trained as an architect at the Melbourne Technical College and University of Melbourne and served in Queensland and Papua New Guinea during World War II in the No. 3 Field Survey Company of the Australian Imperial Force (AIF).[4] A gifted architect, he was also a brilliant and precocious writer, founding the student pamphlet *Smudges* in 1939; and between 1947 and 1953, as director of the RVIA Small Homes Service, he wrote a weekly newspaper column on contemporary architecture in *The Age* newspaper. In 1947 he published *Victorian Modern*, the first history of modern architecture in Australia,[5] and in 1952, the important book *Australia's Home: Its Origins, Builders, and Occupiers*.[6] Remarkably, Boyd was not trained as an art or architectural historian: he was not a specialist. He was an architect who liked to write, and he was ambitious for his talent. Because they formally documented Australian architectural history in its infancy in the 1950s, Boyd's two early books became surrogate histories even though they were stridently polemical.[7] His aim was to jolt everyday Australians and architects into critical reflection on the parlous state of design locally and at the same time, attempt to codify some sort of historical pedigree for what he considered to be the best of Australian modernism at that time.

From the outset, Boyd, purposely targeted his writing to specific readerships, ensuring reception at scholarly, professional, and popular levels, and within local, regional, and international spheres. His ability to cross these boundaries has, in Australia at least, not been equaled since and it can be argued that Boyd's writing, which made him a public figure in Australia, constituted an architectural practice more persuasive than his own considerable talents as an architect.[8] And it was a skill that he would consciously reflect upon in 1957 in an article entitled "These Critical Times" in the *Journal of Architectural Education*, which would show him self-reflectively describing his past and future methodological trajectory as a critic of contemporary architecture.[9]

The search for architectural form

On his first trip to Europe in 1951 as part of a travelling scholarship, Boyd secured an introduction to the editors of *The Architectural Review* (*AR*) and from that date onwards until his early death in 1971 was a regular contributor to the British journal, not just as an Australian correspondent but also as an informed commentator on the state of contemporary architecture and theory. His first article for *AR*, entitled "A New Eclecticism?" – a term which he coined in 1951 to counter "New Empiricism" – was intended to argue the case for the validity of thinking about multiple forms of modernism.[10] Supplementing his argument with references to earlier *AR* articles by Sigfried Giedion and JM Richards, both of whom were promoting expanded definitions of functionalism,[11] Boyd's thesis of a "New Eclecticism" was provocative in its balanced position. Its theoretical message was arguably too radical a concept for an architecture culture still intent on drawing battle lines between rational and organic approaches to the making of architectural form. Yet, others, like Eero Saarinen in his 1953 "Six Broad Currents of Modern Architecture," would later pursue exactly the same argument.[12] Undaunted, Boyd continued to expand upon the issue with articles in *AR* like "Port Phillip Idiom" (on regionalism and the modern Melbourne house, 1951),[13] "The Functional Neurosis" (1956),[14] and importantly, "Engineering of Excitement" (1958),[15] in which he queried the viability of the new shape architecture of the 1950s. His introduction (complete with pun) captured the period's expansive mood:

> The plain but wholesome dough of modern architecture is being flavoured with more and more currants: buildings with warps, waves, folds, droops, and other unexpected shapes sharply outlined against the modular grid background.[16]

For Boyd, these buildings, whose forms were predicated on a special structural principle, were not necessarily more functional or economical than a cube. Their shape was determined by the architect trying to "find something new to say" and, more significantly, by "a pendulum swing against the idea of universality in modern architectural theory and a hankering after the individual poetic expression."[17] But the efforts to create new form resulted in yet another absence of canon: were these buildings valid, rational, or authentic bearers of a new monumentality? Boyd asked:

> How can they and the glass box be right? No one answers these questions convincingly. Surveying the MIT auditorium and his mixed-up confreres of the postwar decade Eugenio Montuori said in 1955: "The mess is complete."[18]

These articles secured Boyd respect, and writers like Reyner Banham, JM Richards, and William Jordy made ready cross-reference to his writings and critique in their subsequent articles in *AR*.[19] Boyd followed up his 1958 survey with another important review of structurally determined buildings in his 1963 article "Under Tension,"[20] which considered the rise of tensile architecture in the light of Frei Otto's recent book, *Zugbeanspruchte Konstruktionen*.[21] He concluded it with the comment that "in this kind of ugliness there may be one of the first really new keys to an escape from the historical vision that has been offered since the eradication of ornament"[22] – a comment that referred to Boyd's own recent contributions to American journals on contemporary American architecture, particularly recent works by Edward Durell Stone and Minoru Yamasaki, writings which had also garnered the respect of his peers.

Boyd's breakthrough to an American readership had come with his tenure as Visiting Bemis Professor at MIT from 1956 to 1957, following introductions through John Ely Burchard and Pietro Belluschi, both of whom had visited Australia previously. Immersing himself in contemporary American architecture culture, Boyd contacted editors Thomas Creighton (*Progressive Architecture*), John Knox Shear (*Architectural Record*), and Douglas Haskell (*Architectural Forum*); subsequently, with a series of articles like "The Pursuit of Pleasingness"[23] and "Decoration Rides Again"[24] for *Progressive Architecture*, *Architectural Record*, *Architectural Forum*, and *Harper's Magazine*, he secured himself a regular place in a broader international readership, even earning the respect of an architect like Eero Saarinen (one of Boyd's idols) as well as a position on the Board of Contributors of *Architectural Forum* from 1965 until 1971.

In his writings, Boyd mapped the increasingly pluralistic path of postwar modern architecture, which the editor of *Progressive Architecture* Thomas H. Creighton would describe in 1961 as a movement and label as "Chaoticism."[25] Boyd highlighted not so much an era of "chaoticism" but the increasing need for architects to consider the significance of design intention in an intellectual climate where questions of monumentality, form, structure, representation, and the dismantling of modernist canons were being accelerated by contemporary conditions of ephemerality, affluence, and spectacle. At this point in 1958, Boyd had determined two different aspects of postwar architecture – decoration and excitement – that begged for analysis and codification. Reflecting upon this in *Architectural Forum* (July 1959), Boyd asked, "Has success spoiled modern architecture?"[26] and highlighted the reluctance of postwar architects (other than Stone) to openly acknowledge aesthetics and beauty:

> It is not yet fashionable to admit purely esthetic [sic] motives. Grilles are justified on the grounds that they reduce air-conditioning loads – as tail fins stabilize a car. Nor is it popular yet to embrace symbolism publicly and un-selfconsciously. Churches shaped like fish are said to get that way inadvertently ....[27]

Boyd concluded with "six different interpretations of beauty," five of which were buildings designed by American architects Yamasaki, Johansen, Mies, Wright, and Saarinen and the sixth being Italian Vittoriano Vigàno raw concrete Istituto Marchiondi Spagliardi, Milan (1955-57), as if to underline the American preoccupation with aesthetics and formalism.[28] Boyd brought these musings together for *Harper's Magazine* in September 1959. In "The Counter-Revolution in Architecture," he acknowledged "the abundant decade of the 1950s" that necessitated "a new affluence in architecture."[29] He suggested that, in reaction to tiring of the technique that had perfected the glazed box, architecture had split into two parts – "a search for new richness on the surface and a new excitement in form" – and that this split was best represented by the recent work of Stone and Saarinen, both of whom had recently graced the cover of *Time* magazine.[30] Invoking buildings cited in previous articles, Boyd described Stone's work as "International Style gift-wrapped" and the Huntington Hartford Museum "with its Venetian arcade and verd-antique marble medallions promising to be as exquisite as a superbly packaged chocolate box."[31] Saarinen's aesthetic progress from Detroit to TWA was described with the important statement that "Saarinen, under the gaze of a lost, impressionable generation of younger architects, developed in a few years from reasoned rectangles to felt space."[32] Boyd went further, clarifying this idea of "felt space":

> The mutual advancement of the spatial expression and the psychological state of a sensitive occupant is more valuable than any ordained symbolism or poetic abstraction. Excitement, in short, should be pertinent.[33]

Boyd's argument for the functional relevance of "excitement" even garnered Saarinen's approval. As Eeva Liisa Pelkonen has discovered, Saarinen, in response to *Progressive Architecture*'s Thomas Creighton's 1959 cataloguing of formal strategies as "The New Sensualism"[34] wrote to Creighton saying:

> I have read your "New Sensualism" article …. and I think you have made too large an umbrella encompassed by one name. (Egocentrically I prefer the division Robin Boyd made in HARPER'S).[35]

Just under two years later in his next article for *Harper's Magazine*, entitled "The New Vision in Architecture" (July 1961), Boyd further expanded his analysis of postwar architecture, describing yet more categories of design strategy in contemporary architecture in simple terms, such as "the suitcase and the bunch of grapes"; "twinship and circle"; and grouping together Le Corbusier's Monastery at La Tourette and Louis Kahn's Medical Research Buildings at the University of Pennsylvania as "singleness out of confusion."[36] While taxonomic in explanation, Boyd was not throwing up his hands in despair at the increase in choice offered to the designer but rather documenting (not endorsing) an updated and ever-increasing spread of possible architectural directions and avoiding the standard surveys which focused on the work of individual architects. As Boyd had said earlier, "the intellectual rat race is faster now. Everyone would like to be a one-man avant-garde."[37]

The significance of these two readerships in British and American journals at a critical moment in postwar architectural history – 1957-1962 – is noteworthy. Boyd is a respected participant at a moment of contemporary crisis in the search for architectural form.

Ugliness and the visual landscape

There were two further outcomes from Boyd's American sojourn. The first was his 1960 book, *The Australian Ugliness*, in which he reflected upon what he regarded as the blight of American consumer culture as it affected Australia's design culture and visual environment.[38] This was also the text in which Boyd coined terms like "Austerica," "featurism," and "arboraphobia," the latter referring to the Australian tendency to indiscriminately lop or remove any existing tree. *The Australian Ugliness* was the logical next step after Ian Nairn's 1955 "Outrage" articles in *The Architectural Review*.[39] Significantly too, it was a bridge between "Outrage," Peter Blake's (then editor of *Architectural Forum*) 1964 *God's Own Junkyard*,[40] and Belgian architect Renaat Braem's 1968 *The Ugliest Country in the World* (*Het Lelijkste Land ter Wereld*).[41] Blake's book drew much from Nairn's agenda but it is also difficult not to draw comparisons between the covers of Boyd's and Blake's books; we may even observe that Boyd's earlier hand-drawn caricatures had the same subject matter.

While Boyd's book went into multiple reprints, even as recently as 2010 – and came to resemble more and more Blake's book – and had significant aesthetic influence in Australia in terms of affecting everyday house design and an emerging environmental consciousness in the 1960s and 1970s,[42] *God's Own Junkyard* – particularly its photographs, most of which were taken by Blake himself – had an interesting side effect in the United States. As Blake noted in the 1979 introduction to his book's reprinting:

> In some ways *God's Own Junkyard* seems to have provoked a number of interesting polemics. It didn't just (predictably) mobilize the garden clubs; it also mobilized the pop-garde. *Its* members felt that much of what I had assailed was, in fact, not to be sneered at, at all![43]

The power of Blake's photographs in America had a completely different effect from that of Boyd's caricatures, which were a combination of Osbert Lancaster's satirical drawings of the 1940s and Gordon Cullen's drawings for Ian Nairn. Robert Venturi, for example, though he'd written much of *Complexity and Contradiction in Architecture* in 1962, had in its eventual publication in 1966 famously appropriated – among others – Blake's photographs of the commercial strip. But Boyd's *The Australian Ugliness* was different. It was not just an assault on the visual plight of the Australian urban environment but also a damning commentary on the state of Australian popular taste. What makes it therefore original for the period was the combination of its book-length interpretation of Ian Nairn's *Outrage* (1955) images but made in text, John Betjeman's withering critiques of British taste, Osbert Lancaster's caricatures of style, and Russell Lynes's important 1954 book, *The Tastemakers: The Shaping of American Popular Taste*.[44]

Boyd's *The Australian Ugliness* therefore needs to be seen, as scholars such as Aitchison, Heynen, and Gosseye have recently begun to do,[45] within a broader international context of various and sometimes linked regional discourses that in the period 1955-1967 broached the common question of popular taste and the status of urban environment as a visual landscape – a discourse that should naturally include Christopher Tunnard, Ian Nairn, Gordon Cullen, Jane Jacobs, Peter Blake, JB Jackson, Donald Gazzard, Renaat Braem … and Robin Boyd.

One of "the army of scribes"

The second outcome of Boyd's American stay was a recommendation through Walter Gropius for Boyd to be commissioned as an author for the 1962 monograph on emerging Japanese architect Kenzo Tange[46] in the George Braziller

"Makers of Contemporary Architecture" series.⁴⁷ Boyd had been a regular correspondent with Gropius since the latter's 1954 visit to Australia; in Boston, their friendship was cemented and then consolidated through more than a decade of correspondence. It was clear that the elder statesman of the profession held Boyd in high regard.⁴⁸ The book on Tange placed Boyd in a new position, aligning author and subject with orthodox contemporary American architecture culture. In 1962, Tange joined Buckminster Fuller, Philip Johnson, Louis Kahn, and Eero Saarinen as leading contemporary architects; simultaneously, Boyd joined John McHale, John Jacobus, Vincent Scully, and Allan Temko as a leading contemporary commentator. Boyd thus joined the growing band of Western writers commenting – albeit often with limited knowledge and with narrow and often biased views – on contemporary Japan, like Udo Kultermann, John Ely Burchard, JM Richards, and Peter Smithson, and he would continue to write as a balanced commentator on contemporary Japanese projects for American journals throughout the 1960s. While this reflected a general global shift in attention toward postwar Japan, in Boyd's homeland his writings encouraged a new generation of Australian architects to look not so much to Great Britain and the United States for inspiration but to their immediate region, and especially to Japan. Boyd also wrote the book *New Directions in Japanese Architecture* in 1968.⁴⁹ In doing so, he took part in another series devised by George Braziller, side by side with other notable international contributors such as Royston Landau, Robert Stern, Vittorio Gregotti, and Stanislaus von Moos.

In reviewing *Kenzo Tange* and other books in the series, English architect Fello Atkinson grumbled at Braziller's choice of architects, exclaiming, "why such a Yankee bias – four Americans and one Japanese?"⁵⁰ Yet, while Atkinson was critical of Boyd's writing style, he could not think of others who might justify inclusion in the series other than Arne Jacobsen and Egon Eiermann. Atkinson at least acknowledged the significance of the series, writing that through it "modern architecture not only becomes international but inter-cultural."⁵¹ In reviewing the subsequent Braziller series, the "New Directions in Architecture" monographs, Reyner Banham in 1970 was similarly intellectually snobbish and unkind about the idea of a nationally focused series (which he argued demonstrated "sloppy thinking") but did admit to Braziller's commercial success with mini-monographs during the 1960s that have:

> proven highly profitable both to publishers and to the army of scribes that has penned the prefatory essays and selected bibliographies that are the sandwiching around the slices of architectural photography that form the real meat of most of them.⁵²

For Banham, the "New Directions" series "so far – contains more original hits than routine misses"; furthermore, he reserved fair praise for Boyd, describing him (despite his "off-shore view" of Japan) as:

> A deeply involved tourist with strong professional connections in the field (as architect for the Australian exhibits at the Osaka Expo), and his present relationship to the Japanese situation seems almost ideal for a summary interpretation of that situation's present condition. The result is the most straightforwardly readable and most directly satisfying of the four texts under consideration, but whether it will stand up as an historical document in ten years time (as Gregotti's will) remains to be seen.[53]

What Banham in fact was alerting readers to was the dearth of and the limits of criticism to be found in the proliferation of the scholarly picture book, indicative of a particular phenomenon where discourse of the day was largely to be found across a brace of journals, and with multiple voices – of which Boyd was one, and who also appeared in two Braziller series as one of "the army of scribes." For the architectural historian today, this phenomenon between c. 1950 and 1970 highlights the importance of international journals in this period as a key locus of discourse and serves as evidence that voices from the margins, like Boyd and others, were able to participate and make a substantial contribution to a global conversation.

Complexity and contradiction in The Puzzle of Architecture

Boyd's architectural relativism, tinged always with a "moral anchor," was brought together in his 1965 *The Puzzle of Architecture,* a book positively reviewed by Philip Johnson among others but emulated in graphic format and eclipsed a year later by the New York Museum of Modern Art's (MoMA) publication of Robert Venturi's *Complexity and Contradiction in Architecture* (1966).[54] The problem with Boyd's book was that while it was accompanied by his relaxed journalistic writing style and personable sketches and was stunningly accurate in its chronological account of 1950s and 1960s architecture culture, it reached no firm conclusion. It was no manifesto.

Johnson's review of *The Puzzle of Architecture* was glowing, stating that "[Boyd's] description of the situation today in the world of architectural design is completely convincing."[55] He recommended that "every architect read every word" and that "every architect must have this book."[56] Apart from criticism of Boyd's occasional moralizing tone and a telling correction of Boyd's startling omission of the axially symmetrical entrance door to his own Glass House, Johnson concluded with the comment that "postage stamp size photographs would surely have done as well" as Boyd's hand-drawn sketches (the only illustrations in the book),[57] including just such photographs in his own review article as if to prove the point.

Venturi's book, almost certainly in layout stages at the time of the Johnson review, followed the latter's advice directly. In layout, it was almost identical to Boyd's text, but glossier and with postage stamp-sized photographic images; it was also published by MoMA, a more powerful launderer of discourse than Melbourne University Press. Unlike Boyd's book, it was not a historical account of form but an analytical account of design approaches to the latter, and its first chapter had as its title "Nonstraightforward Architecture: A Gentle Manifesto." Complete eclipse of Boyd's work however was clinched by Venturi's inclusion of twelve of his own projects in the conclusion to his book, in effect demonstrating his thesis through design.

Despite positive reviews, part of the problem of Boyd's book was its lack of penetration in terms of distribution. Published by an Australian university press, the book was doomed to face a largely local readership, where the breadth of Boyd's scholarship would not have been appreciated. The book's lack of photographs and, significantly, its inability to articulate a future design direction for architecture would have been frustrating to the practicing architect. As such, *The Puzzle of Architecture* was in large part a commercial and critical flop. At the same time, both the books by Boyd and Venturi may be seen as capping moments to the late 1950s search for architectural form that catalyzed around 1962, rather than as polemical projects that suggested future action. Indeed, Venturi, in his 1977 note to the Second Edition, stated that he wished that "the title had been *Complexity and Contradiction in Architectural Form*, as suggested by Donald Drew Egbert. In the early 1960s, however, form was king in architectural thought, and most architectural theory focused without question on aspects of form."[58]

Expos, exhibitionism, and anti-architecture

Boyd's *The Puzzle of Architecture* could be regarded as being stranded at a theoretical frontier – the English end of a fading Brutalist discussion just at the moment when English critic Reyner Banham published his 1966 book on Brutalism, an endpoint which Boyd himself recognized (see for example, his 1967 *AR* article "The Sad End of New Brutalism"[59]), the waning influence of the American formalists (Paul Rudolph, John Johansen, and Edward Durell Stone), and the end of the postwar functionalist debate perpetuated by Sigfried Giedion and Boyd's mentor Walter Gropius. Boyd's writings, while openly aware of the Smithsons, excluded Team 10 and the Italians. He also excluded Vincent Scully and Robert Venturi, even though he knew of their emerging influence. But like older critics such as Arthur Drexler and JM Richards, Boyd included Japan and, like Giedion, he also included Jørn Utzon.

Perhaps chastened by the mixed reviews of *The Puzzle*, Boyd in the late 1960s focused his international criticism on expo design, "anti-architecture" and the ongoing debacle of the Sydney Opera House,[60] i.e., on things closer to home and on areas in which he himself had international design interests such as in his role as exhibits designer for the Australian pavilions at Montreal (1967) and Osaka (1970). For example, his Fishbowl Takeaway Fish restaurant, South Yarra, Victoria (1969), bore an uncanny resemblance to the base of the 1958 Brussels Atomium.

Boyd's 1968 article entitled "Anti-architecture" and his series of articles on expos and exhibitionism reveal an openness to architecture's changing profile in the late 1960s.[61] Writing on Habitat, Frei Otto, and the Japanese architects at Expo 70, Boyd is cautious, even ambivalent in his attitude towards rapidly changing definitions of architecture. Admitting that "anti-architecture promises a more radical revolution than that of any new style," Boyd was among the first (in 1968) to attempt to make distinctions between Archigram (which he classified as "anti-architecture") and the Japanese Metabolists (which he classified as "architecture [far out, but loyal to Vitruvian principles]"); between Venturi ("edging always closer to anti-architecture and [who] will finally eliminate his own contradictions only when he actually achieves it") and Charles Moore and "all the New Barnists."[62] In March 1970, in his article "A Glimpse of the Future" in *Architectural Forum*, Boyd described Noriaki (Kisho) Kurokawa's Takara Beautilion,[63] a free-form steel pipe frame multistory assembly at Expo 70, as "a glimpse, as through a glass polarized darkly, of what a building of the future might look like."[64] Boyd was speculating on what mechanisms and design tactics were brought to bear to destroy the architectural identity of a system. Here, Boyd offered the most frank and prescient critique of what contemporary Japanese architecture was offering to the world:

> Suffocation by its own servants may be the future of architecture: a Frankensteinian end, as many have been hinting. The Takara building actually demonstrates the possibility for the first time; and demonstrations like this are among the best justifications for World Fairs.[65]

Listening to the margins

Robin Boyd died in October 1971 – aged 52 – too early and with no time in which to develop his various theses and pithy commentaries into longer polemical works. At one level, it could be argued that his strength in capturing contemporary aesthetic concerns in eloquent smaller texts was not translatable into an authoritative voice internationally – despite his sustained presence in journals and various book series over more than twenty years. His early death, his commitment to architectural practice, and his lack of a full-time academic position at a time when architectural history and theory had become specialized disciplines in university education all meant an irrevocable positioning at a hinge point in a shifting landscape of discourse. In 1971 contemporary architectural discourse and its framing had simply moved on. At the same time, his contribution was on some level recognized as internationally significant. In 1973 the American Institute of Architects awarded him posthumously the AIA Architecture Critic's Medal.[66] Boyd's last books were concerned with Australia and, at others' urging, his own architectural work.[67] Since that time there has been no detailed international review of Boyd's theoretical and critical contribution to postwar architectural discourse. His biography (1995) by historian Geoffrey Serle[68] was authorized by the Boyd family, and documentation and analysis of his work, both built and written, has largely been undertaken by Australian scholars in the form of journal articles and conference papers.

The centers of discourseframing architecture culture are necessarily biased. But today hindsight requires acknowledgement of a broader selection of voices to be heard. For Anglophone architecture culture, Boyd's criticism of global architectural events and the simultaneous promotion of Australian architecture were important. As an impartial observer, he was a key bridge between 1960s British and US architecture culture. His voice also represents a different axis of architecture culture in the 1950s and 1960s. Boyd is important as representative of, as in his own words, "Australian culture [as] something like a sturdy little boat battling across lonely waters surging with cross-currents from Europe and America."[69] At the same time, Africa, Asia, and Oceania, and hence places like Canada and South Africa, deserve inclusion, and recent scholars like Mark Crinson, Łukasz Stanek, Chang Jiat-Hwee, Anoma Pieris, Peter Scriver, Rhodri Windsor Liscombe, Justine Clark, and Paul Walker have made important contributions to constructing postwar histories for locations that lacked a figure such as Boyd.[70]

Such histories require looking transnationally, across boundaries, away from the canons and asking whether intellectual and design sustenance was to be found elsewhere. Architectural history and theory continue to perpetuate gaps in the theorizing and documenting of architectural production, especially in Africa, Southeast Asia, and the Pacific, where the concerns often were and continue to be different from those of the Anglo-American and European mainstream. Like architectural design culture, which lionizes its design geniuses, so too architectural history culture perpetuates the celebration of its own creators. For too long, figures like Nikolaus Pevsner, Sigfried Giedion, and Henry-Russell Hitchcock dominated the construction of modernism's discourse. Their inheritors like Reyner Banham and later Manfredo Tafuri amongst others did much to broaden the discussion in the 1960s and 1970s, but, in many respects, they consolidated an already canonical reading of modernism. The globalization of postwar discourse and the mechanisms of its dissemination require broader and more complex networks of diffusion to be recognized and documented.

Robin Boyd played a key role in trying to place Australian architecture in an international setting, attempting to insert one form of local production into the prevailing international conversation. He sought to describe the situation as it was, not as it should be. He took part in a sustained dialogue about architectural form that was focused heavily within architectural journals in the late 1950s and 1960s. He took part in an emerging discourse about the visual landscape of urban environments. He was part of the phenomenon of the 1960s scholarly picture book. He documented the 1960s move toward the dissolution of the architectural canons, especially through Expo 67 and Expo 70 and his familiarity with and sustained exposure of contemporary Japanese architecture. He was not without flaws, but he was a constant presence. And he was not alone. Like the voices of several others – Udo Kultermann, Sibyl Moholy-Nagy, and Noburo Kawazoe, to name just a few – those of an apparent critical second tier, Boyd's voice, albeit from the margins, deserves to be heard in the ongoing documentation and analysis of 1950s and 1960s architectural discourse.

Notes

1. The phenomenon of architects writing about architecture for architects forms the basis for the historiographic periodization of two key anthologies of postwar discourse: Joan Ockman, ed., *Architecture Culture, 1943-1968: A Documentary Anthology* (New York: Rizzoli, 1993) and K. Michael Hays, ed., *Architecture Theory since 1968* (Cambridge, MA: MIT Press, 1998). While these volumes include some articles written by architects, most of the contributions were written within an academic field by architectural theorists without a personal grounding in practice.
2. See Tom Avermaete, Christoph Grafe, and Hans Teerds, eds., *Alan Colquhoun: Architect, Historian, Critic, OASE 87* (December 2012), especially Kenneth Frampton, "'Not Individual Property': The ideas of Alan Colquhoun," *OASE 87* (December 2012): 25-39.
3. Daniel J. Naegele, ed., *The Letters of Colin Rowe: Five Decades of Correspondence* (Des Moines: Architecture Books [Iowa State University], 2015), 4; Nigel Whiteley, *Reyner Banham: Historian of the Immediate Future* (Cambridge, MA: MIT Press, 2001), 9-17.
4. Neil Clerehan, "Boyd, Robin Gerard Penleigh (1919-1971)," *Australian Dictionary of Biography* (Canberra, ACT: National Centre of Biography, Australian National

University, 1993), http://adb.anu.edu.au/biography/boyd-robin-gerard-penleigh-9560/text16841.
5. Robin Boyd, *Victorian Modern* (Melbourne: Victorian Architectural Students Society, 1947).
6. Robin Boyd, *Australia's Home: Its Origins, Builders and Occupiers* (Carlton, Vic.: Melbourne University Press, 1952).
7. At the time of the publication, for example, of Boyd's *Australia's Home* in 1952, Morton Herman's *The Early Australian Architects and Their Work* (1954) had not been published and it was not until 1968 that J. M. Freeland's *Architecture in Australia: A History* appeared.
8. See Philip Goad, "Robin Boyd and the Art of Writing Architecture," in *Semi-Detached: Writing, Representation and Criticism in Architecture*, ed. Naomi Stead (Melbourne: Uro Media, 2012), 182-96.
9. Robin Boyd, "These Critical Times," *Journal of Architectural Education* 12, no. 2 (Summer 1957): 33-36.
10. Robin Boyd, "A New Eclecticism?" *The Architectural Review* 110, no. 657 (September 1951): 150-53.
11. In proposing a "New Eclecticism," Boyd was supporting Sigfried Giedion's insistence upon the ability "to leap from the rational-functional to the irrational-organic" and JM Richards's call for "the logical next step, the functionalism of the particular," wherein Richards stated "There is no call to abandon functionalism… but to (relate) it ever more closely to the essential particulars of time and place and purpose." See Sigfried Giedion, "Alvar Aalto," *The Architectural Review* 107, no. 638 (February 1950): 77-84 and JM Richards, "The Next Step?" *The Architectural Review* 107, no. 639 (March 1950): 170-78.
12. Eero Saarinen, "The Six Broad Currents of Modern Architecture," *Architectural Forum* 99, no. 1 (July 1953): 110-15.
13. Robin Boyd, "Port Phillip Idiom: Recent Houses in the Melbourne Region," *The Architectural Review* 112, no. 671 (November 1952): 309-13.
14. Robin Boyd, "The Functional Neurosis," *The Architectural Review* 119, no. 710 (February 1956): 84-88.
15. Robin Boyd, "Engineering of Excitement," *The Architectural Review* 124, no. 742 (November 1958): 294-308.
16. Boyd, "Engineering of Excitement," 295. The "currants" were a direct reference back to Saarinen's "six broad currents" of 1953. See Eero Saarinen, "The Six Broad Currents of Modern Architecture," *Architectural Forum* 99, no. 1 (July 1953): 110-15.
17. Boyd, "Engineering of Excitement," 296.
18. Ibid., 296. Boyd borrowed the Eugenio Montuori phrase from Bruno Zevi. See Bruno Zevi, "Three Critics Discuss MIT's New Buildings," *Architectural Forum* 104, no. 3 (March 1956): 157.

19. Reference to Boyd's writings is made, for example, in JM Richards, "US Domestic," *The Architectural Review* 110, no. 658 (October 1951): 221-31; JM Richards, "Architecture after 1960," *The Architectural Review* 127, no. 755 (January 1960): 9-10; Reyner Banham, "1960: Stocktaking," *The Architectural Review* 127, no. 756 (February 1960): 93-100; William Jordy, "The Formal Image: USA," *The Architectural Review* 127, no. 757 (March 1960): 156-65; Reyner Banham, "The Perret Ascendancy," *The Architectural Review* 127, no. 760 (June 1960): 372-75.
20. Robin Boyd, "Under Tension," *The Architectural Review* 134, no. 801 (November 1963): 324-34.
21. Frei Otto, *Zugbeanspruchte Konstruktionen: Gestalt, Struktur und Berechnung von Bauten aus Seilen, Netzen und Membranen* (Frankfurt: Verlag Ullstein, 1962).
22. Boyd, "Under Tension," 334.
23. Robin Boyd, "The Search for Pleasingness," *Progressive Architecture* 38, no. 4 (April 1957): 193-205.
24. Robin Boyd, "Decoration Rides Again," *Architectural Record* 122, no. 3 (September 1957): 183-86.
25. In a series of three features in *Progressive Architecture* (March, April, and May 1961), editor Thomas H. Creighton conducted a symposium by correspondence with more than forty American architects. Creighton framed questions to participants around "a design philosophy, a comparatively new, self-conscious architectural point of view, a movement which might be called 'Chaoticism' – the acceptance and practice of the principles of chaos." See Thomas H. Creighton, "The Period of Chaoticism," *Progressive Architecture* 42 (March 1961): 108.
26. Robin Boyd, "Has Success Spoiled Modern Architecture?" *Architectural Forum* 111 (July 1959): 98-103.
27. Boyd, "Has Success Spoiled Modern Architecture?" 99.
28. The six buildings were: 1) decorative use of structure: Wayne University (1958) by Minoru Yamasaki; 2) plastic structural elements: US Embassy, Dublin (1958) by John Johansen; 3) refinement of steel cage: Crown Hall, IIT, Chicago (1955) by Mies van der Rohe; 4) organic cellular structure becomes integral ornament: proposal for Arizona State Capital (1957); 5) brutalist use of raw concrete: Istituto Marchiondi Spagliardi, Milan (1955-57) by Vittoriano Vigàno; 6) the search for new form: Yale Hockey Rink, New Haven, CT (1958) by Eero Saarinen. Boyd, "Has Success Spoiled Modern Architecture?" 102-3.
29. Robin Boyd, "The Counter-Revolution in Architecture," *Harper's Magazine* 219, no. 1312 (September 1959): 40-48.
30. Boyd, "The Counter-Revolution in Architecture," 44.
31. Ibid.
32. Ibid., 47.
33. Ibid., 47-48.

34. Thomas H. Creighton, "The New Sensualism I," *Progressive Architecture* 40 (September 1959): 141-47 and "The New Sensualism II," *Progressive Architecture* 40 (October 1959): 180-87. See also Joseph Rosa, ed., *Glamour: Fashion, Industrial Design, Architecture* (New Haven: Yale University Press, 2004).
35. Eero Saarinen, letter to Thomas H. Creighton, September 8, 1959, Eero Saarinen Papers, Yale University. Quoted in Eeva-Liisa Pelkonen, "The Search for (Communicative) Form," in *Eero Saarinen: Shaping the Future*, ed. Eeva-Liisa Pelkonen and Donald Albrecht (New Haven and London: Yale University Press, 2006), 87.
36. Robin Boyd, "The New Vision in Architecture," *Harper's Magazine* 223, no. 1334 (July 1961): 73-81.
37. Boyd, "Has Success Spoiled Modern Architecture?" 102.
38. Robin Boyd, *The Australian Ugliness* (Melbourne: Cheshire, 1960).
39. Ian Nairn, *Outrage: On the Disfigurement of Town and Countryside*, special issue of *The Architectural Review*, 1955 (London: The Architectural Press, 1956).
40. Peter Blake, *God's Own Junkyard: The Planned Deterioration of America's Landscape* (New York: Holt, Rinehart & Winston, 1964).
41. Renaat Braem, *Het Lelijkste Land ter Wereld* (The Ugliest Country in the World) (Leuven: Davidsfonds, 1968).
42. For example, the architect-designed project house phenomenon that thrived in the 1960s with progressive, affordable modern houses provided by commercial builders such as Pettit and Sevitt in New South Wales and Merchant Builders in Victoria and their accompaniment with indigenous designed landscapes was profoundly influenced by Boyd's *The Australian Ugliness* (1960). See Judith O'Callaghan and Charles Pickett, *Designer Suburbs: Architects and Affordable Homes in Australia* (Sydney: NewSouth Publishing, 2012). A more immediate influence could also be seen in Ian McKay et al.'s survey of Australian housing, *Living and Partly Living: Housing in Australia* (Melbourne: Thomas Nelson, 1971).
43. Peter Blake, foreword to 1979 edition of Peter Blake, *God's Own Junkyard: The Planned Deterioration of America's Landscape* (New York: Rinehart and Winston, 1979), 14.
44. Russell Lynes, *The Tastemakers: The Shaping of American Popular Taste* (New York: Harper, 1954).
45. See, for example, Matthew Aitchison, "Ugliness and Outrage: The Australian Townscape," in *Proceedings of the Society of Architectural Historians, Australia and New Zealand: 30, Open*, ed. Alexandra Brown and Andrew Leach (Gold Coast, Qld: SAHANZ, 2013), 407-17; Janina Gosseye and Hilde Heynen, "In Search of the Ugliest Country in the World: Australia vs. Belgium; On Robin Boyd, Renaat Braem, Regionalism and Post-war Modernism," in *Proceedings of the Society of Architectural Historians, Australia and New Zealand*, 419-31.
46. Robin Boyd, *Kenzo Tange* (New York: George Braziller, 1962).

47. See Philip Goad, "Robin Boyd and the Post-war 'Japanization' of Western Ideas," *Architectural Theory Review* 1, no. 2 (November 1996): 110-20.
48. Boyd-Gropius correspondence held by the Robin Boyd Foundation, Melbourne, and the Walter Gropius Papers, Houghton Library, Harvard University.
49. Robin Boyd, *New Directions in Japanese Architecture* (New York: George Braziller, 1968).
50. Fello Atkinson, book review of the "Makers of Contemporary Architecture" series, *The Architectural Review* 134, no. 798 (August 1963): 80.
51. Atkinson, book review of the "Makers of Contemporary Architecture" series, 80.
52. Reyner Banham, book review of "New Directions in Architecture" series, *The Art Bulletin* 52, no. 3 (September 1970): 344.
53. Banham, book review of "New Directions in Architecture" series, 345.
54. Robin Boyd, *The Puzzle of Architecture* (Carlton, Vic.: Melbourne University Press, 1965); Robert Venturi, *Complexity and Contradiction in Architecture* (New York: Museum of Modern Art, 1966).
55. Philip Johnson, Review of Robin Boyd, *The Puzzle of Architecture* (1965), in *Architectural Forum* 124, no. 5 (June 1966): 72.
56. Johnson, Review of Robin Boyd, 72, 73.
57. Ibid., 93.
58. Robert Venturi, "Note to the Second Edition," April 1977, in Robert Venturi, *Complexity and Contradiction in Architecture* (London: The Architectural Press, 1977), 14.
59. Robin Boyd, "The Sad End of New Brutalism," *The Architectural Review* 142, no. 845 (July 1967): 9-11.
60. Robin Boyd, "Utzon: The end," *Architectural Forum* 124, no. 5 (June 1966): 90; and posthumously published, Robin Boyd, "A Night at the Opera," *Architecture Plus* 1, no. 7 (August 1973): 48-54.
61. Robin Boyd, "Experimenting with Boxes: Habitat's Cluster," *Architectural Forum* 126, no. 4 (May 1967): 29-41; Robin Boyd, "Germany," *The Architectural Review* 142, no. 846 (August 1967): 129-35; Robin Boyd, "Antiarchitecture," *Architectural Forum* 129 (November 1968): 84-85; Robin Boyd, "Expo and exhibitionism," *The Architectural Review* 148, no. 882 (August 1970): 99-100, 109.
62. Boyd, "Antiarchitecture," 84-85.
63. The Takara Beautilion at Expo 70 in Osaka was the pavilion of the Takara Group of four furniture companies.
64. Robin Boyd, "A Glimpse of the Future," *Architectural Forum* 132, no. 2 (March 1970): 32-35.
65. Boyd, "A Glimpse of the Future," 33.
66. "A.I.A. Awards," *New York Times*, March 25, 1973, 8.
67. See Robin Boyd and Mark Strizic, *Living in Australia* (Sydney: Pergamon, 1970).
68. Geoffrey Serle, *Robin Boyd: A Life* (Carlton, Vic.: Miegunyah Press, 1995).

69. Robin Boyd, "Australia," in JM Richards, ed., *New Buildings in the Commonwealth* (London: Architectural Press, 1961), 17.
70. See for example, Mark Crinson, *Modern Architecture and the End of Empire* (Burlington, VT: Ashgate, 2002); Łukasz Stanek, "Architects from Socialist Countries in Ghana (1957-67): Modern Architecture and *Mondialization*," *Journal of the Society of Architectural Historians* 74, no. 4 (December 2015): 416-42; Chang Jiat-Hwee, *A Genealogy of Tropical Architecture: Colonial Networks, Nature, and Technology* (Abingdon, Oxon: Routledge, 2016); Anoma Pieris, *Architecture and Nationalism in Sri Lanka: The Trouser under the Cloth* (London: Routledge, 2013); Peter Scriver and Amit Srivastava, *India: Modern Architectures in History* (London: Reaktion Books, 2015); Rhodri Windsor Liscombe, *Architecture and the Canadian Fabric* (Vancouver: UBC Press, 2011); Rhodri Windsor Liscombe and Michelangelo Sabatino, *Canada: Modern Architectures in History* (London: Reaktion Books, 2016); Justine Clark and Paul Walker, *Looking for the Local: Architecture and the New Zealand Modern* (Wellington: Victoria University Press, 2000).

CHAPTER 3

Contaminations: Art, Architecture, and the Critical Vision of Lara-Vinca Masini

Peter Lang

Lara's own personality reveals, (…) the coexistence of two forces, one tending towards instinctive, spontaneous form, the other instead inclined towards the design project, and largely guided by reason, and it is precisely this union between bursts of vitality and interior rigor that constitutes the peculiarity of her character as scholar and the difficulty of her identifying with one precise critical direction.

Laura Lombardi[1]

In the early sixties, Lara-Vinca Masini succeeded in cementing Florence's reputation as a vibrant and alternative center for Italian postwar contemporary art and architecture. Throughout her active career Masini strove to support Florence's homegrown creative talent, while inviting renowned artists and architects from abroad to Tuscany. Masini engaged the city's galleries, museums, and alternative spaces. She wrote prolifically, worked as an editor, a publisher, and remains to this day an outspoken critic of all things Florentine. Masini played a pivotal role from the outset in the emergence of the *Superarchitecture* movement that would spawn radical groups like Superstudio, Archizoom, and successively, UFO, 9999, Zziggurat, and others.[2]

Over the years, Lara-Vinca Masini achieved several impressive curatorial successes in cities around Italy. Her accomplishments included the cofounding of the Progressive Museum of Contemporary Art in Livorno, "one of Italy's most experimental projects of those years."[3] In 1978, Lara-Vinca Masini was appointed one of principle curators by the Italian Commission for the Visual Arts and Architecture Section for the Venice Biennale (Fig. 1).

In 1980, Masini also curated the controversial Florentine exhibition *Umanesimo, Disumanesimo nell'arte europea 1890/1980: Dai Simbolisti al Nouveau Réalisme*

Fig. 1. La Moglie di Lot, Superstudio, (the Wife of Lot), The Salt Magazines, Zattere, Venice Biennial 1978. From left to right: Piero Frassinelli, Cristiano Toraldo di Francia, Adolfo Natalini. (Courtesy of the Superstudio Archive)

("Humanism and Inhumanism in European Art 1890/1980: From the Symbolists to Nouveau Réalisme").[4] She would go on to win the prestigious Lincei Prize for Criticism in Art and Poetry in 1986.[5]

It is nonetheless perplexing that someone as productive and as accomplished as Lara-Vinca Masini did not achieve serious international acclaim for her contributions to art and architecture criticism. Evidently Masini worked in a field dominated by men, but she, like many women in her circle, had successfully assumed key directorial and curatorial roles in Italy's dynamic postwar art culture.[6] While Masini did not purposely make gender an issue in her work, she did promote women artists, mainly in the interest of her long-term research.[7] Several of her female contemporaries would later join feminist movements, like the art critic Carla Lonzi, who quit the art world altogether in 1970 to dedicate herself solely to political feminism,[8] or Lea Vergine, who through her writings and curating defined "Body Art" in Italy, and launched the major exhibition *The Other Half of the Avant-garde*, which toured in Italy and Sweden in the early nineteen-eighties.[9]

Though Masini wrote on a range of historical and contemporary subjects, it would not help that most of her essays and books were published inside Italy and in Italian. Yet, if her publications were not that well distributed abroad, Masini could nonetheless call upon an impressive network of internationally based artists and architects to participate in her curatorial projects. She was, according to the architect and exhibition designer Piero Sartogo, the first to introduce the Viennese architect Hans Hollein to the Italian public.[10]

It may very well be that none of these issues so far mentioned count as much as Masini's personal curatorial philosophy, which she stuck close to throughout her entire career and which is a highly unique vision on the arts and architecture. Recognizing a degree of interdependency, Lara-Vinca Masini often sought to emphasize how art and architecture *"contaminated"* one other.[11] Throughout her career Masini built up a respectable track record in both the arts and in architecture. And as should become more evident here, Masini would be one of the few to recognize how modern Florentine culture ushered in an era of radical design experiment. Florence's burgeoning creative culture emerged hand in hand with a third world inspired political ideology promoted by the city's unusual mayor, Giorgio La Pira, who personally labored to put Florence at the center of the non-aligned nations movement. Throughout the fifties and early sixties, La Pira promoted international film and art festivals, along with peace programs, workers' rights, and new housing projects.[12] Yet everyday Florentines remained stubbornly attached to their Renaissance heritage, setting off the kind of cultural wars that would make the city increasingly inhospitable to Masini and her artistic vision.

Masini drew her strength from this paradoxical Florentine culture, but it would come with a cost to her reputation. Her way of working did not reveal unified trends, or as some critics were wont to do, channel different creative strains into a single recognizable movement. Consider how Germano Celant and Achille Bonito Oliva, two of the most reputed Italian art critics among her younger contemporaries, are bound, respectively, to *Arte Povera* and the *Transvanguardia*. From a purely architectural perspective, if we look across the same years that culminate around 1980, the neo-rationalists and the post-modern classicists were the ones who would pull out ahead under the determined tutelage of Aldo Rossi, Manfredo Tafuri, and Paolo Portoghesi.[13] Kenneth Frampton, when he became disillusioned with the eclectic nature of the postmodernist project, sought instead a more nuanced alternative that would lead to his comprehensive theory on critical regionalism.[14] Yet Lara-Vinca Masini steered clear of these kind of big assertions, probing instead the intimate processes of creative reason as she worked in dialogue with the exhibitionary context.

Having studied philosophy at the University of Florence, Lara-Vinca Masini began as an editor for the prestigious art journal "*sele*Arte" published by Adriano Olivetti, working for the journal from 1959 to 1965. At its highpoint, the magazine published fifty thousand copies per issue. The founder, Ludovico Ragghianti, played an instrumental role in organizing the legendary exhibitions at the Palazzo

Strozzi in Florence on the architecture of Frank Lloyd Wright (1951), Le Corbusier (1963), and Alvar Aalto (1965).[15]

One of Masini's early prominent exhibitions, produced together with Marco Dezzi Bardeschi, was the *Prima Triennale Itinerante d'Architettura Italiana Contemporanea* ("First Itinerant Triennial of Italian Contemporary Architecture"), later assembled into a comprehensive catalogue published in 1965.[16] This sweeping vision on Italian architecture, delineating an early postwar Italian eclecticism, should be read as a significant *prise de position* by Masini vis-à-vis the Italian postwar architecture context. The exhibit included over two dozen architecture studios and travelled to fourteen Italian cities. Each architecture office was afforded ample documentation and accompanying texts, often featuring their most experimental projects on housing and public buildings. But the exhibit/catalogue project went further, introducing essays by several of the participating architects, original theoretical essays by important critics, assessments on "housing" and an overview on "local debates," clearly engaging with the cities hosting the exhibition's extensive tour through Italy.[17]

While it is amply evident that Masini mastered the subject of contemporary Italian architecture early in her career, her pursuit of more unorthodox approaches to architecture and its complex but poetic relationship to the arts continued to fascinate her and stimulate her research. While working on the *Prima Triennale Itinerante*, she was concurrently involved in making other exhibitions. One that jumps to the front is *Parabola 66*, which opened in the Bilico Gallery in Rome in 1966. Curated by Marcello Fagiolo, the exhibition brought together an architect, a painter, and a sculptor. The common theme that cut across the three contributions, or the three "parables," was about the intersection and dynamic potential of geometric form making in and around public architectural and urban spaces.[18]

It turns out, however, that *Parabola 66* was a fallback solution: Masini's original intention was to make something far more multidisciplinary. At the beginning of her catalogue essay, Masini felt dissuaded from pursuing her original vision for the project:

> When with Paolo Portoghesi, Enzo Mari, Cosimo Carlucci, with poets Renato Pedio and Nanni Balestrini, with electronic music composers Pietro Grossi and Vittorio Gelmetti (and we wanted to add even more names) we tried to hypothesize an interdisciplinary operation whose results would be presented in an exhibition we had in mind to organize in Florence, we realized just how much we could still risk talking about interdisciplinarity when we want to try formerly, abruptly and totally without pretensions either within the context we were already considering, with all the arts (in that case the experiment implied architecture, sculpture, programmed plastic compositions, poetry, music) …[19]

This multidisciplinary collective bringing together multiple practices in the arts, media, music, architecture, and design can be interpreted here as one of the principle curatorial frameworks underpinning Masini's visionary philosophy on the arts and architecture. Her two most significant curatorial projects, the 1978 *Topologia e Morfogenesi* ("Topology and Morphogenesis") produced for the Venice Biennale, and the 1980 *Umanesimo, disumanesimo* in Florence are both heavily invested in transcending boundaries between artistic and architectural practices.

For the 1978 Biennale (B78) Lara-Vinca Masini was invited to the Venice Art Biennale together with Enrico Crispolti and Luigi Carluccio to collectively develop a critical vision dedicated to Italian art, but their original unified theme gave way to three very independent positions, with their own distinct narratives. Crispolti developed *Natura Praticata* ("Nature Practiced," which might be translated better as "Nature Performed"), Carluccio put forth *Natura come immagine* ("Nature as Image"), while Masini led with the theme *Topologia e morfogenesi* ("Topology and Morphogenesis"). These three curatorial efforts would share the same Italian pavilion space with the international selection curated by Achille Bonito Oliva, who had come up with the pavilion's overarching title, *Utopia e crisi dell'antinatura* ("Utopia and the Crisis of Anti-Nature").[20]

The difficult job of resolving these disparate curatorial visions within this one space was assigned by Achille Bonito Oliva to Piero Sartogo, known for having designed the display for the groundbreaking exhibition in Rome also curated by Oliva (the 1973 *Contemporanea*, where Sartogo re-envisioned the newly completed underground parking garage by the architect Luigi Moretti). In Venice, for the Italian Pavilion, Sartogo introduced a "virtual" grid, which he overlaid throughout the building, using segmented walls and ceiling and floor markings to organize the many artists' interventions.[21] Sartogo further distinguished the three sections through his selection of materials, organic wood for *Natura Praticata*, Venetian plaster for *Natura come immagine,* and concrete for *Topologia e morfogenesi.*[22]

But unexpectedly midway through the planning process, Masini was asked by the Biennale commission to expand her exhibition on the visual arts to include a separate section on Italian architecture in another venue at the *Magazzini di Sale* (the Salt Warehouses). Masini had no reservations about expressing her annoyance at having to work out this unexpected request. But, as she goes on to note in her catalogue introduction, she ended up accepting the challenge to work on a second, architectural venue, "to demonstrate how the visual arts and architecture could be shown in reciprocal manner."[23]

The exhibition morphed, nonetheless, into a conflicted survey on the schism enveloping the postmodern architecture movement. Masini's two categories, *Topology* and *Morphogenesis*, at the *Magazzini del Sale* served to divide architects and their projects into two competing programs (Fig. 2). It is helpful to understand how these two significant divisions were defined in the two principle chapter headings in Masini's catalogue:

> TOPOLOGY: In intuitive terms (...) the meaning of "topology" is assumed in the relationship with the anthropological and sociological situation, like the search for mental "territories," utopian, not controlled and discriminated upon by "systems" (disciplinary, professional, aesthetic...), and implicates ideology, the process of history and its calculated errors and judgment.[24]

> MORPHOGENESIS: The form does not develop itself in an autonomous manner, but is the result of the interaction between genetic code (project), laws of natural formativity, entropic characteristics, (levels of psycho-physical, relations with transformational systems) responses to more complex systems of the environment within its historical components, social political, economic anthropological... In metaphoric sense of the term it applies itself, as reference, to all types of architectonic re-foundation...[25]

Masini stuck to her original intent to match these categories to their respective artistic and architectural expressions, giving examples in her catalogue text of both artists and architects whom she associated with one or the other philosophical position. Her original selection of artists installed in the Italian pavilion in the Giardini reflect the conceptual and the esoteric, and their work is consciously connected—though not actually intended to share the same spaces—with the architects who she considered as "existential and utopian," or those she felt were linked to "anthropological memory" or to "future or historical archaeologies."

But this logic did not carry through for Morphogenesis: no artists were selected for the main Italian pavilion to represent what Masini deemed to be the opposing ideological current as she had set out in her introductory essay published in the Biennale catalogue. Masini was most likely, as her introduction proclaimed, short on time to fully integrate the architectural program with the art program she was initially charged with developing.[26] Again, according to the catalogue intro, she accepted the late challenge to curate an important section on architecture at the *Magazzini del Sale* as a way of testing her approach.

Masini's method was primarily conceptually based and did not lend to the opposition's reactionary form of architecture. She was never particularly comfortable with the way she assembled the architects who made up the Morphogenesis group; Masini valued them less for their drive towards autonomy and more for their merging of formal practices within the sociopolitical historical environment.[27] This might have satisfied Masini's view of their position in history, but still fell short of this group's primary message, that these architects were staunchly reclaiming

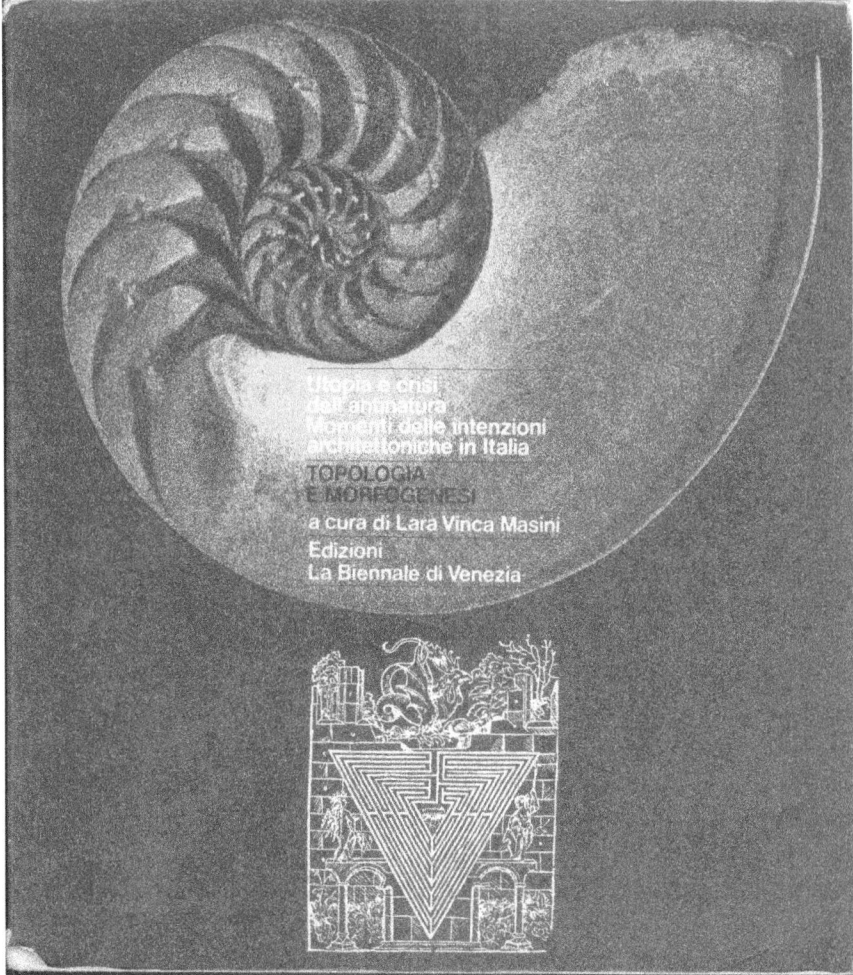

Fig. 2. Catalogue cover, *Topologia e Morfogenesi, Utopia e crisi dell'antinatura. Momenti delle Intenzioni architettoniche in Italia*. Edited Lara-Vinca Masini, La Biennale di Venezia, 1978. Cover image of a spiral shell and labyrinth.

their independence as a discipline. From inside the *Magazzini del Sale*, Masini's exhibition presented a much more balanced view, where scores of architects representing the rationalist and *neo-tendenza* movements had ample space to exhibit their projects along with participants contributing to her section on Topologia. But in 1978, the architects gathered under the Morphogenesis label were in the ascendant and clearly not given the recognition they believed they deserved.[28] Masini likely underestimated how deep this anti-modernist current actually went. It would be hard not to read this as a major shortcoming in Masini's critical method, one that would come back to haunt her.

Masini's section *Topologia and Morfogenesi* did not rise above the fray in a Biennale that in 1978 was deeply marked by strongly opposing ideologies, or what many at the time saw as an epic conflict between a waning conceptual vanguard and a rising conservative rear guard. In general "B78," as this year's Biennale was often referred to, solicited stern reviews in the art journals. Jan Van der Marck, writing in *Artforum*, was aware that the exhibition came too late to resuscitate the avant-garde in the face of a rising tide of neo-conservativism:

> …yet since the disappearance of the avant-garde is symptomatic of an ominously growing conservatism in the arts that is bound to determine the future of this and other art events, it makes sense to pause and situate it in that broader context. Ultimately, the spirit of the times—conditioned by economic, political and historic factors, expressed by our creative community and experienced by all consumers of art—is responsible for the ups and downs in the fate of the Venice Biennale. The new conservatism is not that incidental naysaying to difficult or untried art, mostly a reflection of the popular consensus, we have come to expect from critics of the popular press.[29]

While still on the "right side of history," Masini could not reverse this changing cultural tide. Yet paradoxically, her visual arts installation in the Italian Pavilion was immortalized when her exhibit was visited in the wryly comedic film *Intelligent Vacations*, created by the comedian, actor, and director Alberto Sordi (best known for his 1954 comedic masterpiece "An American in Rome").[30] Accompanied by his stage wife Anna Longhi, playing the characters Remo and Augusta, Roman shop owners, they tour the gardens and main Italian pavilion attempting to understand the conceptual works around the biennale. Another actor, playing an unnamed critic, is followed around by a group of stone-faced visitors as he recites esoteric descriptions on the conceptual art installations before them. The couple doesn't quite get it, but they do their best to fit in. While the scene could be read as a humorous dismissal of high art, there is a certain degree of fascination that makes this walkthrough among the artworks so memorable.[31]

Two years later, Lara-Vinca Masini brought her focus back to Florence, unleashing one of the most comprehensive, groundbreaking, and controversial exhibitions to be staged in the postwar Tuscan city. *Umanesimo, Disumanesimo nell'arte Europea 1890/1980* spread itself out across several venues around Florence (Fig. 3). Its principle exhibition space was the Palagio di Parte Guelfa, but there were also ten public installations by artists and architects in and around the city center, occupying mainly Renaissance era courtyards, along with several interventions found elsewhere in the city. The germinal concept behind the exhibition grew out of a general reaction against an incessant parade of celebratory exhibitions and events on the Renaissance culture of the

Fig. 3. Catalogue cover, *Umanesimo, Disumanesimo nell'arte Europea 1890/1980*. Edited Lara-Vinca Masini, Florence, Silvana Ed. Cover image of a stone carved bracket of a monkey and a shell.

Medici, productions that made no mention of the darker and more deviant aspects of Medicean rule. Masini's title *Umanesimo, Disumanesimo* takes the word humanism and stands it on its head, creating a dialectical relationship between humanism and its opposite. The In-humanism term originates in the study of an anti-renaissance, brought forth by the historian Eugenio Battisti, who taught in Florence and was also active in the contemporary art scene.[32] But Masini also makes sure to tie this research to Italy's bloody street revolts, the rise of extra-parliamentary politics, and the devastating bomb attacks afflicting the peninsula during the postwar period.

In Lara-Vinca Masini's introductory essay to the show's catalogue, "The Coin and its Reverse," she states: "The concept of in-humanism is born from humanism.

A denunciation of the situation, expressed in a sense of emptiness and melancholy, deriving from the knowledge of the uselessness of action, was to be reached when history and myth were annulled into symbolism."[33]

The show grew out of a series of discussions with Giuseppe Chiari, the Florentine Fluxus artist and musician, and Fabio Mauri, the artist and close friend of Masini, both of whom were strong skeptics of the complacent fad for Florence's renaissance revival. As Masini emphasized in a recent interview, their meetings together brought them to formulate a complex and critical response to these clearly commercial and speculative trends, by making use of expressionist art that grew in reaction to rising German nationalism – as the vehicle to critically interrogate artistic responses to this superficially idealized society.[34] Their choice to work in the arts, architecture, music, and philosophy was intended to demonstrate the value of an unvarnished richness in contemporary culture. By taking these critical and unsettling propositions directly into some of the most coveted of Renaissance era palaces and courtyards, Masini succeeded in hitting a major nerve in Florentine society.

Superstudio member Piero Frassinelli, selected by Masini to design and install the exhibition, came up with an "anti-perspective" staircase to the main entrance to the exhibition venue. The staircase was deformed using a forced perspective with its dimensions determined by Le Corbusier's *modulor* man – recalling the Renaissance ideal on the "measure of man." Superstudio cofounder Adolfo Natalini developed a set of Renaissance directional "signs," bar castings based on Brunelleschi's moldings from the Hospital of the Innocents, pointing to exhibit locations around the city. Music from the period 1890-1980 could be heard in the Palagio di Parte Guelfa when visiting a series of small rooms located within the interstices among black and white "zig zag" partitions designed to hold and display the artwork.[35]

The most controversial part of *Umanesimo, Disumanesimo* was the artists' and architects' installations in a selection of Renaissance era palace courtyards, scattered across Florence's historic center. Masini scouted out the courtyards in different parts of the city and assigned them to a selection of artists and architects to create installations that would connect back in very physical terms to the expressionist critique at the heart of the exhibition. Haus Rucker Co., which was founded in Vienna, created an immense freestanding "foldable" laundry rack, with large white sheets hanging out to dry (Fig. 4). The intention was that over time these would become soiled while exposed in the atmosphere, transforming the way the courtyard, (Cortile palazzo Montauti-Niccolini) would be experienced.[36]

Hans Hollein, on the other hand, working in the Cortile Palazzo Pazzi-Quaratesi, chose to create a sort of war zone, with sandbags and barbed wire, and a row of hospital beds facing them (Fig. 5). The German artist Wolf Vostell releasing a chicken among a bed of feathers (Cortile Palagio di Parte Guelfa), the

CHAPTER 3. LARA-VINCA MASINI   91

Fig. 4. Haus Rucker Co., Laundry Racks, Palazzo Montauti-Niccolini Courtyard installation, overscale laundry racks and white sheets. (Courtesy of the Masini Archive)

Fig. 5. Hans Hollein, Palazzo Pazzi Quaratesi Courtyard installation, wartime scene: sandbags and empty beds. (Courtesy of the Masini Archive)

Austrian artist Hermann Nitsch's pagan-like performance among slaughtered animal carcasses (Chiostro delle Obiate), and the German artist Rebecca Horn's tearful funerary ode to the little boy painted in gold from Vasari's history (Cortile Palazzo Frescobaldi) shocked the conservative Florentine public, who even tried to barricade the entrances to these spaces. And accounts in the local press were just as unfavorable. Though Nitsch's work was an action and not meant to last, Vostell's was closed down almost immediately.[37]

The program also included a reflection on the destruction of Florence's historic center, featuring Piero Frassinelli's re-imagining the Risorgimento style central post office at Piazza Repubblica that stands on the former site of the Jewish ghetto. Frassinelli's intervention on the nineteenth-century post office consisted of a series of hung fabrics painted with images from the Alinari photo archives, documenting the streets from the medieval era that vanished to make way for this imposing arcaded structure. There was also a comprehensive study using the Alinari archives, curated by Marco Dezzi Bardeschi, on the false restorations of Florentine Renaissance era buildings, aptly titled *Quale Firenze... Ideologia e pratica dell'infedele* ("Which Florence... Ideology and Practice of the Infidel").

Among the projects critical of Florence's contradictory imaginary, none would be so condemning as Fabio Mauri's intervention at the Vasca della Palazzina Reale, located to the rear to the Santa Maria Novella rail station completed in 1934 (Fig. 6). The design of the Palazzina Reale, designated for official State visits, is attributed to the interwar era Gruppo Toscano, led by the architect Giovanni Michelucci, whose collective won the public design competition. Mauri focused in on the formal reflecting pool as it opened towards the side of the city. This end of the composition included a marble portico, seated statuary, a reflecting pool with flagpole, and a narrow exedra to the side, rendered in stripped down classicist style. The Palazzina Reale was pointedly the site for the welcoming ceremony greeting Hitler's visit to Florence in 1938. By choosing this part of the train station, Mauri bluntly reminded Florentines of Hitler's notorious reception in their city. The artist transformed the reflecting pool into a fountain of red tinted water, while the flagpole was draped in a long white sheet that extended into the pool, absorbing the bloodlike color like a stained bandage.

The concluding event was the conference *Valore, non-valore* ("Value, Non-Value"), a philosophical debate examining the complex legacy of humanism in Florence. Presided over by the art critic and historian Giulio Carlo Argan, the published list of speakers included Giuseppe Chiari, Fabio Mauri, and Hans Hollein, together with critics and historians Marco Dezzi Bardeschi, Gillo Dorfles, Achille Bonito Oliva, Pierre Restany, and Lea Vergine, among others. Florentines stayed away while the audience, mainly from outside Florence and beyond flocked to the event. If one looked past the local dissent, *Valore, non-valore* should be considered as

Fig. 6. Fabio Mauri, Vasca della Palazzina Reale, Santa Maria Novella. The water in the fountain pool is tinted blood red. (Courtesy of the Masini Archive)

one of the most important gatherings of intellectuals to be organized in the city's postwar history.

In one opinion from 1980 published in the conservative newspaper *Il Giornale*, the reviewer, Pier Carlo Santini, writes, "The exhibition in its totality is organized by Lara-Vinca Masini, who is not new to this kind of undertaking, it is meant ' to rupture'..."[38] From the other perspective, writing in the left-wing paper *La Repubblica*, Valerio Eletti observes, "the show is a must see, an 'intelligent' exhibit curated by Lara-Vinca Masini that from the start is in polemic with the pompous excesses of the (previous) exhibit on the Medici, by taking the lead to excavate in the art of the last century the values of the 'negative'."[39]

The impressive collective effort to embed the exhibition into the physical and psychic landscapes of Florence did not have the desired effect, in the end, of swaying Florentines into becoming more critically aware of their city's questionable past. According to Masini, were it not for a few local educational classes and a stream of foreign visitors, there was very little public presence.[40] Masini knew this project would be a provocation, but nonetheless she had not anticipated the degree to which Florentines would react negatively.[41] *Umanesimo, Disumanesimo* was nonetheless a ground-breaking exhibition, and as of this writing there is renewed interest in revisiting its history.[42] But it is also evident that Florentines remain far too beholden to the city's historic legacy and its unidimensional tourist economy to embrace innovation in the arts and architecture, at least in the way Masini envisioned it.

Masini's long and prestigious legacy as a critic and curator seems to have fallen short of achieving the kind of international stature that someone with such noteworthy accomplishments would normally merit. As in Venice in 1978, and in Florence in 1980, Masini always carefully tailored her projects to a specific question through a very personal applied philosophy, pioneering a curatorial style that did not conform to one or another predetermined position. She was constantly seeking out expressions that reflected the issues she was most concerned with, rather than formulating a signature style or pursuing greater prominence. But whereas her capacity to weave together art and architecture and her concern for operating in the public realm set her outside the emerging trends of the eighties, there are clear, if somewhat indirect signals that Masini anticipated a long-term shift towards critical artistic and architectural interventions in the contemporary city. In other words, Lara-Vinca Masini seems to have intuited a working method concerned with criticizing public perceptions of the urban condition, a site-specific approach to cities that would increasingly concern curators over the coming decades.

For example, the famed urban sociologist and pedagogue Lucius Burckhardt participated in a project called the Biennale Urbana – a series of housing initiatives based in Kassel in the early 80s. Burckhardt wanted to intervene in public spaces of the inner city and succeeded in folding his project by 1982 into Documenta 7. The initiative led to a myriad of urban-based proposals for Kassel's center city. Yet it may not have been until the Dutch curator Hedwig Fijen established the Manifesta organization in the early nineties that something similar to what Lara-Vinca Masini had been pursuing began to take more recognizable shape. Fijen speaks about using a trans-disciplinary model in pulling together their biennial curatorial teams, and in Manifesta 9 she "introduced the trans-historical model" that Fijen describes as "a method in which curators make interventions in a historical context, and start-up a dialog between contemporaneity and the historical."[43] Not only does this sound very familiar, but the problems that Hedwig Fijen's curatorial teams encountered reflect working obstacles similar to those often faced by Masini. This would become most evident when Manifesta 6 came to Cyprus, where government intransigence effectively shut the biennial down. "That's what I am a little bit proud of," Fijen observed, "that we saw an opportunity for the curators to innovate, to experiment. And specifically, how can you do an experiment which is actually even able to fail?"[44]

The brilliance of Masini springs from her ability to produce exhibitions that are about activating spaces, getting artists, architects, and designers to respond viscerally to the environment in which they are set, by creating critical projects that are at once contaminated and contaminating. Other exhibitions curated by architectural critics from the same period tended to pursue more constrained objectives. Take for example Bruno Zevi's exhibition from 1978, *Brunelleschi anti-classico*, which occupied the cloisters of Santa Maria Novella in Florence. Zevi introduced large scale installations designed by Piero Sartogo that were meant to upend existing tropes about Brunelleschi's understanding of geometry and modularity.[45]

The exhibition by Zevi can be taken as a historical corrective, providing through its carefully articulated narrative an alternative account on Brunelleschi's prescient architectural development. But the exhibition, besides amplifying the architect's position as lone genius, leaves little for interpretation. Zevi did not probe deeper into the vicissitudes of Florentine society; nor did he question how Brunelleschi would be interpreted by his peers and successors.

Masini, on the other hand, would not have missed the opportunity to take such an inquiry further afield, as she went on to do two years later when she came down hard on the glorified celebrations of Medici Florence. To Masini, these previous exhibitions exalting the figures and architecture of the Renaissance would merely play into the hands of those whose livelihoods were most dependent on the city's highly profitable tourist trade. Lara-Vinca Masini fought long and hard to keep Florence from becoming an urban boutique, and she made quite a number of enemies along the way. But the lingering question is whether Masini fell short as a critic, and whether her vision would be able to stand the test of time. There I think the answer is more nuanced, depending largely on how narrowly architecture is defined as a form of creative expression. Masini took the broad perspective, and we should give her view renewed consideration.

Notes

1. Laura Lombardi, "Lara Vinca Masini e la critica d'arte a Firenze, una città dura," in *Artiste della Critica*, ed. Maura Pozzati (Mantua, Corraini, 2015), 76.
2. Lara Vinca Masini spoke in an interview of her close relations to Ettore Sottsass Jr. and Nanda Pivana (interview by author, September 26, 2016).
3. Petition on behalf of LVM 2016 (https://www.artribune.com/professioni-e-professionisti/didattica/2016/12/lara-vinca-masini-appello-gentiloni-franceschini-vitalizio/). The Livorno project should have had its equivalent in Florence, but Masini never could overcome the provincial resistance she encountered in her effort to make a modern museum of art in Florence.
4. From start to finish, the latter exhibition was largely scorned by mainstream Florentine society despite being well received outside the city and beyond. Alessandra Acocella, "Un itinerario urbano per ripensare Firenze, *Umanesimo, Disumanesimo nell'arte europea*

1890-1980," in *Arte a Firenze 1970-2015: Una città in prospettiva,* ed. Alessandra Acocella and Caterina Toschi (Macerata: Quodlibet, 2016).
5. Premio Lincei, "Critica dell'arte e della poesia," 1985. https://www.lincei.it/it/premio-ministro-1961-2011-classe-smsf.
6. The historian and curator Maura Pozzati brings together essays on twelve noted female art critics, including Lara-Vinca Masini, Lea Vergine, Carla Lonzi, and Palma Bucarelli. Maura Pozzati, ed., *Artiste della Critica* (Mantua: Corraini editori, 2015).
7. For example, as documented by Alessandra Acocella, Masini would be instrumental in arranging for a major retrospective of the work of Ketty La Rocca at the Venice Biennale in 1978, though as La Rocca worked in a photographic medium, for Masini it made more sense for it to be exhibited in the section curated by Luigi Carluccio. Cited in Alessandra Acocella, "Tra utopia e disincanto. Le mostre di Lara-Vinca Masini alla Biennale 1978," in *Presenze toscane alla Biennale Internazionale d'Arte di Venezia,* ed. Flavio Fergonzi (Milan: Skira, 2017), 135.
8. Martina Corgnati, "Carla Lonzi, Da Autoritratto all Gibigianna e oltre," in Pozzati, *Artiste della Critica*, 93. See also Laura Lamurri, *Un margine che sfugge: Carla Lonzi e l'arte in Italia 1955-1970* (Macerata: Quodlibet, 2016).
9. Francesca Alfano Miglietti, "Lea Vergine, la signora della body," in Pozzati, *Artiste della Critica*, 117.
10. Interview with Piero Sartogo by author, June 20, 2017, Rome. While there were repeated contacts with Austrian architects by the late sixties, specifically in Graz during the Trigon and at Alvin Boyarsky's IID in London, it would be Lara-Vinca Masini who would organize the first serious exhibitions of their work in Florence in 1980 in her exhibition on Humanism.
11. Interview with Lara-Vinca Masini by author, July 29, 2003, Florence. "While before architects used art like some appendix, I think what today we call shifts, or contaminations, comes out of this…this is the impact of the radicals…Today so much architecture reflects the world of art. And vice a versa so many artists are working on space… It's not that one becomes the other but that there is this shift, this exchange, from the sciences, and poetry."
12. Masini's commitment to interdisciplinarity reflects the core values that shaped Florence after the war, beginning in the 1950s, when Giorgio La Pira assumed the city mayor's office, introducing in the process a pious form of humanist government. In the years that ensued, the city would host world film festivals, promote international cultural exchanges, and lead an effort towards global peace. One of La Pira's capstones was bringing the European University Institute to Florence. "La Pira, Communities of Europe and the World: Foundation Stones of Dialogue," posted November 2014, European University Institute, https://www.eui.eu/Research/HistoricalArchivesOfEU/News/2014/11-04-LaPiracommunitiesofEuropeandtheworldfoundationstonesofdialogue.

13. This was certainly the case in the following Venice Biennale, when Paolo Portoghesi would curate *The Presence of the Past*. See Léa-Catherine Szacka, *Exhibiting the Postmodern: The 1980 Venice Architecture Biennale* (Venice: Marsilio Editore, 2017).
14. See Stylianos Giamarelos, "Intersecting Itineraries beyond the Strada Novissima: The Converging Authorship of Critical Regionalism," *Architectural Histories* 4 (July 2016). https://journal.eahn.org/articles/10.5334/ah.192/.
15. Lombardi, "Lara Vinca Masini e la critica d'arte a Firenze," 64.
16. Lara-Vinca Masini and Marco Dezzi Bardeschi, eds., *Prima Triennale Itinerante d'Architettura Italiana Contemporanea* (Florence: Edizioni Centro Proposte, 1965).
17. Some of the more outstanding essays included Renato De Fusco on the teaching of modern architecture, Lara-Vinca Masini on a proposal for a new critical language, Filiberto Menna on *Architettura Programmata*, and Vittorio Gregotti's *Fruition and Significance*, to name but a few.
18. The painter Marcolino Gandini's geometrically generated frescoes were fused to large freestanding concrete slabs set in unremarkable urban peripheries; the sculptor Cosimo Carlucci's outdoor works were made of multilayered overlapping space-age aluminum wings that reflected the sky and channeled the wind, while Paolo Portoghesi presented highly intricate geometrically shaped buildings with their study sketches. See Catalogue: Marcello Faggiolo, ed., *Parabola 66* (Florence: Edizione centro proposte, 1966). *Parabola 66* includes essays by Giulio Carlo Argan, Marcello Fagiolo, and Lara-Vinca Masini.
19. Lara-Vinca Masini, untitled essay, in *Parabola 66*, 14.
20. "The theme Anti-natura was not my theme but was introduced by Achille Bonito Oliva." Interview with Lara-Vinca Masini by author, July 29, 2003, Florence.
21. While Achille Bonito Oliva lauded Sartogo's architectural installation, he remained dismissive about the exhibits by these three curators. Achille Bonito Oliva, ed., *Between Art and Architecture: Piero Sartogo e gli Artisti, 1968-1978* (Turin: Allemandi Publishers, 2014), 193.
22. Cited in Acocella, "Tra utopia e disincanto," 138.
23. Lara-Vinca Masini, ed., *Topologia e Morfogenesi: Utopia e crisi dell'antinatura, Momenti delle intenzioni architettoniche in Italia* (Venice: La Biennale di Venezia, 1978), 5.
24. Quoted from Masini's blurb on the chapter "Topology." Ibid., 17, translated by author. Here is a sample list of writers, critics, artists, and architects exhibited under the section "Topology": Werner Ruhnau on Yves Klien, Walter Pichler, and the architect designers Hans Hollein, Franco Raggi, Andrea Branzi (Archizoom Associati), Lapo Binazzi (UFO), Adolfo Natalini (Superstudio) 1977, Ettore Sottsass, Gaetano Pesce, Ugo La Pietra, Gianni Pettena, Gruppo 9999, Alessandro Mendini, Riccardo Dalisi, Almerico de Angelis, Gruppo Strum, Remi Buti, and Cavart.
25. Quoted from Masini's blurb on the chapter "Morphogenesis." Ibid., 103, translated by author. Especially telling were the contributions by those who were leading the *neo-ten-*

denza movement, with fundamental texts by Giorgio Grassi, Vittorio Gregotti, Franco Purini, Constantino Dardi, Carlo Aymonino, Manfredo Tafuri, Aldo Rossi, Massimo Scolari, Bruno Reichlin, Fabio Reinhart, Mario Botta, and Aduino Cantafora.

26. Lara-Vinca Masini, "Introduction," in *Topologia e Morfogenesi*, 5.
27. Masini, *Topologia e Morfogenesi*, 11.
28. See Léa-Catherine Szacka, *Exhibiting the Postmodern: The 1980 Venice Architecture Biennale* (Venice: Marsilio Editore, 2017). Szacka gives the most detailed history to date on the first independent Architecture Biennale in Venice, "The Presence of the Past," curated by Paolo Portoghesi, held in 1980. This exhibit was dominated by the very same group of eclectic postmodernists.
29. Jan Van der Marck, "The Venice Biennale: Can It Rise Again?" *Artforum*, September 1978, 74.
30. Stefano Vanzina (Steno) Titanus, *Un Americano a Roma* (Rome: Minerva Film, 1954), film starring Alberto Sordi.
31. Film excerpt from Alberto Sordi with Anna Longhi in the scene from the Venice Biennale from the film *Dove vai in vacanza?* ("Where Do You Go for Vacation?", 1978), episode "Le vacanze intelligenti" ("Intelligent Vacations"), directed by Alberto Sordi, https://youtu.be/lj438bBpX9w.
32. Acocella, "Un itinerario urbano per ripensare Firenze," 161.
33. Lara-Vinca Masini, "Introduction," in *Umanesimo Disumanesimo nell'arte europea* (Milan: Silvana Editoriale), 16.
34. Interview with Lara-Vinca Masini by author, September 26, 2016, Florence.
35. A short list of artists in the exhibition provides a sense of Lara Vinca Masini's Dionysian vision: Kazimir Malevich, Henri Fauconnier, Erich Mendelsohn, Piero Manzoni, Constant, Fernandez Arman, Oskar Kokoschka, Egon Schiele, Marcel Duchamp, Raul Hausman, Meret Oppenheim, Frederick Kiesler, Jean Debuffet, Frei Otto, Asger Jorn, Giacometti, Franz Roh …
36. Haus Rucker Co., in *Umanesimo Disumanesimo nell'arte europea*, 143.
37. The full list of courtyard installations are as follows: Sandro Chia, Giuseppe Chiari, Luciano Fabro, Haus-Rucker-Co, Hans Hollein, Rebecca Horn, Fabio Mauri, Hermann Nitsch, and Wolf Vostell.
38. Pier Carlo Santini, "Una Discutibile manifestazione fiorentina: Umani disumani e un po' strani," in *Il Giornale*, Milan, October 17, 1980.
39. Valerio Eletti, "Dal Simbolismo all'informale: A Firenze un Europa 'disumana'," in *La Repubblica*, October 16, 1980, Rome.
40. Interview with Lara-Vinca Masini by author, November 10, 2017, Florence.
41. Ibid.
42. An excellent exhibition was recently displayed at the Villa Romana in Florence curated by Alessandra Acocella and Angelika Stepken, entitled *Umanesimo Disumanesimo 1980/2017: Lara-Vinca Masini e il senso della crisi nell'arte europea*, 9.11-15.12.2017,

Villa Romana, Florence Italy, http://www.villaromana.org/front_content.php?idcat=69&idart=1149&lang=1.
43. Agnese Čivle, "A Nomadic Event with a Permanent Impact: An interview with Hedwig Fijen, the Director of Manifesta – The European Biennial of Contemporary Art," in *Arterritory. Baltic, Russian, and Scandinavian Art Territory* (08/05/2016). Accessed on July 29, 2018. http://www.arterritory.com/en/texts/interviews/5571-a_nomadic_event_with_a_permanent_impact/.
44. Ibid.
45. On the Zevi exhibition in Florence, see Sartogo Architetti Associati, "Brunelleschi Anticlassico: mostra nei chiostri di Santa Maria Novella per il quinto centenario della nascita di Filippo Brunelleschi/ Brunelleschi Anticlassico: Exhibition for the Fifth Centenary of the Birth Of Filippo Brunelleschi – Florence," no date of publication. Accessed on August 22, 2018. http://www.sartogoarchitetti.it/index.php?/esposizioni/brunelleschi-anticlassico/.

CHAPTER 4

Architecture Becomes Programming: Invisible Technicians, Printouts, and Situated Theories in the 1960s

Matthew Allen

I will begin with a slightly unusual telling of a much-rehashed narrative in the history of architectural theory.[1] In a 1957 essay, John Summerson suggested that architects would need to reconstruct their discipline around programming – they should give up designing *form* and start to think about organizing *patterns of activity*.[2] A few architects took Summerson's advice to heart. Christopher Alexander wrote software to manipulate architectural programs; Cedric Price seems to have spent most of his time gathering data and drawing diagrams.[3] Two senses of the term "programming" developed simultaneously in this era. In architecture, programming referred to the practice of organizing functional spaces,[4] while in the field of computation, programming referred to the practice of creating software.[5] The craze for "spatial location-allocation" software around 1970 is one example of how these two senses of programming came together: computer programs could be used to manipulate architectural programs.[6] Price's Fun Palace (1964), with its computer-controlled flexible spaces, went so far as to imagine that computer programming and architectural programming are fundamentally the same thing.[7]

But just as some architects embraced programming in the 1960s and '70s, a branch of architecture theory (which I will refer to as "Theory"[8]) gained traction precisely in opposition to this trend. Peter Eisenman's famous 1976 editorial described how over the previous centuries "architecture became increasingly a social or programmatic art," just as Summerson had noted. Contrary to Summerson, however, Eisenman suggested adopting a "non-humanistic attitude" that begins with the "negation of functionalism."[9] Colin Rowe, writing with a different focus but within the same intellectual milieu, equated programming with "naive scientism" and worried that architects would be sidetracked by an "orgy of expensive but impeccable interdisciplinary collaboration" and end up perpetually "waiting for printout."[10] If Eisenman and Rowe represent the common opinion of Theory circa 1980, the famous debate in those years between Alexander and Eisenman can be seen as the moment when Theory "won." While Alexander's buildings might have been pleasant and functional, they were also, as Eisenman argued, boring. And worse, they seemed to be part of an insidious program of social engineering.[11] The buildings advocated by Eisenman, on the other hand, aimed to provoke inhabitants to question their own deeply held values. In the following decades, this sort of architecture (call it "critical architecture") became associated with Theory, at least in the East Coast North American academic context that played such a large role in setting the intellectual standards and agendas during this period.[12] Summerson's argument in favor of programming had been tried, tested, and repudiated.

However true the foregoing historical sketch may be, it certainly must be qualified. The Theory that repudiated programming is embodied, for example, in the essays collected in K. Michael Hays's *Architecture Theory since 1968*.[13] This theoretical lineage runs through Frankfurt School critical theory, and as such it views programming (in both the architectural and computer science senses) as instrumental and normalizing. Theorists in this vein typically suspect that the rationalism required to conform thought to the dictates of computer logic or functional requirements is akin to totalitarianism.[14] In fact, they seem to have regarded a particular *habit of thought* as the true enemy. When the uncompromising Frankfurt School figure Theodor Adorno moved to Los Angeles, he saw authoritarian thinking everywhere.[15] From the perspective of North America, consumer culture and technocracy were certainly forces to be reckoned with. Hence the urgent need for opposition, particularly from the intellectual bastions of the East Coast – and particularly via "autonomous" activities such as art and the formalist architecture that aligned itself with art.

Suspicion regarding programming still lingers today. We should note, however, that Alexander and other proponents of programming were not naive functionaries. To the contrary, many were very theoretically minded. This chapter begins with the premise that it is worth questioning the distinction whereby *Theory* upholds standards of critique while (minor, ad hoc) *theories* are tied down by the contingencies of practice. This concerns another détente of the Cold War era. It was precisely through the combative, oppositional mode of Eisenman and his cohort that all sorts of minor theories were occluded behind the Iron Curtain of Theory.

An expanded history of theory should begin by noting that programming and its associated theories did not disappear even after they were excluded from Theory. A thriving subculture of programming congealed around computers – in technical classes and computer centers at architecture schools, in computer groups at corporate firms, and in a global network of nomadic computer consultants.[16] The tradition of programming in architecture continued as a subdiscipline through the 1970s and '80s, finally rejoining the mainstream with the digital architecture of the 1990s.[17] Once the distinction between *Theory* and *theories* is set aside, we can begin to locate the situated knowledge that has been obscured and to think about how to reincorporate it into the history of theory. (This applies not only to the subculture of programming. Hays has suggested that the 1960s saw the end of the illusion of a single shared "architecture culture," and that the 1970s were the beginning of an era of fragmentary, insular subcultures.[18] Thus there are likely many subcultures and situated theories waiting to be rediscovered.)

With digital culture becoming second nature across the discipline, now is a particularly good time to uncover and reconsider the theories that accompanied its emergence. A postulate of cultural techniques may help us to identify these situated theories: namely, that *practices precede concepts*.[19] The usual example is that people made marks of one sort or another long before the concept of "writing" solidified.[20] Likewise, assemblages of processors and input and output devices were used before "the interactive computer" or "computer-aided design" or "digital modelling" became stable concepts.[21] If theories are situated in contexts of practice, cultural techniques stand out as figures of knowledge that mark the former.

This line of reasoning poses problems, however. Does every instance of practice engender its own concepts? If so, then what is the basis for believing that a concept is shared by more than one person? These are particularly pressing questions in the case of early electronic computers because it is not obvious how or why computer-related concepts would have spread. Architects conducted many isolated and ephemeral "experiments" using computers before the 1990s, but few recognizable buildings were produced. Computers themselves did not move at all: until the 1980s, computers were big, immobile boxes to which few people had access. Computers in the 1960s and 1970s are a straightforward case of what Bruno Latour calls "centers of calculation."[22] Following Latour's argument, we can imagine that early computers gained their power through the diffusion of "immutable mobiles" – that is, words and images on paper that circulate in lieu of computers themselves. The hypothesis of this chapter is that evidence for shared computer-related concepts in architecture can be found in printouts.

As a methodological point, the approach of cultural techniques assumes that theory can exist in a situation even if it is not explicitly articulated. This raises the question of what exactly a theory is. My working definition is rather broad: theory is about understanding.[23] Newton's theory of gravitation allows us to understand the motion of planets and why things fall to earth. Theories of programming allow us to understand architecture in certain ways. A theory works this way even if it is never written down or explicitly articulated.[24]

Cultural techniques thus play a mediating role between printouts and theories. Traditionally, aesthetics have often been called upon to play a similar mediating role – to translate subjective judgments of singular things into the shared values of a "community of taste."[25] Commenting on Immanuel Kant's aesthetic philosophy and updating it for the mid-twentieth century, Hannah Arendt described the specifically *political* role of aesthetics. Aesthetic judgments, Arendt says,

> share with political opinions that they are persuasive; the judging person—as Kant says quite beautifully—can only "woo the consent of everyone else" in the hope of coming to an agreement with him eventually. [...] Culture and politics, then, belong together because it is not knowledge or truth which is at stake, but rather judgment and decision, the judicious exchange of opinion about the sphere of public life and the common world, and the decision [regarding] what manner of action is to be taken in it, as well as to how it is to look henceforth, what kind of things are to appear in it.[26]

Expanding on Arendt's insight, we could add that some aesthetic/political judgments are also decisions about which *theories* are allowed to appear in shared life. Though I will need to substantiate this in the following pages, I suggest at the outset that printouts can be productively analyzed in terms of aesthetic schema (which I take to be equivalent to figures of knowledge) on the way to making judgments about them. I will return to the important role of aesthetics for the history of theory in the conclusion.

The following cases are presented as a guidebook to some of the aesthetic categories that can be found in the subculture of architect-programmers in the 1960s. There are several excellent guidebooks on the topic of older printing methods (woodcuts, engravings, etc.); the one by William Ivins that has been around since 1943 is especially perceptive at providing hints about how image types and techniques are related to historical figures of knowledge.[27] Such guidebooks are lacking for computer-generated printouts.[28] I will structure my own modest contribution around a 1964 conference presentation by an IBM technician named Christopher Smith.[29] I will illustrate the five printing methods Smith identifies, grouped into three sections: *X Y Plotter* and *Drafting Machine* output, *Standard Printer* and *Modified Printer* output, and *CRT* output.[30] To connect this with what was going on in architecture, I will correlate Smith's examples with images created at a computer center that operated at Harvard's Graduate School of Design. The Laboratory for Computer Graphics and Spatial Analysis (LCGSA), as it was called, is best known for the mapping software it created,[31] but it also developed dozens of smaller programs covering many aspects of design in the 1960s and 1970s. Researchers at the LCGSA took advantage of its location in an architecture school to collaborate with architects (including Charles Correa and The Architects Collaborative [TAC]),[32] to work across media (from color prints to kinetic art), and to experiment with the wide array of output devices available in the period. The LCGSA's projects are collected in a binder called the *Red Book*;[33] it is from here that I will pull images.

X Y plotter and drafting machine output

If there has been a single "great device" of graphic output for architecture, it is the plotter. Plotters in the 1960s produced not pixels, as they do today, but lines: the pen moved in the X direction while the paper moved in the Y direction. Rather than recreating a one-to-one matrix of pixels, plotters operated through a language of instructions for creating vectors. As Claus Pias so eloquently puts it, "computer graphics of this kind might therefore be described as choreography, as the notation of movements to be performed."[34]

In the mid-1960s there were, in fact, two choreographic languages for plotters: one for common plotters and another for what were called drafting machines. For Smith, what set these devices apart was their precision. Common plotters were less precise because they could only understand instructions for creating straight lines. Drafting machines, on the other hand, could create complex curves.

These devices understood different sets of instructions because they were used quite differently – though neither was originally used by architects. Plotters were inexpensive, everyday devices for engineers and scientists, but they were still beyond the means of most architects. In any case, plotters lacked the graphic refinement an architect could easily produce by hand (Fig. 1). The common plotter was a device of expediency for those who could afford the luxury and lacked the manual skill.

The drafting machine was a more refined device, but it too did not suit the needs of architects. Drafting machines could accommodate several pens and different line weights and they could draw complex curves, but they lacked a software environment that could handle architectural notation.[35] They operated on a low-level language derived from descriptive geometry and tailored to aerospace fabrication.

The development of the language of drafting machines was a pivotal moment in the history of computation. In the postwar period, a torrent of funding for defense-related research washed over American academia, with the Massachusetts Institute of Technology (MIT) among the largest recipients.[36] A series of grants at MIT to develop manufacturing techniques combined with research surrounding electronic computers, resulting in the Automatic Programmed Tool language (APT).[37] APT quickly became the preferred language for controlling fabrication

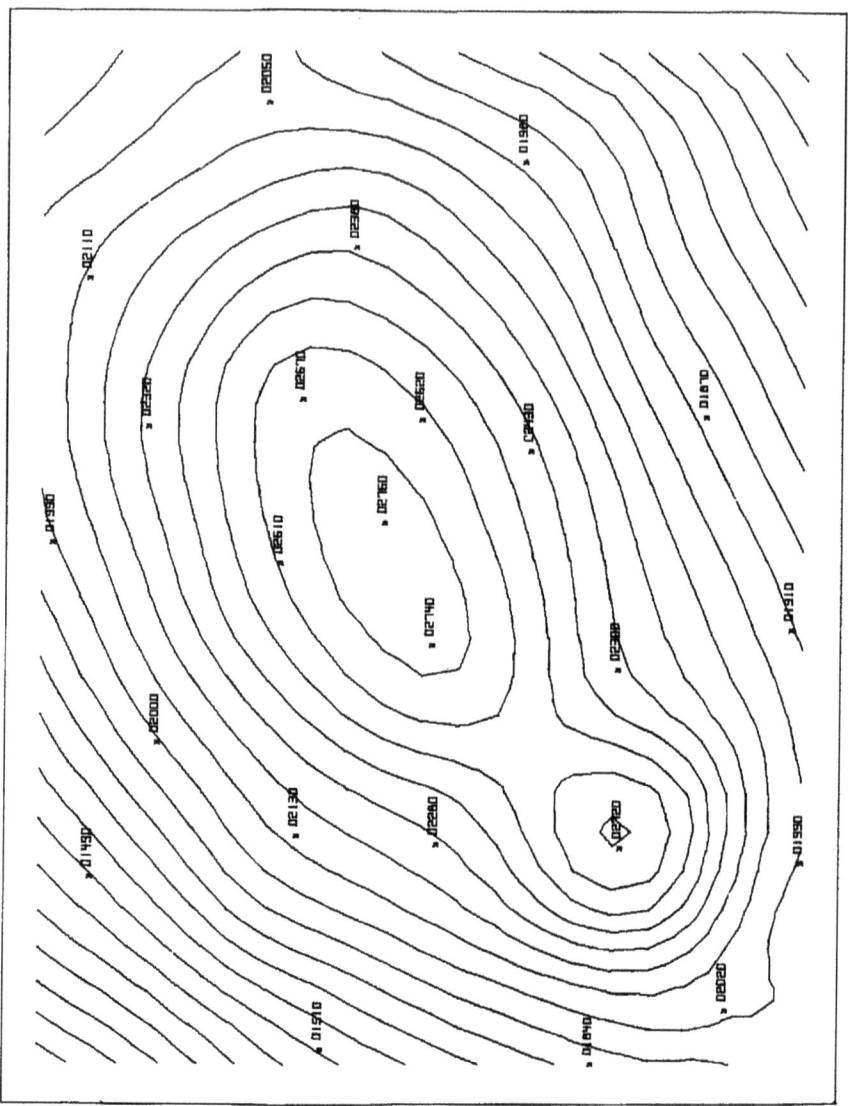

Fig. 1. X Y plotter output reproduced in Christopher P. Smith, "Graphic Data Processing" (1964)

machines, which originally were run directly from punched-tape programs. The CAD Project of 1959 aimed to bypass this step and to "provide an efficient mechanism for going almost directly from the requirement for a machined part to the finished product."[38] One result of the CAD Project was Sketchpad, which became the first proof of the concept of the general-purpose interactive computer. At Sketchpad's conceptual core was APT, the language of drafting machines.

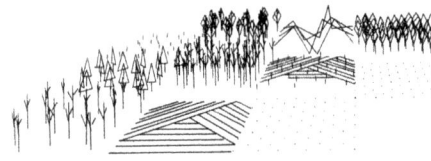

Fig. 2. Perspective Simulation of Development in the Landscape (Spring 1968), from *Selected Projects* (Courtesy of the Frances Loeb Library, Harvard University Graduate School of Design)

One Magnificent Mile comprises three hexagonal concrete tubes bundled together for structural stability. Using the same computer graphics system as for the other studies shown here, the structural engineers were able to display the deflected shape (exaggerated) of the building under wind loading.

The drawing was created utilizing SOM's Structural Data Management System (SDMS) that was initiated 10 years ago. With the system, a data base is developed that describes the structure, its elements, and the loadings placed upon them. A standard language was developed to describe structures of all kinds regardless of the analysis techniques or programs to be employed. This language can deal with all sorts of "goofy" geometries. It has a library of standard elements: configurations, properties of sections, load distributions, etc. The SDMS can take a list of all the members that have loads on them and turn it into input for STRUDL, STRESS or other analysis programs. The engineer never has to deal with understanding the specific formats for all the different analysis programs. SDMS produces input that is sent to whatever computer happens to run that program.

ARCHITECTURAL RECORD *Mid-August 1980* 87

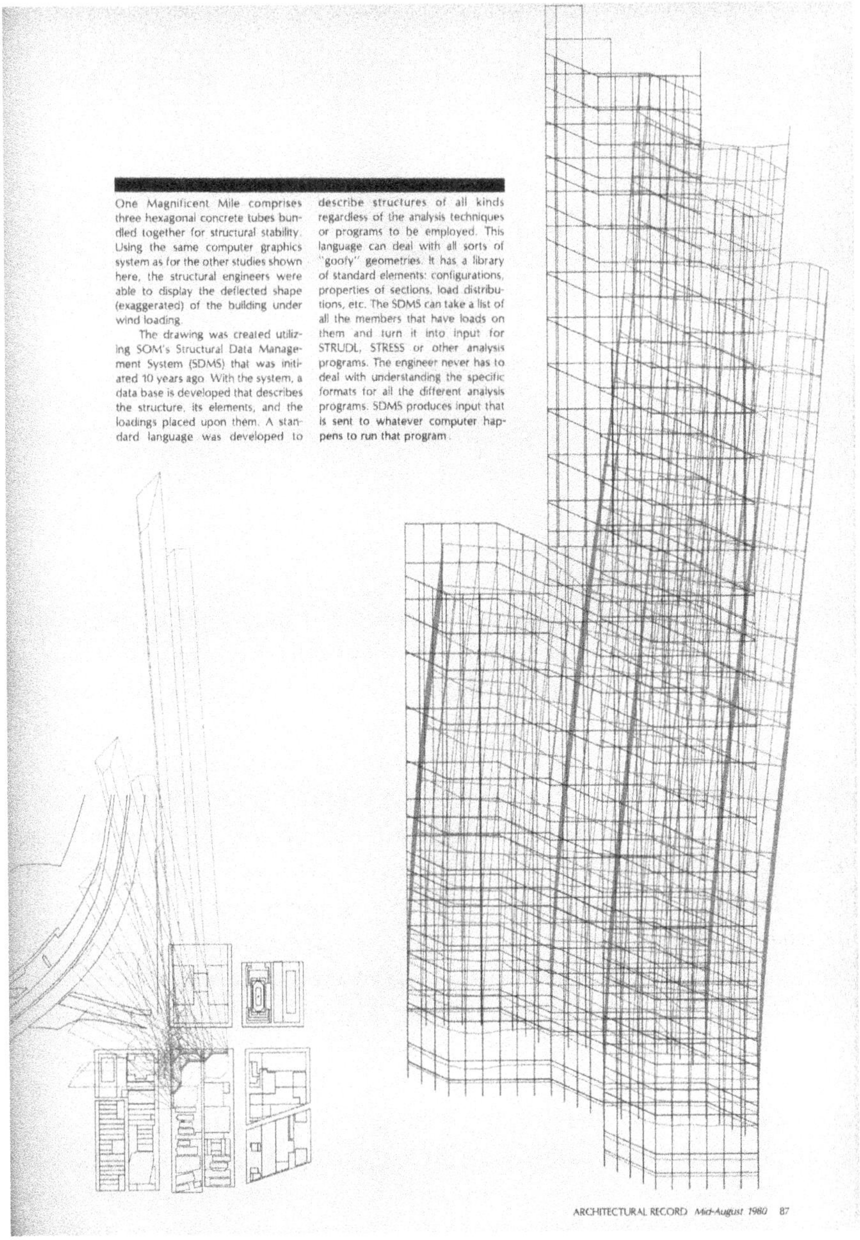

Fig. 3. Page from "SOM's Computer Approach," *Architectural Record* (Mid-August 1980)

I tell this well-known story as a reminder that CAD drawings in the 1960s should not be thought of as bare-bones architectural drawings, though that might be what they look like. Rather, they were something like performances of sets of instructions for a manufacturing process. A drafting machine and its drawings would have had an aura similar to that of a supercollider or a space shuttle: they were feats of big engineering used by large, technically sophisticated institutions.

Many of the drawings in the Harvard lab archive were produced by common plotters. They generally have only one line-weight and are made up of a series of line segments – no curves (Fig. 2). Some show evidence of device modification. One drawing creates a Moiré effect though the superimposition of lines made with pens of different widths. Another was plotted with several colors of ink. There is a story about a programmer at the LCGSA who used a plotter to draw dots rather than lines; his idea had to be scrapped, however, because it replaced the usual soothing *whoosh whoosh* rhythm of the plotter with a jarring *Thunk Thunk Thunk Thunk* soundtrack as it slammed the pen into the paper hundreds of times.[39]

One LCGSA researcher notes that "watching a plotter was an impressive experience," like watching a superhuman draftsman.[40] Plotter drawings in the 1960s pointed towards a techno-social future of human-computer symbiosis[41] in which "the computer will […] aid man in the creative process, making it possible for him to generate wealth with very little labor and emancipating him for activities that are commensurate with his humanity and his spirit."[42]

We should emphasize that plotter drawings were usually unnecessary from a practical point of view; generally speaking they could just as well have been drawn by conventional means. Plotters were nevertheless used by architects because, as one researcher noted, they added a "commercial value in marketing the product."[43] The LCGSA came out with a series of books to convince corporate managers that they could use computer graphics to sell their computational expertise to clients. The public relations value of plotter drawings held for decades. One key moment was a 1980 article in *Architectural Record* that featured two-color plotter drawings by Skidmore, Owings & Merrill (SOM) (Fig. 3).[44] What was most impressive was not the drawings themselves but the fact that SOM had the corporate wherewithal to orchestrate their design process around the computer. Some have argued that seeing images in specialized ways and asking others to see them in the same way is a foundation of professional expertise;[45] others have argued that the postwar period was an era in which ideals of "trained judgment" held sway in many disciplines.[46] The plotter drawings of SOM and Harvard's LCGSA therefore constructed and publicized the expertise and judgment of the architect-programmer.

In these plotter drawings we see a distinct figure of knowledge emerging: the wireframe. Wireframe drawings present a visual logic stripped of superficial details. As with Iakov Chernikhov's drawings half a century earlier, they seek maximum spatial-analytical punch with minimal graphic means.[47] The jarring colors suggest a lack of sophistry and an attunement to modern, mechanical functionality. We are allowed to see through buildings with a penetrating intelligence, all the way to their underlying structures and forces. I want to emphasize that these are aesthetic effects: wireframe images seem rational, but they present rationality without explanation. The viewer is left with the *feeling* of rationality.

The concept most closely associated with the wireframe aesthetic is the canny combination of deep-structural rationality with public relations value: the idea that it is an *image* of architecture that is most important, but rather than an image of a building, what is offered is an image that gestures towards a building's structural rationality and performance. The wireframe aesthetic is a distinct aesthetic category or schema and is a key figure of knowledge used by those who approached architecture as programming.

CRT output

If the plotter was important in the 1960s and '70s and remains so today, there is another device that was just as ubiquitous but that has since disappeared. This device is the microfilm plotter. Microfilm plotters came in a variety of forms, but all were variations on the theme of a camera mounted to a screen (Fig. 4). As the

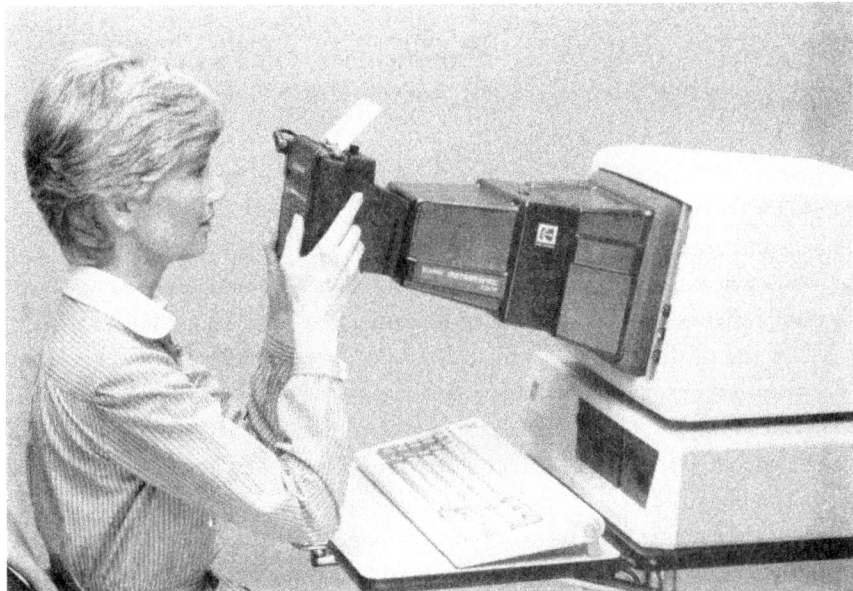

Fig. 4. Kodak Instagraphic CRT print imager illustrated in John Lewell, *A-Z Guide to Computer Graphics* (1985)

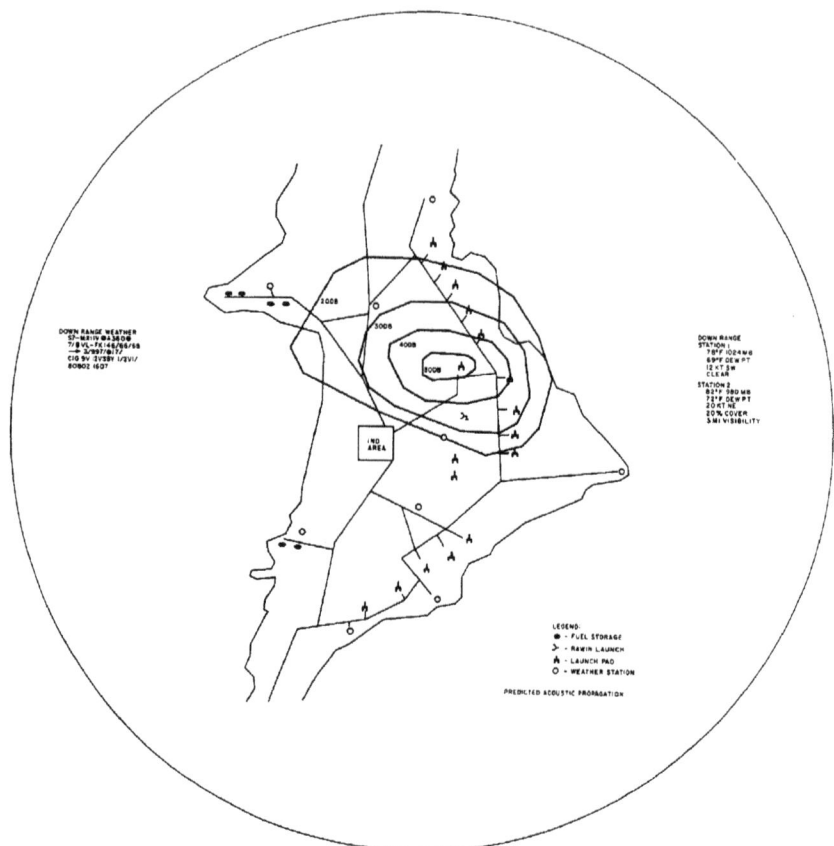

Fig. 5. Cathode ray tube output reproduced in Christopher P. Smith, "Graphic Data Processing" (1964)

phosphor coating on the cathode ray tube lit up, this light would be captured on film. Smith notes that "the primary characteristic of the Cathode Ray Tube as a graphic device is speed. [...] Drawings that might take 15 minutes or an hour on a drafting machine or x y plotter can be produced in seconds on a CRT."[48]

The first microfilm plotters were developed alongside the first CRT screens. They were very expensive and were found only in large research centers.[49] As CRTs and microfilm plotters became less rare in the late 1960s, the conventions of CRT drawings followed two paths. One direction was towards drawings that looked similar to plotter drawings. Several of the examples given by Smith, for example, could have been produced on a drafting machine. One example, however, gestures in the other direction (Fig. 5). This is a geographic drawing of some kind, with a circle around it, which directs our attention towards the round screen from which it came (most screens in the '60s were round rather than rectangular). I will focus

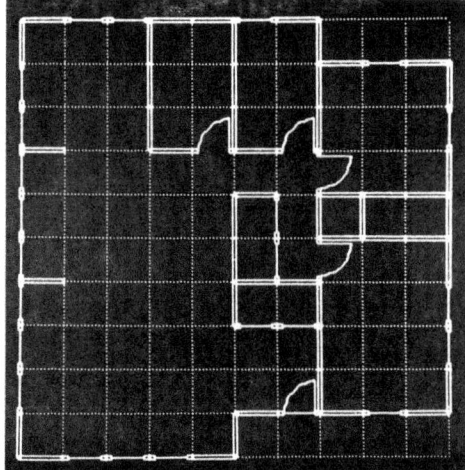

Fig. 6. Interactive Architectural Applications on a CRT (Cathode Ray Tube) (1967-1968) from *Selected Projects* (Courtesy of the Frances Loeb Library. Harvard University Graduate School of Design)

on this second set of conventions – conventions that emphasize that CRT drawings are images *from a screen*. Using today's terminology, I will call these "screenshots."

Only two images in the LCGSA's *Red Book* clearly came from CRTs. Both have white lines on black backgrounds, an inversion of the pen-on-paper look common to architectural drafting (Fig. 6). The color scheme of light lines on a black background is one convention of 1960s screenshots. Others include: showing incomplete or partial views, which emphasizes that the computer screen offers a framed view of a virtual object with a reality beyond any particular representation; showing examples of what software can do rather than a single definitive image of a project; implying that what is shown in the image involves computation in some way, often by including unnecessary annotations; and a look that is, by the standards of other media, unpolished and without the normal niceties of visual communication. These conventions add up to an image type that represents "the interactive computer" and the process of using one.[50] In an era when most computer use involved punch cards and printouts – with no screen and no interaction – screenshots conjured an unusual situation.

The shift towards interaction and simulation opened new possibilities for many disciplines, including architecture.[51] Donald Greenberg, a faculty member at Cornell and pioneer in computer graphics, included dozens of screenshots in a 1977 article in *Architectural Record*.[52] He created the first "flythrough" (of a new I. M. Pei building) and produced colorful photorealistic renderings (of Le Corbusier's Ronchamp) – techniques that fit nicely with the reigning architectural

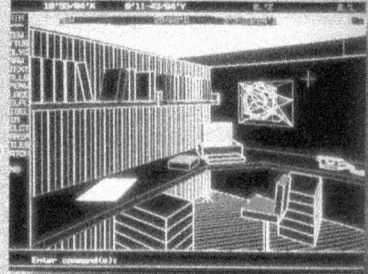
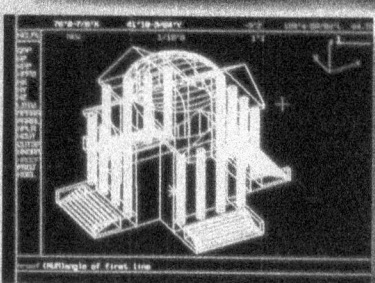

Fig. 7. Advertisement from *Architecture* (February 1987)

phenomenology of the period.[53] By 1987, an issue of *Architecture* focusing on computers was chock full of advertisements featuring screenshots of new CAD software (Fig. 7).[54] Screenshots serve as a reminder that computers are not reducible to "tools" or "electronic brains," which were persistent tropes already in the 1960s.[55] The computer came to be seen also as a window into a simulated world and a means by which to manipulate the latter as one would a physical model.

Some of the conventions of 1960s CRT drawings have been carried forward into contemporary screenshots. We now typically bypass the camera and create bitmap images with the press of a button, but the vestigial menu bars and default colors of screenshots still represent the idea that something is native to the computer. Just as the snapshot aesthetic of the 1950s captured everyday urban life,[56] the screenshot aesthetic conveys the supposed authenticity of the digital environment at the center of contemporary architectural production.[57]

The main theoretical postulate involved in the screenshot aesthetic is that finished buildings are less important than the methods and technologies of architectural production. The idea is that architecture resides not in well-composed physical objects but in the processes that precede them, which can only be grasped and manipulated through the computer screen. The screenshot aesthetic draws the viewer to empathetically imagine using an interactive computer.

Standard printer and modified printer output

Although screenshots are among the easiest images to produce with a computer today, they were rare in the 1960s. In terms of popular appeal, the 1960s equivalent of the screenshot was output from what Smith calls a standard printer. Also known as chain printers, these devices operated much like typewriters: through the impact of ink and metal on paper. They were fast and cheap, and they were the only output device every computer center could be expected to have.[58]

With a little imagination and programming, a chain of standard characters can produce a drawing. The graphic coherence of standard printer drawings seems to congeal despite their flimsy material support (Fig. 8). The flowcharts and graphs that Smith gives as examples use elements outside the normal grammar of graphic design. Repurposed characters fall on a regular grid, forming into lines and shapes seemingly against their own will. The effect is of a shimmering field with figures just barely coming into focus.

After standard printers, Smith describes modified printers, which add special characters for business, engineering, or scientific graphics that allow relatively sophisticated drawings of molecules, circuit diagrams, and the like. Modified printers supplied the look of the made-in-house business and scientific graphics of the 1960s.

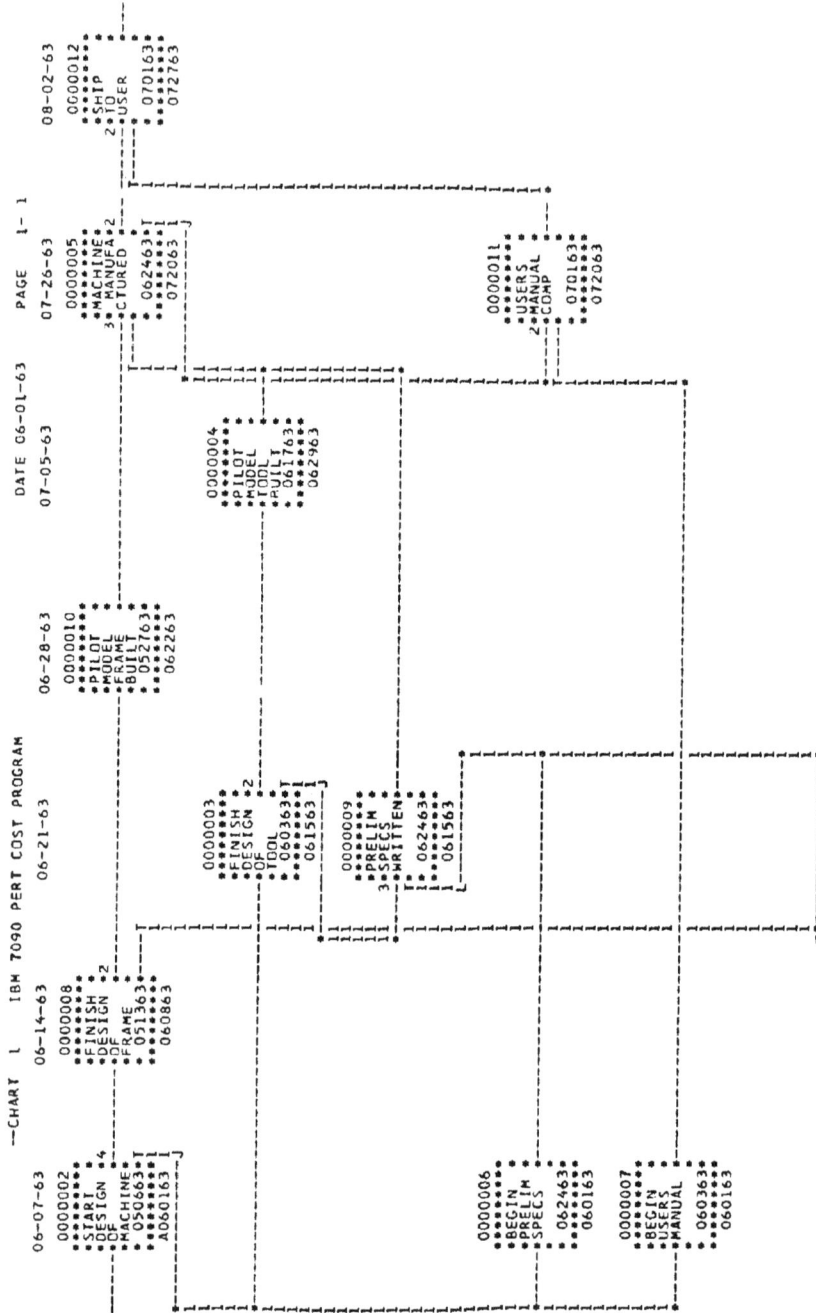

Fig. 8. Standard printer output reproduced in Christopher P. Smith, "Graphic Data Processing" (1964)

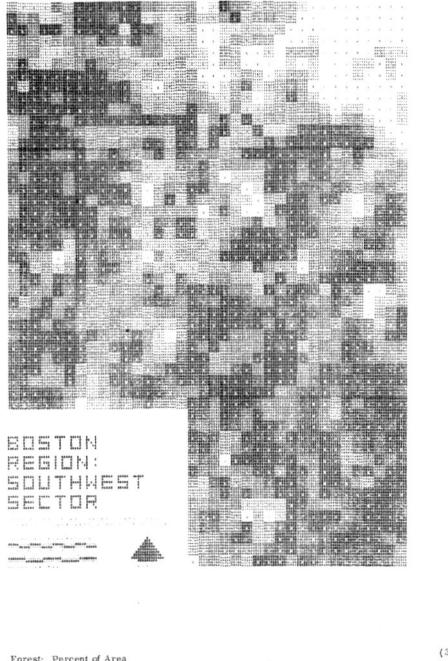

Fig. 9. Boston Region: Southwest Sector (Fall 1967), from *Selected Projects* (Courtesy of the Frances Loeb Library, Harvard University Graduate School of Design)

In its desire for popular relevance, Harvard's lab developed its own form of modification for standard printers. Rather than requiring a chain of special characters, programmers used a trick that allowed characters to be printed over the top of one another. A period or a zero would make a light spot; several characters – O X A V – printed on top of one another would make a dark spot (Fig. 9). By obliterating recognizable characters, this technique brought printers closer charcoal on paper – the impressionistic realm of tone. Drawings could now be produced through pixels, long before raster monitors or the concept of the bitmap were common.[59] A great deal of the LCGSA's theoretical and programming activity went into defining and smoothing tone-based boundaries – much like the bitmap filters that would later help make Photoshop so popular. While plotters required programmers to think in terms of a choreography of lines, standard printers asked them to think in terms of an even field of data.

Programmers at the LCGSA incessantly explored the visual potential of their printers. They wrote routines to create drop shadows, for example, and ran their paper through their printers multiple times with different colored ribbons (Fig. 10). As much as any other image from this period, these drawings convey the

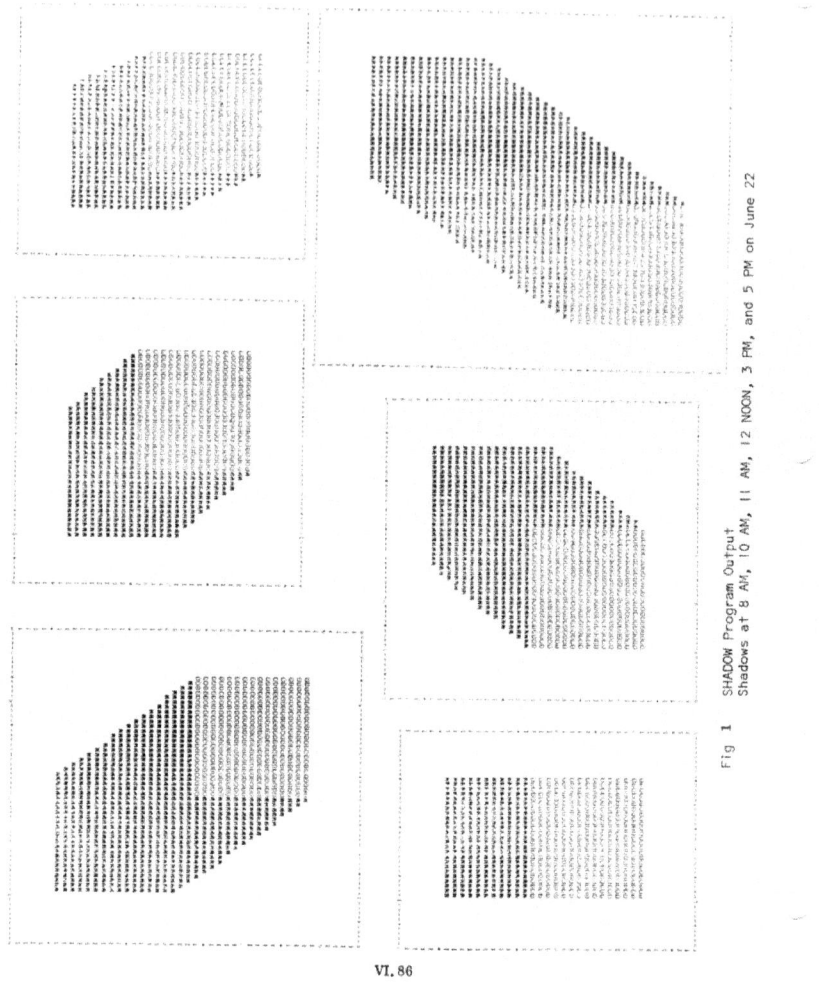

Fig. 10. Shadow (1971) from *Selected Projects* (Courtesy of the Frances Loeb Library, Harvard University Graduate School of Design)

atmosphere of 1960s hacker culture: extracting the furthest range of surprising possibilities from the limited equipment available. These printouts also certainly take part in the information aesthetic – "the 'pleasure' of thinking" and "the excitement of discovering new rules, laws, and limitations"[60] – that drove much experimentation in computer art in this period.[61] LCGSA researchers looked for patterns in the built environment by obsessively studying the figures created by overlapping layers of information.[62] When Colin Rowe later poked fun at "the enthusiasts for data collection," it was certainly people like the researchers at the LCGSA that he had in mind.[63]

The theory involved in standard printer drawings could be characterized as positivist: the information aesthetic certainly depends on belief in the value of empiricism, that knowledge is cumulative, and that societies and environments are undergirded by patterns and laws. Time spent obsessively computing the connections between activities and rooms in a suburban house, for example, contributed a small but solid brick to the edifice of human knowledge.[64] It is also important, however, to understand that practitioners of the information aesthetic were typically driven to put such knowledge in hands of "the people." In other words, the work of Harvard's lab fit the technocratic ethos of the 1960s, but it was also a forerunner of the countercultural ideals of the personal computer era.[65] To understand the information aesthetic, it is important that these contradictory ideas be kept in tension. We might add, more generally, that theories often contain such internal contradictions, and that aesthetic categories sometimes stand as figures that mark these irresolutions.

Conclusion

According to Smith, the methods listed above exhaust the computer output methods available in 1964. Smith's list is confirmed by the LCGSA archive: all the images in the *Red Book* were originally output by devices that fall into his categories.[66] They thus appear to provide a reasonably accurate window onto the 1960s subculture of architect-programmers.

Some printouts that originated in the LCGSA circulated outside of this subculture, largely in the hands of a new class of professionals in the world of architecture: computer consultants. Allen Bernholtz and Eric Teicholz are representative figures here.[67] Both were trained as architects, and both spent time as researchers in the LCGSA during its early years. Bernholtz joined the lab shortly after it was founded in 1965. He worked on a series of architectural projects with Marshall McLuhan, SOM, Perkins and Will, and several other smaller firms, and ended up employed by Canada's Ministry of State for Urban Affairs in 1972. Teicholz likewise worked on a string of projects with Ivan Sutherland, Charles Correa, TAC, and other smaller firms in Boston, and developed a suite of architectural software that he sold to Digital Equipment Corporation before moving into the world of facilities management. During their stints at the LCGSA, Bernholtz and Teicholz wrote essays for journals such as *Design Quarterly* and *Architectural Forum*, presented at trade conferences (for both architecture and computation), and met one-on-one with countless clients and colleagues. If programming was their common mode of practice, printouts were the objects they placed at the center of attention. Indeed, Bernholtz opined that computer programming would make architectural programming into "an explicit exercise where we could sit down and point to these differences and have the designers discuss it, argue it, and eventually come to some compromise regarding the building program."[68] He argued for a new subdiscipline of programming within architecture, calling himself a "programmatic engineer" – a job he described as "some mix of architect, engineer, [and] computer-psychologist type."[69] This professional ideal was developed in a shared subculture and became visible to wider audiences via printouts.

Once aesthetic techniques begin to circulate outside the context in which they were first developed, they tend to be used with little regard for the ideals of their original context. Historians, who are inclined to be aware of the many ways that theories tag along with practices, are often called upon to remind architects of the contexts they may have forgotten. I hope that the foregoing historical sketch suggests just how difficult this sometimes is. If every situation of practice – every subculture – has its own concerns and theories, historians have a lot of recontextualization work to do. Compounding the difficulty, historical theories often conflict with the theories and convictions held by historians themselves. If we do not subscribe to a particular theory, we might not find it worth our time to examine it. If we are committed to critical theory, we might have trouble seeing the value of "instrumental" theories and elaborating them on their own terms.

As I suggested above, aesthetics offers a method by which to approach such forgotten, questionable, subcultural theories. Between a singular History of Theory and isolated microhistories of theories, aesthetic categories stand as figures of knowledge that allow us to map the local situations of theories in terms of the larger cultural territory they share.

This approach requires us to think about aesthetics in a slightly unusual way, however. In the quotation above, Arendt agrees with Kant that aesthetic judgment is the moment when taste becomes public. The problem is that Arendt assumes that it makes sense to talk about "the public," "universal" judgment, and a singular culture. Kant and Arendt (and aesthetic philosophers generally[70]) are biased towards the universal. For Arendt, Greece and Rome stand in for all human values. She worries about how the singular culture she evidently loves (so-called Western culture) appears to be in the process of dissolution under the pressure of mass culture (which, she says, is not culture at all but "entertainment" – what culture becomes when it is instrumentalized).

It is helpful to situate Arendt in the mid-century discourse of "the crisis of man," a term I borrow from Mark Greif.[71] Writing on the heels of several decades of catastrophe, critics such as Arendt tended to think in terms of enormous existential conundrums. "Mankind" and "culture" were universal values to be defended, and they was often seen in terms of sweeping binary paradigms: culture versus civilization (Paul Ricœur and Kenneth Frampton), autonomy versus instrumentality (Adorno and Eisenman), or even, most strangely, the Japanese high cultural "snob" versus the American subcultural "animal" (Alexandre Kojève). Such antinomies could only work for polemic and caricature. Last century's age of crisis continues to resonate today (Frampton, for one, has repeatedly updated Arendt's paradigm), but it is showing signs of age. We have now passed through a several-decades-long celebration of multiculturalism, and cultural constructionism has become the lingua franca of the humanities. Champions of a singular, universal "culture" are looking more and more like relics of the Cold War.

The Kantian aesthetics we have inherited from figures such as Arendt aim towards the universal, but such an aim is not necessary. Why not update aesthetics? Can we imagine aesthetic judgments to be shared but not universal?

One direction would be to see aesthetic schemas as analogous to emotions, with all their variety and culturally situated complexity. William Reddy describes emotions as "loosely connected thought material" that we come to name and categorize through a long process of enculturation. In other words, the connotations of and boundaries between emotional schemas depend on our upbringing in a specific culture.[72] Once such a system of schema is in place, it provides templates or shorthands for rapid response to situations encountered in everyday experience. I suggest that aesthetic categories should also be understood as loosely connected thought material that are put into schemas that we share with the people around us and use to make quick judgments.

Once we see aesthetic judgments as not universal but subcultural, we can also see a finer grain of aesthetics categories. Arendt, like Kant, generally limits her discussion to beauty. Kant sometimes also writes about the sublime;[73] Rozenkratz added ugliness to the repertoire.[74] Writing about the world of postindustrial labor, Sianne Ngai adds the cute, the zany, and the interesting.[75] In a significant update to aesthetic theory, Ngai argues that

> our aesthetic experience is always mediated by a finite if constantly rotating repertoire of aesthetic categories [...], which are by definition conceptual as well as affective and tied to historically specific forms of communication and collective life.[76]

As an example of what this expanded cast of aesthetic categories might look like, we could turn to Benjamin Buchloh's analysis of the fine-tuned aesthetic work done by conceptual artists in the postwar period.[77] In order of appearance, he lists:

the aesthetic of administration
the aesthetic of the speech act
the aesthetic of linguistic convention and legalistic arrangements
the aesthetic of the handcrafted original

the aesthetic of administrative and legal organization and institutional validation
the aesthetic of contemplative experience
the aesthetic of mural painting
the aesthetic of Conceptual Art
the aesthetic of permutation
the aesthetic of the studio
the aesthetic of production and consumption
the aesthetic of declaration and intention
the aesthetic of the newly established power of administration
the aesthetic of anonymity

The foregoing analysis suggests a specific role for aesthetics in the history of theory: to describe concerns and concepts in a way that is schematic and shared but not universal. Rather than reflect on (universal) culture, we could investigate situated processes of cultural production. Confronted with practices and images that seem to be attached to some theoretical content within a subculture, we could begin by identifying a set of aesthetic categories that appear to be at work. We could then elaborate the "thought material" with which they are associated. In this way, aesthetic categories can be taken as figures of knowledge that mark situated theories.

Looking at the printouts that emerged from the subculture of architect-programmers in the 1960s, we can see evidence of theoretical investment that goes well beyond the trope of computers as mere tools or calculators. Other concepts present themselves. Wireframes point towards theories of the deep structure of architecture and the expertise required to control it. Screenshots are evidence of theories of interactivity and the idea that finished buildings are less important than the processes of architectural production. Screenshots came along with techniques of simulation that matched contemporaneous architectural phenomenology. The clunky pixelizations of chain printer drawings were developed alongside theories of information and visualization and countercultural ideals of hacking. They habituated architects to thinking about drawings as fields of data. New aesthetic categories encapsulated these situated theories, and printouts were the medium by which they spread.

Returning to the observations with which I began, I will reiterate that situated theories and Theory share a common denominator: they are about understanding. One big difference has to do with the attitudes that characterize them: localized, operative theories are usually characterized as "positive" while Theory is "critical." Rather than linking positivity with positivism and scientism, I suggest linking it with desire. The situated theories I outlined above do not begin with a hermeneutics of suspicion; unlike the model offered by the Eisenman/Alexander debate, they do not imagine theory as a battlefield. Why not take a cue from aesthetics and approach theory – initially, at least – in terms of pleasure and appreciation? Historians of theory could begin by grappling with situated desires to understand worlds of practice on their own terms and save judgment for theorists of theory.

Notes

1. I would like to thank Hilde Heynen and Sebastiaan Loosen for their insightful comments on my manuscript and Laura Frahm for her advice and encouragement on this project from the beginning.
2. John Summerson, "The Case for a Theory of Modern Architecture," *The Journal of the Royal Society of British Architects* 64, no. 8 (June 1957): 307-13.
3. Molly Wright Steenson, *Architectural Intelligence: How Designers and Architects Created the Digital Landscape* (Cambridge, MA: MIT Press, 2017).
4. Architects still refer to "the program" of a building even though the term "programming" did not catch on. Books that promoted programming include, e.g., Benjamin H. Evans and Clarence Herbert Wheeler, *Architectural Programming: Emerging Techniques of Architectural Practice* (AIA, 1969).
5. On the distinction between programming and software engineering, see Federica Frabetti, *Software Theory: A Cultural and Philosophical Study* (Lanham, MD: Rowman & Littlefield, 2014). On the history of programming and the software industry, see Martin Campbell-Kelly, *From Airline Reservations to Sonic the Hedgehog: A History of the Software Industry* (Cambridge, MA: MIT Press, 2003).
6. A bibliography of "the field of computerized location-allocation in environmental design" from 1972 lists 473 relevant publications. Erich Bunselmeier, *Computerized Location – Allocation. Exchange Bibliography no. 414* (Monticello, Illinois: Council of Planning Librarians, 1972).
7. Stanley Mathews, "The Fun Palace: Cedric Price's Experiment in Architecture and Technology," *Technoetic Arts* 3, no. 2 (September 2005): 73-91.
8. The other field where "Theory" means the same thing is literary studies. See, e.g., "Theory: Death is not the End," *n+1* 2 (Winter 2005).
9. Peter Eisenman, "Post-Functionalism," *Oppositions* 6 (September 1976).
10. Colin Rowe, "Program vs. Paradigm," *The Cornell Journal of Architecture* 2 (1982): 8-19.
11. Christopher Alexander and Peter Eisenman, "Contrasting Concepts of Harmony in Architecture," *Lotus International* 40, no. 67 (1983): 60-68.
12. See, e.g., Louis Martin, "History, Theory, Criticism," and Mary McLeod, "1968-1990: The End of Innocence: From Political Activism to Postmodernism," in *Architecture School: Three Centuries of Educating Architects in North America*, ed. Joan Ockman (Cambridge, MA: MIT Press, 2012).

13. K. Michael Hays, ed., *Architecture Theory since 1968* (Cambridge, MA: MIT Press, 1998).
14. An extreme version can be seen by bringing together Hannah Arendt's "Crisis in Culture" and *Eichmann in Jerusalem*: her arguments set up a certain affinity between the philistine who approaches art in terms of use value and Adolf Eichmann, the Nazi officer who perpetrated genocide under the guise of bureaucratic logistics. (Arendt was not part of the Frankfurt School, though she shared many concerns and was in the same generation as, e.g., Adorno.) Hannah Arendt, *Between Past and Future: Six Exercises in Political Thought* (New York: Viking, 1961) and *Eichmann in Jerusalem: A Report on the Banality of Evil* (New York: Viking, 1963).
15. See, e.g., Theodor Adorno, *The Stars Down to Earth* (Abingdon: Routledge, 2001).
16. How exactly this happened is part of a longer story in which – to point out just two factors – corporate modernism and "popular" postmodernism were construed as theoretically shallow and curricula in architecture schools segregated technical and practical courses at a significant distance from courses in history and theory.
17. Antoine Picon suggests that before the "digital culture" of the 1990s, architects took part in the "computer culture" of the preceding decades. Antoine Picon, *Digital Culture in Architecture: An Introduction for the Design Professions* (Basel: Birkhäuser, 2010).
18. K. Michael Hays, "Introduction," in *Architecture Theory since 1968*.
19. Bernhard Siegert, "Introduction: Cultural Techniques, or, The End of the Intellectual Postwar in German Media Theory," in *Cultural Techniques: Grids, Filters, Doors, and Other Articulations of the Real* (New York: Fordham University Press, 2015).
20. Thomas Macho, "Zeit und Zahl: Kalender- und Zeitrechnung als Kulturtechniken," in *Bild, Schrift, Zahl*, ed. Sybille Krämer and Horst Bredekamp (Paderborn: Wilhelm Fink, 2003).
21. Michael Mahoney argues that the various devices that have been lumped into the category of "computers" should be disaggregated and approached through the histories of the groups that used them. Michael Mahoney, "The Histories of Computing(s)," *Interdisciplinary Science Reviews* 30, no. 2 (June 2005).
22. Bruno Latour, "Drawing Things Together," in *Representation in Scientific Practice*, ed. Michael Lynch and Steve Woolgar (Cambridge, MA: MIT Press, 1990).
23. More specifically, for the purposes of this paper, I subscribe to Michael Friedman's rather minimalist "global view of scientific understanding," in which a theory is a concise, singular mental construct that stands for or "explains" many other mental constructs (observations). In this view, the reduction from multiple unexplained phenomena to coherent figures of knowledge is the hallmark of theory. Michael Friedman, "Explanation and Scientific Understanding," in *Theories of Explanation*, ed. Joseph Pitt (Oxford: Oxford University Press, 1988).
24. In the following pages I will not fully elaborate the theories I discuss. Rather, I will provide reference to primary sources that expand the theories in further detail and secondary sources that explicate their historical context.

25. Charlton Payne, "Kant's Parergonal Politics: The *Sensus Communis* and the Problem of Political Action," in *Kant and the Concept of Community*, ed. Charlton Payne and Lucas Thorpe (Rochester, NY: University of Rochester Press, 2011).
26. Arendt, *Between Past and Future*, 222-23.
27. William Ivins, *How Prints Look: Photographs with a Commentary* (New York: Metropolitan Museum of Art, 1943).
28. The closest are books such as John Lewell's *A-Z Guide to Computer Graphics* (New York: Mcgraw-Hill, 1985) and Martin Jurgens's *The Digital Print: Identification and Preservation* (Los Angeles: Getty Conservation Institute, 2009). What is missing in both are concise accounts of why particular visual techniques might be chosen: what are their connotations and affordances? Generally, it is the field of visual studies that is pursuing this sort of question most vigorously; see, e.g., James Elkins, *Visual Practices across the University* (Paderborn: Wilhelm Fink, 2007).
29. Christopher Smith, "Graphic Data Processing," *DAC '64 Proceedings of the SHARE Design Automation Workshop* (1964).
30. Though most readers are probably familiar with printers and plotters, CRTs are decidedly obsolete. CRTs or "cathode ray tubes" were the dominant screen technology until the advent of flat-panel screens (LCDs and LED displays).
31. Nick Chrisman, *Charting the Unknown: How Computer Mapping at Harvard Became GIS* (Redlands, CA: ESRI Press, 2006).
32. Interview by the author with Eric Teicholz, March 4, 2017.
33. Harvard University Laboratory for Computer Graphics and Spatial Analysis, *Selected Projects*, held at Harvard University Graduate School of Design Loeb Library. http://id.lib.harvard.edu/aleph/004662797/catalog.
34. Claus Pias, "Point and Line to Raster: On the Genealogy of Computer Graphics," in *Ornament and Abstraction: The Dialogue between Non-Western, Modern, and Contemporary Art*, ed. Markus Bruderlin (Köln: DuMont, 2001).
35. Advertisements in trade magazines in the 1960s and 1970s show that there was a market for innovative techniques to save drafting time using preprinted elements (often furniture and annotations).
36. Arindam Dutta, "Linguistics not Grammatology," in *A Second Modernism: MIT, Architecture, and the "Techno-Social" Moment*, ed. Arindam Dutta (Cambridge, MA: MIT Press, 2013).
37. Daniel Cardoso Llach, *Builders of the Vision: Software and the Imagination of Design* (Abingdon: Routledge, 2015).
38. Douglas Ross, *Computer-Aided Design: A Statement of Objectives*, Technical Memorandum 8436-TM-4 (Cambridge, MA: MIT Electronic Systems Lab, 1960).
39. Chrisman, *Charting the Unknown*, 142.
40. Ibid., 79.

41. J. C. R. Licklider, "Man-Computer Symbiosis," *IRE Transactions on Human Factors in Electronics* HFE-1: 4-11.
42. Steven Coons, "Computer Aided Design," *Architecture and the Computer: Proceedings / First Boston Architectural Center Conference / 1964* (Boston: Boston Architectural College, 1964): 28.
43. As I will describe in a moment, most of the LCGSA's early software was designed to use inexpensive chain printers for output, which, the researcher said, "as a research and learning tool […] provided everything I needed to know and was more efficient both time- and money-wise than plotter output." Allen Bernholtz, "Spatial Allocation in Design and Planning," *Proceedings of the 9th Design Automation Workshop* (1972).
44. "SOM's computer approach," *Architectural Record*, mid-August 1980.
45. Charles Goodwin, "Professional Vision," *American Anthropologist* 96, no. 3 (1994): 606-33.
46. Lorraine Daston and Peter Galison, *Objectivity* (New York: Zone Books, 2010).
47. Robert Bruegmann, "The Pencil and the Electronic Sketchboard: Architectural Representation and the Computer," in *Architecture and Its Image: Four Centuries of Architectural Representation*, ed. Eve Blau and Edward Kaufman (Cambridge, MA: MIT Press, 1989).
48. Smith, "Graphic Data Processing," 58.
49. Zabet Patterson has written a book about one of the first microfilm plotters, the S-C 4020, which was used by scientists and artists (and the distinction between the two, she notes, is often difficult to make) at Bells Labs in the 1960s. Some of the first computer art was made using this particular device. Zabet Patterson, *Peripheral Vision: Bell Labs, the S-C 4020, and the Origins of Computer Art* (Cambridge, MA: MIT Press, 2015).
50. Matthew Allen, "Representing Computer-Aided Design: Screenshots and the Interactive Computer circa 1960," *Perspectives on Science* 24, no. 6 (November-December 2016).
51. For the case of physics, see Peter Galison, *Image and Logic: A Material Culture of Microphysics* (Chicago: University of Chicago Press, 1997); for architecture, see Sherry Turkle, *Simulation and Its Discontents* (Cambridge, MA: MIT Press, 2009).
52. "Computer Graphics for Architecture: Techniques in Search of Problems," *Architectural Record*, mid-August 1977.
53. Jorge Otero-Pailos, *Architecture's Historical Turn: Phenomenology and the Rise of the Postmodern* (St. Paul: University of Minnesota Press, 2010).
54. *Architecture*, February 1987.
55. On the trope of the "electronic brain," see Paul Edwards, *The Closed World: Computers and the Politics of Discourse in Cold War America* (Cambridge, MA: MIT Press, 1996). For an early example of the "merely a tool" trope, see Christopher Alexander, "A Much Asked Question about Computers and Design," *Architecture and the Computer: Proceedings / First Boston Architectural Center Conference / 1964*, 52-54; for a critical examination,

see Jon Agar, "What Difference Did Computers Make?" *Social Studies of Science* 36, no. 6 (2006): 869-907

56. Geoffrey Batchen, "Snapshots: Art History and the Ethnographic Turn," *Photographies* 1, no. 1 (September 2008).
57. I have written elsewhere about how architects today use screenshots to create an effect of authenticity. Matthew Allen, "Screenshot Aesthetic," *MOS: Selected Works* (Princeton: Princeton Architectural Press, 2016).
58. The IBM 1403 printer came standard with IBM computer installations in the mid-1960s. Evan Ackerman, "Built for Speed," *IEEE Spectrum*, April 2017, http://spectrum.ieee.org/geek-life/history/how-the-ibm-1403-printer-hammered-out-1100-lines-per-minute.
59. For a critical history of raster imaging, see Jacob Gaboury, "The Random Access Image: Memory and the History of the Computer Screen," *Grey Room* 70 (Winter 2018).
60. Christoph Klutsch, "Information Aesthetics and the Stuttgart School," in *Mainframe Experimentalism: Early Computing and the Foundations of the Digital Arts*, ed. Hannah Higgens and Douglas Kahn (Berkeley: University of California Press, 2012).
61. Higgens and Kahn, *Mainframe Experimentalism*.
62. On the importance of "pattern seeing" in postwar architecture, see Reinhold Martin, *The Organizational Complex: Architecture, Media, and Corporate Space* (Cambridge, MA: MIT Press, 2003).
63. Rowe, "Program vs. Paradigm," 15.
64. Allen Bernholtz and Edward Bierstone, "Computer-Augmented Design," *Design Quarterly* 66/67 (1966): 40-51.
65. Fred Turner, *From Counterculture to Cyberculture: Stewart Brand, the Whole Earth Network, and the Rise of Digital Utopianism* (Chicago: University of Chicago Press, 2006).
66. It is worth noting, however, that none of the images are original: all the sheets in the Red Book are photocopies. Electrostatic printing or Xerography has been "the most popular office copying method" since the 1960s (Institute of Museum and Library Services, "Architectural Drawing Reproduction," *Preservation Self-Assessment Program*, https://psap.library.illinois.edu/format-id-guide/archdrawingrepro (accessed May 18, 2017). Interestingly, in an essay from the breakthrough period of "digital architecture," Eisenman argues that the fax machine (a form of electrostatic printer), not the computer, would change architecture. Peter Eisenman, "Folding in Time: The Singularity of Rebstock," in *AD: Folding in Architecture*, ed. Greg Lynn (London: Academy Editions, 1993).
67. The following section is documented in Matthew Allen, "Prehistory of the Digital: Architecture Becomes Programming, 1935-1990" (PhD thesis, Harvard, 2019).
68. Bernholtz, "Spatial Allocation in Design and Planning," 185.
69. Ibid.

70. E.g., Gérard Genette, "What Aesthetic Values?" *Essays in Aesthetics* (Lincoln: University of Nebraska Press, 2005).
71. Mark Greif, *The Age of the Crisis of Man: Thought and Fiction in America, 1933-1973* (Princeton: Princeton University Press, 2015).
72. William Reddy, *The Navigation of Feeling: A Framework for the History of Emotions* (Cambridge, UK: Cambridge University Press, 2001).
73. Immanuel Kant, *Beobachtungen über das Gefühl des Schönen und Erhabenen* (1764).
74. Karl Rosenkrantz, *Die Aesthetik des Hässlichen* (1853).
75. Sianne Ngai, *Our Aesthetic Categories: Zany, Cute, Interesting* (Cambridge, MA: Harvard University Press, 2015).
76. Sianne Ngai, "Our Aesthetic Categories," *PMLA* 125, no. 4 (October 2010): 948.
77. Benjamin Buchloh, "Conceptual Art 1962-1969: From the Aesthetic of Administration to the Critique of Institutions," *October* 55 (Winter 1990): 105-43.

CHAPTER 5

Troubled Dialogues: Intellectuality at a Crossroads at the *Carrefour de l'Europe* in Brussels

Sebastiaan Loosen

Belgium, 1976: the jury of the annual Robert Maskens architecture prize decided not to award a first prize, not due to a lack of quality but because the jury members could not agree on the criteria by which to evaluate architecture.[1] A number of problematic postwar modernist projects had resulted in a raised awareness of architecture's societal complexity and during the 1960s gradually put into question the vocabulary used to discuss the discipline. As this was an internationally wide phenomenon, the jury's choice was symptomatic not only of a bleak Belgian situation, where a shared basis for discussing architecture had been eroded, but also, more generally, of a 1970s architecture culture in search of its own terms. Paradigmatic in this regard was that Belgium's main architecture journal changed its title in 1970 from *La Maison* to *Environnement*, as the concerns of the journal shifted from notions of plan and composition to a more context-driven approach (Fig. 1).

This 1970s situation can be characterized as driven by a search for an adequate knowledge to better architecture's role in society. This knowledge could come from many directions, and indeed many voices offered different ways in which to reach a "societally relevant" form of knowledge, containing the promise to go beyond the perceived flaws of postwar modernist architecture. I would argue that the intellectual malaise was so profound that more than ever these different voices did not only differ in content but might even be found to differ on the fundamental level as to *what* knowledge about architecture actually *is* or *should be*. In other words, different views occurred based on different takes on how architectural knowledge itself stands vis-à-vis society, and hence their legitimacy was drawn from this self-postulated societal merit.[2] This is why this essay points to the epistemological, since these different voices implicitly entail a conception on the nature of knowledge, to the extent that

Fig. 1. Covers of *La Maison* (February 1970) and its successor *Environnement* (March 1970).

arguments alone won't provide the way out of the malaise. The anecdote on the 1976 Maskens prize is emblematic for the stifling effects of such conflicting views, not necessarily of architecture but of knowledge, of how to talk about architecture, and even of what terms are deemed adequate to establish a dialogue. In a time when the need for discussion and conversation was at its height, the art of dialogue stood at an all-time low and more than ever voices claimed their own right independently of each other.

Carrefour de l'Europe being thought

Though emblematic, the Maskens prize debate constituted only a minor point in Belgian history. But the idea of a troubled dialogue due to epistemological differences can be expanded by drawing on the more significant debates surrounding a major episode of Belgian architectural history: the *Carrefour de l'Europe*, or *Europakruispunt* (Europe's Crossroads). Long a triangular void in the heart of Belgium's capital, this site was left open after the working-class district *La Putterie*, or *De Putterij*, was demolished to establish a north-south railway connection (inaugurated in 1952). Located between the newer, upper part and the historical, fine-grained, lower part of the city, the site was desperately in search of an articulation

Fig. 2. The site of Carrefour de l'Europe, 1950s. Photograph by Cas Oorthuys.
Source: Berthe Delépinne, *Dit is Brussel* (Amsterdam: Contact, 1958), 58. © Cas Oorthuys / Nederlands Fotomuseum

to mediate between these two separate worlds. This process was at the time strongly colored by the increasing challenges that automotive mobility was posing to the city; for example, a 1962 masterplan saw the site's future as an infrastructural node of inner-city motorways, hence its name, Europe's Crossroads.[3] By 1967 its fate seemed definitively sealed as it was leased for ninety-nine years with the intention to build a car park.[4]

These developments embodied the harsh side of postwar modernism: in the name of progress and modernization, local authorities endorsed large-scale projects drastically transforming the existing built environment, driven by a stringent economic logic and powerful business interests. As the 1960s waned, the critique on such projects was widespread, and hence the future of the triangular site, left empty at the heart of the capital, was intrinsically entwined with a heightened awareness of the need for public debate on the built environment.[5] Thus, at the dawn of the 1970s, the void turned into a vacuum, absorbing all topical challenges modernity was posing to architecture; as a subject of discussion and proposed solutions, the site intensified into something of an intellectual Petri dish, a test case of different views on how architecture could cope with those challenges.

In short, the capital was harboring a parking lot right in front of its Central Station, so devoid of any imagination that any serious intellectual in Belgium *had* to engage with the topic (Fig. 2). And even if the Carrefour de l'Europe's history spurred many interesting design proposals worth a discussion in their own right, in this essay I mobilize its history only to focus on the debate it triggered, the arguments about architecture that were raised, and the ways in which the different voices framed the societal relevance of their understanding of the site. As such, Europe's Crossroads can be read as a crossroads of Belgian architecture intellectuality.

Dealing as it does with a well-documented case in urban and design history,[6] this essay briefly revisits three important 1970s-1980s voices in the Carrefour de l'Europe discussion, bringing into focus the contours of intellectuality surrounding them. These include an activist-historicist voice (ARAU), a participatory sociologist's (Sieg Vlaeminck), and one with "anti-nominalist" tendencies, pointing to "the real" as a way of reinvigorating architectural criticism (Mil De Kooning). Far from covering the whole range of noteworthy perspectives on the Carrefour de l'Europe (missing out not in the least on those of the involved architects), the three voices under consideration here demonstrate how profound the disagreement could be between the different paths offered in thinking architecture's place in society.

Power

By the fifties, the car heightened the pressure on the inner city, and the default tabula rasa approach towards urban interventions foreclosed the city's future. Against this context, the *Atelier de Recherche et d'Action Urbaines* (ARAU, Workshop of Urban Research and Action) was formed in 1969 by architect and historian Maurice Culot (b. 1937), sociologist René Schoonbrodt (b. 1935), and parish priest of the Maroles neighborhood, Jacques Vander Biest (1929-2016). As an urban activist movement, they set themselves and their students at the Brussels architecture school La Cambre the task of developing counterprojects for each proposal issued by the authorities and developers. These counterprojects were represented in easily understandable and reproducible drawings and had functional mixing (against modernist zoning) as their most basic guideline, in an attempt to counter the tendency of barring residences from the city.

ARAU's first action in 1969 was directed at the symbolic site of the Carrefour de l'Europe.[7] By a specific site-driven instigated polemic on the inclusion of residencies, and counter to a prevalent fatalism regarding the imposed projects among the neighborhood's inhabitants, ARAU managed to initiate a discussion ultimately centered on social imagination: what do we, as a society, choose to plan for?

As Isabelle Doucet has argued, ARAU's counterprojects were consciously drawn to function as discussion objects and should be considered as objects of knowledge in their own right.[8] As such, we may note their radical but clear-cut take on how and what "kind" of knowledge architects should invest in to serve society best: the knowledge that there are other options possible than the urban interventions proposed by the authorities. But more than merely providing an alternative, their "epistemic strategy" consisted of providing alternatives in order to shift the discussion to a societal level. In their counteractive role, ARAU's counterprojects crucially raised the question of what urban life we would like to foster. By relying on abstract volumes in their early drawings, rather than fully detailed projects, ARAU rendered programmatic heterogeneity legible as being the requisite for a valuable urbanity.

In an issue of the Dutch journal *wonen-TA/BK* devoted to ARAU, the historian Francis Strauven (b. 1942) – one of the chroniclers and an early advocate of ARAU – gave a clarifying interpretation of the organization's actions. These did not involve simply opposing certain policies and ventilating protest voices and calls for participation: they were also framed as part of a wider plea for a renewed intellectuality in architecture, in an attempt to better incorporate "the social" in architecture thought: "The criticism [of protest and participation movements] was not only directed against the procedures of town planning, but just as much against the concepts of Modern Architecture, and so against architects. (…) The architects did not discuss the (social) contents of their profession but limited themselves as usual to organizational and formal problems. (…) Apart from one or two private initiatives the formation of theories remained nonexistent in Belgium, and it still remains so."[9]

For ARAU, a crucial factor in this rethinking of architecture's social dimension was its sister organization *Archives d'Architecture Moderne* (AAM, Archives of Modern Architecture), which, through its impressive publication and exhibition activities, was investing in the historical reflection required to formulate a sound critique. Part of this reflection was to reappropriate the modernist legacy, by uncovering an obscured romantic and more artisanal form of modernism, in an attempt to reinvest modern forms with the ideological ideas and societal values they originally contained.[10]

Strongly informed by Marxism, for ARAU – and indirectly for AAM – the political dimension was the ultimate referent in their approach: the process of building is

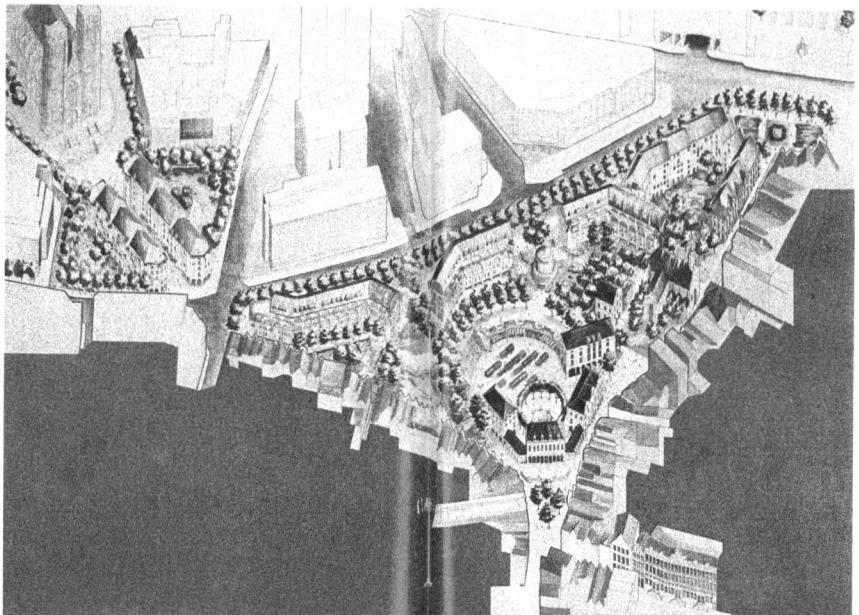

Fig. 3. ARAU's 1976 "aesthetic alternative." Drawing by Marc Gierst and Maurice Culot, cropped. Source: ARAU, "Proposition d'aménagement pour le centre ville de Bruxelles," *Archives de l'Architecture Moderne. Bulletin d'Information*, no. 8 (1976). © ARAU

of a political strategic nature, taking part in an understanding of history as a stage of struggle. René Schoonbrodt was unambiguous in this regard, stating that "all actions by ARAU are aimed at one single goal: to create the possibilities for the birth of a society in which every individual can assert as much power as possible on social life as a whole."[11] Hence the sort of understanding they aimed for in their counterprojects had two goals: on the one hand, exposing by means of a counterexample the existing project's underlying logics (where modernist urban planning was gradually cast on the side of speculation and unbridled capitalism); and on the other, providing an alternative with a clear, different form of urbanity to be used as a tool in a newly instigated debate, to arm the local inhabitants in their struggle to shape their environment.

Thus, the renewed intellectuality ARAU hoped to invigorate was deeply entangled with issues of power. Instead of opting for some form of neutrality when mobilizing their architectural expertise in their actions, they pleaded wholeheartedly for partisanship, never hiding their socialist-communist sympathies.[12] For ARAU, society was in the first place structured by power relations and hence the form of knowledge that could serve society best was one that could serve as a basis for power strategies. In other words, the point at which social relevance is attributed to this specific figure of knowledge lies entirely within the realm of power relations. Only knowledge that renders power accessible to the inhabitants is deemed relevant here – hence their attention to public media and populist strategies. What came to be known as ARAU's architectural hallmarks – their emphasis on historically grown urban tissue and, and in a later stage their reliance on a historicist architectural form (Fig. 3) – both subscribed to this logic.[13]

Thus, for ARAU, architecture knowledge became more and more a matter of tactics, rejecting any idea of an essence being worthy of consideration in its own right: everything is brought back to its tactical dimension in the overarching mission to empower the neighborhood's inhabitants, to shift the production of the built environment more in their direction.

Science

Many of the themes raised by ARAU – participation, revitalizing inner cities, no architecture without ideology – were shared by several of their peers but nevertheless led to differing perspectives on how architecture ought to serve society, and hence what figure of knowledge could best fulfill those aims. The increasing role the social sciences came to play in architecture is a case in point. In Belgium, for example, the sociologist-urbanist Sieg Vlaeminck (1933-2011) came to the fore as an architecture critic in the 1970s, advocating an enlarged role of the social sciences in architecture. Though he joined ARAU in their critique on modernist architecture, he remained committed to a rather modernist conception of knowledge: one that implicitly claimed that society is progressing because the various sciences – including the rising social sciences – are increasingly able to understand the mechanisms of the world.

In this worldview, the way out of the impasse posed by postwar modernism and the ensuing intellectual malaise was entirely within science's reach, and Vlaeminck continuously called upon the social sciences throughout the 1970s (and well into the 1980s) to scientifically take into account inhabitants' less tangible needs – those of a psychological and social kind. Towards this aim he continuously pleaded for an "ecology of dwelling," *woonecologie* – a local articulation of the rising field of Environment-Behavior Studies, inspired by the works of William Michelson and Alexander Mitscherlich.[14]

At the same time, accompanying his faith in the potential of a more scientific approach – and arguably taking the upper hand in his writings – was the fierce call for transparency and accessibility of knowledge. In the same spirit, much of his writings in public media were driven by the aim to translate scientific expertise to a wider public, to emancipate the latter by making expertise accessible and understandable.[15]

Notably, Vlaeminck played a role in the unawarded 1976 Robert Maskens prize mentioned in the introduction. Being part of the editorial staff of Belgium's main architecture journal *A+*, he moderated an extensively covered panel discussion between the jury members, in an attempt to delve into the aporias responsible for the troubled debate among them.[16] What the ensuing dialogue between, most notably, architects Jean Barthélemy (1932-2016), Georges Baines (1925-2013), Jan Tanghe (1929-2003), and bOb Van Reeth (b. 1943) made clear was that the jury members were more than ever aware about the complexity of architecture's societal role. What stifled the dialogue was an inability to come to an agreement on how to articulate this societal aspect. In his concluding remarks Vlaeminck points to this inevitable, yet elusive thing called "the social" and ends by stressing "the need for a clear voice and unconcealed analyses of the architectural reality."[17]

Only a few months after the report of this discussion, Vlaeminck shared his understanding of the discussions surrounding the Carrefour de l'Europe, in a way that echoes his earlier concluding remark.[18] He explicitly aimed to address and evaluate the "true meaning" behind the contemporary developments concerning the Carrefour site. The troubled dialogue of the Maskens competition fresh in mind, with "thinking the social" emerging as its most stifling factor, it is hard to read this article otherwise than as an attempt to provide "a clear voice and unconcealed analysis" of one of the most symbolic sites in Belgium.

By then, a whole series of design proposals had emerged for the site, most notably ARAU's so-called "aesthetic alternative," which marked the start of their concern with aesthetics (but formulated in social terms).[19] Remarkably, given this wealth of projects and Vlaeminck's often repeated faith in an objective scientific approach to guide us to a better living environment, he chose not to rely on the social sciences to evaluate the merits of the proposals, choosing instead to uncover the ideologies underlying them. Despite his scientific ideals, he suspended his judgment in order to strip the already existing voices to their ideological basis in terms of how they stand vis-à-vis the existing political order, be it in a conformist, conflictual, or consensual manner (Fig. 4).[20] The absence of the trust in the social sciences so prevalent in his other writings is striking, but it seems he ventured upon this rare piece of ideology critique as an attempt – fruitful or not – to isolate the discussion on the social in its most essential form from the discussion on this specific site.

"The social" here was not tied to an inherent quality of an envisioned way of life, as in ARAU's drawings, but rather to a mode of political progress. The question to be resolved was how we as a society envision change to be possible within an existing political constellation and more specifically how we want the built environment to be produced. Vlaeminck's refusal to evaluate the projects on their own merits indicates his view that at least a substantial part of "the social" escapes architecture and that he could not articulate important aspects of "the social" innate and specific to architecture. Like many other intellectuals of the decade, his calls for a scientific approach explicitly framed architecture as part of a wider environment at the risk of dissolving architecture's specificity.[21]

Fig. 4. Design study by Groep Planning, 1970. The group stood for Vlaeminck's "consensual approach." Source: Sieg Vlaeminck, "Het Europakruispunt te Brussel," *A+*, no. 42 (1977): 15. © Groep Planning / SumProject

In terms of epistemology, Vlaeminck's writings clearly indicate that knowledge's societal relevance lies within the realm of objective science, wherein the scientific approach is seen as a relatively unproblematic form of grasping specific qualities of the human environment. But the shift to his small piece of ideology critique indicates that the societal relevance of such scientific knowledge more specifically relies on the notion of transparency. The plea for more science came with the demand of transparency: making science accessible to a wider public and making political positions of design proposals explicit. Thus, his work was framed by the aim for and belief in an increasing transparency between world and the knowledge thereof. And hence the societal value of knowledge was claimed within a logic of representation rather than within a power field (in contrast to ARAU).

The real

By the 1980s, a whole series of proposals were generated for the Carrefour de l'Europe, one bolder than the next. But what they had in common was a depiction of the site as a void desperately in need of architecture. Many architects sought to "fill" this void, often by resorting to a typo-morphologically inspired method of carefully knitting the surrounding urban fabric together. A number of architects

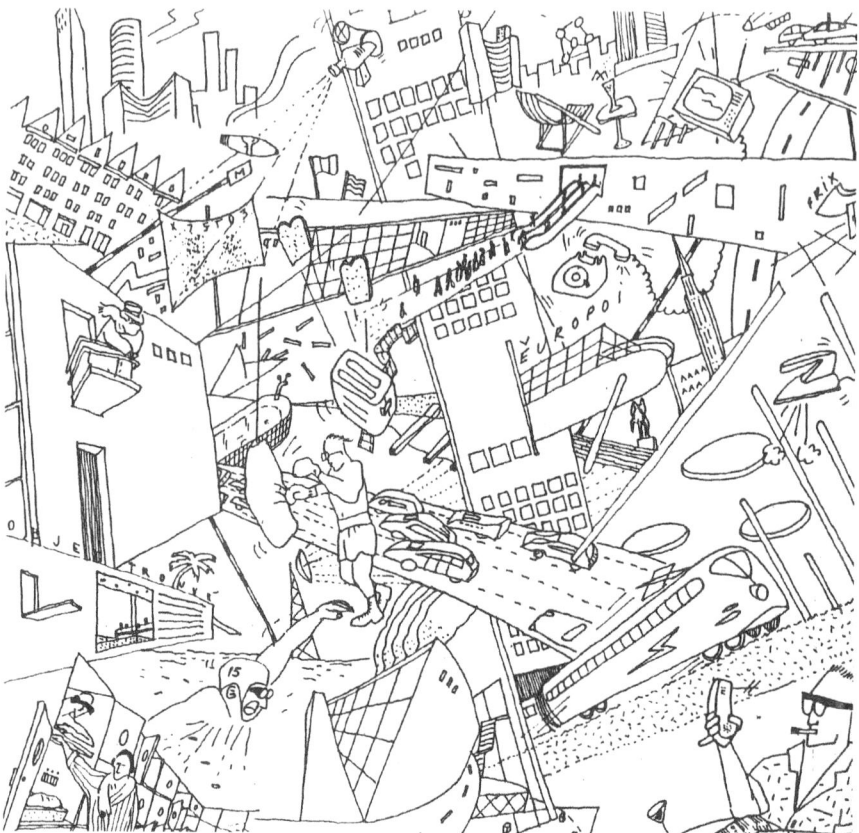

Fig. 5. Impression for the Team Hoogpoort design. Source: Mil De Kooning, "Quand on n'a pas ce qu'on aime on aime ce qu'on a," *Vlees en Beton*, no. 4 (1985): n.p.

and critics, however, deemed this to be an all too easy and insufficient diagnosis of the site. Architecture critic Mil De Kooning (b. 1955), for instance, wrote that "the problem with this site is the rupture caused by the traffic between the upper and lower parts of the city and not some traumatizing lack of architecture."[22] In contrast, he provocatively stressed that the existing car park had more metropolitan qualities than most of the proposals drawn for the site. The major exception, in his view, was the OMA-influenced design entry by Team Hoogpoort – consisting of Stéphane Beel (b. 1955), Xaveer de Geyter (b. 1957), Arjan Karssenberg (b. 1955), and Willem Jan Neutelings (b. 1959) – which instead of seeking to repair the urban tissue opted for a radical gesture of nourishing the urban void and introducing recreative functions via interventions at the site's borders. Thus the design introduced an "urban fact" that generated new potential, which existing typologies would never be able to deliver. For De Kooning, it was the only design capable of articulating this metropolitan sensibility and allowing to experience the qualities of the site (Fig. 5). Thus he gave voice to a new generation that embraced the potential metropolitan qualities of large and radical urban gestures. In later years, the Team Hoogpoort entry, together with its early advocates, was designated by some as the birth of a new architectural culture in Belgium.[23]

Central to De Kooning's view was an argument about intellectuality. For him, seeing and recognizing the potential metropolitan qualities – overlooked by most proposals – was an act of intellectuality, an active engagement with reality that was all too often skipped over in design. Indeed, in the journal and book series he founded, *Vlees en Beton* (Flesh and Concrete), De Kooning showed himself a fierce (and polemical) defendant of a renewed intellectuality. His writings of the early 1980s bore witness to an emerging more self-aware architecture culture and contain lucid reflections upon the shifting role of the intellectual in this fledgling culture. Against those who speak with preconceived ideas (i.e., ARAU's political views and Vlaeminck's social sciences), and perhaps characteristic of a more nuanced younger generation, De Kooning placed those who simply cherish and disclose "that which is."[24] Hence he put architect bOb Van Reeth and even more his mentor, critic Geert Bekaert (1928-2016), on a pedestal in his publications, both of them thinking along similar lines – for instance in the inspiration they took from the Flemish vernacular.

As Christophe Van Gerrewey has noted, central to the ideas of this new architecture culture, was the willful and strategic mobilization of the category of "the real,"[25] as the basis for a relevant intellectuality was seen in its permanent engagement with the latter.[26] Again the arguments over the Carrefour site evidence a shift on the level of epistemology: the debate shifts on where the fundaments of a potentially socially relevant knowledge are seen to be lying. Though De Kooning's and his colleagues' commitment to try and let reality speak for itself has a ring of neutrality to it, their notion of "the real" implies a perspective on what is deemed societally valuable.[27] This is for instance clear in Bekaert's 1970s collaborations with filmmaker Jef Cornelis (b. 1941). In his scenarios, lower class dwellings, such as the pigeon fancier's self-fashioned living environment, were staged as part of a fierce critique on bourgeois architecture's representational aspect, which concealed reality more than doing justice to it.[28]

As the ideal was seen in reality speaking for itself, this embrace of "the real" inevitably came with a solid dose of anti-nominalism, a critique of language and representation. As Van Reeth worded the maxim of this line of thought: "As one speaks, one harms reality."[29] Since words, concepts, and knowledge in general did not coincide with "the real," a continuous caution towards the former was necessary to stay in tune with the latter. It is this continuous caution that was portrayed as the way out of the intellectual malaise of the 1970s by De Kooning and his colleagues. In line with the idea of autonomy,[30] references external to architecture were rendered suspicious, in favor of looking for the criteria that architecture raises by itself. Only in this way a desired form of immediacy could be reached: more than abstract ideals, it is the reality of building that offers the material to constitute its own rules.[31]

This intellectual mobilization of "the real" contained two challenges in terms of knowledge: first of all, how was the critic expected to get in touch with "the real," and second, how was a dialogue possible when words were suspicious from the very start? The first challenge meant a revaluation of the intellectual labor of the critic. The critic's task was redefined as a perennial attempt to put the "unwordable" into words, which, arguably, only the most eloquent managed to do. The plea for a continuous engagement with "the real" follows the structure of the Greek notion of *poiesis*, the creative act of bringing something into being. The intellectual labor of the critic came to be seen as that of a "poet" in that sense, standing eye to eye with bare reality, unmediated by the existing norms and forms we normally resort to in understanding that reality. Thus, the critic's work became that of Heidegger's measure-bestowing poet: gathering a measure of all things from the things showing themselves.[32]

The capacity of the poet-critic to articulate an aspect of reality that a work of architecture managed to put forward was deemed almost of equal importance as the work of the architect itself. Hence it is not surprising that just as architecture intellectuality was promoting "the real" as its unattainable ideal, the figure of the critic entered the limelight, was put on a par with the architect, and became a topic of interest in itself (Fig. 6). In this regard, Bekaert did not simply write for De Kooning's *Vlees en Beton* as an expert writing on architecture but also figured as its subject. The journal staged Bekaert-as-critic in a long interview that discussed his way of writing, his manuscripts being cherished and used as illustrations to the interview; moreover, it was around the same time that De Kooning and others initiated the anthologization process of Bekaert's writings.[33]

The second challenge – how to come to a dialogue when words were suspicious from the start – translated itself into the need for permanent debate. Postulating "the real" as the horizon of intellectuality, always out of reach, equaled the necessity of unceasing deliberation. Accordingly, De Kooning greatly encouraged polemics and was convinced that a strongly articulated position forces others to define their own. Thus, articulated opinions replaced power strategies or a faith in science, and the necessity of debate, rather than power or science, was where societal relevance found its base. Or, as Bekaert formulated it during his editorship of the Dutch journal *Archis*: "Building never escapes the curse of thinking. It needs its story to societally exist. There is no choice, unless the one between lazy thinking, if it can be called thinking, or an exigent thinking that critically questions itself and its world."[34]

Fig. 6. Architect Rem Koolhaas and critic Geert Bekaert on a par. Cover of *Vlees en Beton*, no. 4 (1985).

Conclusion

The argument that surfaces by staging these three voices in a dialogue on the Carrefour de l'Europe is that the troubled debate that characterized the 1970s and 1980s has less to do with argumentative disagreements than with differing, rather implicit, epistemic positions.[35] These latter contain an implicit view on how architectural understanding should relate to practice and could contribute to the social. In other words, they can be considered to contain a conception of what architecture theory ought and can aspire to be. How theory is conditioned by this more pragmatic, epistemological dimension concerning the "status" or "standing" of architecture knowledge within reality – a dimension that somehow precedes the arguments actually made[36] – is often overlooked in architecture theory's historiography and allows us to diagnose more accurately the troubled dialogue so characteristic of the 1970s. Thus, we might recognize in it and in the various ways these different figures of knowledge claimed their relevance for society, the places "where the uncomfortable questions of form and program with respect to society and its political formation were asked; where irresolution rather than resolution was assumed" – to quote from Anthony Vidler's *Histories of the Immediate Present*.[37] As Vidler argues, it are "disruptive moments" such as these that allow us to reassess the process of modernity in architecture culture. Surely these epistemic positions reoccur at different moments in history, but it seems as if when a certain paradigm came to crisis, the stifling effect of these different positions was felt the most and led to the questioning of the established conditions of dialogue.

Notes

1. Sieg Vlaeminck, ed., "Zin of onzin van architektuurwedstrijden," *A+*, no. 40 (1977): 25-36.
2. In a broader cultural historical perspective, Zygmunt Bauman identifies this self-postulated nature as characteristic of intellectuality in a postmodern condition (and most radically articulated by Richard Rorty): "The intellectual activity draws its legitimacy from the intellectuals' own moral conviction as to the value of their work and as to the worthiness of the discourse they are keeping alive and guarding against being stifled or numbed in the cacophony of communal traditions. With such a strategy adopted, the fact that others do not care for the legitimations we offer is no longer a problem. We simply do not offer legitimations." Zygmunt Bauman, *Legislators and Interpreters: On Modernity, Post-Modernity and Intellectuals* (Cambridge: Polity Press, 1987), 198.
3. Francis Strauven, "Urban Transformations of the Innercity of Brussels since the End of the 18th Century," *Wonen-TA|BK* nos. 15-16 (August 1975): 15.
4. Geert Bekaert, *Contemporary Architecture in Belgium* (Tielt: Lannoo, 1995), 194.
5. Michel Didisheim, "L'enjeu du concours," *Environnement: Revue Mensuelle Urbanisme, Architecture, Design* no. 11 (1970): 330-32.
6. "Aménagement du carrefour de l'Europe à Bruxelles: Les enseignements d'un concours," *Environnement* no. 11 (1970): 330-41; Sieg Vlaeminck, "Het Europakruispunt te Brussel: Een eindeloze 'place de misère'? Een nodeloos of een noodzakelijk conflict?" *A+* no. 42 (1977): 13-19; Jan Storms, Hilde Heynen, and André Loeckx, eds., *Forum architectuur van de stad* (KU Leuven, afdeling architectuur, 1985); André Loeckx, "20 jaar ontwerpen voor het Europakruispunt te Brussel, overzicht en kritiek," *Monumenten & Landschappen* 8, no. 2 (1989): 29-48; André Loeckx, "The Eloquence and Silence of an Urban Fragment," *Arkitekturtidsskrift B* no. 51 (1994): 98-109; Robert

Courtois and Pierre Loze, "Het Europa-kruispunt: De grote wonde of de weerstaanbare wederopbouw van het Brusselse stadscentrum," *A+* no. 127 (1994): 44-54; Bruno De Meulder, "The Boulevard de l'Impératrice: An Arena for Brussels Urbanism," *Archis* no. 6 (1998): 52-57; De Meulder, "The Carrefour de l'Europe: Recent Architectural Designs in the Rear View Mirror," in *Vacant City: Brussels' Mont Des Arts Reconsidered*, ed., Bruno De Meulder and Karina Van Herck (Rotterdam: NAi, 2000), 84-99; Christophe Van Gerrewey, "Amnesty for the City: The Hoogpoort Design for the Carrefour de l'Europe in Brussels (1983)," *The Journal of Architecture* 19, no. 3 (2014): 435-53.

7. ARAU, *Quinze années d'action urbaine, ou, Bruxelles vu par ses habitants* (Brussels: ARAU/CFC, 1984), 61.
8. Isabelle Doucet, "Counter-Projects and the Postmodern User," in *Use Matters: An Alternative History of Architecture*, ed. Kenny Cupers (London: Routledge, 2013), 233-47; Doucet, *The Practice Turn in Architecture: Brussels after 1968* (London: Routledge, 2015), chap. 2.
9. Strauven, "Urban Transformations," 17.
10. Maurice Culot and François Terlinden, eds., *Antoine Pompe et l'effort moderne en Belgique 1890-1940* (Brussels: Musée d'Ixelles, 1969).
11. René Schoonbrodt, "Balance and Prospects after Five Years of Struggle," *Wonen-TA|BK* nos. 15-16 (1975): 18-26.
12. Sebastiaan Loosen, "'Le Monopole du Passéisme': A Left-Historicist Critique of Late Capitalism in Brussels," in *Re-Framing Identities: Architecture's Turn to History, 1970-1990*, ed. Ákos Moravánszky and Torsten Lange, East West Central: Re-Building Europe, 1950-1990, vol. 3 (Basel: Birkhäuser, 2016), 261-74.
13. Francis Strauven, "Postscript: Structure versus Architecture," *Wonen-TA|BK* nos. 15-16 (1975): 74-76.
14. William Michelson, *Man and His Urban Environment: A Sociological Approach* (Reading, MA: Addison-Wesley, 1970); Alexander Mitscherlich, *Die Unwirtlichkeit unserer Städte: Anstiftung zum Unfrieden* (Frankfurt: Suhrkamp, 1965); Mitscherlich, *Thesen zur Stadt der Zukunft* (Frankfurt: Suhrkamp, 1971); Sieg Vlaeminck, "Sociaal-ecologische verkenningen," *Extern: Tijdschrift voor Omgevingswetenschappen* 2, nos. 1-3, 11-12 (1973): 46-58, 125-38, 169-79, 753-70, 829-45; Sieg Vlaeminck, "Woonecologie: De interferentie tussen gebouwde omgeving en menselijk gedrag," in *Ruimtelijke planning: Praktijkboek voor stedebouw en stadsvernieuwing, huisvesting en milieu*, ed. Jan Van Alsenoy, vol. II.H.5 (Antwerp: Van Loghum Slaterus, 1985).
15. Sebastiaan Loosen, "Secularized Engagement in Architecture: Sieg Vlaeminck's Plea for *woonecologie* in 1970s Flanders," *International Journal of History, Culture and Modernity* 6 (2018): 1-37.
16. Vlaeminck, "Zin of onzin."
17. Ibid., 36, author's translation.
18. Vlaeminck, "Europakruispunt."

19. ARAU, "Proposition d'aménagement pour le centre ville de Bruxelles," *Archives de l'Architecture Moderne: Bulletin d'Information*, no. 8 (1976).
20. Vlaeminck, "Europakruispunt," 18-19.
21. Reinhold Martin, "Environment, c. 1973," *Grey Room* no. 14 (2004): 78-101.
22. Mil De Kooning, "Quand on n'a pas ce qu'on aime on aime ce qu'on a," *Vlees en Beton* no. 4 (1985): n.p.
23. Bekaert, *Contemporary Architecture*, 195; Van Gerrewey, "Amnesty for the City," 435.
24. Mil De Kooning, "Het vermogen tot herkennen: Een algemene reflectie en een oproep aan de bevolking," *A+* no. 81 (1983): 36-37.
25. Van Gerrewey, "Amnesty for the City,"448.
26. Geert Bekaert, *Rooted in the Real: Writings on Architecture*, ed. Christophe Van Gerrewey, Vlees en Beton 87 (Ghent: WZW, 2011).
27. Elsewhere in this volume, Andrew Toland discusses how these various appeals to "the real" are essentially a restructuring of the relationship between discipline-specific knowledge and our constructions of the world.
28. Jef Cornelis, "Bouwen in België," *Waarover men niet spreekt*, 16 mm, 31 min (BRT, 22 March 1971); Cornelis, "Een eeuw architectuur: België, 1875-1975. Tien taferelen," *Toren van Babel*, 16 mm, 35 min (BRT, 21 March 1976).
29. "bOb Van Reeth in gesprek met Mil en Marc De Kooning en Dirk Jaspaert, 1983-1984," *Vlees en Beton* no. 3 (1985): n.p., author's translation: "Zodra je spreekt doe je de werkelijkheid pijn."
30. For some of the protagonists in the Flemish context, see Caroline Voet et al., eds., *Autonomous Architecture in Flanders: The Early Works of Marie-José van Hee, Christian Kieckens, Marc Dubois, Paul Robbrecht and Hilde Daem* (Leuven University Press, 2016).
31. Geert Bekaert, "Het recht op architectuur," *Wonen-TA|BK* no. 4 (1981): 9-17.
32. Hilde Heynen, *Architecture and Modernity: A Critique* (Cambridge: MIT Press, 1999), 16; Diana Aurenque, "Heidegger on Thinking about Ethos and Man's Dwelling," *Architecture Philosophy* 2, no. 1 (2016): 39-53.
33. Geert Bekaert, "Spreektralie," *Vlees en Beton* nos. 3-4 (1985): n.p.; Bekaert, *Verzamelde opstellen*, 2 vols, ed. Mil De Kooning and Herman Stynen (Brussels: Stichting Monumenten- en Landschapszorg, 1985-1986).
34. Geert Bekaert, "Studenten (pro domo)," *Archis* no. 2 (1992): 11, author's translation.
35. For a more general account of this line of argument, see John Peter Nettl, "Ideas, Intellectuals, and Structures of Dissent," in *On Intellectuals: Theoretical Studies, Case Studies*, ed. Philip Rieff (Garden City, NY: Doubleday, 1969), 53-122.
36. See also Benjamin Aldes Wurgaft, *Thinking in Public: Strauss, Levinas, Arendt* (Philadelphia: University of Pennsylvania Press, 2016), 12-13.
37. Anthony Vidler, *Histories of the Immediate Present: Inventing Architectural Modernism* (Cambridge: MIT Press, 2008), 199.

SECTION 2

Projects of Theory

CHAPTER 6

Institutionalized Critique? On the Re(birth) of Architectural Theory after Modernism: ETH and MIT Compared

Ole W. Fischer

Prelude

A continuous and intensifying criticism of late modernist architecture during the 1960s – against its built environment as much as against its protagonists and theories – led not only to the phenomena of postmodernism in the decades to follow but also to a crisis of architectural education. This chapter proposes that one of the responses to this observed crisis was the internalizing of critique within architectural education as history and theory. Significantly, both the Eidgenössische Technische Hochschule (ETH – Swiss Federal Institute of Technology) in Zurich and the Massachusetts Institute of Technology (MIT) in Cambridge (Mass.) were among the first architectural schools to institutionalize history and theory: the Institut für Geschichte und Theorie der Architektur (gta – institute for history and theory of architecture) was founded at the ETH by Adolf Max Vogt and Paul Hofer in 1967 while the History Theory Criticism of Art and Architecture (HTC) program at MIT by Stanford Anderson and Henry ("Hank") A. Millon followed in 1974, after a longer phase of incubation. Yet these events speak of more than just an ostensible rapprochement with architectural history in the education of architects, which had been questioned since the modernist critique of historicist eclecticism. Rather, there was nothing less at stake here than a revision of modernity as a scientific project (and modernism as its formal expression). The institutional shift of research and doctoral programs from art historic programs where they had traditionally been housed to schools of architecture – and with ETH and MIT being two similarly polytechnic-modernist ones – resulted on the one hand from the changed architectural discourses of the time and, on the other hand, accelerated the criticism by internalizing it.

Situation of the 1960s

Postwar modern architecture faced growing critique both from within as well as from outside the discipline. Representative of the former are books such as *Architettura della Città* by Aldo Rossi and *Complexity and Contradiction* by Robert Venturi, both published in 1966, followed in 1969 by *Meaning in Architecture* by Charles Jencks and George Baird, which introduced semiotics to architecture long before Jencks's epochal collection *The Language of Post-Modern Architecture* (1977).[1] Also, the proliferation of radical small magazines and periodicals around 1968 speaks volumes about the internal reaction against modernist architecture and pedagogy.[2] Exemplary of the external criticism against postwar operational thinking and technocratic optimism in architecture are *The Death and Life of Great American Cities* by Jane Jacobs (1961) and – in the German-speaking discourse – *Die Unwirtlichkeit unserer Städte* by Alexander Mitscherlich (1965).[3]

Of course, multiple trends contributed to the rediscovery of history and theory in schools of architecture: for one, the Society of Architectural Historians (SAH) was founded in 1940 by a group of young US academics (John Coolidge, Walter Creese, Rexford Newcomb, Donald Drew Egbert, etc.) interested in the history of ideas rather than styles. In parallel, Sigfried Giedion – art historian, secretary-general of the CIAM, and bridge between the Swiss ETH and US academic institutions at Cambridge – held the Charles Eliot Norton lectures at the Graduate School of Design at Harvard at the invitation of Walter Gropius, an attempt to provide the (at the time still evolving and expanding) modern movement with (art)historic legacy. As a pupil of Heinrich Wölfflin, Giedion took a distinctively Hegelian dialectic approach to architecture as organic expression of the epoch. His lectures were edited and published as *Space, Time and Architecture* in 1941 and turned within short period into the official historical account of the modern movement (next to Nikolaus Pevsner).[4] In 1956 the German-born art historian Rudolf Wittkower (teacher of both Colin Rowe at the Warburg Institute in London and later of Stanford Anderson in New York) accepted a professorship at the Department of Art History and Archaeology at Columbia University (New York), where he stayed until 1969. There, he spread his formalist comparativist method in interplay with religious-philosophical content, as he explicated in *Architectural Principles in the Age of Humanism* (1949).[5] This study on the Italian Renaissance (which combines diagrammatic analysis with humanist Neo-Platonism and Neo-Pythagorism) enjoyed wide distribution among architects, including Alison and Peter Smithson, Reyner Banham, and Peter Eisenman.[6] The already mentioned Robert Venturi also took note of it and recycled the ideas and image materials he had gathered during his stay at the American Academy in Rome (1961–62) – which manifested into the aforementioned *Complexity and Contradiction* – directly for his teaching at the University of Pennsylvania and then Yale School of Architecture, where he taught, according to his own account, the supposedly first course in architectural "theory" that was unattached to either history or to design studio. Even if this self-assessment does not hold up, his image-saturated teaching style of precedents – fed by his interest in predominantly complex architecture (Mannerism, Baroque, Eclecticism) – and the methodological clues he took from the New Criticism in literature (as his repeated reliance on T.S. Eliot shows) plus the inspiration he drew from Pop Art and pop culture indicate a different type of intellectual engagement with architecture. The Princeton School of Architecture on the other hand, where Venturi had received his education, developed a curricular emphasis on architectural history under Donald Drew Egbert – one of the SAH cofounders (see above) and architect-scholar on medieval art, French Beaux-Arts, and US civilization – and the French-born architect Jean Labatut – who combined Beaux-Arts principles with French modernism of the 1920s and introduced a distinctively French flavored Neo-Thomist phenomenology at Princeton.[7] Labatut – a design instructor and long-time director of graduate studies at Princeton – explored both the experiential qualities of architecture as well as its spiritual existential (specifically Catholic) contents, which allowed for an analytic approach to architectural history beyond stylistic categorization, including that of Modernism. Labatut served as advisor for supposedly the first dissertation at an architecture program in the US in 1958: *Water and Architecture* by Charles W. Moore,[8] who in turn would become one of the most important protagonists and educators of a phenomenologically inspired postmodern architecture.

Since its inception as the Federal Institute of Technology in 1855, the ETH Zurich housed a department of architecture, which in the postwar area was committed to a modernist progressivism.[9] Very similarly, the School of Architecture and Planning of MIT existed since the founding of the institute in 1865, which makes it the oldest architectural department in the US. And after a long phase of imitating the Parisian *École des Beaux-Arts* and *École Polytechnique*, MIT had been a stronghold of modernism since the 1930s and by the 1960s was immersed into a technologically driven optimism of "scientific planning." Yet at the same time, the architecture departments of both ETH and MIT had brought on board ambitious history faculty, who envisioned a role for their subject beyond the obligatory teaching of survey courses.

Events on the way to HTC: CASE and the 1964 Teachers' Conference

In 1964, the *Conference of Architects for the Study of the Environment* (CASE) was founded at the initiative of the young Peter Eisenman, who had just returned to New York City after completing his PhD at the University of Cambridge in

England. By invitation only, CASE convened a small group of young architects, critics, and assistant professors, many of whom soon took on key positions within US academia, such as Kenneth Frampton, Michael Graves, Richard Meier, John Hejduk, Stanford Anderson, Henry Millon, and the English critic Colin Rowe (distinguished already by his senior professor position at Cornell University). Attempts to include Robert Venturi remained fruitless (and may have led to the infamous grey versus white debate in the 1970s). CASE was the breeding ground for both the *New York Five* (Eisenman, Graves, Gwathmey, Hejduk, Meier) and their exhibition plus catalogue at the Museum of Modern Art New York,[10] as well as for the Institute of Architecture and Urban Studies (IAUS) in New York cofounded by Eisenman and Emilio Ambasz, which served as a research, exhibition, publication, and education platform independently from existing universities.[11]

In addition, CASE figures as an important clearinghouse for ideas: besides the question of the "discipline," its core and its limits (the notion of autonomy – a quest that keeps some of its original members busy until this day), the group discussed the relationship of theory to practice, especially from the vantage point of an alternative form of architectural education *different* from modernism. Here the CASE group could rely on some of its members' experience as "Texas Rangers," as the generation of young educators came to be known whom Dean Harwell Hamilton Harris had hired at the University of Texas School of Architecture, Austin, between 1951 and '58. Developing formalist approaches to design, this generation included Colin Rowe, John Hejduk, Robert Slutzky, Werner Seligmann, Lee Hirsche, Bernhard Hoesli (who then joined the ETH Zürich and was instrumental in founding the institute gta), Lee Hodgden, Jerry Wells, John Shaw, and W. Irving Phillips Jr.[12] At CASE the discussions around pedagogy took a slightly different spin towards postgraduate education, because of two architects who had earned PhDs from art history programs: Stanford Anderson (Columbia University) and Peter Eisenman (Trinity College Cambridge, UK). One of the recurring themes was the question of "research in architecture" and how it could contribute to a discipline-specific doctorate (in difference to the existing ones in art history departments). This is significant at a time when none of the architecture programs in America offered a PhD. Eisenman quickly found an answer with the inauguration of the IAUS in 1967 as a platform for "discourse" – as one quickly learned to say – that acted as vessel for research grants, stipends, postgraduate education, donations, etc., and in the early years even design studies for public housing, which dried up quickly because of changes in HUD funding and the looming bankruptcy of New York City. Stanford Anderson took a different approach on "research" and, together with his art-historian colleague Henry Millon, cofounded the HTC program at MIT in 1974 – ten years after he had started his position at MIT in 1964.

In 1964 – the same year as the inaugural CASE meeting – another important conference took place: a teacher seminar on history, theory, criticism held at Cranbrook Academy in Michigan, cohosted by the Association of Collegiate Schools of Architecture (ACSA) – which represents academic architecture programs in North America – and the American Institute of Architects (AIA), the US national professional organization. Chaired and organized by the aforementioned art historian Hank Millon, it included Reyner Banham (London), Bruno Zevi (Rome), Colin Rowe, and Sibyl Moholy-Nagy as distinguished guest speakers. The participants tried to grapple with the problem of how architectural historians should react to a second and third generation of modernists, who imagine themselves as *ahistorical*. The convened group of scholars perceived a crisis of architectural history within architectural education across the US, because most schools had adapted some variation of modernist Bauhaus pedagogy and thereby had incorporated its originating defect. In 1919 Bauhaus founding director Walter Gropius had banned history courses from the curriculum of the revolutionary design school, regarding them as instruction in stylistic eclecticism. The long-lasting result, according to the scholars gathered at Cranbrook, was a fundamental split between architectural history and studio instruction, which had led to a non-reflected resurfacing of eclectic tendencies – if not historicism proper – in the late 1950s and early 1960s, for example in the work of Philip Johnson.[13] The answer, according to most speakers at the seminar, would have to be sought in a redirection of architecture (and architectural history) towards "research," conceived of in the full breadth of both natural and technical sciences as well as the humanities. In retrospect, the discussion set up by Millon seems to have been crafted as a testing ground and as legitimization by his peers in the field for a potential HTC program at his own institution – MIT. Significantly, Millon's younger colleague, the recently appointed architect and art historian Stanford Anderson, held a programmatic lecture in which he applied Karl Popper's scientific theory directly to architecture in order to dissect Reyner Banham's naïve functionalist position on both the methodological and rhetorical levels.[14]

Previous to MIT HTC there has been a pilot for a graduate and PhD program for architectural history established at the College of Architecture at Cornell University, in addition to (and with support of) the existing program in art and architectural history at the Department of Art History at the university's College of Arts and Sciences.[15] There were other precursors, of course, such as the PhD program in urban planning at MIT – and similarly at other schools of architecture, such as Cornell and Princeton – that had resulted directly from a new institute: the Center of Urban and Regional Studies (1957), which was soon after its inception brought into the Joint Center for Urban Studies in cooperation with the Harvard Graduate School of Design (1959). Yet here research studies focused almost entirely on mathematical-cybernetic models and first applications of computers. Exemplary of this approach is the doctoral thesis of the Austrian-born, Oxford-educated mathematician and architect Christopher Alexander.[16] Sociology, economy, politics, and humanities were regarded primarily as providers of data, while one of today's most well-known products, *The Image of the City*[17] authored by Kevin Lynch, with Donald Appleyard, Sydney Brower, Michael Southworth, and György Kepes, the latter of whom had formed a "visual studies" group within the MIT-Harvard Joint Center for Urban Studies, remained rather an exception. It was not until 1967 that Kepes was able to institutionalize the Center for Advanced Visual Studies as an independent unit within MIT.

The first step towards an institutionalization of HTC was the introduction of a bachelor in history theory criticism of art and architecture within the School of Architecture and Planning at MIT in 1966, only two years after the first CASE meeting and the ACSA/AIA teachers' conference. The new undergraduate program instigated two new assistant professors – Wayne Andersen (1964) and Rosalind Krauss (1967), both art historians – which distinguished the MIT HTC from any other school of architecture in the US at that time. The second step was the draft for a PhD program in "History Theory Criticism of Art, Architecture, and Urban Form" (sic) which was soon changed to "History Theory Criticism of Art, Architecture and Environmental Studies" while the program came to be known by the name "History Theory Criticism of Art and Architecture") written up by Hank Millon and Stanford Anderson in 1971.[18] Yet things were complicated because of the leave of Millon to the American Academy Rome in 1973, followed by his final departure to become the founding director of the Center for Advanced Study of the Visual Arts at the National Gallery Washington, DC, in 1979. Rosalind Krauss moved from MIT to Princeton in 1973, so that the emerging HTC program had to be shouldered by the two remaining young professors Stanford Anderson and Wayne Andersen. In 1973, the new hires of Dolores Hayden (who did not have a PhD) and Donald Preziosi, both on assistant professor level, promised support, as did illustrious visiting faculty, but the program did not fully consolidate until the arrival of David Friedman in 1978.

From the MIT HTC program draft one can draw the following points for the discussion of the institutionalization of critique within academia:

First, the authors critique an "engaged" or "operative" (Tafuri) type of architectural history à la Pevsner, Giedion, Zevi or the aforementioned Banham, which Millon and Anderson view as "partisan" (hence not "scientific" in the sense of historiography). Yet the authors position themselves also against the more traditional and conservative mainstream art historians who (according to Millon and Anderson) concentrate on image, form, and meaning rather than addressing questions of materiality, production processes, technique, and the social, economic, and urban contexts and conditions architects must face, simply because art historians lack the competency in design and construction of architecture and urbanism necessary to describe and analyze these aspects.

Second, the authors call for a specific architectural writing of history, which, per Millon and Anderson, should not be housed in art history programs but rather developed in direct confrontation with practicing architects, artists, and students within schools of architecture, with the goal of growing a new generation of architectural historians educated as architects (which was already discussed at the first CASE meeting by Eisenman and Anderson).

Third, the authors propose the triad of History Theory Criticism, each provided with specific roles within architectural education: "History" should be "scientific" in the sense of a general historiography, that is, as (semi-)autonomous with regard to architecture, with its own set of questions and findings (here Anderson's familiarity with the theories of science of Karl Popper and Paul Feyerabend comes into play). "Theory" should address the methods of historical writing, their reflection – especially from a comparative standpoint to other sciences: sociology, anthropology, philosophy, history, and theory of science, via linguistics all the way to informatics and technical sciences – but also include reflections on curricula and pedagogy. "Theory" is per se critical of the logical impossibility of a "universal theory of architecture" (which was directed against modernism and its theoretical underpinnings, such as Giedion's Hegelian claims of the spirit of time in *Space, Time and Architecture*). Furthermore, "Criticism" was understood by Millon and Anderson as a confrontation with design, which is why both authors repeatedly collaborated with designers and wrote on design methods. Anderson's engagement with CASE went so far as to result in an MIT design contribution to the MoMA exhibition *The New City: Architecture and Urban Renewal* in 1967,[19] parallel to his long-term project on a speculative prognosis for the social-cultural framework for the future of architectural practice.[20] In addition, "criticism" should act as a systematic testing ground (or "falsification," in the words of Popper) of the models, methods, and hypotheses developed in architectural history and theory.

Finally, both authors acknowledge the importance of an in-house academic press, which existed independently at MIT since 1962,[21] in order to publish the findings of its research centers and carry the research back into the discipline as well as society at large. They thus helped to establish HTC quickly as a brand name in the academic world and a model taken up by others to this very day.

As a result, the MIT HTC program pursued the *institutionalization* of history, theory, and criticism of architecture in the US in the 1970s and 80s (in parallel, yet independent of the IAUS in New York) as a form of *legitimizing* architecture within a research-intensive technical university such as MIT as well as a form of *intellectualization* of the practice of architecture (based on its own histories and traditions) through a rigorous, systematic, and interdisciplinary research program. It could draw on support from new institutions and programs (such as the CCA in Montreal, founded in 1979, or the Graham Foundation, founded in 1956), grants, and publications, at just that moment when the perceived failure of late-modern architecture collapsed the revolutionary narration and technological determinism of the modern project, which in itself was the first subject for historical analysis and (re-)contextualization, as exemplified by Anderson's own dissertation on Peter Behrens, the *Werkbund*, and the early modern movement.[22]

MIT HTC and Institut gta at ETH Zurich compared

The situation at the architecture department at the ETH in Zurich shows many parallels:[23] despite (or because of?) an academic context characterized by late modernist technological determinism, the founding of the gta in 1967 stands for a return of history and theory within the architecture program, parallel to the expansion of the disciplinary focus on sociology, anthropology, art and literature criticism, philosophy, linguistics, semiotics and structuralism, as well as a renewed interest in popular culture and the vernacular.

Although details remain hidden in the gta archives, the institute gta experienced a shorter incubation period from proposal to establishment in summer 1967 compared to the decade it took to set up HTC at MIT. In close parallel to the reasoning of Millon and Anderson at MIT, the gta started immediately with its own academic outlet – the gta Verlag – as a side product of the forming of the institute in 1967, with the opening address as the first publication of the gta series in 1968.[24] The new institute claimed to cover areas ranging from art and architectural history, theory, to historic preservation, yet already the opening address of the gta shows latent tensions between the linguistic art historical approach of Adolf Max Vogt and the archeological historical building research represented by Paul Hofer.[25] Vogt provokingly argues for texts, images, and ideas stronger than stone – providing as examples the Pythagorean theory of a harmonious order of the cosmos reaching from early high cultures all the way to Le Corbusier's *Modulor*, the example of Abbé Laugier and the notion of the "primitive rustic hut" for the development of neo-classicism, and the example of Serlio's print of Bramante's unrealized regular design for the cupola of St. Pietro in Vaticano echoing in Wren's St. Paul's Cathedral, in Boullée's "église métropolitaine," and even in the redesign of the US Capitol in Washington, DC, in the mid-nineteenth century.[26] Vogt continues this historic trajectory of texts and images prevailing over the material fact of "stones" into the 20th century and identifies both the CIAM and Sigfried Giedion's *Space, Time and Architecture* as potential lines for research: he imagines an analysis of the reception between "theory" (here understood as the "fundamental convictions" of the historian Giedion,[27] that is, as a form of ideology) and "practice" (here understood as the work of the modernist masters described by Giedion as well as the influence of the latter's book on the second and third generation of modern architects). In other words, with his emphasis on "reception" and "effect," Vogt envisions a historization of the modern movement similar to Anderson at MIT, yet with the difference that he still seems to embrace Giedion's "operative" history which Anderson and Millon (and Tafuri) had already criticized and rejected. Hofer, on the other hand, takes the materiality of stone literally and provides an analysis of the techniques of surface treatment of medieval stonemasons in order to date the excavated Romanesque castle in Bern.[28] Even if Hofer positions himself closer to the notion of "*Baugeschichte*" (building history) of the German polytechnic tradition, which is informed by archaeology and natural and building sciences and treats the existing structure as material witness and primary source, the institute gta chose the opposing model of "*Architekturgeschichte*" (architectural history) infused by art historical methods, which used to be primarily text based (archive) and image-centric (drawing, photo). Accordingly, preferred hires up to this day at the ETH gta have been art historians rather than architect-scholars, not to speak of the new type of researchers that Millon and Anderson sketched out in the MIT HTC draft during the same period. No wonder that the docent for built heritage preservation, Albert Knoepfli, who was originally integrated into the gta in 1967, went on to found his own institute (*Institut Denkmalpflege*) at the ETH as soon as he was promoted to full professor status at the department of architecture in 1972. The result of this positioning of the gta firmly on the side of authored "architecture" (rather than "building" and its vernacular, anonymous, and archeological undertones) and on that of art historian methods (form, text, image) has brought a deepening division between practical conservation and building research (with its strong apparatus of natural sciences) on the one side and the institute gta on the other. From its initiation, the institute gta focused on monographic methods, archival research, studies of reception, influences, and discourses – that is, primarily on questions of communication, meaning, and interpretation, which also drove the postmodern movement as critique of the primarily technological, functional, and abstract references of late-modern architecture. On the other end of the spectrum, the institute gta separated history and theory from studio instruction (note the absence of "criticism" in its name!) by prioritizing the educational formats of slide lecture and seminar. In comparison, the MIT HTC proposes an alternative approach – the direct confrontation and involvement with design (even if this has proven to be more complicated in the real existing MIT School of Architecture than in the HTC draft program, as the author noticed during his visiting position at HTC in 2010). Yet one does not even have to go as far as Cambridge, MA, to find that alternative setups would have been possible: in the same year 1967 that saw the founding of the institute gta, Jürgen Joedicke at the Technische Hochschule Stuttgart (today University of Stuttgart), another polytechnic institution similar to ETH and MIT, founded the "Institut Grundlagen der modernen Architektur" (IGMA – the Institute for the Principles of Modern Architecture), which combined historical research (predominantly on the modern movement) with a critique of late modern tendencies and direct involvement in design studios, such as courses in design methodology – clearly in difference to the ETH at Zurich. And since there are various connections between Joedicke and the ETH (via his publications,[29] specifically the CIAM as well as via the Swiss journal *Bauen + Wohnen* where Joedicke served as editor in the 1960s), he must be regarded as part of the network of protagonists rethinking architectural education and pioneering history, theory, and criticism in the 1960s and 1970s in parallel to Anderson and Millon at MIT or Vogt and Hofer et cetera at ETH.[30]

The institute gta also includes an exhibition platform (gta Ausstellungen) and an archive, which received upon inauguration the documents of Gottfried Semper from the ETH library as a first gift, and which has been collecting architects' estates and holds the CIAM papers. In parallel MIT HTC chose a slightly different institutional setup, since the MIT Library Special Collections and the Rotch Architecture Library keep archives and estates and yet are not directly part of HTC. Similarly, MIT set up its own exhibition program at Hayden Gallery (since 1948/50, today MIT List Visual Art Center) that worked in close connection with Kepes's aforementioned CAVS (since 1967) and with MIT Media Lab (since the 1980s) but has its own director and curator(s) independently from the HTC program.

(Instead of a) conclusion: The end of theory?

During the 1960s both the practice and the pedagogy of late modern architecture came into crisis. Once the superstructure of the profession came to be seen as questionable, architecture learned to build a new ideological project out of the very criticism that it encountered: rather than technological optimization or planning for a society to come, the vector of intellectual speculation turned towards history, sociology, philosophy, anthropology, linguistics, feminism, cultural studies, and other humanities (both of the discipline itself as well as the society at large). Significantly, this process of internalization can be tracked with the institutionalization of history and theory (and criticism) within leading schools of architecture, especially those of polytechnic tradition deeply immersed in the technological positivist agenda of that period (MIT, ETH, TH Stuttgart). The combination of the criticism against the modern project, which demanded reconsideration and historization (that is, to be framed as something of the past to be studied), as well as the notion of "research" as common goal at these types of technical universities opened paths towards new programs in history and theory (and criticism) within schools of architecture. Other impulses came from the institutionalization of criticism on the fringes of academia, such as the IAUS in New York, or organizations such as CCA Montreal and DAM Frankfurt. These initiatives fundamentally changed the way in which architecture is conceived, discussed, and written about, but also how it is taught, and eventually how it is practiced.

Today, some fifty years later, this project of internalized critique has itself come under scrutiny. The "long summer of theory" – as the period from the 1960s to the '90s has been dubbed[31] – led to a quick come and go of fashionable "theories,"[32] which after the fall of the Iron Curtain gave away to a pragmatic design engagement around the newly opened global marketplace for architecture that seemed too busy for elaborate readings before the legitimizing role of history and theory shifted over to technology. Accelerated (but not caused) by the hardening grip of the licensing and accreditation bodies (NAAB/AIA in the US, RIBA in UK, the Bologna bachelor and master system in the EU), architectural education has moved towards emphasizing sets of skills and tools, especially in digital applications and representation, in sustainable and resilient bench marks and codes, as well as in material science and fabrication. In parallel, a historization of the 1960s and the emerging postmodern moment, and with it, the "birth" of architectural theory and history, began. The archival interest in the period of the 1960s to 80s recalls the historization of the modern movement by the protagonists of this very phase (e.g. Anderson on Behrens, Joedicke on Häring, Vogt on CIAM, etc.). Yet the question remains: has the institutionalization of criticism in the form of history and theory within architectural education come full circle and are we experiencing another technological driven phase of neo-modernity (or "reflexive modernity" or "liquid modernity" to use the phrases of Beck or Bauman respectively[33])? Or are we on our way towards a very different cultural frame, in which the historization of the previous present indicates a transition to something yet unknown?

Notes

1. Robert Venturi, *Complexity and Contradiction in Architecture* (Garden City: Doubleday, 1966 – The Museum of Modern Art New York Papers on Architecture 1); Aldo Rossi, *L'architettura della città* (Padova: Marsilio, 1966) in English: idem, *The Architecture of the City* (Cambridge, MA: MIT Press, 1982, in the series *Oppositions books*); Charles Jencks and George Baird, eds., *Meaning in Architecture* (New York: Braziller, 1970); Charles Jencks, *The Language of Post-modern Architecture* (London: Academy Editions, 1977).

2. See for example: Beatriz Colomina and Craig Buckley, eds., *Clip, Stamp, Fold – The Radical Architecture of Little Magazines 196X to 197X* (Barcelona: Actar, 2010); for a general account of the situation at architectural schools in the US in the late 1960s see: Joan Ockman, ed., *Architecture School: Three Centuries of Educating Architects in North America* (Cambridge MA: MIT press, 2012), 153ff, 161-85.
3. Jane Jacobs, *The Death and Life of Great American Cities* (New York: Random House, 1961); Alexander Mitscherlich, *Die Unwirtlichkeit unserer Städte: Anstiftung zum Unfrieden* (Frankfurt am Main: Suhrkamp, 1965).
4. Sigfried Giedion, *Space, Time and Architecture – The Growth of a New Tradition* (Cambridge, MA: Harvard University Press, 1941); cf. Nikolaus Pevsner, *Pioneers of the Modern Movement from William Morris to Walter Gropius* (London: Faber & Faber, 1936).
5. Rudolf Wittkower, *Architectural Principles in the Age of Humanism* (London: Warburg Institute, 1949).
6. On the trajectory from Wölfflin to Wittkower to Rowe see: Anthony Vidler, *Histories of the Immediate Present: Inventing Architectural Modernism* (Cambridge MA: MIT Press, 2008); especially "Introduction" and chapter 2: "Mannerist Modernism: Colin Rowe." The method of diagramming had been introduced earlier by Paul Frankl's dissertation thesis, another pupil of Wölfflin, in Paul Frankl, *Die Entwicklungsphasen der neueren Baukunst* (Leipzig, Berlin: Teubner, 1914), with the late English translation: idem, *Principles of Architectural History: The Four Phases of Architectural Style, 1420-1900*, trans. and ed., James F. O'Gorman; foreword by James S. Ackerman (Cambridge, MA: MIT Press, 1968); on the peculiar lateness and timeliness of this translation just parallel to the crisis of modern architecture in the late 1960s, see Ole W. Fischer, "The Birth of Architectural History out of Stylistic Critique? – Paul Frankl and the *Principles*," *EAHN Journal*, 2018.
7. Rajesh Heynickx, "Conceptual Debts: Neothomism and Modern Architecture in Postwar America," *The European Legacy, Toward New Paradigms* 22, no. 3 (2017): 258-77; Samuel O'Connor Perks, Rajesh Heynickx, and Stéphane Symons, "From Inertia to the Absolute with Jean Labatut: On Visuality, Religion and Intellectual Transfers in Post 1945 Architecture," *Architectural Theory Review* forthcoming, 2020. I would like to express my sincere gratitude to Rajesh Heynickx pointing these texts out to me and sharing them, where he and his coauthors highlight the role of the French Catholic philosopher Jacques Maritain for Labatut.
8. Thesis typescript, University of Princeton, 1957, published in an edited version as: Charles Willard Moore, *Water and Architecture*, with photographs by Jane Lidz (New York: H. N. Abrams, 1994); for the influence of Labatut at Princeton and on the development of Postmodernism see: Jorge Otero-Pailos, *Architecture's Historical Turn: Phenomenology and the Rise of the Postmodern* (Minneapolis: University of Minnesota Press, 2010), chapter 2: "Eucharistic Architecture: Jean Labatut and the Search for Pure Sensation."

9. Gwendolyn Wright, "History for Architects," in *The History of History in American Schools of Architecture 1865–1975*, ed. Gwendolyn Wright and Janet Parks (Princeton: Princeton Architectural Press, 1990), 13-52, here 29: MIT as one of the examples of "modernist" programs in the USA, which had reduced history content in their curriculum to a minimum.
10. *Five Architects: Eisenman, Graves, Gwathmey, Hejduk, Meier* [New York] [1972], preface by Arthur Drexler; introduction by Colin Rowe; criticism by Kenneth Frampton, catalogue Museum of Modern Art New York.
11. Cf. Kim Förster, "The Institute for Architecture and Urban Studies, New York (1967-1985): Ein kulturelles Projekt in der Architektur" (PhD thesis Zürich: ETH, 2011); Cf. Suzanne Frank, *IAUS, the Institute for Architecture and Urban Studies: An Insider's Memoir* (Bloomington: Author House, 2011).
12. Cf. Alexander Caragonne, *The Texas Rangers: Notes from the Architectural Underground* (Cambridge, MA: MIT Press, 1995).
13. Marcus Whiffen, ed., *The History, Theory and Criticism of Architecture: Papers from the 1964 AIA-ACSA Teacher Seminar* (Cambridge, MA: MIT Press, 1965).
14. Stanford Anderson, "Architecture and Tradition that isn't »Trad, Dad«," in *The History, Theory and Criticism of Architecture*, ed. Marcus Whiffen (Cambridge, MA: MIT Press, 1965), 71–89; with direct connection to: Reyner Banham, "Coventry Cathedral – Strictly »Trad, Dad«," *New Statesman* 63 (May 25, 1962): 768-69, reprinted in: *Architectural Forum* 117 (August 1962): 118-19.
15. Stephen W. Jacobs, "History: An Orientation for the Architect," in *The History, Theory and Criticism of Architecture: Papers from the 1964 AIA-ACSA Teacher Seminar*, ed. Marcus Whiffen (Cambridge, MA: MIT Press, 1965), 47-69, here p. 62.
16. Christopher Alexander, *Notes on the Synthesis of Form* (Cambridge, MA: Harvard University Press, 1964). This PhD was awarded by the Harvard Graduate School of Arts and Sciences; the Harvard GSD did not start its own PhD program in architecture before 1987.
17. Kevin Lynch, *The Image of the City* (Cambridge, MA: Technology Press, 1960 – later MIT Press).
18. Henry Millon and Stanford Anderson, "Proposal for a PhD Program in History, Theory and Criticism of Art, Architecture and Urban Form," Spring 1971, n.p. *MIT Institute Archives, Series VII*, Departments 1965-85, Box 175, Folder: Dept. of Architecture and Planning, 1969-76/24; quoted after: John Harwood, "How Useful? The Stakes of Architectural History, Theory, and Criticism at MIT, 1945-1976," in *A Second Modernism. MIT, Architecture and the "Techno-Social" Moment*, ed. Arindam Dutta (Cambridge, MA: MIT Press, 2013), 106-43, here: 134.
19. Museum of Modern Art (MoMA), ed., *The New City: Architecture and Urban Renewal* ([n.p.], 1967), see here: the proposal of the MIT group: 42-47.

20. Stanford Anderson, "Possible Futures and Their Relations to the Man-Controlled Environment," Research Project 1966-78 supported by a grant of Graham Foundation and the Institute of Architecture and Urban Studies IAUS New York; published as: Stanford Anderson, ed., *Planning for Diversity and Choice: Possible Futures and Their Relations to the Man-Controlled Environment* (Cambridge, MA: MIT Press, 1968); Stanford Anderson, ed., *On Streets* (Cambridge, MA: MIT Press, 1978).
21. A precursor, the Technology Press, existed since 1932 in cooperation with the commercial publishing house John Wiley & Sons.
22. Stanford Anderson, "Peter Behrens and the New Architecture of Germany, 1900-1917" (PhD Thesis Columbia University, l968); published revised as: idem, *Peter Behrens and a New Architecture for the Twentieth Century* (Cambridge, MA: MIT Press, 2000).
23. Adolf Max Vogt, "Das Institut, seine Aufgabe, seine Verpflichtung," *Institut für Geschichte und Theorie der Architektur: Reden und Vortrag zur Eröffnung, 23.6.1967* (=Schriftenreihe des Instituts für Geschichte und Theorie der Architektur an der Eidgenössischen Technischen Hochschule Zürich, Band 1), (Basel, Stuttgart: Birkhäuser, 1968): 11-19; see also: Ruth Hanisch and Steven Spier, "'History is not the Past but Another Mightier Presence': The Founding of the Institute for the History and Theory of Architecture (gta) at the Eidgenössische Technische Hochschule (ETH) Zurich and its Effects on Swiss Architecture," *The Journal of Architecture* 14, no. 6 (2009): 655-86.
24. Jakob Burckhardt, Adolf Max Vogt, and Paul Hofer, *Institut für Geschichte und Theorie der Architektur an der ETH – Reden und Vortrag zur Eröffnung, 23.6.1967* (=Schriftenreihe des Instituts für Geschichte und Theorie der Architektur an der Eidgenössischen Technischen Hochschule Zürich, Band 1), (Basel, Stuttgart: Birkhäuser, 1968); the gta Verlag started as cooperation with commercial publishers (Birkhäuser Basel/Stuttgart; Ammann Bern; Ernst & Sohn Berlin), before it became completely independent in the 1990s.
25. Both Adolf Max Vogt (PhD in art history at the University of Zurich) and Paul Hofer (PhD in art history at the University of Bern) try to set themselves apart from the Basel tradition of stylistic art history as represented by Jacob Burckhardt and Heinrich Wölfflin, see here for example the obituary for Wölfflin by Paul Hofer, "Heinrich Wölfflins Gegenwart," *Freistudentische Zeitschrift* 27, no. 5 (November 1945), where Hofer describes Wölfflin as a giant of art history – but of the pre-WWI area – whose belief in organic form of the classic periods his generation would look upon with awe and bewilderment.
26. Adolf Max Vogt, "Das Institut, seine Aufgabe, seine Verpflichtung," in Burckhardt, Vogt, and Hofer, *Institut für Geschichte und Theorie*, 11-19; here 13-16.
27. Vogt, "Das Institut," 16-18.
28. Paul Hofer, "Die Haut des Bauwerks: Methoden zur Altersbestimmung nichtdatierter Architektur," in Burckhardt, Vogt, and Hofer, *Institut für Geschichte und Theorie,* 21-51.

29. Jürgen Joedicke, *Geschichte der modernen Architektur: Synthese aus Form, Funktion und Konstruktion* (Stuttgart: Hatje, 1958), translated as, idem, *A History of Modern Architecture* (New York: Praeger, 1959); Jürgen Joedicke, ed., *Dokumente der modernen Architektur, Volume I – XV* (Zurich: Girsberger; Stuttgart: Krämer, 1959-87), which included thematic issues and German translations on: CIAM Otterlo, Brutalism (Reyner Banham), Georges Candilis, and other contemporary architecture, or monographies of the early modern masters such as Hugo Häring, etc.
30. A discussion of Jürgen Joedicke and the institutional history of the IGMA in Stuttgart goes beyond the scope of this paper.
31. Philipp Felsch, *Der lange Sommer der Theorie: Geschichte einer Revolte 1960 bis 1990* (Frankfurt: Fischer, 2016).
32. Today often compiled into readers and anthologies, that is, historicized and turned into a subject for historical analysis itself, like this text and the conference it was written for.
33. Ulrich Beck, *Risikogesellschaft – Auf dem Weg in eine andere Moderne* (Frankfurt am Main: Suhrkamp, 1986); Ulrich Beck, Anthony Giddens, and Scott Lash, *Reflexive Modernization: Politics, Tradition and Aesthetics in the Modern Social Order* (Cambridge: Polity Press, 1994); Zygmunt Bauman, *Liquid Modernity* (Cambridge: Polity Press; Malden, MA: Blackwell, 2000).

CHAPTER 7

Thinking Architecture, its Theory and History: A Case Study about Melvin Charney

Louis Martin

In their introduction to this book, the editors resorted to an analogy with the game of chess to suggest that the history of architectural theory could go beyond the simple description of the "moves" of the theorist by examining "how the rules of the game shifted throughout history."[1]

To address this question, I propose to examine some aspects of the work produced in the 1960s and 1970s by Montreal architect and artist Melvin Charney (1935-2012).[2] Charney's oeuvre, one may argue, is truly representative of the period ranging from the 1960 to the mid-1990, since it reflects a shift – which characterized the passage from "High Modernism" to "Postmodernism" – from an architecture conceived of as an instrument efficiently performing functions (machine) to an architecture conceptualized as a system of signs (language). As described below, Charney scrutinized theoretical dualities inherited from the modern movement and transformed them with the introduction of references external to the field of architecture. In the process, a trajectory emerged that changed the terms of reference and shaped the thematic contents of this dualistic framework.

On a metacritical level, my methodological outlook builds on a crucial distinction Stanford Anderson (1934-2016) made in 1987 between the *internal* and the *external* history of architecture.[3] "Internal history," he explained, "considers what is unique to [the field of architecture]," while "external history demonstrates how the field […] is enabled or constrained by social conditions." The core of Anderson's argument is

> to accept neither complete determination nor autonomy. There is, rather, an intersection between a relatively independent field such as architecture and the enabling and limiting conditions of society. There is some internal order to the field of architecture, but its intersection with a particular society is a matter of historical inquiry, not logical demonstration.

Anderson gave, unfortunately, no clue about what he meant by "internal order of the field." Also open to speculation is how "the enabling and limiting conditions of society" actually affect the internal order of the field. Charney never referred to Anderson's model, but his work suggests hypotheses about these issues.[4] Yet, in the context of this book, the conjunction of both Charney's critique and Anderson's theory may help to assess the assertion of the editors that "the history of architectural theory in the post-war period has been impacted by the coming and going of a series of theoretical frameworks: critical theory, postmodernism, critical regionalism, deconstructivism, pragmatism, and so on."[5]

Image versus process

After architectural studies at McGill University, Melvin Charney completed his education at Yale University in 1959. There, he was deeply influenced by the ideas of Louis I. Kahn, notably, by his distinction between design and architecture. According to Kahn, design proposed formal solutions to a problem formulated *a priori* in a program, whereas architecture started with the "realization" of a problem.[6] Design tended to impose order with exterior forms. In contrast, architecture felt the "existence will" of a need, that is, the form lying undeveloped within that need. In other words, architecture grew out of a need as a plant from a seed. Architecture was the product of an intellectual process rather than a mere preconceived vision. This is why Kahn valued archaic form, which was form still loaded with possibilities. Design was imagery, while architecture was a perpetual process of inquiry into the nature of things.

Following Kahn's advice, Charney travelled in the eastern Mediterranean countries between 1961 and 1963.[7] In looking at how ancient cultures answered architectural problems, the contemporary architect could learn how to get to the core of emerging new societal demands.

In Istanbul – most notably in its historical mosques – Charney found an architecture embodying "construction"; the principle of which was the "build-up" of elements. Separation of small, familiar parts, such as columns, thin walls, and domes, was the "rule of the game" in sixteenth-century Turkish architecture.[8] In this way, buildings retained "a sense of process"; thus, they had meaning for a contemporary architecture similarly made of small, prefabricated industrial elements.

In contrast, the troglodyte architecture of Cappadocia was based on the principle of "excavation"; whereby material was removed from natural rock formations to create inhabitable space.[9] Yet, the landscape of Cappadocia was also characterized by the presence of the discordant image of "constructed architecture" imported by the Christians during the 11th century. While the "plan

Fig. 1. Melvin Charney, partial view of the arcaded porch of St. John the Baptist Church showing a column, arches, and dentils, Cavusin, Cappadocia, Turkey, 1961, gelatin silverprint, 23.0 x 34.9 cm. Collection of the Canadian Centre for Architecture, Montreal, PH1987 :0615 © Melvin Charney / SODRAC (2018).

of a rock-cut dwelling began with the cutting of its spaces," religious architecture "began with an image," the image of a known style, of previous examples. Specifically, rock-cut churches were not "construction," since their sculpted decoration was merely an "image of construction." Charney's archive from his travels includes a photograph he took meant to show that the columns and arches of these churches held nothing up (Fig. 1). What separated the indigenous dwellings and the religious environment of Cappadocia was not a difference of principle – both were realized by way of excavation – but precisely the difference between "process" and "image."[10]

Upon his return to Montreal in 1964, Charney found instances of "process" and "image" in the new architecture that emerged out of the frenetic modernization of his native city. The traditional city of streets and squares was transformed into an environment of dense, vertical clusters of buildings. A detailed analysis of Place Victoria indicated the semi-successful insertion of tall skyscrapers in the urban fabric. Place Victoria and its siblings, such as Place Ville-Marie, presented a special environmental problem, he wrote: their "interior circulation spaces are part of the private building yet because of their size really serve the public as streets and are in a sense an extension of the public city."[11]

This dichotomy, he argued, was not clearly resolved in the planning of these building complexes. Yet, Place Victoria was superior to the other recent Montreal high-rise office towers because it emphasized "a sense of process set up both in the grouping and in the phasing of the elements of this building."[12] By comparison, Place Ville-Marie and the C-I-L House exhibited "an overt formalism and a two-dimensional composition of parts;" their architecture followed a "packaging ideology" which had "all the semblance of cool integration" of technology. "However, in Place Victoria," Charney concluded, "integration has in itself become part of the form; the technology of this tower is realized in architecture, and, as architecture, technology here becomes a human factor."[13]

In his first influential essay, "Grain Elevator Revisited," Charney showed that the dichotomy between image and process was ingrained in the discourse of the modern movement.[14] He was intrigued that Le Corbusier used photographs of American grain elevators to illustrate his famous definition of architecture: "L'architecture est le jeu savant, correct et magnifique des volumes assemblés sous la lumière." He was struck by the fact that Le Corbusier published an image of Montreal's Grain Elevator no. 2 and wrongly situated it in the United States. Moreover, Le Corbusier touched up the photograph: to illustrate his argument, he erased the Bonsecours Market from the background to isolate the volume of the elevator in a void; finally, he marked out the edges of the building to accentuate symmetry.

Charney noticed the discrepancies of the Purist myth. The imposing structures of the port of Montreal were visibly not monuments isolated in the American prairies; neither were they made to stir emotions, as Le Corbusier argued. After he studied their conception, Charney realized that each elevator was a link in a distribution chain, built at the scale of the continent, for the global provision of grain.

He concluded that Le Corbusier and his contemporaries of the 1920s did not understand that the elevators were not buildings but large-scale machines made to keep grain in motion. Because they looked at them merely as images, the "moderns" of the 1920s saw the elevators as formal analogues for a future architecture. In Charney's opinion, contemporary architects made the same aesthetic mistake when they looked at the installations of the Kennedy Space Centre and at Apollo vehicles as a prefiguration of a new lifestyle. For him, "rather than the static and lumpish neo-monuments of yesteryear," the elevators were the image of a process, a "process we must study if we believe that architecture is an involvement with human processes rather than with designed things."[15]

Taking the Pavillon du Québec at Expo 67 as an example, Charney argued that Quebec's architecture was characterized by an overwrought formalism (Fig. 2).[16] His own anti-formalism adhered to the radical discourses of the 1960s, and in particular, to the ideas of the inventor of the Fun Palace, Cedric Price. These discourses in favor of an *"architecture autre"* undermined the very values on which

Fig. 2. Pavillon du Québec, Expo 67, Montreal, 1967. Papineau, Gérin, Lajoie & Durand, architects. Source: BAnQ, Centre d'archives de Québec, Fonds Office du film du Québec, photographer unknown, 1967, E6, S7, P6711680.

modern monumental architecture rested: composition, pre-visualization, permanence, fixity, and ultimately, the very notion of "object," for which was substituted the notion of "process."

An instance of *architecture autre*, Charney's project for the Canadian Pavilion at Expo 70 at Osaka, showed that an alternative to the "object of design as work of art" was the "environmental kit-of-parts," which enabled to anticipate a nomadic and participative architecture, constantly transformed by the users. In other words, here was an "architecture of process" realized by a selection, an appropriation, and a "*détournement*" of industrial products (Fig. 3).[17]

Charney's opposition of "process" and "formalism" echoed the contemporaneous distinction between "instrument" and "monument" George Baird made in 1967 when he compared Cedric Price's Pottery Thinkbelt project and Eero Saarinen's CBS Building in New York City.[18] Baird considered that this dichotomy was an aporia that could be resolved with the introduction of semiology. Following a different path to surpass the dichotomy, Charney resorted instead to Michael Polanyi's concept of "tacit knowledge" to supplement structuralist theories of the sign.

Fig. 3. Melvin Charney, architect, Harry Parnass, architect, Janos Baracs, engineer, Marcel Pageau, engineer. View of the model for a competition entry for the Canadian Government Pavilion, Japan, World Exposition, Osaka, 1967, gelatin silver print, 50 x 66.6 c, Collection of the Canadian Centre for Architecture, Montreal, Purchased with support of the Canada Council's Acquisition Assistance program. DR1997:0004:008 © Melvin Charney / SODRAC (2018).

The contradiction of contemporary architecture

The starting point of his argument was the contradiction of contemporary architecture "between its elitist and repressive condition and its obvious origins in social content."[19] To illustrate this contradiction, Charney compared photographs of two individual houses built north of Montreal.[20] On the one hand, the picture of an architect's house found on the cover of a book on contemporary architecture in Quebec embodied the ideology and failure of "architecture as an institutional system" (Fig. 4).[21] On the other hand, the photo of an anonymous house, which illustrated an article denouncing the ugliness of Quebec's landscape, represented the other repressive side of an elitist cultural institution incapable of seeing in this image "an authentic architecture born of real things and rooted in people's real lives" (Fig.5).

A scrupulous description of the architect's house[22] indicated that its ambiguous formalism detached the building from its environment. In its formal isolation, this house, largely derivative from American precedents of the 1950s, recalled "the language of an aesthetic myth."

Fig. 4. Architect Charles Elliott Trudeau's house in the Laurentians, Quebec, ca. 1966. Reproduced with permission from *Vie des arts*, no. 42 (1966): 32.

Fig. 5. House of an unknown person, n.d., photograph: Jean Saulnier. Reproduced by permission of the Ministère de la culture du Québec from *Culture vivante*, no. 15 (1969): 12.

Found on the side of the road, the other was, on the contrary, totally integrated into its environment. The anonymous house was "specific to its occupants and to its place." Its real significance lay in the fact that it reflected "the condition of those who had to struggle – with a minimum of resources available – to find a way to house themselves." According to Charney, the house belonged to a living popular tradition of medieval origin, which was still alive in the modern age. He derived this line of thought from John A. Kouwenhoven's *Made in America: The Arts in Modern Civilization* (1949), in which the author argued that the vernacular tradition was transformed by industrialization, notably by the invention of balloon framing and prefabrication. According to Kouwenhoven, the vernacular tradition was the real driving force of "an architecture indigenous to modern civilization."[23] But Charney added another layer to this proposition when he maintained: "A tradition refers to an attitude towards building, an attitude rooted in an innate response to the need for organization of physical space and conditioned by the resources available." In presenting popular architecture as an "innate response" of people to their environment, Charney drew an explicit analogy with Michael Polanyi's "tacit knowledge," a form of knowledge acquired in practice, which cannot be expressed otherwise.[24] On that basis, Charney argued: "the source of contemporary architecture in Quebec is in a way of building that has shaped the relationship between people and the built form they inhabit."[25]

With this provocative comparison, Charney added layers to the previous dichotomy between "image" and "process." Obviously, the architect's house represented the image of a foreign modern architecture, a stylistic phenomenon, a packaging ideology. In contrast, the anonymous house illustrated a process, which was the stamp of an authentic modernity rooted in real experience. What was new in this presentation was Charney's contrasting of the authoritarian essence of architecture as an institutional system and of the liberatory potential of popular architecture, an idea, we will see below, invigorated by his reading of Foucault.

From "objets-types" to "images-types"

Also in 1970, Charney conceived the *Memo Series*, a project he submitted to a Canadian competition for a museum to air flight and an air force memorial. The *Series* searched for a commemorative architecture that would not take the form of a building. Charney speculated on the materialization of a Canadian memorial network, which would grant "existence to an architectural concept in the heads of people."[26] The project was based on the idea that meaning emerges in the interaction between people and their environment. The originality and major shift of this pivotal project in Charney's itinerary resided in his replacing of the selection of industrial built fragments (the "objets-types") by a series of found images evocative of air flight (the "images-types"). Consequently, the artifactual bits were selected for their evocative power rather than for their potential as building material for the creation of a built environment.[27]

Charney produced dozens of memos describing a variety of commemorative scenarios, like visits of crash sites, travelling museum planes, meetings of veterans in abandoned sheds, virtual reconstitution of historical flights and of war experiences, and so on. At once memorials and memoranda, the *Memo Series* aimed at putting in place a national network anticipating today's social networks. Commemoration was no longer conceived as a localized monumental design object but rather as a personal experience shared with a vast community: the concept of architecture "in the heads of people" was fundamentally a social fact repressed by the architectural institution, which not only imposed objects but also restricted the way people interacted with the built environment.

Charney's accompanying criticism of power was openly buttressed by the work of Michel Foucault, who exposed the repressive mechanisms of power. The idea that history transforms documents into monuments, found in *The Archeology of Knowledge*,[28] consolidated Charney's innovative handling of images published in the press, the massive diffusion of which participated in the formation of a collective unconscious. Inspired by the practices of Pop Art,[29] he "monumentalized" those images by retrieving them from daily inattentive consumption: he collected them, classified them, and developed a discourse on them in his *Dictionnaire d'architecture*, a work suggesting a possibly inherent, yet unrevealed, structure to the dialectics of liberation and oppression of which architecture is both an instrument and a mirror.[30]

Other monuments

In parallel, Charney explored by way of construction the commemorative potential of the architectural images he found meaningful. His first installation, created in 1975, reconstituted the image of a worker's house targeted for demolition by an urban renewal project for downtown Trois-Rivières (Fig. 6).[31] The image of the building, a hybrid between a house and a tomb, revealed the innate architectural knowledge and the daily heroism of an unknown worker. In accordance with the Freudian definition of a totem, this installation, entitled *Le trésor de Trois-Rivières*, was a substitute for the demolished house (Fig. 7). That reification seemed necessary in order to commemorate a work the value of which the cultural institution was incapable of recognizing. The dialectics of elite and popular architecture implied a dialectical understanding of architectural monumentality, which was the site of a political struggle about memory.

Fig. 6. First page of Hélène Gosselin Geoffrion's article "Trois-Rivières Centre-Ville." Reproduced from *Architecture Concept*, 30, no. 328 (March-April 1975): 22.

Fig. 7. Melvin Charney, *Le trésor de Trois-Rivières*, 1975, wood construction, 3.8 x 2.88 x 4.31 m. On display at the Musée d'art contemporain de Montréal. Fonds Yvan Boulerice.

In contrast, Charney's urban installation *Les maisons de la rue Sherbrooke*, built as part of the cultural program of the 1976 Montreal Olympics, was not a work referring to an antecedent.[32] In this work, building aimed at making visible the collective space of the street as defined by the façades of individual buildings, a space de-structured by demolition and punctuated by the ruins of a disappearing city. For Charney, those surviving fragments were not commemorative of a bygone past but rather comprised the concentrated brief for the future city (Fig. 8). The installation introduced fragments of houses that never existed. As visual duplication of the real houses on the other side of the street, the new fragments inverted the process of erosion of the *quartiers populaires*, "the city of urban knowledge." The work introduced a new ruin and thus materialized the idea that ruins could project the future of Montreal. The ephemeral façade was a reified metonymy of Montreal urban architecture. The fragment reduced the whole to its essential characteristic: that of a construction subsumed by the street, that of a backdrop defining the collective street space.

Yet, the profound significance of *Les maisons de la rue Sherbrooke* surfaced, not without bitter irony, with their very destruction by order of Mayor Jean Drapeau.[33]

Fig. 8. Melvin Charney, *Les maisons de la rue Sherbrooke*, Corridart Montreal, Quebec: view of the installation, 1976. Photographer unknown. Collection of the artist, now at the Canadian Centre for Architecture.

The destruction re-enacted, like in a ritual, the demolition of the *quartiers populaires*, the repositories of an innate urban knowledge. The figurative content of this work and the images of its destruction acted as a catalyst that brought to collective consciousness the fact that the city was the battleground of a real struggle between repressive power and cultural resistance.

Perhaps the most remarkable aspect of Charney's act of urban activism was its worldwide diffusion under the form of a mass media image.[34] The photographs of the rue Sherbrooke installation thus acquired the status, and diffused the message, of the images collected over thirty years by the architect in his *Dictionnaire d'architecture*.

The sign of the sign

By the early 1980s, Charney's analysis of Montreal had evolved as he acknowledged the displacement of the mechanical/biological analogy by a semiologic analogy, which also suggested a structural displacement in the understanding of architecture as a societal practice, since semiology is based on the assumption that there exist shared referential links to which human artifacts convey meaning, and these links, [...], are socially bound: society makes every use a sign of itself.[35]

The 1960s urban renewal project for Montreal was still enacted during the 1970s, as resistance from the residents of the targeted central neighborhoods increased. Two intertwined cities coexisted in tension: the modern metropolis of private superblocks and the fragmented traditional "city of urban knowledge" of the central *quartiers populaires*. If the private commercial interiors of recent superblocks were still an ambiguous extension of exterior public space, they began to incorporate features of the traditional city such as a "square" in the case of Complexe Desjardins and historical fragments in the case of the Université du Québec à Montréal (UQAM). In parallel, renovation, insertion, and gentrification became common practices that helped in preserving the neighborhoods. While the superblocks tended "to automate and normalize sign systems" in their total reproduction of themselves, small-scale interventions in the *quartiers* replicated "things-as-they-are."[36] This unresolved tension was, for Charney, a transitional stage that would lead to "the introduction of textural urban figuration and typologies."

Nonetheless, Charney remained convinced that popular architecture provided the essential model of architectural creation. As a type of natural sign, popular architecture represented the fundamental nature of architecture: true primitive huts "at once both primitive and metaphorical."[37] For him, these huts confirmed:

> the arrival of an architecture that finds its place in the new order of things and that is aware of the images of images, the symbols of symbols and the signs of signs. It is as if architecture starts by refusing to refuse, by wanting to affirm that continuity between art and life.[38]

In the "postmodern" 1980s, however, signs and symbols were reintroduced in "a practice so obviously tied in to institutionalized power" in the name of a return to history and a rediscovery of the sense of place.[39] For Charney, it was "as if the 'innocence' of history were now being advanced in place of the 'innocence' of pragmatic functionalism of the modernist decades."[40] But history was far from being innocent and architecture was far from being a transparent means of representation. In his mind, architecture had to "make obvious what is said and for whom it is said."[41]

The reintroduction of figural content in architecture fostered a new dialectic of sensibilities opposing, on the one hand, a critical "discourse of revelation" seeking to expose that "what is accepted as natural is in fact historically constituted and thus subject to change," and on the other hand, "an insidious exploitation of representational devices to belie the very significations promulgated in the name of history."[42] The first tendency gave rise to a renewed formalism animated by "the very desire to evoke the autonomous life of architectural forms." Symptomatic of the "incipient 'innocence' which pervades practice," the second tendency assumed that architectural meaning emerged from a sense of place. But for Charney,

> There is no such thing as a "Place" other than the sum total of the representations of that place. There are, therefore, no "innocent" sites. There have never been neutral voids to be filled by buildings, other than the destructive imposition of a strategic emptiness. Nor can I relate to such notions as *genius loci* which seems to grapple with the phenomena of constructed presences in pre-contextual, if not in anti-urban terms.[43]

The rediscovery of "architecture as a system of signs" introduced in the discipline a crisis of meaning, which duplicated the contemporaneous Derridean deconstruction of the sign. Nevertheless, Charney was convinced that architectural meaning is not dissociable from life. For him, meaning was constructed by the inherent logic of a narrative that blends images and words. In his artwork of the 1980s, he assumed that meaning emerges from a process of layering in which layers establish correspondences and associations revealing on one side the collective "signs of recognition" of the city, and on the other side the "ciphers of deception" of architecture as an institutional system.

Charney and his contemporaries

Like the theoretical contributions of other major architects/critics of his generation such as Colin Rowe, Peter Eisenman, or John Hejduk, Melvin Charney's critique represents a sophisticated extension of Le Corbusier's didactic lesson encapsulated in his famous slogan "eyes which do not see." Over the course of thirty years he evolved an original dualistic reading of architecture that looked for "the image behind the *image*."[44] For him, architecture was never an aesthetic or formal problem; nor was it the product of an individual genius. Being grounded in real life, architecture resulted from an innate, if unconscious faculty, common to everyone, which gave meaning to collective built forms such as cities. The architectural institution replicated and aestheticized the forms of vernacular architecture, whether popular or industrial.

Like Robert Venturi and Denise Scott Brown, Charney's interest in pop environments led him to consider architecture as a system of signs. But rather than conceiving the built environment as a system of communication, Charney, in a way analogous to but distinct from Aldo Rossi, saw in popular architecture a repository of experience, a reified memory of the heroic struggle for a place realized by people increasingly deprived of their legitimate means of cultural expression by a repressive technocracy. After 1968, at the moment when architectural culture repudiated utopia, the founding notion of the historical avant-garde, Charney affirmed architecture's fundamental political role. Yet, he did not limit architecture to the status of a repressive apparatus, as he believed that it could also be a means of liberation when appropriated by people. In addition, rather than considering architectural figures as heraldic and decorative devices, he saw in architectural images traces of a language rooted in a collective unconscious. Throughout his meditations Charney metamorphosed constantly the "dialectics" of architecture. In the 1980s, his psychoanalytical model drew architecture out of the semiological duality opposing the syntactic (Eisenman) and the semantic (Venturi) sides of the sign. By 1990, architecture could be understood as a dialectics between the reification of a mythical narrative and the *mise en abyme* of this reification by its replication as an architectural image.

Concluding remarks

Our brief survey of Melvin Charney's relentless critique of late modern and postmodern formalism may provide provisional answers to the questions raised by Anderson's essay. By external history, Anderson plainly referred to the technical and economic factors enabling or limiting the realization of buildings by the *profession*.[45] I suggest here that the theoretical constructs of the *discipline*, which Anderson defined as the "growing knowledge that is unique" to the field of architecture, is also affected by external history. Charney's case illustrates how architecture's internal history is transformed by the introduction in the discipline of concepts drawn from external disciplines. Yet, the "internal order of the field" seems to be shaped not in terms of a dialectics to be overcome, but as a duality – or a "contradiction" as Charney put it – echoing previous dualistic models, such as Le Corbusier's distinction between architecture and engineering, Giedion's famous split between "feeling" and "thinking," and Aldo van Eyck's "twin-phenomena," models which reverberate with the post-1968 opposition of phenomenology and structuralism highlighted by K. Michael Hays.[46] In Charney's work, this duality took the form of oppositions of terms ("design vs. architecture," "image vs. process," "institutional system vs. popular architecture," "oppression vs. liberation," "ciphers of deception vs. signs of recognition," and so on), which were framed with notions found outside the field of architecture (Pop art, Polanyi's tacit knowledge, Foucault's archaeology, theories of the sign, Freudian and Lacanian psychoanalysis, etc.).

Still, if Charney's itinerary constitutes a paradigmatic instance of the general shift from a biological to a linguistic analogy during this period, it also shows that this thematic transformation of architectural theory did not abolish the dualistic framework inherited from the modern movement.[47] In Charney's case, thematic transformation seems consolidated, rather than generated, by the import of external notions. An obsession with the contradictions of an architectural institution perpetuating a mythical and inadequate relationship to the "world" has constantly driven his action; consequently, external references enriched and confirmed a critical argument bred by an issue internal to the architectural discipline.

Some exploratory considerations can be drawn from this state of affairs. Firstly, one can ponder what the status is of the different ideas and tendencies launched in architectural theory. Theoretical frameworks, such as critical theory, postmodernism, critical regionalism, deconstructivism, or pragmatism, are not equivalent and interchangeable. Neither are they surface phenomena, whims of fashion, or the result of external influences: the conditions of their appearance are intimately tied to the internal condition of architecture. Therefore, if the history of the theory of architecture is to be more than the reactivation of forgotten manifestos or the application of an ideological framework proclaiming what history should have been, this activity must uncover the latent logic of the field in mapping the relationships between these concepts and explaining their role in the development of architectural "knowledge."

Secondly, the "knowledge" generated by the "importation procedure" seems inseparable from the architect's critical intent. It is this intentionality that distinguishes theoretical works such as Charney's from the "consumption of theory"[48] tacitly endorsed by a conception of theory's history as a "coming and going of a series of theoretical frameworks."[49] Insomuch as meaning springs from the effects sought by the critical project, such "knowledge" certainly has cultural and social relevance but claims no "scientific" value. So, in Charney's case, the critical outlook generated by "the revelation of what the architectural institution represses" is an instance of "recalibration" aiming at disclosing the theoretical distortion perpetuated by dominant models.[50]

Thirdly, the import of new themes in architectural theory since the 1960s has regularly modified the terms of the internal duality of the architectural field, yet the duality persists, showing that the internal order of the field adapts to, but is not determined by, external history. Simply said, the "rules of the architectural game" remain, without a doubt, remarkably stable in the *longue durée* of its history, while its thematic contents change.

This is a possible way of interpreting what Anderson conceived as *the semi-autonomy of architecture*. Other case studies will be necessary to validate this thesis.[51] This, in itself, is a historiographical project.

Notes

1. Sebastiaan Loosen, Rajesh Heynickx, and Hilde Heynen, "The Shifting Contours of Post-War Architectural Theory," in *The Figure of Knowledge: Conditioning Architectural Theory, 1960s-1990s,* ed. Loosen, Heynickx, and Heynen (Leuven: Leuven University Press, 2020). Author's note: I assume that the editors are referring only to the history of Western architecture from the 1960s to the 1990s.
2. This essay draws upon the research published in Louis Martin, ed., *On Architecture: Melvin Charney, A Critical Anthology* (Montreal & Kingston, London, Ithaca: McGill-Queen's University Press, 2013), 496.
3. Stanford Anderson, "On Criticism," *Places* 4, no. 1 (1987): 7-8.
4. Charney first met Anderson at the ACSA Teachers Seminar held in Cranbrook during the summer of 1964. See: Marcus Whiffen, ed., *The History, Theory and Criticism of Architecture* (Cambridge, MA: MIT Press, 1965). Anderson invited Charney to participate in the symposium entitled "Form and Use in Architecture" held at MIT in March 1969. For this event, Charney read his essay "Experimental Strategies: Notes for Environmental Design," which he concurrently published in *Perspecta 12, the Yale Architectural Journal*, 1969; reprinted in Martin, *On Architecture*, 202-16.
5. Loosen, Heynickx, and Heynen, "The Shifting Contours of Post-War Architectural Theory."
6. Louis I. Kahn, "Concluding Remarks to the CIAM Congress, Otterlo, 1959," in *CIAM '59 in Otterlo*, ed. Oscar Newman (London: Tiranti, 1961), 208.
7. Charney's research was of course in synchronicity with the vernacular trend of the period of which Sibyl Moholy-Nagy and Bernard Rudofsky were preeminent advocates. See: Sibyl Moholy-Nagy, *Native Genius in Anonymous Architecture*. (New York: Horizon Press, 1957), and Bernard Rudofsky, *Architecture Without Architects: A Short Introduction to Non-pedigreed Architecture* (Garden City, NY: Museum of Modern Art/Doubleday, 1964). Charney, who visited the Greek Temples of Sicily, was also inspired by the teaching of Vincent Scully Jr. See Vincent Scully Jr. *The Earth, the Temple, and the Gods: Greek Sacred Architecture* (New haven, CT: Yale University Press, 1962).
8. "Elements are units which can be put together in an architectural game to make anything you like. By observing the rules of the game, i.e., a door as a door, a building may be accomplished, adjusted to change, or distorted to suit a whim." Melvin Charney, "A Journal of Istanbul: Notes on Islamic Architecture," (1962) reprinted in Martin, *On Architecture*, 62-71.
9. Melvin Charney, "Troglai: Rock-Cut Architecture" (1963), reprinted in Martin, *On Architecture*, 72-80.
10. Charney's dichotomy between process and image rephrased Louis Kahn's distinction between "architecture as realization" and "design as imagery." See Kahn, "Concluding Remarks."

11. Melvin Charney, "Place Victoria, Montreal" (1965), reprinted in Martin, *On Architecture,* 116-19.
12. Ibid.
13. Ibid.
14. Melvin Charney, "Grain Elevators Revisited" (1967), reprinted in Martin, *On Architecture,* 169-78.
15. Ibid.
16. Melvin Charney, "Modern Movements in French Canadian Architecture" (1978), reprinted in Martin, *On Architecture,* 321-31.
17. With his project for Osaka published in several international magazines in 1969 and 1970, Charney was recognized as a significant, radical architect and was invited to the International Futures Research Conference in Kyoto (1970) to present his work along with Cedric Price, Archigram, and Yona Friedman.
18. Baird's contrast of the "instrument" and the "monument" concurred with Kenneth Frampton's analysis of the 1927 competition for the building of the League of Nations, which distinguished Meyer/Wittwer's radical utilitarianism from Le Corbusier/Jeanneret's more traditional "humanism." Baird's essay illustrates how the duality inherited from the 1920s reappeared under another guise in the 1960s. See: George Baird, "'La 'dimension amoureuse' in Architecture," *Arena: Architectural Association Journal* 83 (June 1967): 25-30, reprinted and modified in C. Jencks and G. Baird, eds., *Meaning in Architecture* (London: Barrie & Jenkins, 1970); and Kenneth Frampton, "The Humanist versus the Utilitarian Ideal," *Architectural Design* 37, no. 3 (March 1968): 134–36.
19. Melvin Charney, "On the Liberation of Architecture: Memo Series on an Air Force Memorial" (1971), reprinted in Martin, *On Architecture,* 236-45.
20. Melvin Charney, "Towards a Definition of Quebec Architecture" (1971), reprinted in Martin, *On Architecture,* 246-264.
21. Claude Beaulieu, *Architecture contemporaine au Canada français.* Coll. Art, vie et sciences au Canada français (Quebec: Ministère des affaires cultures, 1969). The author of the pamphlet, Claude Beaulieu, was an active promoter of modern architecture during the 1960s. At the time, Beaulieu was an editor of the magazine *Vie des Arts,* in which he published an article on the house in 1966. See: Claude Beaulieu, "À Saint-Sauveur-Des-Monts: Une résidence classique dans la nature sauvage," *Vie des Arts,* no. 42 (1966): 31-41.
22. The architect and owner of the house was Charles Elliot Trudeau, brother of then Prime Minister of Canada Pierre Elliot Trudeau.
23. See: John A. Kouwenhoven, *Made in America: The Arts in Modern Civilization* (Garden City, NY: Doubleday, 1949), 95.
24. See: Michael Polanyi, *The Tacit Dimension* (New York: Anchor Books, 1967).
25. Charney, "Towards a Definition."
26. Melvin Charney, "On the Liberation of Architecture: Memo Series on an Air Force Memorial" (1971), reprinted in Martin, *On Architecture,* 236-45.

27. "On the Liberation of Architecture" was introduced with the following epigraph quoting Walter Benjamin's "The Author as Producer": "The tiniest fragment of everyday life says more than..."
28. Foucault's reflection is found in the first pages of Michel Foucault, *The Archeology of Knowledge*, trans. A. M. Sheridan Smith (New York: Routledge, 1972). Charney acknowledged the decisive impact Foucault had on him in Melvin Charney, "Confrontations in Urban Architecture," in *Ville, métaphore, projet: Architecture urbaine à Montréal, 1980-1990 / City, Metaphors, Urban Constructs: Urban Architecture in Montreal, 1980-1990*, ed. Irena Latek (Montreal: Éditions du Méridien, 1992), 99-103. In this connection, see Jean-François Chevrier, "Art as the Reinvention of an Urban Political Form," in *Melvin Charney, Parcours: De la réinvention /About Reinvention* (Caen, France: FRAC-Basse-Normandie; New York: Distributed Art Publishers, 1998), 162-241.
29. Since the early 1960s, Charney shared the fascination of the Pop artists of his generation for the rhetorical function of mass media imagery, which he compared to the techniques of French "nouveau roman." See Melvin Charney, "The World of Pop" (1964), reprinted in Martin, *On Architecture*, 81-87.
30. See: Melvin Charney, "Low-Income Housing into the 70s with Sewer Pipes and Subsidized Speculation" (1972), and "Learning from the Wire Services" (1976), reprinted in Martin, *On Architecture*, 265-69 and 276-80. Also: Melvin Charney et al., *Tracking Images: Melvin Charney, Un Dictionnaire...* (Montreal: Canadian Centre for Architecture, 2000), English, French and Italian, 99.
31. Melvin Charney, "Other Monuments: Four Works, 1970-1976" (1977), reprinted in Martin, *On Architecture*, 291-304.
32. Ibid. Also: Melvin Charney, "Corridart: Art as Urban Activism," reprinted in Martin, *On Architecture*, 314-19.
33. The official line from City Hall was that the art was obscene and constituted a threat to public safety and security. See: Taylor C. Noakes, "The Mayor Who Wouldn't Let Art Ruin His Olympics," *Citylab*, 30 November 2016. https://www.citylab.com/equity/2016/11/the-mayor-who-wouldnt-let-art-ruin-his-olympics/509102/.
34. For instance, *The New York Times* related the incident on July 17, 1976. A year later, Charney described the project in *Architectural Design*, London; see: Melvin Charney, "Corridart: Art as Urban Activism" (1977), reprinted in Martin, *On Architecture*, 314-19.
35. Melvin Charney, "The Montrealness of Montreal: Formations and Formalities in Urban Architecture" (1980), reprinted in Martin, *On Architecture*, 332-41.
36. Ibid.
37. Melvin Charney, "To Whom it May Concern: On Contemporary Architecture in Quebec" (1982), reprinted in Martin, *On Architecture*, 342-60.
38. Ibid.
39. Charney visibly referred to contemporary postmodern theory as it crystallized at the 1980 Venice Architecture Biennale and as framed by Paolo Portoghesi et al. in *The*

Presence of the Past: First International Exhibition of Architecture – Venice 80 (Milan: Electa/Venice: Edizioni La Biennale di Venezia, 1980). On the Biennale, see: Léa-Catherine Szacka, *Exhibiting the Postmodern – The 1980 Venice Architecture Biennale* (Venezia: Marsilio Editori S.p.a, 2016).

40. Melvin Charney, "Sign of Recognition, Ciphers of Deception" (1983), reprinted in Martin, *On Architecture*, 314-19.
41. Ibid.
42. Charney, "Sign of Recognition."
43. Ibid.
44. Catherine Millet, "Interview: Melvin Charney, explorateur de la mémoire collective," *Art Press* 202 (May 1995): 56-60, reprinted in English translation in Martin, *On Architecture,* 419-24.
45. In the same text, Anderson outlined an expanded understanding of architecture as a cultural field, which is not limited to the works produced by professional architects – the *profession*. He conceived this field as a *discipline* that encompasses the activities of protagonists working in the institutions constitutive of the field (schools, museums, publications, libraries, galleries, etc.), Anderson, "On Criticism."
46. See: K. Michael Hays, *Architecture Theory since 1968* (Cambridge, MA: MIT Press, 1998), x.
47. George Baird traced back this "structural" dualism to the origins of modern architecture in the quarrel of the ancients and the moderns, which opposed the tenets of tradition (François Blondel) and the principles of reason (Claude Perrault). See: Baird, "La dimension amoureuse."
48. The distinction between consumption of theory and theoretical work in architecture made by Diana Agrest and Mario Gandelsonas in 1973 is still relevant, although a revision of its epistemological model is necessary. See Diana Agrest and Mario Gandelsonas, "Semiology and Architecture: Ideological Consumption or Theoretical Work," *Oppositions* 1 (1973): 93-100.
49. Loosen, Heynickx, and Heynen, "The Shifting Contours of Post-war Architectural Theory."
50. For a description of this process, see: Louis Martin, "Against Architecture," *Log* 16 (2009): 153–67.
51. For another case study based on the same method, a comparison the architectures of Peter Eisenman and Bernard Tschumi, see: Louis Martin, "Blanc et rouge, ou l'hétéronomie théorique de l'autonomie formelle," *Cahiers de recherche du LEAP / LEAP Research Notebooks*, 2 (Winter 2018): 28-35.

CHAPTER 8

Dirtying the Real: Liane Lefaivre and the Architectural Stalemate with Emerging Realities

Andrew Toland

A road trip into "reality"

It is 14 April 1988. Let us take a brief road trip with Rem Koolhaas. It lasts a day. We are driving through the Dutch "countryside." This scenario implies something rather leisurely – the motoring equivalent of a *promenade architecturale* – but it seems it must have been something far more frenzied, or at least tinged with risk and danger: he is driving (or so he reports the following day) at a speed of 160 kilometers per hour.[1] We feel a little scared, but the effect of the "landscape" is numbing. We skim through two- and three-story sprawl, concrete frames smeared with insulation or disguised behind mirror glass or the pseudo-regionalism of brick and gables.[2] We hurtle past a motorway restaurant called Rick's; Rem says he hears it "broadcasting distant echoes" of Aldo van Eyck's Stadthalle in Deventer.[3] We zip past Schiphol Airport and on to Amsterdam; although it's not really Amsterdam, as Rem wryly points out to us, since the motorway skips by the city center at a tangent, pulling more and more businesses and institutions away from its core and towards its periphery, drawn by the inexorable gravitational pull of its trail.[4] He accelerates, and we speed back out into the highway sprawl sewn into a fabric of polder fields and architectural dross. We're driving at 160 kilometers per hour because, he says, "that's the speed at which this architecture should be experienced."[5]

I want to use this brief vignette to introduce what I label the "dirty real," a conceptual and aesthetic formation that emerged within the architectural, landscape, and urbanist culture of the 1980s and 1990s; it begins with Liane Lefaivre's importation of the term into architecture at the end of the 1980s but has implications beyond that, up to and including the present (hence the need for the differentiating label I propose). This conceptual-aesthetic formation can also be traced backwards into a longer and larger set of discourses on "realism" within architectural culture, a debate that is, in essence, about how to recalibrate the relationship between discipline-specific theories and constructed narratives of "the world outside."

Lefaivre's transitional interpretation signals a continuity with, but also a modification of, earlier discourses of "realism" within architecture, from the 1950s to 1980s. Each of these "realism" discourses sought (through both texts and images) to establish certain conceptual and aesthetic relationships between architecture and its broader settings, but also internally within architecture culture between modernism and claims of a different approach, as well as between "high" aesthetics or design theory and something supposedly more "real." Adopting the language of the editors' framing of this section of the present volume, Koolhaas's road trip vignette enacts certain of the recalibrations of architectural knowledge about and engagement with the world heralded by this new phase of architectural realism – what Lefaivre would recognize as a "dirty realism" but which subsequently mutated into the new variant strain I have termed the "dirty real."

These more recent "realisms" within architecture culture involve significant modifications of the earlier "realisms" at both a conceptual and aesthetic level. On the conceptual level, they fully incorporate the lessons of cultural theories from other disciplines, ranging from literary and art theory to postmodern philosophy and cultural studies, in which "reality" is presented as "constructed" rather than "natural" and in which "the real" (sometimes "the Real") within architecture and landscape takes on a Lacanian and Deleuzian coloring (with greater and lesser degrees of faithfulness to the originals).[6] The aesthetic dimension expresses an affective stance that is both distancing and equivocal, while simultaneously engaging subject matter and imagery that speaks to broader cultural narratives in ways that are compelling, even transfixing. This aesthetic and affective mode, with significant parallels in contemporary art practice (documenta 11 of 2002 is regarded as a seminal moment in this history[7]), signals a particular response of architecture culture to the contradictions presented by the historical conditions rapidly unfolding in the 1980s and 1990s. An examination of the emergence of dirty realism and a subsequent "dirty real," and their position in architectural "realism" discourses more broadly, sheds light on the evolution of architecture's intellectual culture away from internal disciplinary questions towards a situation wherein the architectural disciplines are producing studies on everything from the effects of sexualized imagery to the configuration of military geography.[8] Seen in terms of the broader themes of this volume, it also presents case of a "not-quite" theoretical framework – one that was seen (at least for brief moments) by certain influential figures within the culture as having heuristic promise but has not quite gained the purchase to establish a wider discourse.

"Dirty realism" in architecture

Koolhaas's road trip was presented as a vicarious experience of reality (or "virtual," as we might have said ten or fifteen years ago) in a slideshow presentation he gave at a conference he organized on April 15-16, 1988, at TU Delft entitled "Whether Europe."[9] The trip may or may not have occurred "in reality" the previous day, as he claimed, or at the purported speed of 160 kilometers per hour.

Koolhaas presents the road trip as a kind of landscape transect cutting through two layers of "reality." On the one hand we see the Dutch "natural" landscape of the polders. But behind this layer of landscape that presents the seemingly "visible" "reality" of the Netherlands is another "reality,", the "reality" of "the speculators," a reality in which (in a claim that presages his later, more famous, assertion of "junkspace"[10]) what remains of the land(scape) is being slowly but steadily consumed by this "continuous belt of strange non-architecture."[11] The relationship of "dirty realism" to the history and diction of landscape aesthetics is not insignificant, as will become apparent below.

What interests us here is not so much the conceit of the road trip Koolhaas is using to present a series of claims about OMA's early work, but rather the influence that this presentation, and the symposium of which it formed a part, had in sparking the thinking of the architectural historian and critic Liane Lefaivre – then one of Koolhaas's colleagues at Delft – on the topic of "dirty realism" in architecture, a descriptor she derived by borrowing the term "dirty realism" from a 1983 editorial by Bill Buford introducing a collection of short fiction entitled "Dirty Realism: New Writing From America" in the British literary journal *Granta*.[12] Lefaivre seized on this term from Buford and adopted it as a way of interpreting the work of architects whom Koolhaas had initially selected for his "Whether Europe" conference.[13] Seeing in the work evidence of a broader architectural tendency, in 1989 and 1990 Lefaivre published a series of articles[14] – as well as editing a special issue of *Archithese* on the theme of "dirty realism"[15] – all of which presented "dirty realism" as the heir to contextualism (including the "pop contextualism" of *Learning from Las Vegas*), but one that expressed a "harsher," "more confrontational" attitude appropriate to postindustrial "world cities" in the wake of Reaganomics and Thatcherism (Fig. 1). The significance of Lefaivre's interpretation lies in its attempt to characterize an emerging architectural response to the nascent urban and related cultural effects of the transformations that had their origins in the 1970s and 1980s but accelerated after 1989-1991 and came to dominate discourse in the late 1990s and early 2000s, encapsulated in the (now-overworked) terms "globalization" and "neoliberalism."[16]

Although the influence of Lefaivre's notion of "dirty realism" was relatively limited (in contrast with her formulation, with Alexander Tzonis, of "critical

Fig. 1. Cover of a special issue of *Archithese* 1-90 (1990), guest edited by Liane Lefaivre, on the theme of dirty realism in architecture. Image courtesy of *Archithese* and Fritz Neumeyer.

regionalism" a decade earlier[17]), it was nonetheless invoked periodically across the span of the following two decades as providing a particular lens onto contemporary conditions perceived to be both confronting and expressed through the architectural disciplines.[18] Although several of these invocations proposed modifications to Lefaivre's application of the phrase, they all had in common an attempt to express a shift in collective subjective experience within the changed environments of contemporary globalized cities and media-saturated landscapes. For Fredric Jameson, "dirty realism" encapsulated aspects of new orders of experience within the spatial turn of late capitalist culture;[19] for Paulette Singley, it signified an unprecedented fusion of the real and ideal, planned and informal, that becomes "all too real";[20] for Stan Allen, it spoke to an anti-idealist approach to architectural construction embedded in a model of the vernacular that is not "local, rural, and specific" but rather "global, urban, and total."[21]

Precisely how and why the adjectival modification "dirty" is thought necessary is something worth exploring further. However, we must first acquire some sense of the uses of the notion of "realism" within architectural culture.

Variations of "realism" in architecture

Although not nearly as well-known as a genre classification as in literary studies or art history, a persistent discourse of "realism" (or discourse framed in cognate variations – "reality," "real," "the real") – has also existed in architectural culture. While the deployments of the term "realism" or "reality" in the postwar discourses of architecture and urbanism, especially from the 1960s into the 1980s, have been diverse[22] and can even be contradictory in their details, what these earlier "realism" discourses share is an interest in the use of the term in thinking about the relationship between architecture and the purported "realities" of its typological histories and vernacular building traditions; of its materiality, production, and tectonics; and of the relationships between architecture and its urban and social contexts, particularly after modernism.[23] More recently, a further set of "realism" discourses emerged, especially in Dutch art and design culture. By contrast to the earlier discourses, these emphasized the hybrid form of the artificial and the natural, and the mediated and the material, within contemporary developed global consumer environments.[24] Lefaivre's "dirty realism" offers us a bridge within this particular genealogy, one that helps us understand the continuities as well as the transformations in architecture's realism discourses.

A key aspect of the earlier invocations of "realism" and "reality" is the attempt to reorient architecture away from the individual object towards the collective contribution of architecture to the broader political project of "the city." This is

Mario Biraghi's analysis[25] of Tafuri's interest in architectural "realism" and issues of "reality" – issues most explicitly addressed in Tafuri's 1985 essay "Architettura e Realismo"[26] but which surface at other points in his oeuvre. In *The Sphere and the Labyrinth*, Tafuri asserts that expressions of "realism" and "reality" within architecture mean that it is no longer "an individual work" that is "at stake, but rather an entire cycle of production" as expressed in urban fabric and the interventions of urban planning under the emerging conditions of "late capitalism."[27] This same impulse towards a concern with what is "at stake" at an urban scale within "late capitalism" is clearly present in Lefaivre's writings on dirty realism; it is made particularly explicit in Fredric Jameson's 2007 essay on "Globalization and Architecture," in which he discusses Tafuri and Francesco Dal Co's opposition of two "realities" in their *L'Architettura Contemporaneo* (although Jameson does not explicitly relate it to his earlier interest in Lefaivre's notion of dirty realism in this later essay). The dissolution of the classical opposition between building and city, and the cessation of the building "as a locus of artistic and functional possibilities" under existing political economic conditions (dual architectural problematics Tafuri and Dal Co had identified even in their own time) become, in Jameson's retelling, "realities" that are vastly amplified under conditions of "global postmodernity."[28] This same dilemma around the agency of architecture and urbanism is a core element of Lefaivre's writing on architectural "dirty realism":

> how to combine the construction of lyrical objects that provoke reflection and action in connection with the construction of a world that reflects the social and ecological realities of our cities – realities that are becoming ever "dirtier."[29]

Jameson's judgment (as well as Tafuri and Dal Co's premonition) was, simply, that this was not possible – that as "realities" became "dirtier," the purchase of architecture, its potency with respect to those "realities" loosens.

It is worth, therefore, to focus on the adjectival modifier Lefaivre introduces into this discourse in light of the pattern of subsequent developments in architecture culture. Here, something further begins to emerge. "Dirty," in the formulation of architectural "dirty realism," signals a movement away from the earlier conditions of "realism" in architecture – the conditions of architectural modernism's response to the industrial capitalist or socialist city. "Dirty" instead heralds a fundamental shift on two fronts. Firstly, it registers a shift in the contexts of architecture, now so easily recognized by us (to the point of cliché) as the effects of "globalization" and "neoliberalism" but which had their origins in the wholesale reorganization of Western societies brought about by the retrenchment of the welfare state and termination of the Bretton Woods international trade and financial system in the 1970s. Secondly, it speaks to an intensified media and consumer culture – conditions that contaminate or overwhelm the cultural order of modernity within which the individual architectural object or designed landscape might once have been thought to have meaning or produce social effects. But this engulfment or swamping is not just a function of political economics or the pop culture–mass media complex. In order truly to understand the full implications of the adjectival modifier "dirty," we need to turn to the aesthetic dimension of this emerging new tendency within architecture culture itself that Lefaivre was attempting to capture and express.

Images of the "dirty real"

For both Lefaivre and for Buford before her, part of the powerful allure of the adjective "dirty" when added to "realism" was the expression of a set of aesthetic preoccupations. Buford seemed to relish referencing (and Lefaivre equally relished quoting his description of) "low-rent tragedies ... roadside cafés, ... supermarkets, ... cheap hotels ... a world cluttered with junk food and the oppressive details of modern consumerism ... a curious dirty realism about the belly-side of contemporary life, but ... [a] realism so stylized and particularized – so insistently informed by a discomforting and sometimes elusive irony – that it makes the more tradition realistic novels ... seem ornate, even baroque by comparison."[30] For Buford (and seemingly for Lefaivre) this was a mode in which the artwork was "so spare in manner that it takes time before one realizes how completely a whole culture and a whole moral condition are being represented,"[31] or an art about "how things fall apart and what is left when they do."[32]

In this context, it is worth reflecting on the specific photographs Lefaivre used to illustrate her articles on architectural dirty realism: a skyline of "oppressive mass housing" behind a rubble-strewn foreground; aerial views of jumbles of office buildings, warehouses, and highway overpasses in a triptych of London, Paris, and Berlin; the industrial urban periphery across the fields viewed through the windscreen of a car travelling down a motorway; the vacant lot and blank façade of an inner urban site; a cluttered alleyway framing a faceless Tokyo mid-rise. All of these are expressions of what she describes as the "hard-edged realities" that parallel the "'under belly' of everyday life in the late 20th century" that Buford found crystallized in a particular literary style.[33] Lefaivre clearly saw an equivalent in a distinct materiality of the 1980s city – "chain-link fences, industrial waste-heaps, parking lots, garages, anonymous high rises."[34]

In a later iteration of thoughts on "dirty realism," found in the introductory essay Lefaivre cowrote with Alexander Tzonis for their 1992 survey book *European Architecture After 1968*, the authors develop Lefaivre's earlier claim by explaining the "return to [dirty] realism in architecture" with reference to earlier aesthetic modes valuing and finding attraction in "the negative qualities of hardness, harshness, roughness, and incompleteness," such as the *non-finito* of the early Renaissance, but especially in Kant's explication of the sublime as a "portrayal of the infernal kingdom [that] arouse[s] enjoyment, but with horror," an aesthetic "perhaps associated with the beginnings of the crisis of confidence in the possibility of a perfect world of urbanity."[35] It makes sense that, having slipped the bonds of the individual building and escaped into the domain of the city, Tzonis and Lefaivre invoke what are essentially terms of landscape aesthetics to understand contemporary relationships to the urban landscape. We can see, in this turn to landscape aesthetics – from the crisp object of architecture to the muck of the contemporary city – a parallel to other contemporaneous conceptual realignments "from object to field," but we can also see the influence of themes in contemporary art[36] and photography. The latter is the theme of Ignasi de Solà-Morales's well-known 1995 essay on the mediation of certain urban landscapes, "Terrain Vague."[37] In that essay, he also explores the particular affective role of urban photography in constructing a postmodern urbanized subjectivity, in which he too makes a specific connection to the aesthetic legacies of the "Romantic imagination."[38] We might equally turn to his 1996 introductory essay to the book accompanying the XIX Congress of the International Union of Architects, with its description of the "reality … [of] [m]otorways, airports, integrated transport systems, cloverleaf intersections, shopping centers, theme parks, massive leisure spaces, tourist centers; build-it-yourself residential areas, mobile homes, alternative forms of housing for users different from the traditional family unit; operations of renewal, for the recovery of heritage in terms of ideological demands and intended for mass consumption; parks, obsolete and protected pre-industrial spaces,"[39] an inventory of repetitive and overwhelming "built environment" intensity that finds its visual analogue in, say, the ACTAR-published 2001 *Mutations*[40] and scores of other architectural books of the ensuing decade. These codes of representation that mark out contemporary "global postmodernity" (as Jameson would have it) are one of the characteristics that suffuse the so-called "big books" of architecture from the late 1990s/early 2000s and continue to define almost an entire genre of art and design publishing produced by imprints such as ACTAR, 010, and NAi (now merged), Taschen, Lars Müller, Hatje Cantz … These codes for representing "reality" also frame the claims of "landscape urbanism" and its "infrastructural landscapes," most evident in Alan Berger's *Drosscape*[41] – but also throughout Charles Waldheim's advocacy of the entire landscape urbanism "project"[42] – and continue to find expression in the still-burgeoning architectural, landscape, and urbanist quasi-art publishing project, a project which sees the entire surface of the earth as subject to, in Neil Brenner's words, "planetary urbanization."[43] These representational strategies overlap with and are often used to illustrate the more recent realism discourses in art and design invoked above, constituting the conceptual and aesthetic formation I label the "dirty real."

Conclusion: The ambivalence of the "dirty real"

The significance of situating an architectural mode of the "dirty real" within a broader characterization of evolving aesthetic sensibilities is that it draws attention to the interwoven affective and intellectual dimensions of unfolding responses within architecture culture to the "challenges" of "globalization" and an ascendant "neoliberal" order that is now judged to frame almost all built production and their contexts. But contrary to the hard-nosed, pragmatic, clear-eyed approach that "realism" (and, even more emphatically "dirty realism") implies, attention to the affective reveals the extent to which these positions are suffused with a detached ambivalence or distanced fascination that belies submission rather than resistance.[44]

Lefaivre and Tzonis's invocation of the Kantian sublime and the crisis of urbanity has parallels in recent discussions of contemporary aesthetics, subjectivity, and affect,[45] but within architecture culture, it speaks to a particular tension between the conditions of spatial production and traditions of the social function of architecture. This is most evident in the photographs that so often accompany architectural discourses from the 1990s onwards: urban landscapes where the subject matter is abject but the crafted image triggers conventions of aesthetic appreciation, even "awe" (in the Kantian sublime sense).[46] An account of "dirty realism" and its origins also provides a way of understanding certain aspects of architectural production as a part of broader cultural production within a period that historians and political scientists are only now beginning to bracket, commencing sometime around 1989 to 1990 and ending somewhere between 2008 and the present.[47]

Given this historiographic uncertainty, as well as the inherent dangers of historical periodization, I can suggest only a provisional conclusion. The "dirtying" of architectural "realism" that Lefaivre was registering as a consequence of seismic political-economic shifts in the end of the 1980s and early 1990s, in combination with a landscape aesthetics that paradoxically combines monotony, abjection, and awe, speak to the difficulties of the architectural theory project in a culture that increasingly (often without realizing it) accepts "reality" as both "natural" and "constructed." While "natural" order may be thought to be subject to mastery and progressive improvement through empirical knowledge and technical intervention, a "constructed" order is susceptible to critique, to exposure of the magician's sleight-of-hand. But the aesthetic and affective registers, in particular, of the "dirty real" seem to suggest these two approaches cancelling each other out – on the one hand, drawing attention to the rhetorical construction of the "real" world of the "contemporary" built environment as a totality, but at the same time signaling a sense of powerlessness in the face of that totality. It is that collapse in contradiction that might ultimately be the true contamination, or "dirtying" of the "real."

Notes

1. Rem Koolhaas, "Tempo 160," *Archithese* 20, no. 1 (January/February 1990): 39-43.
2. Koolhaas, "Tempo 160," 39.
3. Ibid.
4. Ibid., 43.
5. Ibid., 39.
6. This is also what distinguishes it (although there are some inevitable overlaps) from the architectural discourses around the "everyday": cf. Deborah Berke and Steven Harris, eds., *Architecture of the Everyday* (New York: Princeton Architectural Press, 1997).
7. See Mark Nash, "Reality in the Age of Aesthetics," *Frieze* 114 (April 2008): 118-125.
8. E.g., see Nicole Kalms, *Hypersexual City: The Provocation of Soft-Core Urbanism* (Abingdon, UK: Routledge, 2017); Pierre Bélanger and Alexander Arroyo, *Ecologies of Power: Countermapping the Logistical Landscapes & Military Geographies of the U.S. Department of Defense* (Cambridge, MA: The MIT Press, 2016).
9. Koolhaas, "Tempo 160," 43.
10. Rem Koolhaas, "Junkspace," in *Harvard Design School Guide to Shopping*, ed. Chuihua Judy Chung et al. (Cologne: Taschen, 2001).
11. Koolhaas, "Tempo 160," 43 (author's translation).
12. The writers included under this title in the issue of *Granta* (no. 8) were Jayne Anne Phillips, Richard Ford, Raymond Carver, Elizabeth Tallent, Frederick Barthelme, Bobbie Ann Mason, and Tobias Wolff. Buford adds in his editorial that a more "comprehensive collection" might also have included Mary Robinson, Ann Beattie, Richard Yates, Jean Thompson, and Stephen Dixon: Bill Buford, "Editorial," in *Granta* 8, "Dirty Realism: New Writing From America" (Harmondsworth, UK: Penguin, 1983), 5. A further issue (no. 19) of *Granta* devoted to this genre (also edited by Buford, but with no editorial) was published in 1986 under the title "More Dirt: The New American Fiction" (Harmondsworth, UK: Penguin, 1986). The writers included in that issue were Richard Ford, Jayne Anne Phillips, Richard Russo, Ellen Gilchrist, Robert Olmstead, Joy Williams, and Louise Erdrich.
13. In addition to Koolhaas himself, Nigel Coates, Jean Nouvel, Bernard Tschumi, Hans Kollhoff, Laurids Ortner, Carel Weeber, Kees Christiaanse, and Zaha Hadid. In her article, Lefaivre also suggested that the interpretation could be extended outside of Europe to American architects such as Frank Gehry, Lars Lerup, Craig Hodgetts, and Morphosis: Liane Lefaivre, "Dirty Realism in European Architecture Today: Making the Stone *Stony*," *Design Book Review* 17 (1989), 18.
14. Liane Lefaivre, "Il realismo sporco nell'architettura/Dirty Realism in Architecture," *l'ARCA* 28 (1990); Liane Lefaivre, "Dirty Realism in der Architektur," *Archithese* 20, no. 1 (January/February 1990): 14-21.
15. *Archithese* 20, no. 1: "Neue Ansichten: Dirty Realism" (January/February 1990).

16. A simple Google Books Ngram search for "globalization"/"globalisation" shows usage following a classic econometric S curve for new product markets, with the most exponential growth occurring between the mid-1990s and mid-2000s, accessed January 12, 2017, https://books.google.com/ngrams/graph?content=globalization%2Cglobalisation&year_start=1980&year_end=2008&corpus=15&smoothing=3&share=&direct_url=t1%3B%2Cglobalization%3B%2Cc0%3B.t1%3B%2Cglobalisation%3B%2Cc0.
17. See Carmen Popescu, "Critical Regionalism: A Not So Critical Theory" [chapter 10 in this volume].
18. In Koolhaas's *S, M, L, XL*, the "dictionary" contains an entry for "Dirty Realism" and a quotation from Buford's 1983 editorial; a section on OMA's project for the Spui, a 200-metre long section of road in the centre of The Hague is also entitled "Dirty Realism: A Mini-Farce" but contains no suggestions on how to approach the interpretation of this title. Lefaivre is not mentioned: Rem Koolhaas and Bruce Mau, eds., *Small, Medium, Large, Extra-Large: Office for Metropolitan Architecture* (New York: Monacelli Press, 1995), 290, 292; 570-75.
19. Fredric Jameson, *The Seeds of Time* (New York: Columbia University Press, 1994). Jameson's discussion of architectural dirty realism is at 144-59.
20. Paulette Singley, "Los Angeles – Between Cognitive Mapping and Dirty Realism," in *Shaping the City: Studies in History, Theory and Urban Design*, ed. Edward Robbins and Rodolphe El-Khoury (New York: Routledge, 2004), 127; Paulette Singley, "Los Angeles's Dirty Realism," in *Forum Annual 2004*, ed. Kazys Varnelis (Los Angeles: Los Angeles Forum for Architecture and Urban Design, 2004), 47–52.
21. Stan Allen, "SANAA's Dirty Realism," in *The SANAA Studios 2006-2008, Learning from Japan: Single Story Urbanism* (Baden: Lars Müller, 2010), 62.
    Independently, in the late 1980s and 1990s, Spanish architect and editor of *Quaderns* Josep Lluís Mateo had also taken inspiration from Buford's attempt to express a particular contemporary literary mode or style that expressed, Mateo later said, "something that I had intuited at the time and which interested me (though I ... still didn't know it at the time)": Conversation between Iñaki Ábalos and José Lluís Mateo, Barcelona, September 17, 2002, accessed December 17, 2015, https://web.archive.org/web/20081121145712/http:/www.mateo-maparchitect.com/02_jlmateo/analysis/01_entrevista_eng.html.
    The term "dirty realism" has also recently been applied by Jesús Vassallo in his study of the relationships between certain contemporary architects and art photographers, although without specific reference to the earlier usage of the term: Jesús Vassallo, *Seamless: Digital Collage and Dirty Realism in Contemporary Architecture* (Zurich: Park Books, 2016).
22. This chapter discusses "realism" discourse in the tradition of literary and art criticism. It does not address the influence of philosophical realism or the pragmatist tradition in philosophy on architectural discourse (although, on the latter, see Joan Ockman,

"Consequences of Pragmatism: A Retrospect on 'The Pragmatist Imagination'" [chapter 14 in this volume]).

23. The most notable of these were articulated in the late 1960s through to the mid-1980s by Manfredo Tafuri (see further below); in the mid-1970s by Martin Steinmann and Bruno Reichlin in Switzerland (see "Realismus in der Architektur," ed. Martin Steinmann and Bruno Reichlin, *Archithese* 19 [1976]), including overlapping contributions by Alan Colquhoun; by Bernard Huet in France (see *L'Architecture d'Aujourd'hui*, "Formalism-Realism," ed. Bernard Huet, 19 [1977]); and over a similar period in *Oppositions* by Rafael Moneo, Jorge Silvetti, and Giorgio Grassi. Aspects of this history have been explored by Silvia Malcovati (see "Realism and Rationalism: An Italian-German Architectural Discourse," *bfo-Journal* 2 [2016], 5-15) and A. Krista Sykes in her 2004 doctoral dissertation under the supervision of K. Michael Hays, "The Vicissitudes of Realism: Realism in Architecture in the 1970s" (PhD diss., Harvard Graduate School of Design, March 2004). Hays had an interest of his own in "realism" in architecture – a topic he explored in his 1995 book on the architecture of Rodolfo Machado and Jorge Silvetti, *Unprecedented Realism: The Architecture of Machado and Silvetti* (New York: Princeton Architectural Press, 1995). Silvetti himself had written an article for *Harvard Architectural Review* in 1980 entitled "On Realism in Architecture," *Harvard Architecture Review* 1 (1980). Hays also included essays by Steinmann, Reichlin, Huet, and Silvetti about architectural "realism" in his influential 1998 collection *Architecture Theory since 1968* (Cambridge, MA: MIT Press, 1998), 246-53; 254-61; 262-83. An earlier strand of realism, originating with essays by Oriol Bohigas and Alejandro de la Sota in the 1950s and 1960s appears to have been influential in Spain, especially in the Barcelona scene centred around the ETSB, later finding expression in Ignasi de Solà-Morales's essay "Weak Architecture" (printed in English translation in Ignasi de Solà-Morales Rubió and Sarah Whiting, *Differences: Topographies of Contemporary Architecture* [Cambridge, MA: MIT Press, 1997]), which draws together the influence of Bohigas and de la Sota and sets them alongside Tafuri's argument in "Architettura e Realismo" (see below). An independent strand of architectural "realism" discourse also emerged in America in the 1980s and 1990s, developed by Michael Benedikt in his pamphlet *For an Architecture of Reality* (New York: Lumen Books, 1987) and a 1988 issue of *Centre* journal he edited entitled "Buildings and Reality: Architecture in the Age of Information" (*Centre* 4 [1988]). At an urban scale, Peter G. Rowe advanced the notion of "civic realism": Peter G. Rowe, *Civic Realism* (Cambridge, MA: MIT Press, 1997).

24. See, for example, Linda Vlassenrood, ed., *Reality Machines: Mirroring the Real in Contemporary Dutch Architecture, Photography and Design* (Rotterdam: NAi, 2003); Joachim Declerck and Dries Vande Velde, "From Realism to Reality. A Future for Dutch Architectural Culture: An Interview with Pier Vittorio Aureli and Roemer van Toorn," *OASE* 67 (2005): 41-50; 112-20; Ole Bouman, ed., *Architecture of Consequence: Dutch Designs on the Future* (Rotterdam, NAi, 2009); Lukas Feireiss, ed., *Testify! The Con-*

sequences of Architecture (Rotterdam: NAi, 2011); and Giampiero Sanguigni, *Triggering Reality: New Conditions for Art and Architecture in the Netherlands* (Amsterdam: The Architectural Observer, 2012). This more recent set of discourses traces a genealogy back to so-called "Dutch pragmatism" and the related "Big Books" of architecture (see further below) and arguably also traces through to earlier Dutch-Belgian realism discourses (see, e.g., Geert Bekaert, *Rooted in the Real: Writings on Architecture*, ed. Christophe Van Gerrewey (Mechelen, Belgium: WZW Editions & Productions, 2011).

25. Marco Biraghi, *Project of Crisis: Manfredo Tafuri and Contemporary Architecture*, trans. Alta Price (Cambridge, MA: MIT Press, 2013), 135.
26. Manfredo Tafuri, "Architettura e Realismo," in *L'avventura delle idee nell'architettura 1750-1980*, ed. Vittorio Magnago Lampugnani (Milan: Electa, 1985).
27. Manfredo Tafuri, *The Sphere and the Labyrinth*, 4th ed., trans. Pellegrino d'Acierno and Robert Connolly (Cambridge, MA: MIT Press, 1995), 287.
28. Fredric Jameson, "Globalization and Architecture," in *The Domestic and the Foreign in Architecture*, ed. Sang Lee and Ruth Baumeister (Rotterdam: 010 Publishers, 2007), 115-19.
29. Liane Lefaivre, "Dirty Realism," 12. The text quoted in English, which is essentially identical to the final paragraph of Lefaivre's editorial in *Archithese*, is taken from Lefaivre's abstract published in the *Summary of Papers* from UIA XVII Montreal 1990.
30. Buford, "Editorial," 5.
31. Buford quoting Frank Kermode describing the work of Raymond Carver: Buford, "Editorial," 5.
32. Buford quoting Jayne Anne Phillips: Buford, "Editorial," 5.
33. Lefaivre, "Dirty Realism in European Architecture Today," 18.
34. Ibid.
35. Alexander Tzonis and Liane Lefaivre, *Architecture in Europe since 1968: Memory and Invention* (London: Thames & Hudson, 1992), 22.
36. See n. 7 above.
37. Ignasi de Solà-Morales Rubió, "Terrain Vague," in *Anyplace*, ed. Cynthia C. Davidson (Cambridge, MA: MIT Press, 1995), 118-23.
38. de Solà-Morales, "Terrain Vague," 121.
39. Ignasi de Solà-Morales Rubió, "Present and Futures: Architecture in Cities," in *Present and Futures: Architecture in Cities*, ed. Ignasi de Solà-Morales Rubió and Xavier Costa (Barcelona: XIX Congress of the International Union of Architects UIA Barcelona 96, 1996), 11.
40. Rem Koolhaas, Stefano Boeri, Sanford Kwinter, Hans-Ulrich Obrist, and Nadia Tazi, *Mutations* (Bordeaux: Arc en rêve, centre d'architecture; Barcelona: Actar, 2001).
41. Alan Berger, *Drosscape: Wasting Land in Urban America* (New York: Princeton Architectural Press, 2006).

42. Perhaps best illustrated in his descriptions of Detroit in conjunction with his use of Jordi Bernado's photographs in *Stalking Detroit* (Georgia Daskalakis, Charles Waldheim, and Jason Young, ed., *Stalking Detroit* (Barcelona: Actar, 2001) and in a chapter that immediately precedes Singley's chapter on Los Angeles's "dirty realism" (Charles Waldheim, "Detroit – Motor City," in *Shaping the City: Studies in History, Theory and Urban Design*, ed. Edward Robbins and Rodolphe El-Khoury [New York: Routledge, 2004]). Jordi Bernado's photographs are at 80-81.
43. Neil Brenner, ed., *Implosions/Explosions: Towards a Study of Planetary Urbanization* (Berlin: Jovis, 2014). This exact same claim (however, without reference to Brenner) is made by the architect Jacques Herzog in claiming the return of "reality": Jacques Herzog, "Introduction," in *The Inevitable Specificity of Cities: Napoli, Nile Valley, Belgrade, Nairobi, Hong Kong, Canary Islands, Beirut, Casablanca*, ed. ETH Studio Basel, Roger Diener, Jacques Herzog, Marcel Meili, Pierre de Meuron, Manuel Herz, Christian Schmid, and Milica Topalović (Zurich: Lars Müller, 2015). It seems no coincidence that many of the photographs that appear in this book were taken by Bas Princen, and that Princen's photography, in conjunction with the architectural work of OFFICE Kersten Geers David Van Severen, is the inspiration for Jesús Vassallo's claim of "dirty realism" in his recent book (see n. 21 above).
44. Curiously, this parallels Tzonis and Lefaivre's interpretation of an earlier historical moment of architectural "populism" in the 1960s (see Alexander Tzonis and Liane Lefaivre, "In the Name of the People," *Forum* 3 [1975], 10-17).
45. See in particular Siane Ngai's repurposing of the Kantian sublime in the form of a modernist/postmodernist aesthetic and affective register she terms "stuplimity": Siane Ngai, *Ugly Feelings* (Cambridge, MA: Harvard University Press, 2005), 248-97.
46. This is intertwined with recent visual conventions in contemporary photography; e.g., see the work of Benoit Aquin, Nadav Kander, Daniel Beltrá, Susannah Sayler and Edward Morris, Mitch Epstein, and, *a fortiori*, Edward Burtynsky.
47. See, e.g., Timothy Garton Ash, "Is Europe Disintegrating?" *The New York Review of Books*, January 19, 2017, accessed January 11, 2017, http://www.nybooks.com/articles/2017/01/19/is-europe-disintegrating/; Andrew J. Bacevich, "The Age of Great Expectations and the Great Void: History After 'the End of History,'" accessed January 11, 2017, http://www.tomdispatch.com/post/176228/tomgram:_andrew_bacevich,_how_we_got_here/.

CHAPTER 9

Between Making and Acting: The Inherent Ambivalence of Arendtian Architectural Theory

Paul Holmquist

In the rise of contemporary architectural theory, Kenneth Frampton (b. 1930) and George Baird (b. 1939) were among the key theorists and critics who sought to grasp and recover the meaning of architecture in terms its sociopolitical relation to the public realm. For Frampton and Baird, modern architecture's crisis of meaning stems from the loss of an inherent relation to the public realm, and therefore to the possibilities for an affirmative human politics at once critical of, and alternative to, the hegemony of capital. Yet, while drawing inspiration from the critical theory of the Frankfurt School, both Frampton and Baird look to the phenomenological political philosophy of Hannah Arendt to understand how architectural making, insofar as it contributes to the constitution of a common world, is a precondition for the possibility of acting politically and thus a means of potentially recovering an authentic public realm. At the same time, in adopting Arendt's political philosophy to envision a theory of architectural making aimed at the political possibilities of others, Frampton and Baird tacitly interpret her critical analysis of politics in modernity as the basis for a projective and productive theory of architecture.[1] In so doing, they elide the fundamental distinction that Arendt makes between work, the productive activity of making, and action, comprising the activities of creating and sharing a public realm and political life as the realization of human freedom. Although Frampton and Baird traverse the divide between making and acting in different ways and to varying degrees, I argue that they both induce a potentially fatal contradiction between the necessity inherent to making and the freedom essential to politics, which threatens to defeat in advance the recovery of an authentic public realm in Arendt's terms. Frampton's and Baird's architectural theories are therefore marked by a profound ambivalence as to architecture's capacity to take what Baird calls the "ethical risk" of acting towards the political possibilities of others.[2]

Accordingly, in this essay, I examine Frampton's and Baird's adaptation of Arendt's philosophy to architecture in order to reconfigure the bases of architectural knowledge to take account of architecture's relation to the public realm, and how contradictions arise between making and acting in their respective theories that threaten to compromise the freedom at stake within it. I then show how the development of their theories can be understood as attempts to reconcile such contradictions, and how they both ultimately come to sacrifice either action or making and to negate their inherent interrelationship. I conclude, however, that the ambivalence of their Arendtian architectural theories does not signal the failure of architectural theory, as such, to reconcile disciplinary knowledge with philosophical insight but rather reveals the fundamental ambivalence of architecture itself as a projective, productive practice in late modernity, as well as the potential limitations of architectural agency in addressing the political dimension of human life.

As architectural critics, historians, and theorists, Frampton and Baird are heteroclite thinkers who marry complex and sometimes contradictory sources of thought within a theoretical conception of architecture's public dimension that takes its primary impetus from Arendt's seminal work of political philosophy, *The Human Condition* (1958).[3] In this treatise, Arendt reaches back to the origin of the Western political tradition in ancient Greece to recover key concepts by which to critique the development of politics in modernity and the loss of a meaningful public realm. Central to this critique is her original concept of action as the actualization of human freedom in speaking and acting for the sake of a shared, public world of human affairs.[4] For Arendt, action is the constituent activity of politics and the public realm. It is categorically distinct from the activities of work (the constructive and reifying activity that produces the tangible human world) and labor (the productive activity to sustain human biological life), which are both governed by causality and necessity.[5] In speaking and acting publicly, according to Arendt, men and women appear to each other freely by virtue of their concern for what is truly public, and disclose who they truly are as individuals by transcending the exigencies of their private lives. For Arendt, a "space of appearance" arises between men and women whenever they speak or act together, which comprises the essence of the public realm in which human freedom can obtain the fullest, most tangible worldly reality.[6]

Key to Frampton's and Baird's adaptation of Arendt's philosophy is the inherent relation she posits between action and the products of work. The work of fabrication constructs the common world of things that is the concrete precondition for the public realm, and thus the very possibility of politics.[7] By virtue of its commonality, the world allows for the objective sense of reality necessary for speaking and acting to become meaningful, arising out of the plural and diverse perspectives that individuals have of it.[8] But the world is also the communicative context of art and architectural monuments that testify to, memorialize, and orient human action, and whose sheer durability allows it to transcend individual lifespans to become an enduring frame for, and testament to, otherwise ephemeral speech and deeds.[9] The common world thus sustains, conditions, and gives reality and relative permanence to the opening of a meaningful public realm in which people can reliably and freely appear to one another in action and speech. In turn, the meaning of the world of things depends upon its being the concern of action and speech taking place within it.[10] The love and care for the world, as both the concrete environment and the realm of human affairs inhering within it, is thus the central concern of politics for Arendt.[11]

With the rise of contemporary mass society, however, the durability and meaningfulness of the world have dissolved into the totalizing processes of production and consumption as modes of labor.[12] The original distinction between public and private has been lost in the rise of what Arendt calls the social realm, in which once private concerns for biological life, such as economic interest and well-being, assume public significance as the object of politics.[13] With the loss of the common world and an authentic political culture came that of a properly political public realm, in which one could appear other than as a producer or consumer for the sake of life. For Arendt, a world of processes, rather than things, cannot sustain the common, objective reality born of plural perspectives necessary for politics, nor can it testify to, memorialize, or give orientation to action. Without such a shared reality and meaningful frame, the very possibility of action as Arendt understands it comes into question. The space of appearance so vital to authentic public life cannot reliably come into being, nor can human freedom, as the essence of politics, obtain worldly reality.

Frampton and Baird both take Arendt's philosophical theory and account of the loss of a shared world as the basis for critically analyzing modern architecture's crisis of meaning in their primary Arendtian works, including Frampton's "Labour, Work, and Architecture" (1969), "Industrialization and the Crises of Architecture" (1973), and "The Status of Man and the Status of his Objects" (1979) and Baird's *The Space of Appearance* (1995) and other essays.[14] Both look to her theory for an intrinsic relation between architecture and an otherwise intangible public realm as the sphere of political life. In so doing, Frampton and Baird go so far as to interpret Arendt's "space of appearance" and the public realm itself as integral to architectural space. Architecture embodies the public realm by giving durability, form, and expression to man's "public being" in monuments, civic buildings, and urban spaces and articulating the distinction between the public and private realms.[15] In their view, architectural language expresses cultural values to provide the meaningful setting and ground for Arendtian action as public, civic life. In particular,

Frampton draws upon Arendt's theory to define "architecture" according to its public role as the product of work, in contrast to mundane and vernacular "building" as the product of never-ending construction processes, akin to those of labor for the sake of merely living.[16] He goes so far as to assert that a "political reciprocity … must of necessity maintain, for good or ill, between the status of men," as the capacity to live fully human lives through action, "and the status of their objects," in which the role of communicative architectural form is paramount.[17] Baird, on the other hand, emphasizes architecture's expressive and framing relation to public space in terms of its potential to accommodate human action within it. He writes that "the form of the built world … [should] become an architectural analogy of the plurality of the human condition itself," prioritizing architecture's capacity to embody human plurality, Arendt's essential condition for political life, and the common sense of "worldly reality" inhering within human social situations.[18]

Following Arendt, Frampton and Baird see modern architecture's crisis of meaning in the loss of the common world, and above all in the loss of a political, public realm as its proper object in the rise of mass consumerist society. They take up Arendt's critique of utilitarianism to condemn the dominance of functionalism, technological instrumentality, and aestheticism in modern architecture culture, which they blame for the incapacity of architecture to express cultural values other than those of a universal, industrialized consumer society. Yet, in so doing, Frampton and Baird tacitly implicate modern architecture culture in the loss of the public realm through its failure to sustain architecture's inherent reciprocity with public life. Their response to architecture's crisis of meaning is then to recognize and recover the former's responsibility for the public realm, and thus for the possibility of political life. The reconstitution, as it were, of a vital public realm by giving form, expression, and reality to the latent potentiality of public life – the possibility of Arendtian action in a democratic society – thus becomes the central task of architectural making.[19]

Frampton's and Baird's implicit project to recover the public realm as the object of architecture represents in turn a tacit translation of Arendt's critical theory of politics in modernity into a projective and productive theory of architecture. In looking to political philosophy to understand the relation of architecture to sociopolitical reality, they seek to actualize this new self-knowledge in architectural practice. Thereby, they depart significantly from Arendt's thought to posit a theory of making that is also a theory of acting politically – to achieve through making what she reserves exclusively for action, namely, constituting the sphere of common concern, meaning and potential appearance that is the public realm. This shift is especially evident in their earliest writings, where Frampton and Baird both figuratively characterize how architecture "acts" with respect to the public realm to give it form, substance, and reality, as a precondition for political action. They each identify architectural making with acting in different ways, and to different degrees. For Frampton, architecture is a concrete and expressly political act of making, whereby the meaning of the public realm as fundamental cultural values is given tangible, expressive architectural form. For Baird, on the other hand, architecture imbues a certain tangibility and durability to the worldly reality of action itself, by reinforcing and formalizing the social conditions and relationships in which it consists. Yet for both, the meaning and reality of the public realm itself becomes subject to the projective and productive agency of architectural making. As a result, architectural making and architectural objects threaten to supplant the agency that Arendt reserves solely for human actors to collectively constitute the public realm through their own speaking and acting.

Frampton's conception of making-as-acting appears throughout his key, early Arendtian texts, wherein he develops his view of the "political reciprocity" between making and acting in such a way as to confer a near equivalency upon them.[20] In "Labour, Work, and Architecture," he refers to architectural making as a "building act" existentially predicated on properly political action in Arendt's sense, but on whose "inherently public character" and "agency" in creating a permanent human world "the very act of human public appearance depends."[21] In "The Status of Man and the Status of his Objects," he goes on to describe how architecture actualizes this reciprocity between architecture and politics by reifying the space of appearance itself – the essential space of politics, and of meaning – in order to physically manifest man's "public being" in built form.[22] Architectural making for Frampton thereby not only prepares for and memorializes public action through representing collective values in civic form but also effectively becomes the medium of action itself, thus assuming its originary capacity and significance. The creation of an architectural "space of public appearance" expressing the reality and meaning of the public realm here appears as an expressly political act of making that threatens to displace the role of human actors itself.[23]

Baird is much more circumspect than Frampton in identifying architectural making explicitly with acting, asserting instead an analogy with speaking. In "*La Dimension Amoureuse* in Architecture" (1969), Baird draws upon Saussurean semiology to characterize "design acts" as communicative gestures, which as "*parole*" articulate particular instances of the deeper cultural "*langue*" of architecture.[24] Here, architecture itself is an inherently meaningful "language," spoken through form rather than by human actors in order to embody and express cultural meaning and values and evoke the public realm in which actions and speech attain significance. If for Frampton the meaning of the public realm is reified in fabricating the common world, for Baird worldly reality itself is reified through design acts as the condition for human action.[25] In "The Dining Position: A Question of *Langue* and *Parole*" (1976), Baird takes up Arendt's conception of the common world as analogous to a table separating and relating people within a shared, objective, and political sense of reality and calls upon architecture to reify the relational structuring of social situations in communicative form and space as the common world.[26] He charges architecture to foster the qualities of publicity that Arendt demands of the world and the public realm – its capacity to be seen from a plurality of perspectives – such that it becomes an "analogy of the plurality of the human condition itself."[27] In so doing, however, Baird would have architects assume the reality-forming role otherwise reserved by Arendt for acting men and women themselves from their diverse perspectives on the common world, and architecture becomes the concretization of human relations otherwise constituted plurally through action.

By conceiving of architectural making within the domain of Arendtian action, whether explicitly or implicitly, and supplanting human action with that of architecture, Frampton and Baird risk the very freedom at stake in the public realm and invite defeat in advance of their project to recover it. At first glance, associating architectural making with political action would seem to be unremarkable in contemporary theory, having been *de rigueur* for the strand of modern architecture extending from Claude-Nicolas Ledoux in the late 18th century through the early modern avant-garde, and remaining all but unquestioned throughout much of the 20th century. For Frampton and Baird, architecture's presumed capacity for political making falls well within their general orientation to the critical theory of the Frankfurt School. But acting in the mode of making is cataclysmic for Arendt. The radical freedom of action distinguishes it from the making of work. According to Arendt, work entails a single actor who controls the process of making to culminate in a preconceived result, within the ineluctable framework of causality, means, and ends.[28] Making in the realm of politics denies the freedom of plural actors to constitute the world of human affairs and its meaning through their own actions by applying its singular, non-plural conditions of making to politics: one actor, one perspective, and one reality.[29] Furthermore, subjecting action to the causality and instrumentality of making destroys the essential freedom of action and its potential meaning, which is axiomatically undeterminable. To the extent that Arendtian concepts are fundamental to Frampton's and Baird's theory, their framing of the public realm as an object of architecture – a condition to be intentionally achieved, if not actually made, through an exercise of architectural making – jeopardizes, in principle, the very freedom it depends upon. According to a strict reading of Arendt, merely positing the recovery of the public realm as a goal entrains it within the framework of ends and efficient means, cause, and necessary effect and condemns it to failure. In light of the danger posed to freedom through the identification of architectural making with acting politically, Frampton's and Baird's theory appears profoundly ambivalent and places architecture's intentionality and agency in the realm of politics squarely in question.

The radical yet highly conditional freedom that Arendt ascribes to public life has become all but untenable in modernity. Although Frampton and Baird do not acknowledge the contradiction between making in acting implicit in their approaches, they do recognize the danger of acting through architecture upon the political lives of others. Both reject the stridently utopian strands of modernism along with much of the tradition of the modernist avant-garde. Frampton bleakly acknowledges the limits of architecture given the loss of an authentic political culture and public realm in late modern consumer society: "Whether architecture ... will ever be able to return to the representation of collective value is a moot point. At all events, its representative role would have to be contingent on the establishment of a public realm in the political sense."[30] For his part, Baird stresses both the dialogical contingency of architecture with respect to the cultural ground and the danger that attempting to manipulate the experience or meaning of architecture poses to its collective validity.[31] In criticizing Eliel Saarinen's CBS Building as a ruthlessly simplified *Gesamtkunstwerk* and Cedric Price's Potteries Thinkbelt as a "life conditioner" in which students become part of the "servicing mechanism," he decries the "dictatorship of designers" – through either presumption or indifference – in which attempts to manipulate consciousness inevitably fail and impoverish the public realm.[32] "Design acts," Baird writes, are "inescapably partisan."[33] However, he commends architects such as Machado and Silvetti for negotiating architecture's inherent "ethical risk" of presumption or domination by refusing to directly manipulate experience and meaning.[34]

In spite of architecture's limitations and risks, the recovery of aspects of an Arendtian public realm, in some fashion and to some degree potentially latent in contemporary social life, remains the tacit object of Baird's and Frampton's theories as they were subsequently developed over their careers. This development, in fact, can be understood as the attempt to overcome the political ambivalence between architectural making and acting in their thought and to resolve the contradiction between them. In this endeavor, both Frampton and Baird look beyond Arendt to other theorists for help in reconciling her thought to both the potential and limitations of architectural practice. In "On Reading Heidegger" (1975), Frampton locates the public realm in a conception of place that takes its departure from Martin Heidegger's notion of world, and in which the particular forms and values of a culture emerge out of a historical, dialectical relation to natural environment through building.[35] But it is only with "Towards a Critical Regionalism: Six Points for an Architecture of Resistance" (1983) that Frampton concludes that architecture can attempt to compensate for the loss of an authentic underlying political culture and supply new "permanent values" of society for the work of reification.[36] Through resistance to the universality of technology and late capitalist consumer society, architecture can recover a meaningful public dimension and potentially instigate a new political culture. Frampton theorizes how the Heideggerian cultivation of autochthonous "place-form," now in a dialectical relationship with universal technology, allows for an authentic embodiment and expression of particular cultures within globalized society. Through its formal and constructive logics, architecture effects and expresses the identity and values of a people, manifesting their transformative engagement with the natural environment over time, while the boundedness of public place-form is now what allows for and shelters the space of appearance.[37] Architecture "acts" by giving form to the relationship of a people and their way of life grounded in natural needs and modulated according to topography, climate, and light, against the alienating meaninglessness of techno-scientific consumerist civilization.

Here, architecture as fabrication assumes an autonomy for Frampton that, in direct contradiction to Arendt's theory, aspires to the freedom of properly political action in which making – as the transformation of nature according to human needs – possesses an inherent meaning. In this view, architecture is in effect the reification of itself as work, and the public realm is constituted in relation to natural necessity, rather than freedom. Frampton likewise returns human action to a natural basis in order to recover pre-alienated political experience. He asserts that the sensual, bodily experience of material and constructed place-form, as exemplified in Alvar Aalto's Säynätsalo Town Hall, can provide the basis for cultivating an authentic, if resistive, civic and political culture and public realm.[38] Yet it is architecture that finally realizes the meaningful autonomy of action for Frampton in his conception of tectonics as capable of opening a human world through symbolic, constructed form. In "*Rappel à l'Ordre*: The Case for the Tectonic" (1990) and *Studies in Tectonic Culture: The Poetics of Construction in Nineteenth and Twentieth Century Architecture* (1995), Frampton draws upon the philosophy of Giambattista Vico and the architectural theory of Gottfried Semper, among others, to invoke the "critical myth of the tectonic joint" embodying the "existential truths residing in the human experience."[39] To the extent that these "truths," as cultural values, embody the memory of Arendtian work, rather than action, and remain determined and fixed through their tectonic specificity outside of the capacity of actors to freely inflect, transform, or disregard, the ambivalence between making and action is abolished in architecture only for it to become all-acting in constituting the underlying reality and meaning of the common world, effectively leaving human actors to dwell passively within its mythic aura.

While Frampton propounds the agential potential of form, Baird remains wary of architecture's "ethical risk" of impinging on the freedom of action through imposing too strong a form and determinate meaning onto public life. In "*La Dimension Amoureuse*," he writes that architects should rather "offer ... 'ideal' images of human existence, 'ideal' frames for human action,"[40] seeing them as orientational settings for public life that at the same time tangibly reinforce and manifest the relational structure of social reality.[41] Consequently, Baird's theory and criticism into the 1990s turns increasingly towards urban public spaces, framed within a communicative architecture that evokes a potential public realm. He lauds Machado and Silvetti's unrealized projects for public squares in Genoa, Houston, Providence (Rhode Island), and Leonforte (Sicily), proposed in the late 1970s and 1980s, for their "aspiration to *civitas*" and invocation of a shared public life, through a nuanced, abstract language of monumental form and everyday urban "object-types."[42] Baird notes how Machado and Silvetti utilize traditional urban type-forms such as stairs, colonnades, walkways, bleachers, overlooks, and plazas to create "apparatuses of possible urban exploration," which multiply and elaborate the conditions in which a mass public in Benjaminian distraction might attain revelatory, plural perspectives on itself.[43] Architecture here "amplifies the expansive, public potentialities of the subconscious, sensory mobility of bodies in space" to induce a "delirious" provocation of momentary self-awareness.[44] The potential public realm evoked within these projects is not fixed formally or visually but is rather left open to the unfolding of action itself, promising to be, as Baird writes at the conclusion of *The Space of Appearance*, one of "passionate symbolic reinterpretations, the precise social meaning of which we will not be able to determine by ourselves, or in advance."[45]

Yet Baird's tentative optimism fades as he turns increasingly to Walter Benjamin's notion of "distraction" to account for the nature of architectural experience in relation to contemporary mass society, in which action alone can no longer resuscitate a viable public realm. But architecture's power to affect the public unconscious and condition its behavior now presents a heightened danger of manipulation, and Baird eschews any assertion of instrumental or ameliorative agency for it.[46] He instead focuses his theory on the nature of public space itself, conceiving it in terms of a perceptual and experiential spectrum that spans between the poles of distraction and Arendtian action to account for the sheer variety of public social life and behavior.[47] In *Public Space: Cultural/Political Theory: Street Photography* (2011), Baird calls upon art, rather than architecture, to "act" – instrumentally and amelioratively – within public space. He cites the public and gallery installations of artist Dennis Adams and architects Elizabeth Diller and Ricardo Scofidio for their capacity to manipulate the "thresholds of consciousness" of a distracted public to provoke moments of self- and other-awareness in which political action may be possible.[48] Architecture, on the other hand, is relegated to the formal role of mutely ordering and conditioning urban social space to allow for varying degrees of visibility, propinquity, and spatial continuity, and ceding priority to the lived dynamic of a potential public life that can only be discerned, and remembered, through photography.[49] The public realm now appears in his theory beyond architecture's capacity to evoke, let alone propose or recover. Baird ultimately overcomes architecture's so-called ethical risk, and the ambivalence of making and acting, by effectively giving up making itself for the sake of the potential action of spectators that may never be actualized.

Frampton and Baird are finally unable to fully overcome the inherent ambivalence of their Arendtian theory without one side of the making-acting dichotomy prevailing over and nullifying the other. For Frampton, architectural making becomes an expressly political act of resistance, capable of supplying the permanent, authentic cultural values within industrialized, consumer society by becoming their source. Tectonics comes to triumph, however, over all properly political action to constitute the cultural meaning of the public realm as embodied by architecture. Baird reasserts the primacy of action in social situations and relationships over an architecture that becomes increasingly formal, passive, and mute, while ceding its provocative and communicative role to the practice of art. Architectural making eventually retreats from producing things to formally conditioning public social space, ultimately yielding its communicative agency wholly to action. In sacrificing either action to making, or making to action, the development of Frampton's and Baird's theories ultimately fails to sustain the interdependence that Arendt sees between the two, the "reciprocity" between architecture and public political life that they originally discovered in her philosophy.

In responding to the crisis in architectural meaning by appealing to Arendt's political theory, Frampton and Baird reconfirmed the intrinsic relation between architectural making and sociopolitical reality that had long formed a part of traditional architectural knowledge but had little support in modern social and political theory. As David Leatherbarrow has written, the embodied practical knowledge of the structure and patterns of human life had historically comprised what he calls architecture's "ethical reason."[50] Furthermore, self-reflective architectural knowledge, or theory, had always accounted for architecture's disciplinary capacity to accommodate sociopolitical life as a technical, fabricative practice.[51] Addressing the challenges to the historiography of Vitruvianism, Dalibor Vesely has written that "creative architectural thinking is possible only in collaboration with other disciplines, such as philosophy, astronomy, music, geometry, and rhetoric," so that architectural theory's relation to the primary cultural tradition can be illuminated.[52] In appealing to Arendt's political thought, Frampton and Baird renew this longstanding relation, albeit through a critical, analytic framework of knowledge. They rely upon her thoroughgoing critique of political modernity, and of the modern subsumption of political action within the mode of making, for the means by which to reconcile architectural knowledge with the reality of modern political life and the public realm. Yet the development of modern architecture itself was predicated on this very political modernity, in defining itself to various degrees since the late 18th century by presuming a sociopolitical agency of making. In spite of Frampton's and Baird's critical rejection of many aspects of modernist architectural ideology, this agential capacity of architecture remains a latent, if understated, intuitive premise of their theories that is nonetheless refuted by the very philosophy they turn to in order to confirm it.

If the historiography of architectural theory can trace the dialogue it enters into with other forms of knowledge, a key historiographical challenge lies in comprehending and clarifying the points of intersection and exchange so as to contribute to the ongoing project of architecture's disciplinary self-knowledge. The tracing of Frampton's and Baird's engagement with Arendt's thought reveals neither a failure of architectural theory nor a failure of the sociopolitical aspiration of architectural making, per se. To some extent, it reveals how Arendt's understanding of the capacity of making to account directly for, and bear creatively upon, political life may not be as rich or complete as the disciplinary tradition of architectural theory has long held. Arendt's conception of making in *The Human Condition* stems largely from a critical reading of Plato and the ideal city of *The Republic*, rather than other thinkers such as Aristotle, for instance, whose revelatory, poetic, and worldly conception of making was championed by her former mentor Heidegger.[53] Yet Arendt's critique of acting in the mode of making from Plato through the modern era has much to do with her rejection of the remedy it would seem to provide for the unpredictability of action and the chaotic uncertainty of the world of human affairs by controlling action to produce determined ends. However, Arendt acknowledges that architecture, as a public art, in fact requires *prudentia*, the politician's wisdom and foresight with respect to human affairs, and thus is capable of negotiating their relative unpredictability while preserving the essential freedom of action.[54] As such, it is the certainty with which architectural making presumes to address the structure and meaning of human sociopolitical life, let alone the utopian impulse to act directly on this life, that is in turn revealed through Arendt's thought as a limitation of architecture in modernity.

In light of this view, it may be fruitful to conclude by turning yet again to Arendt for an alternative remedy for the unpredictability of action that may further inform architectural knowledge. Against the "frailty" and uncertainty of human affairs she poses the making and keeping of promises, which she argues establish "islands" of relative stability amid the boundlessness of action.[55] Arendt's notion of the promise freely made – and freely kept or abandoned – may offer ways to reconsider the agential dimension of architecture and its potential to address political life without recourse to the aspiration for certainty inherent in the mode of making. Within this new Arendtian framework, architecture might overcome the ambivalence of making and acting only by foregoing any presumption of sovereignty or emancipatory claims, for the sake of the much more radical freedom of others to act.

Notes

I wish to thank the organizers of "Theory's History, 196X-199X. Challenges in the Historiography of Architectural Knowledge" for the opportunity to present an earlier version of this essay for the panel "Leaning on Philosophy," chaired by Filip Mattens of KU Leuven. The comments I received from him and those attending were very helpful in developing the paper for this publication. I would also like to thank Hilde Heynen and Sebastiaan Loosen for their careful reading of the manuscript, and for their questions and suggestions that were invaluable in refining and clarifying the arguments. I am very grateful to Florencia Fernandez Cardoso and the entire editorial team for their dedication, care, and attention throughout the review process. Finally, I wish to acknowledge the generous support of my early research for this essay by the Azrieli School of Architecture and Urbanism at Carleton University and the Peter Guo-hua Fu School of Architecture at McGill University.

1. I use these terms in their general senses to distinguish Frampton and Baird's architectural theory from Arendt's analytic and explanatory political theory.
2. George Baird, "On Publicness and Monumentality in the Work of Machado and Silvetti," in *Writings on Architecture and the City* (London: Artifice, 2015), 245.
3. Hannah Arendt, *The Human Condition* (Chicago: University of Chicago Press, 1958). All subsequent citations refer to the second edition, published in 1998 (see note 4). Frampton and Baird were both active in the extraordinary intellectual architectural scene in London during the 1960s, which along with that of Venice, according to K. Michael Hays, played a central role in the emergence of contemporary architectural theory as it is known today (Francesco Garofalo, Introduction to Baird, *Writings*, 8). They both made seminal contributions to *Meaning in Architecture* (1969), edited by Baird and Charles Jencks, along with other important critics and theorists such as Françoise Choay, Reyner Banham, Joseph Rykwert, Alan Colquhoun, and Christian Norberg-Schulz. In addition to Hannah Arendt, Frampton and Baird have been similarly influenced by the key figures of the Frankfurt School such as Theodor Adorno, Max Horkheimer, and Jürgen Habermas, and the phenomenology of Martin Heidegger and Maurice Merleau-Ponty.
4. Hannah Arendt, *The Human Condition*, 2nd ed. (Chicago: University of Chicago Press, 1998), 7-8; see also ch. 5, "Action," 175-247.
5. Ibid., 7-8; see also ch. 3, "Labor," 79-135, and ch. 4, "Work," 136-74.
6. Ibid., 198-99; Hannah Arendt, "What is Freedom?" in *Between Past and Future: Eight Exercises in Political Thought* (New York: Penguin Books, 2006) 147, 153, 167.
7. Arendt, *The Human Condition*, 50-58.
8. Ibid., 57.
9. Ibid., 94-96, 173.
10. Ibid., 204.

11. Hannah Arendt, "Introduction *into* Politics," in *The Promise of Politics*, ed. Jerome Kohn (New York: Schocken, 2005), 106.
12. Arendt, *The Human Condition*, 230.
13. Ibid., 38-49.
14. Kenneth Frampton, "Labour, Work and Architecture," in *Meaning in Architecture*, ed. Charles Jencks and George Baird (London: Barrie & Rockliff, The Cresset Press, 1969), 150-68; "Industrialization and the Crises in Architecture," *Oppositions* 1 (September 1973): 57-82; "The Status of Man and the Status of His Objects," in *Labour, Work and Architecture* (London: Phaidon, 2002), 25-43; George Baird, *The Space of Appearance* (Cambridge, MA: MIT Press, 1995).
15. Frampton, "The Status of Man," 42.
16. Frampton, "Labour, Work and Architecture," 151-54; "The Status of Man," 26.
17. Frampton, "The Status of Man," 42.
18. George Baird, "The Dining Position: A Question of *Langue* and *Parole*," in *Writings on Architecture and the City* (London: Artifice, 2015), 50; 46-50.
19. It should be made clear that nowhere do Frampton or Baird express what they would be the first to denounce as the "naïve" intention to recover or reconstitute the public realm solely through architecture, or indeed, to recover a lost political culture. They are all too aware of Arendt's own view on this, in her writing that "the activity of work…although it may not be able to establish an autonomous public realm in which men *qua* men can appear, still is connected with this space of appearance in many ways" (Arendt, *The Human Condition*, 212). Yet Frampton and Baird also recognize that the fabricated common world must be "fit for appearance" (Arendt, *The Human Condition*, 173, 204) and that absent an authentic political culture in contemporary consumerist society, this fitness can take an anticipatory, evocative, provocative, and invocative – if not exactly productive – stance in their theory with respect to the ever-present potentiality that Arendt reserves for action and the space of appearance itself.
In addition, both Frampton and Baird trained and worked as architects; they have also spent their careers educating architects. They remain dedicated to the critical, but "operative," role of architectural history and theory in support of contemporary practice, and the critical capacity of architectural practice itself to constructively engage the political realm (see, for instance, Baird's "'Criticality' and its Discontents," *Harvard Design Magazine* 21 [Fall 2004/Winter 2005]: 16-21). Their Arendtian critiques of modern and contemporary architecture can only be seen as serving the wider ambition to recover, albeit with some ambivalence, a properly public, and truly political vocation for architectural practice. In this ambition, architecture's own public address of a potential public life could plausibly be understood as constituting a tentative, provisional public realm, according to its more conventional understanding as socially invested, public space. It is for these reasons that I claim that Frampton's and Baird's theories effectively, if not expressly, aim at the recovery of the public realm

as the object of architecture, and that this recovery amounts to the reconstitution, in some fashion and to some degree, of a public realm from the latent potentiality of Arendtian action.
20. On this point, see also Jorge Otero-Pailos, *Architecture's Historical Turn: Phenomenology and the Rise of the Postmodern* (Minneapolis, MN: University of Minnesota Press, 2010), 224-26.
21. Frampton, "Labour, Work and Architecture," 151.
22. Frampton, "The Status of Man," 42.
23. Properly speaking, there can be no "space of appearance" that arises out of and through architecture for Arendt, as it only comes into being "wherever men are together in the manner of speech and action, and therefore predates and precedes all formal constitution of the public realm" (Arendt, *The Human Condition*, 199). Arendt furthermore states that the public realm itself is "the potential space of appearance between acting and speaking men" (Arendt, *The Human Condition*, 200), whose meaning does not consist of cultural values but in being "the realm where freedom is a worldly reality" (Arendt, "What is Freedom?" 153). Lastly, there is no properly political – i.e., truly free – agency that can be ascribed to nonhuman actors, as action is "the only activity that goes on directly between men without the intermediary of things" (Arendt, *The Human Condition*, 7).
24. George Baird, "*La Dimension Amoureuse* in Architecture," in *Writings on Architecture and the City* (London: Artifice, 2015), 22-24.
25. Baird, "The Dining Position," 42-43, 46, 48.
26. Arendt, *The Human Condition*, 52.
27. Baird, "The Dining Position," 50.
28. Arendt, *The Human Condition*, 140-44.
29. Ibid., 220-30. Arendt emphasizes that the attempt to do away with the plurality of actors – as when action is subsumed within the mode of work – "is always tantamount to the abolition of the public realm itself" (ibid., 220).
30. Frampton, "The Status of Man," 40.
31. Baird, "*La Dimension Amoureuse*," 23.
32. Ibid., 28-29.
33. Ibid., 43.
34. Baird, "On Publicness and Monumentality," 245.
35. Kenneth Frampton, "On Reading Heidegger," *Oppositions* 4 (October 1974), n.p.
36. Kenneth Frampton, "Towards a Critical Regionalism: Six Points for an Architecture of Resistance," in *Labour, Work and Architecture* (London: Phaidon, 2002), 77-89.
37. Ibid., 85.
38. Ibid., 88-89.

39. Kenneth Frampton, "*Rappel à l'Ordre*: The Case for the Tectonic," in *Labour, Work and Architecture* (London: Phaidon, 2002), 103; *Studies in Tectonic Culture: The Poetics of Construction in Nineteenth and Twentieth Century Architecture* (Cambridge, MA: MIT Press, 1995), 1-27.
40. Baird, "*La Dimension Amoureuse*," 34.
41. Baird, "The Dining Position," 47-48.
42. Baird, "On Publicness and Monumentality," 244-45.
43. Ibid., 244.
44. Ibid., 243-44.
45. Baird, *The Space of Appearance*, 347.
46. George Baird and Mark Lewis, *Queues, Rendezvous, Riots: Questioning the Public in Art and Architecture* (Banff, AB: Walter Phillips Gallery, 1994), 6; George Baird, *Public Space: Cultural/Political Theory: Street Photography* (Amsterdam: SUN, 2011), 10, 25.
47. Baird, *Public Space*, 52.
48. Ibid., 133.
49. Ibid., 94-131.
50. David Leatherbarrow, "Architecture is Its Own Discipline," in *The Discipline of Architecture*, ed. Andrzej Piotrowski and Julia Williams Robinson (Minneapolis, MN: University of Minnesota Press, 2001), 86.
51. Ibid., 95.
52. Dalibor Vesely, "The Architectonics of Embodiment," in *Body and Building: Essays on the Changing Relation of Body and Architecture*, ed. George Dodds and Robert Tavenor (Cambridge, MA: MIT Press, 2002), 30-31.
53. Martin Heidegger, "The Question Concerning Technology," in *The Question Concerning Technology, and Other Essays* (New York: Harper & Row, 1977), 6-12.
54. Arendt, *The Human Condition*, 91.
55. Ibid., 243-47.

CHAPTER 10

Critical Regionalism: A not so Critical Theory

Carmen Popescu

One year after the much disputed *Strada Novissima* at the Venice Biennale in 1980, which promoted history as one of the chief actors in conceiving of architecture and its meaningfulness, a new concept proposed a different way to deal with the same idea of architectural meaning.

Labelled "critical regionalism," the new concept appeared as a response to Paolo Portoghesi's installation (and its misuses of history), but, above all, as a solution to the ongoing architectural crisis. Its criticality was to be understood particularly in this sense: an upgraded version of historic regionalism, called upon to fight the causes of the persisting architectural crisis, as well as its devious byproducts, such as postmodernism and its decried use of history.

If critical regionalism proved to be a pervasive, if not powerful tendency, it succeeded thanks to a carefully crafted theory, built up through a series of programmatic texts whose various authors (historians and critics) turned the new current into a major expression of contemporary architectural thinking. I will explore here how this theoretical apparatus was shaped, by briefly considering its prehistory (as a legitimizing starting point) and by analysing its further development through the contributions of the major figures of critical regionalism. By doing so, I will interrogate the very construction of the concept (which one may term a "travelling concept," problematic in that it is not fully assimilated, or too diluted),[1] in order to decipher the agenda of the statements at stake. Focusing on the epistemological construction – on the background of an abridged chronological evolution, which might give the impression of a linear narrative – and on its inconsistencies will allow me to address the question of how "critical" critical regionalism actually was.

(Re)considering regionalism

It is a shortcut of modernist historiography to present modernism and regionalism as two opposed stances. Certainly, several reasons led to the establishment of this shortcut, the apex being most probably the clash between the two at the International Exposition of Art and Technology in Modern Life (Paris, 1937), whereby modernist architecture was relegated to a secondary position by the monumental neoclassicism of the main building and the picturesqueness of the *Centre régional*.[2]

Thus, it might have appeared as paradoxical when the most significant actors of the Western architectural scene gathered in the wake of World War II in a symposium organized by the Museum of Modern Art, New York (MoMA) to consider how regionalism could rescue modernism.[3] Propelled by a chronicle Lewis Mumford had published a few months before in *The New Yorker*,[4] the symposium frontally addressed the question of modern architecture's crisis, thought to originate in its capacity (or lack thereof) to convey expressiveness and a certain humanism. Mumford's essay addressed this issue, noting that there was an ongoing change both in Europe and America which proved that modern architecture was "past its adolescent period" and "its assertive dogmatism," that it was ready to go beyond the machine. As an example, he pointed to the Bay Region style, "a free yet unobtrusive expression of the terrain, the climate, and the way of life on the Coast," insisting on how such an architecture could provide a "native and *human* form of modernism."[5]

As the debates revealed the lack of meaningfulness as the most critical problem of the crisis of modern architecture, the logical remedy, according to historian Henry-Russell Hitchcock, was to enhance its capacity to convey "expressiveness."[6] In his intervention to the symposium, Hitchcock singled out several architectural expressions, insisting on two of them, namely "monumentality" and "domesticity," both directions to be massively explored in the postwar years. Theorized in the early 1940s by Sigfried Giedion, with Josep Lluis Sert and Fernand Léger, and debated in a 1948 special issue of *The Architectural Review* (responding somehow to the MoMA symposium), monumentality would embrace several different paths in the coming decades, often flirting with history.[7] As for what Hitchcock called "domesticity," it evolved in a straight connection with the concept of site (understood as an inhabited place), rekindling many of the (forgotten) values of regionalism. Labelled as "new" or, later, "critical" in order to distinguish it from its (banned) historic form, this rekindled regionalism was to be developed as a "humanized" modernism.

This might be seen as the beginning of the travelling journey of the concept of critical regionalism. The MoMA symposium marked a (pre)founding moment, which cut – implicitly or explicitly – the connections with the history of architectural regionalism, a move that would later affect its (travelling) legacy.

(New/critical) regionalism reloaded: An incomplete brief history

The paradox of the MoMA symposium embracing regionalism was all too obvious, and several of the participants knew it very well. When presented with the "novelty" of the Bay Region style, Walter Gropius manifested his surprise, stating that expressing the terrain, the climate, and the way of life was "almost precisely, in the same words, the initial aim of the leading modernists in the world twenty-five years back."[8]

That modernism and regionalism were not that irreconcilable was an unspoken truth. The connection with the site and its materiality, the interest in tradition as transmission of an essential architectural thinking was interpreted in various degrees and various manners by several main figures of modern architecture, from Adolf Loos to Le Corbusier, from Marcel Breuer to the Spanish GATEPAC or the Italian group around Giovanni Pagano, to name only few. But if the concern already existed, it had little – if any – theoretical grounding. This latter developed progressively by numerous contributions that laid, often disparately, such theoretical foundations.

One of the most influential in this sense was Martin Heidegger's lecture at the Darmstadt Fifth Colloquium in 1951. Arguing that space does not have a value per se if it is not understood as place, that is, in its multilayered physicality and spirituality,[9] Heidegger's discourse was perceived by the architects attending the colloquium as a leading thread. Its inspirational impact was particularly instrumental for the further development of two architectural directions, which were to evolve in close proximity: regionalism (in its critical version) and phenomenology.

The notions of place and dwelling were already of interest to the architectural community. Three years after the Darmstadt lecture, two historians addressed them in their own manner: Sigfried Giedion exhorted a "new regionalism" while Sibyl Moholy-Nagy praised "anonymous architecture."[10] Both texts introduced several pivotal elements for the future discourse on critical regionalism: the input of the regional diversity, the connection with the site, the necessity to understand space as place, and the importance of tradition seen as continuity.

Written as a militant text, Giedion's essay represented an updated alternative to his previous engagement with "New Monumentality." The historian saw in the "new regionalism" a "developing trend," explaining it as a space-time conception, whose motivating force was the "respect for individuality and [the] desire to satisfy the emotional and material needs of the area" and finally "cosmic and terrestrial conditions." The new trend was described as a clear acknowledgement of otherness, both because of its relation to "the so-called 'technically underdeveloped areas'" and of its attempt to repair the long-lasting injustice of a dominating Western culture. For its part, Sibyl Moholy-Nagy's "anonymous architecture" provided another point of view on otherness and marginality. In her essay, she analysed the vernacular examples from the Heideggerian perspective of the connection between man and his site and recommended them as a source of inspiration for contemporary architects. According to Moholy-Nagy, vernacular and the tradition it encapsulated were the closest to an essential thinking in architecture.

Attempting to look beyond the Western architecture, Giedion and Moholy-Nagy aimed in fact to infuse meaning to this latter. Meaning would be precisely one of the key notions debated by numerous architectural publications. Among these, the journal *Perspecta* played a decisive role by introducing Heidegger, through Kenneth Frampton and Christian Norberg-Schulz, to a large architectural audience, thus preparing the scene for the emergence of new sensibilities, able to "deal with the progressive disenchantment of the world."[11]

When critical regionalism was launched as a concept in 1980-1981, its positioning took advantage of both a certain existing familiarity with the issues it would convey and of the novelty of its being wrapped up in a new packaging. The concept was launched by Alexander Tzonis and Liane Lefaivre through two texts – "Die Frage des Regionalismus" and "The Grid and the Pathway" – to be considered later as the founding texts of critical regionalism.[12] Before they came up with the label, Tzonis and Lefaivre guest-edited a special issue of *Le Carré Bleu* in 1980, overtly attacking historicism as the central source of crisis in contemporary architecture. In their introductory essay, they sketched a possible alternative to all these recent deviations; unnamed as yet, this alternative was referred to simply as "the new architecture."[13] The same year, while a student at Harvard and working under Tzonis, Anthony Alofsin wrote "Constructive Regionalism," a plea for a nuanced understanding of regionalism as composed of a multitude of meanings.[14] The young Alofsin expressed his "hope" that "an incisive clarity would render regionalism a constructive tool in the production of architecture."

What happened next is easily imaginable: Tzonis and Lefaivre replaced "constructive" with "critical" – a highly hot term and attitude at the time – thus finding a name for their "new architecture" and at the same time coining a label that would become iconic. The iconicity of the latter was to further increase when the concept was embraced by Kenneth Frampton in 1983.[15]

The consecration: Pomona meeting

But what turned critical regionalism into a real concept (though it was the third stage of its journey as I have followed it here), akin to a paradigm, was the so-called Pomona meeting.

Organized in 1989 by Spyros Amourgis,[16] the event was presented as "The First International Colloquium on Critical Regionalism" and aimed to proclaim the new current as the architectural path to be followed, both for its ethical values and its long-lasting legitimacy. As Marvin Malecha, dean of the Pomona College of Environmental Design, remarked in his preface to the proceedings, the colloquium was "not so much about a new movement as about the renaissance of long-forgotten values."[17] In his view, there was an urgent need to revive the latter in order to again include "the social imperatives in the process of design" and thus to forge a "coherent philosophy" for a new architecture.

That was precisely Amourgis's goal, who deplored the "formalistic approach and narrowing perspective of architectural ideology" that led, according to him, "to a search for security in the past and the coalescence of the 'Strada Novissima' of the Venice Biennale."[18] As Amourgis noted, the real problem was not history, but the lack of an appropriate study of it, resulting in a young generation "historically confused and with misconceptions about the modern legacy." Deprived of philosophical training, young architects were thus left "ideologically naked."

In this context of theoretical emergency, critical regionalism was presented as "the first theoretic statement since the last meeting of Team X," which recommended it as the valid alternative to the confusion ruling over the architectural field. The meeting acknowledged Lefaivre and Tzonis as the generators of critical regionalism's theoretical foundations, while presenting Frampton as the creator of an "embryonic canon," with his list of six points offered as a definition of the current.

The discussions outlined several important features for defining critical regionalism: its relation to the place (understood as a complex concept bringing together context, environment, history, and culture), its criticality (both against "meaningless modernization" and "vernacular sentimentalism"), and, above all, its capacity to signify. While the latter appeared as the main scope to be pursued – "the continuation of this discourse in search of meaning" – it was obvious that the speakers had different understandings of what this meant. Amourgis singled out three tendencies in his introduction to the proceedings, emphasizing either the environment, the historic and cultural values, or the social ones. And he insisted on the different orientation of the speakers from the "Old World" and those from the "New World": the first favoured the "ingrained historic roots and values," while the second privileged "the natural environment as a predominant reference system." The cover of the proceedings enhanced this theoretical haziness: surprisingly for a colloquium held in California, home of the Bay Region Style, the new current was represented by the Torre Velasca in Milan.

However, as stated by Tzonis and Lefaivre during the meeting,[19] critical regionalism was expected to leave behind any possible dissonances and go beyond its natural (and regrettable) attachment to identity issues in order to be able to respond to global problems.

Theorizing critical regionalism

By making this statement, Tzonis and Lefaivre clearly intended to project critical regionalism onto the international scene, pushing it outside its somehow obvious role of a niche architecture for "so-called 'peripheral' regions." They insisted on this position particularly because the global problems they referred to, "anomy and atopy," were, in their view, most urgent in "superdeveloped parts of the world."[20]

From this perspective, which set an ambitious agenda for critical regionalism, it was imperative to theorize it and at the same time demonstrate that its capacity of meaning was the opposite of postmodernism's irresponsible use of symbols. This somehow echoed Karsten Harries's reflection on meaning in architecture and authenticity (the topic of the 1983 *Perspecta* issue), that he understood as a matter of recovering "architecture's natural symbols" instead of "play[ing] with the symbols of the past."[21]

Aiming to proclaim critical regionalism as the solution to the architectural crisis, Tzonis and Lefaivre endeavoured both to define its criticality and to shape a consistent narrative of its historicity. This latter, covering the entire history of architecture, from Vitruvius and the primitive huts to contemporary examples, was meant not only to state the legitimacy of regionalism but also to dispel any possible controversy related to it. Hence, Tzonis (in charge of the historical discourse) condemned most of the nineteenth- and the early twentieth-century regionalist architectures for being "chauvinistic" and manipulative in their use of history. By doing so, he perpetuated the cliché of a conflictual relationship between modern and regionalist architecture. Being afraid of possible misappropriations of the term, he insisted on its resignification, while providing a mystified narrative of its former use: "Regionalism was *not* the term that architects themselves were referring to. It was a conceptual device that we choose to use as a tool of analysis. To make the argument more accurate and explicit we combined the concept of regionalism with the Kantian concept *critical*."[22] Moreover, he confessed that together with Lefaivre, they thought to go even further: "we even publicly suggested that the concept of regionalism should be abandoned and replaced by realism, hereby erasing the middle part of re-'gion'-alism."

Introducing the notion of realism into the equation was a clever move, which was actually already anticipated by Frampton in 1981: it meant not only that the new current inherited one of the major modernism's principles (essential for the very doctrine of the twentieth-century modernity, as explains Alain Badiou) but also that it reflected the new ways of understanding "reality."[23] Additionally, it was a manner for Tzonis and Lefaivre to affirm their reformist convictions, by challenging the existing hegemonies: "Realism was highly appropriate in reflecting a commitment to the exploration of the identity of the particular (of each case), rather than the generalities of the doctrines."[24] Alleviated from its picturesque hollow frivolity (staged since the 18th century) and from its "chauvinistic" bias (related to nationalist claims), critical regionalism was ready to endorse the role of the perfect rescue solution. Not just a providential solution, but the right answer for actual needs, since it solved the architectural crisis by mediating "the impact of universal civilisation with elements derived indirectly from the peculiarities of a particular place."[25]

Tzonis and Lefaivre borrowed this last statement from Kenneth Frampton, whom they acknowledged in Pomona as "the critic whose writings have helped raise and spread the issue of Critical Regionalism more than any other in the last ten years." Indeed, starting with his "Prospects for a Critical Regionalism" published in the 1983 issue of *Perspecta* on authenticity, Frampton imposed himself as a theoretical authority of the new current.[26] His positioning, soon to be endorsed by the very wide readership of his *Critical History of Modern Architecture*, was founded on a twofold approach.[27] On the one hand, he built his theoretical apparatus on strong philosophical references, such as Heidegger's distinction between space and place, Hannah Arendt's "space of public appearance," and Paul Ricœur's reading of a "hybrid world culture" as a cross fertilisation between rooted culture and universal civilisation.[28] Building on these references, Frampton imagined critical regionalism as a "culture of resistance," one which is dialectical and fights against a centric discourse, seeking to "self-consciously … deconstruct universal modernism in terms of values and images which are locally cultivated, while at the same time adulterating these autochthonous elements with paradigms drawn from alien sources."[29] Such a reading enabled the historian to situate critical regionalism and to distinguish it both from former regionalist expressions (the simplistic evocation of a sentimental vernacular) and from current possibly related architectures (the demagogic populism and the ironical use of the vernacular).

On the other hand, Frampton reinforced the impact of his theoretical construct by translating it into an articulated scheme. He introduced this scheme already in 1983, presented as "six points for an architecture of resistance," analysing the substance of critical regionalism through a series of notions: culture and civilisation/ the rise and fall of the avant-garde/ critical regionalism and world culture/ the resistance of the place-form/ culture versus nature: topography, context, climate, light, and tectonic form / visual versus tactile.[30] Expanded to ten points, and further on reduced to five couples of opposed notions – space-place / typology-topography / architectonics-scenography / artificial-natural / visual-tactile – the scheme appears as a manifesto, clearly alluding to Le Corbusier's "five points towards a new architecture" (1927).[31]

But while complexifying the notion of resistance, in explicit opposition to the domination of a hegemonic discourse, Frampton progressively internalised his understanding of critical regionalism. He accomplished this shift in a 1990 essay that went far beyond the limits of critical regionalism in its attempt to recover the essence of architecture as both practice and discipline.[32] The new concept Frampton forged for the occasion, the "poetics of construction," allowed a different angle for fighting futility in architecture ("resist the contemporary tendency to reduce architecture to scenographic efforts"), grounding in a more consistent manner the lasting values of the discipline. By taking this shift, the historian at the same time reinforced his belief that critical regionalism should be seen as an attitude and not as a matter of style, expanding through the idea of grounding both its materiality and its spirituality. This subtle displacement in Frampton's approach, comparable to Juhani Pallasmaa's exhortation in favour of a "regionalism of the mind" instead of a geographical one,[33] signalled already a fissure in the foundations of critical regionalism.

A problem? Is there a problem?

Despite their relatively different positions – Frampton more on a theoretical ground and Tzonis and Lefaivre more as "hagiographers" – the three main defenders of critical regionalism aimed to reach a similar goal. Defending its agenda went beyond an "ideological taxonomy"[34] or a simple remapping of the architectural landscape; what they hoped for was to reframe the values of (contemporary) architecture and, as a consequence, to reframe the historiographical discourse.

But as Keith Eggener noted in his "critique against critical regionalism," this discourse laid on a problematic intellectual construct.[35] The historiographic reframing appeared to be less efficient than imagined, showing signs of malfunctioning on multiple levels. The first problem could be seen in the very fact that, while attempting to reform architectural historiography, critical regionalism was not a historiographic category but rather a label forged on the scene (and in the context) of architectural criticism. This uncontrolled displacement from concept to labelling opened the door both to a misuse of the notion (by its authors and its further adepts) and a loss of its working force. Frampton seemed aware of this danger, hence his thorough labour on the theoretical background followed by the eventual shift to tectonics, which he thought to be a more powerful category for embodying a culture of resistance.[36] On their side, Tzonis and Lefaivre attempted to avoid a heuristic problem by articulating their narrative via two distinctive voices – Tzonis embracing regionalism as a resilient flow running through the entire history of architecture with Lefaivre anchoring it in the present of architectural criticism.[37] But if this twofold approach succeeded in dissimulating the clash between the two different epistemological logics of history and criticism, it could not solve the confusion created by the conflation between meaning and intention, two key elements in assessing regionalism.

On the front of peripheral architectural production, the historiographic impact of critical regionalism appeared as even more problematic. While defending peripheries, critical regionalism reinforced their geopolitical belonging, stressing their marginality. As a niche narrative of alternativeness, it was reduced to a mere ply within the manifold discourse of an illusionary global history of architecture; meanwhile its intended particularization singularised yet again peripheries for their specificities. Furthermore, their differences could be perceived as a cultural marketing in the context of late capitalism. Commenting on the strange crisscrossing between technology and authenticity – brought together since Giedion's "new regionalism" – Alan Colquhoun remarked when the concept was launched that what was celebrated through critical regionalism "would seem to be more the loss of authenticity than its recovery."[38]

Indeed, the very theorization of critical regionalism came from a central position, which ironically resumed a certain intellectual colonisation in terms of architectural thinking.

To conclude: A disputable criticality

The theoretical bubble produced around critical regionalism attempted to embody both more and less than it actually entailed. Fuelled by a background of crisis, critical regionalism involved a militant dimension, explicit since the first writings attempting to theorize it: Frampton made clear his position defining it as a "call to arms."[39] "New" and later "critical" regionalism were presented as a "good" architecture, as opposed to a "bad" architecture, this latter embodied alternatively (or altogether) by the devious tendencies in contemporary practice and/or the hegemonic discourse attempting to flatten architectural thinking. Paradoxically enough, the bubble around critical regionalism has undoubtedly contributed to this flattening, through its shift into a highly fashionable phenomenon (nurtured, constituting another paradox, by Tzonis's and Lefaivre's writings).

But the disputable criticality of critical regionalism has its origin in its misformulation. On the one hand, the *longue durée* defended by Tzonis and Lefaivre managed to create the illusion of a travelling concept, thus concealing its indefectible connection with modernity, and more precisely with the modernist crisis, whose mutations were in fact responsible for the urge for a "meaningful" architecture. On the other hand, the condemnation of "historical" regionalism – reduced to its historicist aesthetic and its nationalist claims – engendered a misunderstanding of the current, which emerged as a critical response from the very beginning, without waiting for the modernist crisis to posit itself critically. Hence, though "critical" appeared as an instrumental notion for defining critical regionalism, the term suddenly faded. Insisting on the historicity of an unchangeable idea, Tzonis and Lefaivre dropped it and went back to the generic "regionalism."[40] Frampton went also beyond the labelling, either turning critical regionalism into a mere facet of his more complex "constructed poietics" or reframing it as "the salient importance of landscape."[41]

Seen from these entangled perspectives, critical regionalism seemed to have failed its role of providential solution, proving to be a mere "refolution," to paraphrase Charles Jencks.[42] Ironically enough, Jencks used this invented term, borrowing it from the political scientist Timothy Garton Ash, to comment on postmodernism as "critical modernism."

I would argue that critical regionalism could be seen as a version of this critical modernism. When the concept was launched, it aimed to save the modernist doctrine and to legitimize it on a renewed basis. Hence its stubbornness to fight history – modernism's main adversary. Eggener actually related the arrival of critical regionalism on the architectural scene to the rise of resurgent nationalism worldwide.[43] From Giedion to Tzonis and Lefaivre, and partially to Frampton, the doctrine of the renewed regionalism was explicitly shaped against the resurfacing of history in architecture. Fighting against historicist excesses and its formalist approaches (what Frampton labelled as "scenography") was finally a manner of evacuating history through geography, a way of opposing the vertical hegemony of History (in the Hegelian sense) with the embracing horizontality of Geography (as a Herderian response) – culture versus civilisation.[44]

So perhaps critical regionalism was less an architecture *of* resistance than an architecture *meant to provide* resistance – a disguised manner of keeping a certain hegemonic discourse alive.

Notes

1. See Sibylle Baumbach, Beatrice Michaelis, and Ansgar Nünning, "Introducing Travelling Concepts and the Metaphor of Travelling: Risks and Promises of Conceptual Transfers in Literary and Cultural Studies," in *Travelling Concepts, Metaphors and Narratives: Literary and Cultural Studies in an Age of Interdisciplinary Research*, ed. Sibylle Baumbach, Beatrice Michaelis, and Ansgar Nünning (Trier: Wissenschaftlicher Verlag, 2012), 1-21. If it is difficult to consider critical regionalism as a travelling concept from an interdisciplinary perspective; however, its transnational authorship and the reinterpretation of its long genealogy constitute strong arguments in favour of its travelling fortune.

2. Jean-Louis Cohen, ed., *Les années '30: L'architecture et les arts de l'espace entre industrie et nostalgie* (Paris: Editions du Patrimoine, 1997); Jean-Claude Vigato, *L'architecture régionaliste: France 1890-1950* (Paris: Norma Editions, 1994); Deborah Hurtt, "Conciliation and Controversy: Regionalist Architecture at the 1937 Paris Exposition," in *Genius Loci: National and Regional Architecture, Between History and Practice*, ed. Carmen Popescu and Ioana Theodorescu (Bucharest: Simetria, 2002), 224-29.
3. [MoMA], "What Is Happening to Modern Architecture?" *The Bulletin of the Museum of Modern Art* XV, no. 3 (Spring 1948). Retrieved from Vincent B. Canizaro, ed., *Architectural Regionalism. Collected Writings on Place, Identity, Modernity and Tradition* (New York: Princeton Architectural Press, 2007), 293-307.
4. Lewis Mumford, "The Sky Line: Status Quo," *The New Yorker* 23 (October 11, 1947), 104-10.
5. My emphasis.
6. [MoMA], "What is Happening to Modern Architecture?" 299.
7. Sigfried Giedion, "The Need for a New Monumentality," and "Nine Points for Monumentality," in Sigfried Giedion, *Architecture, You and Me. The Diary of a Development* (Cambridge, MA: Harvard University Press, 1958), 25-39, 48-51; Gregor Paulsson, Henry-Russell Hitchcock, William Holford, Sigfried Giedion, Walter Gropius, Lucio Costa, and Alfred Roth, "In Search of a New Monumentality: A Symposium," *Architectural Review* (September 1948): 117-28.
8. [MoMA], "What is Happening to Modern Architecture?" 301-2.
9. Martin Heidegger, "Building, Dwelling, Thinking," in Martin Heidegger, *Poetry, Language, Thought* (New York: Harper and Row, 1971), 143-62.
10. Sigfried Giedion, "New Regionalism," in Giedion, *Architecture, You and Me*, 138-51; Sibyl Moholy-Nagy, "Environment and Anonymous Architecture," *Perspecta*, no. 3 (1954).
11. K. Michael Hays, "*Perspecta* 11-22: Searching for Authenticity," in *Re-Reading Perspecta: The First Fifty Years of the Yale Architectural Journal*, ed. Robert A. M. Stern, Alan J. Plattus, and Peggy Deamer (Cambridge MA: MIT Press, 2004), 780-86.
12. Alexander Tzonis, Liane Lefaivre, and Anthony Alofsin, "Die Frage des Regionalismus," in *Für eine andere Architektur*, ed. Michael Andritzky, Lucius Burckhardt, and Otto Hoffmann (Frankfurt: Fischer, 1981); Alexander Tzonis and Liane Lefaivre, "The Grid and the Pathway," *Architecture in Greece*, no. 5 (1981).
13. Alexander Tzonis and Liane Lefaivre, "Narcissisme et humanisme dans l'architecture contemporaine," *Le Carré Bleu*, no. 4 (1980), 1-15.
14. Anthony Alofsin, "Constructive Regionalism," in Canizaro, *Architectural Regionalism*, 369-73. The text was written in 1980 and revised in 2005.
15. A 2019 issue of *Oase. Journal for Architecture* (no. 103: "Critical Regionalism Revisited"), edited by Tom Avermaete, Veronique Patteeuw, Hans Teerds, and Lea-Catherine

Szacka, examines the canonical role of Kenneth Frampton's concept of "Critical Regionalism," reaching beyond its traditional interpretation.
16. Of Greek origin, Spyros Amourgis was an architect and planner who rotated between Greece, Great Britain, and the US. His involvement with the Pomona meeting might be understood as a consequence of the "Greek connection" opened by Tzonis and Lefaivre through their article "The Grid and the Pathway." As a matter of fact, Amourgis himself seemed to have been already sensitized to the dialogue between architecture and its site, as one of the positions he occupied in Greece was as a secretary general for the National Tourist organization (http://www.rethinkathenscompetition.org/uploads/juries-2nd/Amourgis%20CV.pdf, retrieved September 5, 2019). This sensibility was probably enhanced while in Pomona, surrounded by the examples of the Bay Region style.
For what I called the "Greek connection" and its impact on developing critical regionalism as a travelling concept, see Stylianos Giamarelos, "Intersecting Itineraries beyond the Strada Novissima: The Converging Authorship of Critical Regionalism," *Architectural Histories* 4, art. 11 (2016): 1-18. DOI: http://dx.doi.org/10.5334/ah.192.
17. Marvin Malecha, "Preface," in *Critical Regionalism. The Pomona Meeting – Proceedings*, ed., Spyros Amourgis (Pomona, CA: College of Environmental Design, California State Polytechnic University, 1991), iii.
18. Spyros Amourgis, "Introduction," in Amourgis, *The Pomona Meeting*, vii-xii.
19. Alexander Tzonis and Liane Lefaivre, "Critical Regionalism," in Amourgis, *The Pomona Meeting*, 3-28.
20. Tzonis and Lefaivre, "Critical Regionalism."
21. Karsten Harries, "Thoughts on a Non-Arbitrary Architecture," *Perspecta* 20 (1983), 10-20.
22. Tzonis and Lefaivre, "Critical Regionalism"; Alexander Tzonis and Liane Lefaivre, *Critical Regionalism: Architecture and Identity in a Globalized World* (Munich: Prestel, 2003).
23. Kenneth Frampton, "Du néo-productivisme au post-modernisme," *L'Architecture d'Aujourd'hui*, no. 213 (1981): 2-5; Alain Badiou, *Le siècle* (Paris: Seuil, 2005). In the quoted article, Frampton associated regionalism to realism, by quoting Oriol Bohigas's "Towards a Realistic Architecture" (1967). For the 1980s-1990s interpretation of "reality", see Lefaivre's adopting from literary theory the concept of "dirty realism" (thus a truly travelling concept) in Andrew Toland, "Dirtying the Real: Liane Lefaivre and the Architectural Stalemate with Emerging Realities" [chapter 8 in this volume].
24. Alexander Tzonis, "Introducing an Architecture of the Present. Critical Regionalism and the Design of Identity," in Tzonis and Lefaivre, *Critical Regionalism*, 10.
25. Tzonis and Lefaivre, "Critical Regionalism," 22.
26. Kenneth Frampton, "Prospects for a Critical Regionalism," *Perspecta* 20 (1983): 147-62. Frampton touched upon regionalism in 1981 when writing "Du néo-productiv-

isme au post-modernisme," where he already associated it to a "subtle and stubborn resistance."
27. Kenneth Frampton, *A Critical History of Modern Architecture*, 3rd ed. (London/New York: Thames and Hudson, 1992).
28. Kenneth Frampton, *Labour, Work and Architecture: Collected Essays on Architecture and Design* (London/New York: Phaidon Press, 2002).
29. Frampton, "Prospects for a Critical Regionalism."
30. Kenneth Frampton, "Towards a Critical regionalism: Six Points for an Architecture of Resistance," in *The Anti-Aesthetic: Essays on Post-Modern Culture*, ed. Hal Foster (New York: The New Press, 1983), 17-34.
31. Frampton rewrote his 1983 essay in 1986; this new version was published in its French translation in 1997. Kenneth Frampton, "Ten Points on an Architecture of Regionalism: A Provisional Polemic," *CENTER*, no. 3, "New Regionalism" (December 1987): 20-27; Kenneth Frampton, "Cinq points pour une architecture de résistance," *Poïesis*, no. 5 (1997): 177-83.
32. Kenneth Frampton, "Rappel à l'ordre: The Case for the Tectonic," *Architectural Design* 60, no. 3/4 (1990): 19-25.
33. Juhani Pallasmaa, "An Archipelago of Authenticity. The Task of Architecture in Consumer Culture," in *Architecture, Ethics and the Personhood of Place*, ed., Gregory Caicco (Hanover/London: University Press of New England, 2007), 41-49.
34. Frampton, "Du néo-productivisme au post-modernisme," 5.
35. Keith Eggener, "Placing Resistance: A Critique of Critical Regionalism," in Canizaro, *Architectural Regionalism*, 395-407.
36. Kenneth Frampton, *Studies in Tectonic Culture. The Poetics of Construction in Nineteenth and Twentieth Century Architecture* (Cambridge, MA: MIT Press, 1996).
37. Tzonis and Lefaivre, *Critical Regionalism*; Alexander Tzonis and Liane Lefaivre, *Architecture of Regionalism in the Age of Globalization. Peaks and Valleys in the Flat World* (London/New York: Routledge, 2012).
38. Alan Colquhoun, "Regionalism and Technology," in Alan Colquhoun, *Collected Essays in Architectural Criticism* (London: Black Dog Publishing, 2009), 228-29; originally published in *Casabella*, no. 491 (May 1983).
39. Frampton, "Du néo-productivisme au post-modernisme," 5.
40. Tzonis and Lefaivre, *Architecture of Regionalism in the Age of Globalization*.
41. Kenneth Frampton, *Five North American Architects: An Anthology by Kenneth Frampton* (New York: Columbia University GSAPP/Lars Müller Publishers, 2012).
42. Charles Jencks, *Critical Modernism: Where is Post-Modernism Going?* (Chichester: Wiley-Academy, 2007), 7, 10.
43. Eggener, "Placing Resistance."
44. Carmen Popescu, "Space, Time: Identity," *National Identities* 8, no. 3, "Space, Time: Identity," ed. Carmen Popescu (2006), 189-206.

SECTION 3

The Misuses of History

CHAPTER 11

The Historiographical Invention of the Soviet Avant-Garde: Cultural Politics and the Return of the Lost Project

Ricardo Ruivo

A problem that seems to escape the notice of most who study the field of Soviet architecure is the fact that since the 1960s Western thought on – and indeed, the entire established historiography of – Soviet architecture has historically developed within a specifically Western conceptual framework. While issues surrounding translation from Russian, as well as those of accessibility to sources, have always been on the mind of researchers and historians, the more fundamental problem of translation between conceptual frameworks has never really registered among the producers of what is today a mainstream historiographical narrative. As in the field of social sciences, conceptual frameworks in architecture are developed, among other things, through the production of historiography. As such, there is an evident contradiction inherent in the production of a historiography of architecture in socialism by Western academics over the period in which liberal politics replaced Marxism as the dominant framework of what could be called the academic "lefts." This contradiction is not only problematic for the field of the history in question but also represents an interesting condition in and of itself from the point of view of a critique of historiography as a critique of ideology.[1] Here it will be argued that, within the Western liberal framework, this historiography of Soviet architecture became a tool for the consolidation of a specific, currently dominant, architectural ideology, which is linked to the ascension of a liberal alternative to the left in cultural studies and politics since the 1960s effective demise of class politics in Europe.

The contemporary version of this established narrative has recently had a particularly noticeable presence in London. In 2012, a resurgence of interest in the topic placed the historiography simultaneously at the level of serious research and at that of architectural pop-culture.² This interest continued until 2017, when a veritable explosion of attention to the topic predictably took hold of the city's cultural institutions in the context of the centenary of the Soviet revolution. This happened in the same year when liberal politics seemed to be imploding, particularly in the Anglo-American world, a backdrop within which the tension between cultural politics and class politics seemed accentuated.

We should frame our critique of this historiographical narrative as being intrinsically connected to different understandings of politics, functioning precisely along the line that separates class politics, understood within a Marxist framework, and cultural politics, understood as its liberal-bourgeois alternative that became dominant after the 1960s. This distinction operates through historiography in architectural discourse today, which is well expressed in the London 2017 celebration of the cultural conquests of October. As one small but typical example, one could look at the description for an event in the Royal Academy of Arts in London in April 2017, part of a series on the Soviet "avant-garde." The text says:

> "*Byt*" is a Russian term that encompasses daily life, domesticity, and lifestyle. After the revolution of 1917, architecture had to create the material conditions that would lead to the new "socialist" individual and corresponding "*byt*." The term therefore carries the ambition of utopian projects of the past and invites us to consider how contemporary architecture can serve, or indeed facilitate, a way of life for our time.
> In post-revolution Russia, communal housing was the primary mechanism to create a truly collective society and eliminate the bourgeois domestic sphere. (…)
> (…) There are many who see communal living or co-living as the ideal solution to the housing crisis, regarding a communal lifestyle as socially beneficial, sustainable and economically viable. The idea of pooling funds, space and resources for greater shared gains is becoming increasingly enticing and many are willing to give up on privacy to achieve these benefits.³

One sees here how the Russian concept of *byt*, historiographically imbued with revolutionary potential, morphs into a form of cultural resistance to the economic tragedy of late neo-liberal capitalism and its crisis.⁴ This resistance, far from being a political one, culturally embraces the scarcity created by the crisis of the profit margins and fetishizes its social consequences, presenting overcrowding and poverty as progressive opportunities. So the explicit politicization of the Soviet "avant-garde" becomes an ideological facilitator for an architectural cultural project of what could be called neo-liberal communalism. One could also add as an aside that this method of achieving a certain kind of metaphysical "meaning" in architectural discourse is a sort of inverse Heideggerian proposal; substitute a German word-to-meaning relationship with a Russian one, and the idealist, essentialist metaphysics are now suddenly revolutionary instead of reactionary.

"The avant-garde" and "the project"

Here we propose that this particular ideological articulation is historically constructed from the 1960s onwards through two key categories, "the avant-garde" and "the project."

The category of "the project" is meant here as the one Manfredo Tafuri attacks between 1968 and 1973, from his *Teorie e Storia* to his *Projetto e Utopia*. There is no need to describe his argument here in detail; a quick summary will suffice. "The project" emerges in an embryonic form in 1968 in *Teorie e Storia*, in the context of a critique of ideological deformations in architectural historiography that Tafuri calls "operative criticism." But it only becomes a central category for him in the following year's essay "*Per una Critica dell'Ideologia Architettonica*," where he expands his critique of ideology in architecture in more explicit Marxian terms. The category of "the project" is, in the context of his critique, a specific ideological entity of the architectural discipline that ascribes to itself the messianic capability of producing a social future. Tafuri understands "the project" as a central element of "avant-garde" thought, emerging from the structures of disciplinary autonomy in development in bourgeois society already since the Italian Renaissance, and defines it as an ideological veil through which architects and architectural historians perceive social/historical structures and their transformation. Through this veil, the cultural intellectual idealizes their role as supra-historical and independent of class interests; the cultural agency of the architect is able to replace politics as the mode of transformative social praxis, replacing political struggle with the design of solutions that smooth over and harmonize the contradictions of history. As such, "the project" simultaneously reproduces existing social structures while pretending to alter them and ascribes to the architect a privileged position in society as a designer of futures. The defense of this privileged position is perceived by Tafuri consistently as a defense of architects' own class interests as liberal intellectuals, as well as protecting the notion of a special quality of intellectual labor in the context of revolutionary politics that would do away with such privilege.[5]

The category of "the avant-garde" is more difficult to define with precision, and indeed, that is a crucial point of the argument. "The avant-garde" takes on many meanings from the 1960s onwards, yet at the same time always denotes the same kind of meaning. It presents itself mostly as a fixed category, while in fact being incredibly diverse in its associations. It is simultaneously a precise historiographical category, corresponding to a strict periodization – the interwar period

– and an aesthetic meta-category that goes as far back as the category of art itself. It carries an implicit political undertone and at the same time may be defined on a strictly formal, art-historical level. Its politics are anti liberal-bourgeois (whether revolutionary or fascist, depending on the historical conjuncture); at the same time, it is associated to an elite of a liberal profession and imbued into contemporary liberal aesthetic discourse. It is anti-mainstream, while being the vanguard of the mainstream.

Many would revel in the ambiguities here listed, and indeed the contemporary proliferation of the category does precisely that. But a rigorous historicization of the category permits identifying in these ambiguities the conceptual mechanisms producing precisely the ideology of "the project." These ambiguities are structural and foundational to the use of the category; they are not simply a later distortion of an original more rigorous use, and they are constructed and articulated historiographically. It is through the decisions made in the practice of history writing – its conceptual frameworks and divisions and periodizations – that the wider uses and ideological functions of such a category develop and become established in their broadest ways.[6] In the definition of these uses and functions, the role of the historiography of the Soviet "avant-garde" is instrumental in the specificity of its political articulation.

There is no need to produce here an account of the history of the category of "the avant-garde" from its Saint-Simonian origins to the eve of the 20th century. While such history is interesting and already points to what will be the central problematic of this essay, it is sufficient to tackle the history of the category from the moment it resurfaces in aesthetic discourse after World War II. One should say resurfaces because the category all but disappeared after World War I. While many people are aware of this, it is never a waste to state it as explicitly as possible: the term "the avant-garde" is not a term generally used by those who are identified as such by current historiography. This is especially true for the Soviet "avant-garde," operating in a context where the vanguard role was clearly attributed to the party as a political agent, and certainly not to cultural agents. Agents of what we call "the avant-garde" generally thought of themselves as part of the specific trend or movement they were organized around – they were supremacists, constructivists, formalists, etc., and they fought for their school against others. The notion that, despite their quarrels, they all had a fundamental commonality that enables us to place them in the same categorical box is never fully generated by those agents themselves, but it does emerge slowly from the political struggles they engage in, initially around the term "constructivism." For example, in 1930 the Soviet architectural group OSA – the group self-identifying as "constructivist" – established an alliance with their historical enemies in the remainders of the old ASNOVA – a previous group that they accused of "formalism" – in the context of OSA's political dominance in Moscow's architectural circles and their push for a unification of all movements under their wing in the new group VANO.⁷ We see also how the newer group VOPRA – a later group of younger architects trained in postrevolutionary academia who had also joined OSA and ASNOVA in 1929 in a joint declaration (defending what we could today call "modernism" – another category that had no general use at the time) – denounce the traditionalist architecture produced by several old established architects of the prerevolutionary period, reject VANO, and make the constructivists their main target immediately aftwards. However, a clear periodization that matches what we now call "the avant-garde" does not really become formalized until after World War II, and it comes, curiously enough, as an article of "Stalinist" critique. While the younger generation of architects who led VOPRA did establish the "constructivism" of their elders as their enemy and accuse them of being just as "formalist" as the ASNOVA "formalists" that OSA critiqued, "constructivism" was for them specifically the constructivist group OSA, not a general umbrella term for every single architectural trend and movement founded before theirs. It becomes so only with the emergence of the category of "socialist-realism," which isn't really formulated with great precision before the short period when Soviet cultural policies were defined by Andrei Zhdanov, Stalin's minister of culture from 1946 to 48.⁸ "Constructivism" as a meta-category for, essentially, all architectural and visual arts groups from the revolution to the early 30s is then the first form of "the avant-garde" and defines it as a periodization, but it comes from its enemies, the term itself becoming kind of a slur. It remains so till the end of the Stalinist period and keeps its negative associations even in the context of the posterior denunciation of "Stalinism" by his successor, Nikita Khrushchev. The Khrushchevite critique of "Stalinist" aesthetic guidelines, produced between 1954 and 1956,⁹ made no break with the category of "socialist-realism" and merely joined a condemnation of "Stalinist" monumentalism to the already-established condemnation of "constructivism." Till the mid-1960s, both "constructivist" flights of fancy and "Stalinist" kitsch monumentalism were considered "formalist." "Constructivism" as a category only starts being rehabilitated in the early 1960s in Soviet academia and is only really the object of serious interest towards the turn to the 1970s.¹⁰ This is also the time when an interest in historicizing Soviet architecture, particularly that of the first couple of decades, develops in the West, part of the general interest in historicizing "modernism" as a whole.

Historiographies and origin stories

It is useful to separate the Western historiography of Soviet architecture into two distinct phases, one from the mid-60s to the early 80s, and one from then onwards. This distinction can be defined specifically through the use of the explicit term "the avant-garde" – while it is mostly absent in the first phase, its generalization effectively defines the second.[11] The second phase comes with a merger of two very different bodies of historiography that develop in the first phase, bodies that don't really interact much and are mostly defined by disciplinary areas. Specifically, there is one body of Western historiography of the Soviet "avant-garde" that constructs the first accounts of the developments in the visual-arts, and one that deals with architecture. They have different agents, different concerns, and above all, different ways of articulating aesthetics and politics.

They both start at the turn to the 1960s, and both then lay dormant till the eve of 1968. The visual-arts historiography begins firmly in England, with the efforts of Camilla Gray from 1959 onwards.[12] The architectural historiography begins in Italy, with issue 262 of C*asabella-Continuità* in 1962 fully dedicated to a first attempt at a comprehensive historicization of Soviet architecture from 1917 to the present, followed the next year by Vittorio de Feo's *URSS: Architettura 1917-1936*, effectively the first Western book on the subject.

It is however only around 1968 that interest in early Soviet art and architecture – again, the term "avant-garde" was not yet in general use – really explodes in Britain, Germany, France, and on the American East coast. The first of a huge wave of exhibitions of late Russian and early Soviet visual arts happens in Berlin in 1967 and continues to 1973.[13] Starting in 1971, a similar wave of articles in arts journals in the same countries cover the same materials, and several books compiling Russian texts are published by American authors after 1973.[14] Again, English is the language that mainly dominates the visual-arts historiography. Meanwhile, the architectural historiography remains in Italian and French. Anatole Kopp's landmark work begins in 1967 with the publication of *Ville et Révolution* and goes on till 1978, while a wave of Italian books starts with Vieri Quilici's *L'Architettura del Costruttivismo* in 1969.[15]

Within the architectural historiography there are important differences between the approaches of the Italians and that of Kopp,[16] but here we will address only the crucial difference between the continental historiography of early Soviet architecture and the mostly Anglo-American historiography of early Soviet visual arts. That difference lies in what could be called the "origin stories" of what would become known as "the avant-garde," which is directly linked to the specific meaning of the term "constructivism" for each of these two bodies of work. Essentially, the meaning of the term is so different as to effectively constitute two different "constructivisms" as historiographical objects, which in turn have a relation to two different "constructivisms" as historical objects.

A particularly good example of this is the way Lissitzky's work is used. This most cliché of objects is useful here simply because he served in 1966 as the first contact the Anglo-American architectural circles had with the historiography of visual-arts "constructivism" and simultaneously the preferred object through which visual-arts historians broached architecture.[17] For their historiography, Lissitzky is simply an architectural manifestation of "constructivism," and through him the historiography nearly covers early Soviet architecture from its own visual-arts point-of-view.[18] For the continental architectural historiography, Lissitzky lies mostly outside of "constructivism," for he is entirely unrepresentative of the problems that define the Soviet architectural debate in the late 1920s and early 30s. To understand the complicated nature of the terms, one should realize that Lissitzky was indeed a part of the international "constructivist" movement, self-identifying with the term, in the early years of the revolution between Russia and German-speaking Europe. But he was also part of the architectural group ASNOVA – albeit a distant one – against which the OSA constructivists organized themselves after 1926. As such, it is useful to note that there are not one, but two historical Soviet "constructivisms": one in the visual arts till the early 1920s, and one in architecture from the 1920s onwards. The "constructivisms" don't mix and their agents are largely different. They are mutually incompatible for reasons not to be listed here but that can be summed up by stating that architectural "constructivism" forms in 1926 in a large measure as a critique of visual arts "constructivism."[19]

The different ways of understanding this category, crucial to the definition of a periodization, have a direct relation to what was referred to as "origin stories." The continental architectural historiography puts the genesis of what will be later called "the avant-garde" firmly as a political beginning intrinsically connected to October. "Constructivism" is for these continental historians ascribed mostly to OSA, the category then being first and foremost a specific movement, be it one that is generally perceived to be the most advanced and sort of final form of the professional "project" of architecturally articulating socialist politics. The inherent political character of "constructivism" puts it, for these historians, as the vanguard of the vanguard; with this, architecture would fulfill its mission to plan the reorganization of the built environment to produce the new man of the future. The narrative of this continental historiography should be read as a case of "operative criticism" in Tafurian terms, protecting contradictions inherent to "the project" of "the avant-garde." Where the revolution is understood as a cultural one more than as a political and economic one, architecture, specifically that of "constructivism," would be the central subject of the plan rather than an object of the plan. More than "Soviets and Electrification," as in Lenin's famous formula, socialism would instead be the path towards a new collectivist way of life; architecture, as a cultural and technical agent, would be the direct organizer of this new social structure. That this cultural "project" of liberation failed is then taken as sign of totalitarian counter-revolution. As such, the fate of "constructivism" as a cultural "project" is intrinsically tied to the revolutionary political project. The historiographers of architectural "constructivism," especially Kopp, do not find a similar "project" anywhere else, nor can they – they simply take the role of the defeated *true* revolutionary that was betrayed by the development of *real* events. According to this, "constructivism" must carry the meaning of this specific political dimension and cannot function as an umbrella term – the one used by these historiographers is the more neutral term "the '20s."

The Anglo-American visual arts historiography exists in stark contrast to the above. It has a more formal definition of the object it studies, extending the genealogy of the latter into the late 19th century; the revolution is something that seems to mostly just happen to this object and it sort of ends up dealing with and wading through the revolution, ultimately failing. Naturally, "the '20s" is not their umbrella term, for the period it focuses on lies mostly before the start of that decade. While this historiography initially lacked a specific term– for Gray it is simply "the Russian experiment" – "constructivism" eventually begins to serve this role, in more or less the same way it did in the Soviet debate after the 1940s. However, this historiography, because it has a more formal art-historical, and less political, understanding of its historical object, manages to have at the same time more empirical rigor, but with this, less historiographical substance and less precision when it comes to periodization. Some authors present "constructivism" as a tradition of formal innovation coming from the last decades of the 19th century, while others present a "tradition of constructivism"[20] that extends away from revolutionary Russia to the post–World War II West. This stretching of the historiographical category into the present of the historian should be looked at as another, different case of what Tafuri calls "operative criticism" and is achieved precisely by depoliticizing categorical connotations.

Lost project returned

The contrasting origin stories and categorical associations brings us both to the full consequences of the second historiographical phase and to the final point of the argument. As already mentioned, the second phase comes in the early 1980s with a merger of two different historiographical bodies that developed during the first phase. This merger is produced, very specifically, in London, and led by the architectural discipline, and even more specifically, in and around the Architectural Association. In that school, starting in 1974, "Russian constructivism" had begun being introduced through design teaching, mostly in Diploma Studio 9 running at the time under Elia Zenghelis and Rem Koolhaas.[21] Zenghelis and Koolhaas combine references from the visual arts and architectural historiographies in a way serious historiographical work had yet to do.[22] Eventually, starting in early

1978, a series of more scholarly events on the subject took place, led by Catherine Cooke who starts presenting her research, the first in the Anglo-American circles to tackle the specificity of Soviet architectural production outside the extremely limited framework provided by the established visual arts historiography. These efforts, following Soviet historians' own attempts at historicizing "constructivism" and the British attention given to them,[23] become canonical via their publication in *Architectural Design* between 1983 and 1991. Here, architectural history is finally mixed with the work of the Anglo-American authors of the visual-arts "constructivism" historiography, with Christina Lodder's articles and the Costakis collection lying side by side to Cooke's own articles on what becomes firmly identified and crystallized as the Soviet "avant-garde" in explicit fashion.[24]

With this, we reach the final form of the Western historiography of Soviet architecture, which we have referred to until now as "the avant-garde." This final form brings with it a wave of extremely valuable work and empirical research, which becomes invaluable after the dissolution of the USSR and the increased ease of access to the relevant material. However, this comes at the cost of historiographical precision, for as the two historiographies merge, so too do the properties of each of the two "constructivisms" they separately dealt with. The intrinsic cultural politicality of the "project" of "constructivism," as understood by the continental architectural historians, is fused with the relative imprecision, via depoliticization, of the umbrella term "constructivism" of the Anglo-American historians of the visual arts. As such, an aura of implicit politicality becomes associated with the vague definition of "the avant-garde" as a new meta-category that really does not require any specific articulation with any actual politics. As the AA studio masters migrate to America at the end of the decade, the new narrative gets fed into design as a historiographical legitimator from a revolutionary past. In 1978, Koolhaas identifies himself with a "constructivist" swimming pool arriving at and slicing through a *Delirious New York*. In 1988, Koolhaas, Tschumi, and a whole panoply of rising stars are identified as the "avant-garde" of a new "deconstructivist architecture" at the MoMA exhibition of the same name curated by serial depoliticizer Philip Johnson, an exhibition that pairs the works of the Western "heirs" with those of the Soviet forerunners.[25]

Here we must return to Tafuri and his critique of "the avant-garde" and its "project." The implicit political character carried within the category of "the avant-garde" is one that is historiographically constructed in the span of a few decades, between the mid-1960s and the '80s. Tafuri points out how the historical defeat of "the avant-garde" comes as the material conditions for real planning develop, architecture being revealed to be not the subject of the plan but its object – leaving unsaid the obvious point that the subject is politics.[26] Such is the failure of the cultural "project," and its architectural manifestation in the '30s. One should add that for Tafuri the very category of "the avant-garde" with which he works is itself a historiographical version of "the project" he attacks until 1973, being effectively a migration of "the project" from cultural practice to the academic discipline of cultural history. The meta nature of the category and its ambiguities facilitate the confusion between political struggle and cultural proposal, or in other words, effectively substitute class politics with cultural politics. The Soviet "avant-garde" is an incredibly strong historiographical object for this purpose, and this purpose is embedded in the development of its Western historiography. The continental effort of politicizing architecture via "the project," and the Anglo-American tradition of depoliticizing it, each through its own historiographical practice, merge in a new grand narrative; this results, effectively, in the depoliticization of the very idea of the politicization of architecture.

"The project" itself reaches its final form in this way. From a cultural "project" aimed at expressing and, in so doing, replacing political praxis, it becomes a redemptory rhetoric imbued with an aura of revolutionary politicality practices that, by the standards of most historical agents of "the avant-garde," would be called "formalistic" and therefore reactionary. The "project" of the past "avant-garde," pregnant with the specter of communism, is historiographically brought back to redeem the present "avant-garde" from the sins of its "formalism."

It is therefore not surprising, in an age when the field of the left has become dominated by cultural studies and cultural politics instead of political economy and class politics, to see a cultural interpretation of revolutionary politics, constructed around the term *byt* and presenting, in the face of the crisis of capitalism, an architectural alternative of cultural commonality to an actual political praxis of working class organization.

In the words of the exhibition text this paper started with: "In post-revolution Russia, communal housing was the primary mechanism to create a truly collective society and eliminate the bourgeois domestic sphere." This is a nonsensical affirmation for any who deal with the political struggles of the time. In post-Revolution Russia, the primary mechanism was workers' control over the means of production and elimination of the bourgeois state. In a true manifestation of "the project" of architectural practice migrated to historiographical narrative, the architectural tendency of culturalizing the revolution in the past amounts to its neutralization in the present. That this ends up merely fetishizing capitalist relations instead of combating them is but the contemporary manifestation of the problem Tafuri was attempting to tackle in the short period from 1969 to '73. This is the ultimate face of "the project" that the historiography of "the avant-garde," and especially the Soviet "avant-garde," carried into our present under the guise of radical culture. In effect, it is naught but a liberal shackle on an operative politicization of the architectural discipline.

The historical problem today is in the ideology of the discipline of architecture and, to paraphrase Le Corbusier, *byt* or revolution. Architects tend to prefer *byt* because it matches their disciplinary liberal-bourgeois subjectivity. The current sociopolitical trends however, like those of the 1930s, are demolishing in front of our very eyes such liberal illusions. In such a context, the false hope for a nonpolitical cultural progress that *byt* brings is an objective accomplice of reactionary politics. Just as the Soviet "avant-garde" was historiographically turned into an ally of the "formalism" of Hadid and Schumacher, so *byt* is turned into an ally of the neo-liberal stage of capitalism of both Clinton and Trump. And, in the inevitable failure of its ideological insistence on nonpolitical cultural utopianism, it tends to favor Trump. Given the fact that the center fails and liberal capitalism is at the gates of a fascist turn, architects and historians would do well to abdicate from the "avant-garde" delusions of an architected cultural progress and opt instead for architectural concerns that, instead of fetishizing austerity, are put in the service of organized political transformation.

Notes

1. This approach could easily be understood as residing at a confluence between the concerns of the architectural historian and theorist Manfredo Tafuri and those of the historian and theorist of history Reinhardt Koselleck – between the category of "operative criticism" of the first (essentially representing ideology in the specific field of architectural history) and the category of "conceptual history" of the second, a field that, by historicising concepts, frames the production of historiography as a historical object in itself.
2. See particularly the exhibition *Building the Revolution: Soviet Art and Architecture 1915-1935*, held at the Royal Academy of Arts from October 2011 to January 2012, the culmination of a series of exhibitions taking place between 2007 and 2009 between Moscow, New York and Thessaloniki, joining together a selection from the Costakis collection, period architectural photographs of the Soviet "avant-garde," and Richard Pare's recent photographic coverage of the aging buildings that still stand today. This series of exhibitions produced several books in the form of extended catalogues, with the distinguished collaboration of Jean-Louis Cohen. See particularly the catalogue of this last London exhibition: Tom Neville and Vicky Wilson, eds., *Building the Revolution: Soviet Art and Architecture 1915-1935*, exhibition catalogue (London: Royal Academy of Arts, 2011).
On the other end of the research-to-pop-culture spectrum, one may note the English language publication of *Zaha Hadid and Suprematism*, again an extended catalogue for an exhibition of the same name held in 2010 at Galerie Gmurzynska in Zurich, where

the work of the London-based architect is paired with Malevich's as a sort of direct heir to its tradition of "avant-gardism." See: Galerie Gmurzynska, *Zaha Hadid and Suprematism* (Zurich: Galerie Gmurzynska/Hatje Cantz Books, 2012).

3. Introductory text to *A New Communal: Быт – Way of Life*, an event at the Royal Academy of Arts programmed for April 10, 2017. From:
"A New Communal: Быт – Way of Life," Royal Academy of Arts, accessed December 31, 2016, https://www.royalacademy.org.uk/event/a-new-communal.

4. "Byt" has become a somewhat trendy concept through which to look at the cultural history of the Soviet Union for the past couple of decades. It provides a framework of "Russianness" that favours perceiving class warfare during the Revolution as a sort of revolutionary cultural war to destroy old bourgeois "forms of life" and construct a socialist "identity." See, for example: Irina Gutkin, *The Cultural Origins of the Socialist Realist Aesthetic: 1890-1934* (Evanston, Illinois: Northwestern University Press, 1999).

5. Tafuri produces this argument mainly in the works identified. However, a particularly strong and clear version of his argument is present in his seldom read text of 1971, *Il Socialismo Realizzato e la Crisi delle Avanguardie*, an article focused specifically on the Soviet "avant-garde" written for a volume coedited by himself. See: Manfredo Tafuri, "Il Socialismo Realizzato e la Crisi delle Avanguardie," in Alberto Asor Rosa, Manfredo Tafuri et al., *Socialismo, Città, Architettura URSS 1917-1937: Il Contributo degli Architetti Europei* (Rome: Officina Edizioni, 1976).

6. Tafuri himself produces a sort of relativist form of this point on the mutual dependence between historiography and theory in his introduction to *La Sfera e il Labirinto*, but the most poignant body of work addressing it at a theoretical level is that of Reinhart Koselleck, who advocates the need for a history of concepts. It is also a crucial problem for one of the first and most influential theorists of "the avant-garde," Peter Bürger, who spends the first two dozen pages of his 1979 *Theory of the Avant-garde* on the historical condition of historiographical categories, taking profuse amounts of help directly from Marx. See: Reinhart Koselleck, *The Practice of Conceptual History: Timing History, Spacing Concepts* (Stanford: Stanford University Press, 2002); Peter Bürger, *Theory of the Avant-Garde* (Minneapolis: University of Minnesota Press, 1984).

7. VANO, the Scientific All-Union Association of Architecture, itself came as a partial success after the failed attempt in 1929 to establish the same kind of unification through a Federation of Revolutionary Architects.

8. And constructivists held positions of power till just after this moment. Viktor Vesnin, the most politically connected of their ranks, was only removed from the presidencies of both the Academy of Architecture and the Union of Architects in 1949, and it is hard to ascribe this purely to political reasons since he was by then sixty-seven.

9. Mainly in the series of debates taking place between the Builder's Conference of December 1954 and the Congress of the Union of Architects of November 1955. These are entirely published in Soviet journals at the time and systematically covered

in the British journal *Soviet Studies*. See, for example: Robert William Davies, "The Builder's Conference," *Soviet Studies* 6, no. 4 (April 1955): 443-57; Robert William Davies, "The Building Reforms and Architecture," *Soviet Studies* 7, no. 4 (April 1956): 418-29.

10. With one of Selim O. Khan-Magomedov's first works, a paper entitled "On some of the problems of Constructivism," showing in 1964 a positive evaluation of the early period, an evaluation that was positively received by the Architectural Theory Section of the Moscow Section of the Union of Architects. See: Stephen V. Bittner, *The Many Lives of Khrushchev's Thaw* (New York: Cornell University Press, 2008), 133.

11. This is not to say the term is not used earlier. Clement Greenberg already used it famously in his *Avant-garde and Kitsch* in 1939, in *The Partisan Review*, which could be regarded as an early form of a historiography of "the project." It also comes up every once in a while in the 1960s and 1970s, mainly in the visual arts, and was dominant in Italy. A particularly relevant example of an early historicisation of the category is Donald D. Egbert's "The Idea of Avant-garde in Art and Politics," in *The American Historical Review* in 1967. But it is not anywhere near the universally conventioned term in its contemporary categorical function. See: Clement Greenberg, "Avant-garde and Kitsch," *The Partisan Review* 6, no. 5 (1939): 34-49; Donald D. Egbert, "The Idea of 'Avant-garde' in Art and Politics," *The American Historical Review* 73, no. 2 (December 1967): 339-66.

12. She published a few articles in British arts journals: "The Genesis of Socialist Realist Painting" in *Soviet Survey* in 1959, "The Russian Contribution to Modern Painting" in *The Burlington Magazine* in 1960, and "Lissitzky" in *Tipographyca* also in 1960. Three exhibitions follow between 1959 and 1962 in London, presenting the work of early Soviet artists: *Kasimir Malevich, 1878-1935* at the Whitechapel Art Gallery in 1959, *Larionov and Goncharova*, organized by the Arts Council in 1961, and *Two Decades of Experiment in Russian Art: 1902-1922* at the Grosvenor Gallery in 1962. This bleeds over a bit into architecture via an article by Kenneth Frampton on Lissitzky published in *Architectural Design*, which is based on one of Gray's articles and as such doesn't really cover much specifically architectural at all. See: Kenneth Frampton, "The Work of El Lissitzky," *Architectural Design* (November 1966): 564-66.

13. The list of the exhibitions is too extensive to cover here. It must be noted that the term "the avant-garde" does show up already in a few of them, particularly in the very first one, *Avantgarde Osteuropa 1910-1930*, organized by the German Society of Fine Arts and the Academy of Arts in Berlin, as well as *Osteuropaische Avantgarde bis 1930* at Galerie Gmurzynska in Köln and *Russian Avant-Garde 1908-1922* at the Leonard Hutton Galleries in New York in 1971. It is however still far from being a universal term.

14. The more impactful authors are Stephen Bann and John E. Bowlt who, after coediting *Russian Formalism: A Collection of Articles and Texts in Translation* in 1973, each go on to publish their own collection of translated texts in 1974 and 1976 respectively with *The*

Tradition of Constructivism and *Russian Art of the Avant-Garde: Theory and Criticism 1902-1934*.

15. Kopp follows his inaugural book with *Changer la ville, changer la vie* in 1975 and *L'Architecture de la pêriode stalinienne* in 1978. His is still probably the most widely read take on the subject. The Italian production is wider and more diverse, with *La Costruzione della Città Sovietica* by Paolo Ceccarelli in 1970, *Socialismo, Città, Architettura* edited by Manfredo Tafuri in 1971, *La Città Sovietica* by Marco de Michelis and Ernesto Pasini in 1976, and *Cittâ Russa e Cittâ Sovietica* by Vieri Quilici also in 1976.

16. Among which is the fact that Italy is the one country in the world where the category of "the avant-garde" is universally used, though is fiercely debated. Tafuri, for example, fully rejects it simply as a periodization of the cultural and artistic production of the 1910s to the 1930s, seeing it instead as a mechanism prevalent in bourgeois art since its Italian Renaissance inception.

17. The first piece of writing trying to historicise early Soviet architecture in an architectural publication was "The Work of El Lissitzky" by Kenneth Frampton, published in *Architectural Design* (November 1966), coming as a direct importation into architectural circles of Camilla Gray's 1960 article on Lissitzky published in *Typographica* no. 16 and two exhibitions on Lissitzky in 1965, one a retrospective that toured Europe and a later show at the Grosvenor Gallery in London.

18. Another popular object for that purpose is Yakov Chernikhov, whose manifesto book *The Construction of Architectural and Mechanical Forms* of 1931 is a very late sort-of-architectural expression of the visual arts trends of 1917-1922, being completely obsolete for the architectural debate happening at the time. As such, it helps maintain the impression that architecture is being covered, while in effect being fully ignored.

19. The gradual architecturalization of the historical "avant-garde" is a large topic that will not be addressed here, but it is an important one. As the "art-unto-life" ideology of "productivism" becomes more central in the Soviet debate, so too does architecture as organizer of life become the dominant field, as opposed to the artistic-symbolic mere expressions of a new life the visual arts were capable of. The Anglo-American focus on the visual-arts "avant-garde," and its presentation of vaguely proto-architectural actors like Lissitzky and Chernikhov as the architectural expression of this trend, could be seen as a symptom of an unwillingness to deal with the more radical "avant-garde" critique that eschews "art-as-institution," as Bürger puts it in his *Theory of the Avant-garde* in 1974, and moves from representation towards organization. Continental Europe, where a revolutionary left exists, does not suffer from the same ideological impediments. The tendency of the historical "avant-garde" to drift towards architecture is noted by authors such as Gray or Bann but only really fully addressed by Tafuri in all its implications, mainly in his already mentioned *Il Socialismo Realizzato e la Crisi delle Avanguardie* from 1976.

20. This is obviously referencing Stephen Bann, ed., *The Tradition of Constructivism* (New York: Da Capo Press, 1974).
21. In which Zaha Hadid, incidentally, who fashioned herself as worthy heir to Malevitch, was at the time studying. Bernard Tschumi was also introducing this material in his Diploma Studio 12.
22. From the constitution of a "Malevich group" in the academic year 1975-1976 to a series of seminars on the "social condenser" at the end of the first term of the previous academic year. It's important to note that while Malevich is practically nonexistent in the Continental histories of Soviet architecture at the time, he was heavily treated by Anglo visual-arts historians; conversely, the OSA concept of the social condenser is entirely absent from the Anglo-American histories of Soviet visual-arts is but central to Continental architectural history.
23. See the special February 1970 issue of *A.D.* dedicated to *Building in the USSR*, edited by Oleg Shvidkhovsky, and the following English publication of his book of the same name in 1971. Selim O. Khan-Magomedov would then see his work regularly translated into English through the 1980s and 1990s, precisely during Cooke's period of greatest activity.
24. Cooke wrote several articles during this period, as well as guest editing four special issues entirely dedicated to the subject, entitled *Russian Avant-Garde: Art and Architecture* in 1983; *Iakov Chernikhov* in 1984; *Uses of Tradition in Russian and Soviet Architecture* in 1987; and *The Avant-Garde: Russian Architecture in the Twenties* in 1991.
25. Just as Zaha Hadid would do again in her Zurich exhibition of 2010 and the subsequent book of 2012.
26. In Manfredo Tafuri, *Architecture and Utopia* (Cambridge Massachusetts and London: The MIT Press, 1976), 100.

CHAPTER 12
Effete, Effeminate, Feminist: Feminizing Architecture Theory

Sandra Kaji-O'Grady

The counter-critical and anti-theoretical arguments that emerged at the turn of the second millennium cast the theoretical project of the 1980s and 1990s, and its authors, as effete or effeminate. Which is not to say that the figure of theoretical knowledge in architecture took female form. Rather, the figure that was conjured was a male architect-writer whose impotency was exposed by the action-oriented pragmatism of the architect-builder. These attacks used the very same gendered dichotomies that feminist theorists had sought to expose at the heart of architectural discourse. Anti-theoretical tracts followed a decade during which female theorists had published widely and been professionally rewarded with positions in elite architectural academies. This paper seeks to reveal and understand the relationship between the "effeminizing" of architectural theory and the broader context of divisions of academic labor and institutional regulatory regimes, feminist backlash, loaded metaphors, and territorial disputes between gendered actors. It questions the effects of these attacks, not just on architectural theory and its venues, but for women practicing architectural theory.

Effete theory

Michael Hays and Alicia Kennedy observed in 2000 that the "anti-theoretical rants" that were then gathering force came "from deep within the theoretical camp."[1] They may well have been thinking about Michael Speaks. Speaks obtained a doctorate in literature at Duke University under the supervision of Fredric Jameson in 1993, completing a dissertation titled *Architectural Ideologies: Modern, Postmodern, and Deconstructive*. Adept in the lingua franca of critical cultural and architectural theory, Speaks, nevertheless, came to repudiate theory and the belief, treasured by the leftist avant-garde, that architecture could critically refuse to accept things as they are. In 2000 Speaks wrote, "Architecture should no longer recoil from the degraded world of business and corporate thinking; on the contrary, it should aggressively seek to transform itself into a research-based business."[2] He provocatively celebrated the "managerial avant-gardists" or "class of doers" showcased in business lifestyle magazines. Two years later, in an essay ostensibly advocating for intelligent solutions to the development of the World Trade Center site after September 11, Speaks collapses Deleuze's writings on Spinoza with the utterings of the management theorist and former Shell Oil Company strategist Arie de Geus.[3] Here, Speaks launches an argument for entrepreneurialism, adaptability, innovation, formal diversity, and rapid prototyping, as if these were interchangeable aspects of the real – a position reminiscent of certain arguments from the 1970s which saw in the "real," be that Las Vegas or Manhattan, opportunities for architecture to gain renewed relevance and an expanded audience.

There were more philosophically astute assessments of the trajectory and positions of the architectural avant-garde, such as that delivered by Charissa Terranova to the 2002 ACSA annual conference, which disappeared from view.[4] But Speaks's essay, along with several others published around the same time of a post-ideological, post-theory character, attracted much attention and were given longer lives by their subsequent inclusion in architectural theory compendiums and curricula. By 2004, George Baird in "'Criticality' and its Discontents" characterized the situation in terms of a generational struggle, brought about by "the understandable career efforts" of the protégés of architect Peter Eisenman "to cut loose from him."[5] Baird and others observed that trajectories such as that taken by Speaks, while announcing theory's end, could equally be seen as evidence of its success, given that he and others drew heavily on its precepts and techniques. With greater distance, we can now also add that Speaks's defection proved a savvy career move. In the context of an increasingly conservative and managerially attuned academic sector, rhetoric around enhanced professional relevance and industry engagement is more enthusiastically received than is talk of autonomy and resistance. Taking up a deanship at Syracuse University in 2014, Speaks emphasized his ongoing commitment to the vocational aspect of architectural training over what he describes as an Ivy League approach characterized by "an art historical inquiry into the fundamentals of the discipline."[6] He insists that architecture students should be conversant in the language of real estate, finance, and development as a practical matter, enabling them to act.[7]

Speaks came to this position via a doctoral dissertation that, in its scope and references, would anticipate a quite different conclusion. In it he cites Barthes, Althusser, Jameson, Foucault, Deleuze, and Derrida, and literary theorists and writers such as Linda Hutcheon, Kathy Acker, and Robert Siegle. His dissertation is very much concerned with textuality, the relationship between writing and architecture, and the possibility of a "type of architectural writing which, rather than producing representations of significations, is itself a virtual architectural form [...]."[8] Speaks revered Bernard Tschumi's La Villette Project in Paris and praised Derrida's reading of its competition drawings and models as an example of "a new, theoretical, ideological architecture."[9] Derrida had impressed upon his enthusiastic readers, and we can include Speaks in this group, that philosophy cannot be extricated from the rhetoric it uses, in large part due to philosophy's dependence on metaphor. There can be no speaking directly, no action that evades or precedes text.

It is not unreasonable, then, given his education and interests, to assume that Speaks's choice of words in "Design Intelligence: Part 1, Introduction" (2002) is deliberate and, if it is not, that he would in any case appreciate the deconstruction of this text. Like Derrida, this essay latches onto one troubling word that has not been subject to interrogation in the retrospective consideration of Speaks' text and its historical moment in architecture. It is the word *effete*. Speaks writes contemptuously of the intellectual arguments of the 1980s and 1990s that proposed architecture's autonomy from the imperatives of capitalism. "Whether *effetely* Derridian or ponderously Tafurian, theoretically inspired vanguards operated in a state of perpetual critique," Speaks fumes; they were "incapacitated by their own resolute negativity."[10] This caricature of the Derridian as effete is, it will be argued, symptomatic of a battle for the right to theorize, to speak of, and for, architecture.[11]

"Effete" once described a person or group of people that are enfeebled and powerless, who lack strength or courage. Alternatively, it meant to be affected and pretentious, degenerate and decadent. Etymologically derived from the Latin "ex" meaning out, and "fetus," effete refers in the Latinate sense to one who is worn out by bearing young. Despite its roots in childbearing, the word "effete" is not typically used to describe old women. Indeed, like the word "butch," its power lies in the gap between gender assignation and gendered expression. As the Oxford Living Dictionary observes, in its contemporary use effete describes a *man* who is weak, or unmanly, a man who is *effeminate*. The Macmillan Dictionary tells us that the word effete is now "used about a man who looks or behaves like a woman."[12] The Oxford English Dictionary applies the term effete to one "that has become like a woman: Womanish, unmanly, enervated, feeble; self-indulgent, voluptuous; unbecomingly delicate or over-refined." The notion that to be like a woman is to be feeble and delicate is obviously contestable; nevertheless, this is the stereotype conjured by the epitaph "effete." The effete has also been linked to literary writing and a particular cliché of queer identity. Alan Sinfield situates the implosion of the categories of aestheticism, literariness, aristocracy, homosexuality, and effeminacy with the 1895 trials of Oscar Wilde.[13] From here on, the epitaph "effete" is one of a chain of words that inculcate writing itself. More recently, we might refer to Harvard Professor Niall Ferguson's assertion that the economist John Maynard Keynes "would take this selfish world view because he was an 'effete' member of society." Ferguson proposes that Keynes' economic philosophy is flawed by lack of interest in the future, a selfish worldview he ascribes to Keynes's lack of children and alleged homosexuality.[14]

Use of the term *effete* to deride Derrida and the Derridian was not new. Mark Edmundson, for example, discerns in the New Critics gathered around Harold Bloom a tendency to dismiss Derrida as "an effete textualist."[15] The quality of being effete does not relate to Derrida's social or sexual life but is ascribed to the fact of his attending to and reveling in the textual, of being caught up with the surficial and aesthetic effects of words and literary modes and styles. It is not Derrida's power[16] or masculinity[17] that is on trial. Nor perhaps even what he argues, but *how* he argues. Derrida's enthusiasm for etymology, onomatopoeia, alliteration, metaphor, grammar, translation, and syntax—all of these interests are philosophically suspect and *unmanning*.

Derrida, naturally, is alert to the use of masculine and feminine terms and concepts in philosophical texts. Indeed, one could say that he fixates on the ways in which gender, sexuality, sex, and procreation play out in language and metaphysics – a fixation exemplified by the essay *Spurs: Nietzsche's Styles* (1978). As the theorist of difference, he is much interested in the implications of the conventional binary concepts of man and woman, masculinity and femininity in philosophy. He often adopts paradoxical lexemes, hymen, for example, that are startlingly gendered while proffering them as a way to think beyond binaries. He sees the failure and impurity of sexual norms as something like an opportunity for their redescription. Derrida is also adept at repeating and twisting these norms in ways that confuse readers seeking a clear moral or political position on feminism and criticism. For example, in *Spurs*, he "translates" Heidegger's description of the philosopher of art as one who "even though he at times fancies himself an artist producing works, is content merely to gossip about art, he is a woman—and what is more he is a sterile woman […] impotent, a sort of old maid."[18] It is something like this assertion that Speaks compresses into the word "effete."

Derrida is also sensitive to the ways in which writing, and poetic writing especially, are dismissed. Richard Rorty claims that Derrida explains "why writers are thought effete in comparison with scientists – the 'men of action' of our latter days." Rorty believes that Derrida exposes the roots of Kant's desire to show directly rather than through the thick veil of writing,[19] arguing that Derrida's treatment of philosophical texts allows us to see the Kantian versus non-Kantian contrast as that "between the man who wants to take (and see) things as they are, and thus make sure that the right pieces go in the right holes, and the man who wants to change the vocabulary presently used for isolating pieces and holes."[20] The work of the Kantian, Rorty continues, "is no effete paradise, but one who does his share in the mighty time-binding work of building the edifice of human knowledge, human society, the City of Real Men [...] the non-Kantian is a parasite, flowers could not sprout from the dialectical vine unless there were an edifice into whose chinks it could insert its tendrils. No constructors, no deconstructors."[21] (It is remarkable, that in a discussion about Derrida, Rorty himself seems to repeat the Sartrean metaphor of empty holes so vulnerable to accusations of sexism.[22]) The gendered view of the Kantian man-of-action as edifice-builder to the theorist's vine, emanates, Derrida claims from the "castrated delusions of virility" evident in philosophy's dogmatic belief in "truth, science, and objectivity." Derrida could well be speaking of the projective or pragmatic turn in architecture.

The use of "effete" here is not an isolated instance of Speaks resorting to feminizing insults. In "Two Stories for the Avant-garde" he describes both Sanford Kwinter and the "theory avant-garde" more generally as "hysterical."[23] The word's origins are in the Greek *hysterikos*, of the womb, and it was adopted in the 19th century to describe a neurotic condition thought to be caused by dysfunction of the uterus.[24] The gendered distinction between interpretation, criticism, and theorizing, and the straightforward action of building, making, and acting directly on the world that words such as "effete" and "hysterical" effected went largely unnoticed at this time. Perhaps it was because this gendering was furthered in quite subtle ways, a word here, a metaphor there. Take Whiting and Somol's argument for projective architecture in "Notes around the Doppler Effect" (2002). Drawing from Dave Hickey's obituary on Robert Mitchum, they pitch Robert De Niro's "laboured" method acting – their equivalent of critical architecture's reflective and narrative approach – against a "rakish, lascivious" action-oriented Robert Mitchum.[25] De Niro is emasculated, Mitchum is hyper-masculine.[26] Whiting and Somol repeat Hickey's claim, that as an actor Mitchum *performs* and that performance is delivered, not expressed or represented. Because he performs with his entire body, Mitchum is plausible and surprising. In contrast, with De Niro's style of acting, you can see the struggle and the construction of the character. De Niro, adhering to the "Method'" style of acting, constructs the character out of details. Both actors played the same role in versions of the film *Cape Fear*. Where in the 1991 remake, the film opens with De Niro's character exercising, in the 1962 original, Mitchum enjoys a cigar and is shown "checking out two women as they leave the courthouse, cool as the breeze."[27] The critical architecture of the 1980s and 1990s that Whiting and Somol repudiate is, like De Niro's acting, "one where architecture represented its procedure of formation."[28] Whiting and Somol call for an architecture that delivers performance and "never looks like work."[29] Several years hence, Robert Somol dismissed writing in no uncertain terms, stating "despite the common wisdom of recent history and theory, architecture is a verbal, not textual discipline."[30] In 1999, writing for Peter Eisenman's *Diagram Diaries*, Somol, who had not trained or practiced as an architect, dramatically heralds the diagram as having emerged as the "final tool … for architectural production and discourse."[31]

Real effects

It is not, however, Derrida's personal reputation that is at stake in Speaks's essay, nor even of deconstruction, but the status of architectural theory and of its practitioners. Derrida himself had, in a 1992 discussion with an architectural audience at Columbia University insisted, "[d]econstruction was not primarily concerned with discourse, with text in the trivial, traditional sense but with institutions, that is with the solid, real, building of social constructs in which discourse, texts, teaching, culture, literature, are produced."[32] While it is possible to discern here, too, the relegation of the text to an inferior role to building, what Derrida is pointing at is the intersection between institutions, social constructs, and texts. Deconstruction for him is not limited to a form of literary criticism but is an exposé of the rational and essentialist structures of philosophy, and of the political institutions and discourses that follow. The idea that the discourse around the "death of theory" is the product of an internal intellectual argument *unrelated* to social events, authors, and institutional structures is one of those philosophical fantasies that does not hold up under interrogation. So, why was the projective argument and the pronouncements of architecture theory's end so compelling at the time? Why were they not seen as symptoms of a newly invigorated free market liberalism and a backlash against all progressive ideologies, especially those around diversity?

The answer lies partly in the resonance such announcements had with contemporaneous critical theory debates beyond architecture. These debates were colored by a pervasive sense of doom; theory's impotence was seen to be related to global events. In 2003, the editorial board of *Critical Inquiry* held a conference to debate the future of the journal and theory more broadly. W. J. T. Mitchell observed of the timing of that conference that it "occurred at the very same moment that the United States was plunging into an unprecedented preemptive war against Iraq, without the approval of the United Nations and in the face of overwhelming opposition from great multitudes of people around the globe."[33] The events provoked questions about how theory might "counteract the forces of militarism, unilateralism, and the perpetual state of emergency."[34] It led, Mitchell postulated, to the more difficult question as to the value of "intellectual work in the face of the deeply anti-intellectual ethos of American public life…"[35] In other words, the self-doubts that paralyzed theorists at the beginning of the second millennium mirror the withdrawal of public confidence in intellectual pursuits. There was a growing feeling that theory's concerns, modes, and arguments were shaped by external factors to a degree that made the critic's onlooker stance untenable. Bruno Latour, in "Why has Critique Run out of Steam? From Matters of Fact to Matters of Concern" (2004), reprimands the critic's assumption of a position outside of societal conditions and their influences. He asks how it is that sociologists and cultural studies academics can argue the social construction of, say, science, religion, power, or sport, but "not one of us readers would like to see our own most cherished objects treated in this way."[36] Of course, the situatedness of the critic, her gender, class, race, and embodiment had been central to feminist arguments, including those made in architecture. The rights of minorities to speak and participate in architectural discourse, to celebrate and articulate difference, was at the heart of architectural theory in the 80s and 90s. It behooves us then to see the gendering of theory as effete as part of a wider struggle about the political value of intellectual reflection and a larger struggle for women's rights. Such a struggle tends to be expressed, as Speaks would have it, as a question of how to influence and contribute to society at large – how to be effectual, rather than effete.

Yet, what were the effects of this shift in discourse on practice, beyond the reification of Dutch architecture, with its seemingly pragmatic and data-driven aesthetics? The so-called "effete" and idealistic critical avant-garde – Tschumi, Eisenman, and Libeskind, for example – found themselves leading commercially successful practices delivering large projects for institutions, corporations, and the state. Those who repudiated architectural theory – Somol and Speaks, for example – continued to build their careers around writing, theorizing, and academia. The whole affair could be dismissed as the striking of inconsequential poses. Yet, there were effects. Careers were forged or faltered around the changing fortunes of architectural theory. Many theorists moved sideways into history and what has come to be called the architectural humanities. Others dropped out altogether. I am particularly interested in the dilemmas faced by female theorists as theory became "effete."

Women and the critical margins

As Anne Freadman, Elizabeth Grosz, Meaghan Morris, Sneja Gunew, and many of the French feminists active in the 1980s argued, feminism and post-structuralism shared the conviction that writing, through formal experimentation and interrogation of the conditions of writing, opens up new speaking positions. Gunew, for example, claimed that to "speak as a feminist critic means no less than to be alert to the ways in which 'woman' is constructed in various signifying practices, and to use this awareness to deconstruct texts," adding that it followed that one would also be a writer of texts.[37] For Grosz, feminist writers explored "the transgressive borders or margins of tolerance between philosophy and writing."[38] More than that, women claimed a critical advantage as outsiders. Take Diana Agrest's statement from 1988: "It is from that outside that we can project better than anyone the critical look [...] Woman, representing both the heterogeneity of matter through her body and the historical negation of her gender, is in the perfect position to develop such a discourse."[39] Many women saw themselves as critically enabled by the historic marginalization of the feminine and of female bodies in the discipline and in the academy. In a period in which marginality was seen as an instrument of political subversion and transgression, women made their marginalization a place of intellectual prospect from which experimentation could be advanced. They took the outsider status to which they had been historically relegated as muse and model, and redescribed the situation as an opportunity – to claim the coveted space of criticality for women.

Writers who were doubly outsiders, as women and as outsiders to the discipline, were among the first to write about gender and architecture. Half of the contributors to Beatriz Colomina's *Sexuality and Space*, an edited volume of proceedings from a 1990 Princeton University conference of the same name, came from outside architecture. Laura Mulvey, Patricia White, and Lynn Spigel are film theorists, Molly Nesbit is an art historian, and Meaghan Morris and Elizabeth Grosz are philosophers. These women created a space for post-structuralist theorizing and for the question of gender and identity in architecture. In 1996, Cynthia Davidson's Anyone Corporation held its annual conference *Anybody*, in Buenos Aires, around the implications of new understandings of the body, including those emerging out of "the raised consciousness of the female body." The year 1996 also saw the publication of multiple anthologies of architectural theory dedicated to questions of gender and sexuality: Coleman, Danze, and Henderson's *Architecture and Feminism*; Francesca Hughes's *The Architect: Reconstructing Her Practice*; Diana Agrest, Conway and Kanes Weisman's *The Sex of Architecture*; McCorquadale, Ruedi, and Wigglesworth's *Desiring Practices: Architecture, Gender and the Interdisciplinary*; and Joel Sanders's *Stud: Architectures of Masculinity*. Kate Nesbitt includes a section titled "Feminism, Gender, and the Problem of the Body" in her 1996 anthology, *Theorising a New Agenda for Architecture: An Anthology of Architectural Theory 1965-1995*.

While there had been a trickle of prior texts, the year 1996 can be seen as a triumph of feminist theory in architecture, as well as a significant moment for women in architectural academia. Four of the above books were published by Ivy League presses – Yale, MIT, and Princeton – where several of the female contributors had advanced successful careers as architectural theoreticians, Peggy Deamer, Jennifer Bloomer, and Sylvia Lavin among them. But as audiences for their critical writings grew and institutional rewards accrued, the situation became paradoxical and disorienting. Beatriz Colomina, writing in the last issue of *Assemblage*, recalled that in the journal's heady days in the late 1980s and early 1990s, the contributors were "more or less all disenfranchised. Nobody at the time had more than an assistant professor job. In fact, the majority didn't have a real job at all. By the time we became more or less established, I wanted to end the magazine."[40] In 1999, Sylvia Lavin spoke of the benefits of the marginalization of theory in the university, a situation she found "abets critical theory's claim to be the origin of radical design" and allows theory to maintain its "criticality through institutional marginalization."[41] In 2000, Catherine Ingraham wrote that theory is "still seeking the edge although the edge keeps moving out from under it."[42]

The retrospective *feminization* of architectural theory breaks this détente, but in ways that ultimately deny and misread the historic place for the feminist project of speaking from the outside. In place of Agrest's picture of women enabled by their peripheral condition, we find instead narratives that approximate the breakup moment of the "bromance genre," as if the debates about theory's end or future were a matter for men to decide between themselves. The situation as Karen Burns describes it is one of homophobic irruptions in the exclusively homosocial address of men's bonding to men in architecture.[43] Or as Reinhold Martin writes, "whether the name of the father is Peter or Rem, the postcritical project is deeply Oedipal."[44] It is a matter of sons and fathers, of exchanges between men. Speaks's argument is, thus, not with Bloomer, the most overtly Derridian of the theorists of the period, or even with Derrida, but with his rivals and mentors.

Conclusion

I have focused on the ways in which stereotypes of masculinity and femininity were used to diminish the value of theory in architecture, and of women's contributions to theory. It is undeniable that feminine attributes were used derogatively to undermine critical theory. It is, though, another leap, and perhaps a paranoid one, to suggest that declarations of the end of theory were, at base, a backlash against feminism and the ways in which women had, through critical theory, turned their outsider position in architectural history to advantage. If one accepts that this is plausible there are several contradictory conclusions one could arrive at. The first is that the response was overzealous, something like killing the dog to eliminate the fleas, for the eminence of female theorists, perhaps of theory itself, was, even at its height, not assured. In the venues where theory's death was being debated, men still held the reins. The journal *Architectural Design* had an editorial board consisting of nineteen men and two women. Its special issue on "Theoretical Meltdown" in

2009 engaged twenty-eight male contributors and just five women. The outpouring of publications on questions of gender and sexuality in architectural practice and theory in the year 1996, could, against this fact, be seen as a failed revolution. Catherine Ingraham seemed to succumb to this pessimistic assessment when she wrote that "it was inevitable that the field of architecture would retake its practice from the various practitioners of something other than architectural practice in order to revive empiricist and formalist approaches to material and (now-digital) technology in architectural practice."[45]

A second conclusion would take heart from the skirmish, noting that the gendered and homophobic narrative of "post-criticism" confirms the very weaknesses in architectural discourse that feminist theorists had sought to expose. Projective architecture failed to escape from binary oppositions between writing and building, resistance and complicity. It failed to recognize its own hubris in believing the architect could work productively to temper and modulate the aesthetic and social casualties of free-market libertarianism. Its contemporary flag bearer is not so much the parsimonious architecture of the Dutch, as the post-capitalist excesses and Trumpisms of Patrik Schumacher. Meanwhile, theoretical discourse about architecture has not disappeared but remains more necessary than ever.

Notes

1. K. Michael Hays and Alicia Kennedy, "After All, or the End of 'the end of'," *Assemblage* 41 (2000): 6.
2. Michael Speaks, "Two Stories for the Avant-Garde," in *Archilab: Radical Experiments in Global Architecture*, ed. Frédéric Migayrou and Marie-Ange Brayer (Orleans, France: 2000). http://www.archilab.org/public/2000/catalog/speaksen.htm.
3. Speaks writes at length of the similarity between Deleuze's book *Spinoza: A Practical Philosophy* (1970) and De Geus's *The Living Company* (1997) in "It's Out There…: The Formal Limits of The American Avantgarde," *Architectural Design* 133 (1998): 26-31.
4. Charissa Terranova, "An Architecture of Animal Spirits: Contemporary Architecture and the Condition of the Avant-Garde Promise" (*Proceedings* of the 90th ACSA Annual Meeting, New Orleans Louisiana, April 11-14, 2002, 479). In 2002, Terranova was a doctoral candidate under the supervision of Michael Hays at Harvard University in the Advanced Studies Program on Architecture, Landscape Architecture, and Urbanism.
5. George Baird, "'Criticality' and its Discontents," *Harvard Design Magazine* 21 (Fall-Winter 2004): 16-21.
6. "Deans List: Michael Speaks of Syracuse Architecture," *Archinect* (April 13, 2015). https://archinect.com/features/article/124988136/deans-list-michael-speaks-of-syracuse-architecture.

7. "Michael Speaks of Syracuse Architecture."
8. Michael Speaks, "Architectural Ideologies: Modern, Postmodern and Deconstructive" (PhD diss., Duke University, 1993), xiii.
9. Ibid.
10. Michael Speaks, "Design Intelligence: Part 1, Introduction," *A+U* (December 2002): 16.
11. The pairing of "ponderous" and Tafuri in Speaks' essay is a quite different insult. Ponderous derives from the Latin, *ponder*, meaning weight; it is related to the word pound. It could refer to a turgidity of writing, a pessimistic worldview, or heaviness of person, none of which assail Tafuri's masculinity or authority.
12. "Effete," Macmillan Dictionary, http://www.macmillandictionary.com/dictionary/british/effete.
13. Alan Sinfield, *The Wilde Century: Effeminacy, Oscar Wilde, and the Queer Moment* (New York: Columbia University Press, 1994).
14. Niall Ferguson, Laurence A. Tisch Professor of History at Harvard University, spoke at the Tenth Annual Altegris Conference in Carlsbad, California, on the second of May, 2013. His remarks were reported in the *Financial Advisor*, http://www.fa-mag.com/news/harvard-professor-gay-bashes-keynes-14173.html.
15. Mark Edmundson, *Literature against Philosophy, Plato to Derrida: A Defence of Poetry*, (Cambridge: Cambridge University Press, 1995), 227.
16. In 2002, Derrida was aged seventy-two and not yet diagnosed with the pancreatic cancer that would kill him two years later. He was still very much sought out and powerful, teaching at the University of California, Irvine, where he had been Professor of Humanities since 1986, and serving as a regular visiting professor at several other major American and European universities.
17. A heterosexual man and father of three, Derrida was not known for decadence or dandyism. His penchant for wearing "well-tailored suits" was attributed to his being French. Nathan Kandall, "Jacques Derrida, Abstruse Theorist, Dies at 74," *The New York Times*, October 10, 2004, http://www.nytimes.com/2004/10/10/obituaries/jacques-derrida-abstruse-theorist-dies-at-74.html.
18. Jacques Derrida, *Spurs: Nietzsche's Styles* (Chicago: University of Chicago Press, 1979), 77.
19. Richard Rorty, "Philosophy as a Kind of Writing: An Essay on Derrida," *New Literary History* 10, no. 1 (1978): 156.
20. Ibid., 157-58.
21. Ibid.
22. Sartre discusses slime and holes in *Being and Nothingness*, declaring "the obscenity of the feminine sex is that of everything which 'gapes open.' It is an appeal to being as all holes are." Jean-Paul Sartre, *Being and Nothingness* (New York: Philosophical Library, 1956), 613. His claims infuriated numerous feminists. See Christine Daigle, "Where Influence Fails: Embodiment in Beauvoir and Sartre," in *Beauvoir and Sartre: The Riddle*

of Influence, ed. Christine Daigle and Jacob Golomb (Bloomington: Indiana University Press), 2009. Also, Margery Collins, "Holes and Slime in Sartre's Psychoanalysis," in *Women and Philosophy: Toward a Theory of Liberation*, ed. Carol Gould and Mark Wartofsky (New York: Putnam, 1976), 112-27.
23. Speaks, "Two Stories for the Avant-Garde."
24. Ibid.
25. Dave Hickey, "Mitchum Gets Out of Jail," *Art Issues* (September/October 1997): 10-13.
26. Robert Somol and Sarah Whiting, "Notes around the Doppler Effect and Other Moods of Modernism," *Perspecta* 33 (2002): 76-77.
27. Somol and Whiting, "Notes around the Doppler Effect," 76-77.
28. Ibid., 77.
29. Ibid.
30. Robert Somol, "Pass it on …", *Log* 3 (Fall 2004): 5.
31. Robert Somol, "Dummy Text, or the Diagrammatic Basis of Contemporary Architecture," in *Diagram Diaries*, ed., Peter Eisenman (London: Thames and Hudson, 1999), 6.
32. Jacques Derrida and Mark Wigley, "Jacques Derrida: Invitation to a Discussion, Moderated by Mark Wigley," *D: Columbia Documents of Architecture and Theory* 1 (1992): 11.
33. W. J. T. Mitchell, "Medium Theory: Preface to the 2003 *Critical Inquiry* Symposium," *Critical Inquiry* 30, no. 2 (Winter 2004): 327.
34. Mitchell, "Medium Theory," 327.
35. Ibid.
36. Bruno Latour, "Why Has Critique Run out of Steam? From Matters of Fact to Matters of Concern," *Critical Inquiry* 30, no. 2 (Winter 2004): 240.
37. Sneja Gunew, "Feminist Criticism: Positions and Questions," *Southern Review* 16, no. 1 (March 1983): 153.
38. Elizabeth Grosz, "Derrida and the Limits of Philosophy," *Thesis Eleven* 14, (1986): 26-38.
39. Diana Agrest, "Architecture from Without: Body, Logic, and Sex," *Assemblage* 7, (October 1988): 37.
40. Beatriz Colomina, "Farewell to Assemblage," *Assemblage* 41 (April 2000): 19.
41. Sylvia Lavin, "Theory into History; Or, the Will to Anthology," *Journal of the Society of Architectural Historians* 58, no. 3 (September 1999): 497.
42. Catherine Ingraham, "The Course of the Discourse," *Assemblage* 41 (2000): 33.
43. Karen Burns, "Ex Libris: Archaeologies of Feminism, Architecture and Deconstruction," *Architectural Theory Review* 15 (2010): 255-56.
44. Reinhold Martin, "Critical of What? Toward a Utopian Realism," *Harvard Design Magazine* 22 (Spring/Summer 2005): 105.
45. Catherine Ingraham, *Architecture, Animal, Human: The Asymmetrical Condition* (New York: Routledge, 2006), 93.

CHAPTER 13

Anthologizing Post-Structuralism: Architecture Écriture, Gender, and Subjectivity

Karen Burns

> ... the majority of writers in this quasi-generation of architectural theorists are women.
>
> Mark Wigley, *Assemblage*, August 27, 1995[1]

Archives

The late 1990s rush to anthologize postwar architectural theory produced theory as an archival project. Like all archives, the anthology volumes were incomplete and "fragmentary, contingent traces of historical experience."[2] The gaps in this archive – its missing boxes – and its contingency come to light when we try and search the archival filing system for boxes marked subjectivity and gender. Five mainstream architectural theory anthologies were published in English between 1996 and 1999. However, these volumes included few essays on feminism or gender studies.[3] This omission is surprising because during the late 1980s and '90s, "gender and subjectivity" was hailed as one of the primary topics of the new theory formation by the editors of *Assemblage*, a key North American architectural theory journal published between 1986 and 2000.[4] This chapter examines the presence and absence of the category "gender and subjectivity" within the anthology archives. It sets the disappearance of gender against the intense interest in the question of the theorist's own subjectivity in the period 1984 to 1997 and focuses on the presence and performance of subjectivity in the period's experimental writing projects. I trace the ways in which post-structuralism's topics of subjectivity and gender were reframed by gendered archival practices and by the presence of the neo-conservative North American "Culture Wars." The question of the theorist's authority and mastery remains pertinent today. Social norms of gender, race, class, sexuality, ethnicity, and religion structurally reproduce themselves in architectural theory, above and beyond the "intentions" of individual theorists.

L'écriture

Writing was a powerful medium for staging the encounters between architecture and post-structuralist theory. Oral and written texts were experimental sites. In lecture rooms, symposia, and on the page, speakers and writers played with conventions of language, genre, and typography. By the mid-1990s, however, writing came to be excoriated and cast as a visible sign of theory's difference from building. This paper is not interested in rehearsing the binary opposition of building and writing. Rather it establishes the significance of the experimental writing medium for a range of high-profile architects and theorists. It analyses the value of this medium for metaphysical inquiries into subjectivity – including the theorist's own – and examines the subsequent marginalization and feminization of the writing genre in theory's anthology system.

An experimental architectural genre was borrowed, shaped, and emerged from post-structuralist writing originating in literature, philosophy, and psychoanalysis. "Post-structuralism" describes the reception and interpretation of new French philosophy of the 1960s and 1970s in regions outside France, particularly in North America.[5] Post-structuralism is a set of procedures for rethinking key metaphysical concepts, most sharply those concerned with language, subjectivity, being, and essence. Key exponents of post-structuralist French philosophy and literary theory forged a new theory genre by drawing on techniques developed in modernist texts: notably in the work of James Joyce, as well as Mallarmé, Woolf, and Dadaist writings, among other sources. This genre brings the relationship between the oral and the textual to the fore by emulating the spoken voice and unconscious on the page. Writers use stream of consciousness techniques, divergences, disruptions, and rapid changes of tone, jokes, and dialogue. By mimicking process, writing emphasizes borrowings and language conventions to reveal the subjectivity of the author who writes and the force of protocols in constructing language, "thought," and writing. Notably it is highly form driven: it is an experiment in the physical forms of writing. It is characterized by the interplay of fictional and essayistic genres, mixing fragments of autobiography and extant philosophical texts, experiments in typography, and page design. French writers developed this experimental writing genre in order to work against the metaphysical practices embedded in the very material fabric of writing.

An early architectural example can serve to illustrate the key practices of this genre. In 1984 the London-based architectural journal *AA Files* published

Daniel Libeskind's "Notes for a Lecture: Nouvelles Impressions d'Architecture."[6] Libeskind's essay refuses the protocols of a lecture's coherent structure, narrative, or conformity to rules of argument. His text exposes the *genre* of the lecture as a constructed, social artifact. "Notes for a Lecture" is also a theoretical investigation into the self, subjecthood, and sovereignty. The essay plays up its performance mode, collaging fragments of texts and collectibles to mimic the stream of consciousness of remembrance and personal memories from the individual lecturer's interior world. These techniques foreground the author's intellectual genealogy, revealing the over-riding force of memory and collecting in the formation of ideas. The piece undoes assumptions about the creative self as an original fount of new ideas by constructing the self as a site of texts and artifacts made by others. This lecture questions theory's attachment to the "history of ideas" genre, with its privileging of mastery and rationality as operating concepts.

Outside architecture this writing practice was sometimes described according to a problematic term devised by French writer Hélène Cixous as *"l'écriture féminine."* This designation has proved troublesome for many and remains a source of confusion in the English-speaking world. *L'écriture féminine* uses a metaphor of the feminine to describe writing that is radically different from established protocols, that speaks otherwise. The voice of l'écriture can belong to either male or female authors because the text is a not a natural outpouring but a highly polished performance. Language mimics the interlocking operations of existing texts, including oral textual forms, all signaling to the reader that writing is a constructed artefact rather than a transparent medium of communication. The act of composition – the physical construction of the text – and the composition of authorial identity become intertwined.[7] Form and content are inextricably meshed.

1976-1993

This new writing practice began to enter the discipline of architecture around 1975 before flowering in the architectural mainstream from 1984 to 1997. The genre survives today in less visible parts of architectural writing and performance, notably in feminist works.[8] Fragments of architecture écriture first appeared around 1976, when this French writing practice jumped the channel and made its way to 36 Bedford Square, Bloomsbury, London, home of the AA (Architectural Association) school. The genre asserted its presence in the 1976-1977 studio run by Bernard Tschumi and entitled "Joyce's Garden," a project set in nearby Covent Garden, a historically significant area rescued from threats of demolition and redevelopment. Tschumi gave the students portions of James Joyce's *Finnegan's Wake* to use as briefs for sites at thirty-six locations, sites chosen randomly from the intersecting points of an ordinance survey grid. The use of fiction and chance to select site and brief radically undermined the rhetoric of rationality as the guiding factor in architectural decision-making. Many of the project descriptions, including Tschumi's, however, are remarkably sober. *Finnegan's Wake* appears to have left few traces on the genre of design project description, with the exception of Will Alsop, who wrote: "You are invited to attend a meeting on the corner of the West Central Street and Museum Street for the purpose of arriving at a collective agreement that the proposed building for that site already exists."[9] Handing out briefs consisting of a piece of fiction implicitly questions the normative protocols used for brief writing. The random fictional brief challenges the technocratic function of writing and language in architecture, the assumption that writing communicates – that it exists as a vehicle for communication – and that it occupies a service function in the field of architecture.

By 1984 this writing practice began to appear simultaneously on both sides of the Atlantic. In May 1984, Libeskind's *AA Files* piece was published and in July-August 1984, a special architectural edition of the Atlanta-based *Art Papers* guest edited by Jennifer Bloomer and Robert Segrest featured Segrest's "The Perimeter Projects: Notes for Design," an essay that would be revised and included two years later in the first issue of *Assemblage*.[10] "Perimeter Projects" mixed fictional and factual genres, challenging authorial originality by incorporating pages of quotations and questioning the "authority" of architecture and its privileging of the object. The first issue of *Assemblage* featured a newly translated Kurt Schwitters poem, "The Onion, Merz Poem 8." By publishing the Segrest and Schwitters pieces in its founding issue, the journal declared a commitment to writing experiments and modernist literary innovation. *Assemblage* gave this writing form a long-term home for over a decade. The journal published forty-one issues in total, spanning the years from 1986 to 2000. In volumes one to thirty-two, twenty-one of the issues contained at least one example of the experimental writing genre.[11] From August 1997, no writing of this genre appeared again in *Assemblage* magazine, although whispers of it echoed in the final issue. By 1998, even those writers who'd been strongly associated with this genre, such as Jennifer Bloomer and Ann Bergren, were writing in *Assemblage*'s pages in a much more established (and conventional) academic voice.[12] The public withdrawal of this experimental writing form was unsurprising, given how strongly it had been attacked in the preceding years.

In May/June 1993 the question of architectural writing and its function was put center stage in the first issue of *Any*, whose founding issue was devoted to the question of "writing in architecture." The two editorial pieces and an accompanying diagram clearly linked writing to architectural practice. In the second editorial piece Michael Speaks asserted that "writing becomes architectural [and that is] by producing architecture."[13] The year 1993 was the fever pitch year for contestation over the *Assemblage* project and the new theory formation. Trenchant critiques had been gathering. Andrea Kahn made the problem of architectural theory (or post-structuralist architectural theory) the subject of a plenary address at SUNY Buffalo in 1991. When the lecture was subsequently published in early 1994, she used the epithet "terrorist" in her analysis of Mark Wigley's work.[14] By 1993 the mood was grim. The April 1993 *Assemblage* issue "Violence and Space," featuring material on race, colonialism, class, and gender, was attacked by a *Casabella* editorial and a lecture by Peter Eisenman at Harvard, *Assemblage*'s institutional home.[15] In these contests writing was cast as the opposite of building; its otherness was emphasized. In 1995 Mark Wigley, a prominent theorist, noted that the "writing on trial" paradigm was about institutional control over architecture's debate. He called out the disproportionate scale of the "wildly overdetermined reactions": "You can count all the writers who fit the critics' definitions of post-structuralist theory on one, maybe one and a half, hands. (…) But these people [i.e., the critics of theory] have big enough boom boxes that they can make sufficient noise for the self-appointed watchdogs of the discourse to be convinced of some kind of global conspiracy."[16] These skirmishes contest the view of later anthology commentaries that the "critical project" became "exhausted."[17] It was embattled, which is an entirely different historical frame.

In 1992 North American theorist Bob Somol linked the "powerful backlash against theory, a return to disciplinary rigor, of which the architectural concern of 'making it' is only one manifestation" to a larger "neo-conservative" project, known as "the Culture Wars."[18] These issues burst the boundaries of academia and attained public prominence in 1993, with criticism from the left (in a *Harper's Magazine* essay entitled "The Left Lost in the Politics of Identity") and from the right in the contestations around the 1993 Whitney Biennial (exhibited from February to June 1993).[19] *New York Times* art critic Robert Hughes derided the exhibition as "a saturnalia of political correctness" and *ARTnews* dubbed it "The Whitney's PC Theme Park."[20] The Culture Wars were a series of conflicts over a broad swathe of progressive issues in North America, including abortion, art, affirmative action, race, evolution, family values, feminism, and pornography. Neo-conservatives frequently describe these clashes as a "battle for the soul of America."[21] The increasing importance of identity – a term which refers to the categories around which social groups organize and identify, such as race or class or gender – was both asserted and contested in these battles. "Identity politics" became a major point of contention in these cultural clashes, as critics asserted that identity affiliations undermined universal categories, such as human rights, "common humanity," or national categories.[22] Today, "identity politics" remains a derisive term. It is often used in derogatory ways to dismiss the usefulness of identity categories. Detractors can conflate quite different identity affiliations into a new overarching category called identity.[23] This homogenising category elides difference. Moreover the term "politics" in "identity politics" shifts the focus away from analysis of specific social, systemic, and structural acts of discrimination towards *politics*, with implications of partisanship, party-based systems, lobbying, and voter choice.

The term identity politics slowly crept into architecture. In his introduction to the theory anthology *Architecture Theory Since 1968* (1998), editor K. Michael Hays notes that "there have been important developments in architecture theory not covered by this anthology," and the footnote to this sentence reads: "Feminism and identity politics are only the most obvious of themes that have produced massive numbers of studies since 1993 not primarily concerned with reification."[24] The term used by Hays in his jointly written *Assemblage* editorials was "gender and subjectivity," but now this phrase has been replaced with the much more loaded term "feminism and identity politics." This is a significant shift. The category of gender covers gender norms around men, women, masculinity and femininity, and gender nonconforming identities. Although feminism's core business is the challenge to gender norms, feminism has traditionally advocated on behalf of women subjects. Now the question of subjectivity, once relevant to all theorists, has been shelved and race, a topic of burgeoning concern in 1990s whiteness studies, seems absent but perhaps veiled by the catchall term "identity politics."

Writing a co-history of the decade would include these institutional struggles within architecture schools and journals and their intersection with the sociopolitical landscape of the culture wars. Too often, the anti-theory turn has been framed as an internal shift within the discipline of architecture. For example, the conference call for papers for the 2017 symposium "Theory's History" locates the "crisis" of theory as a crisis internal to theory by noting the "presence of coexisting and even contradictory paradigms derived from very different epistemic domains (anthropology, philosophy, linguistics, social sciences, etc.) led to a setback of theory (...)."[25] (Once again the responses to extra-disciplinary forces are figured through the metaphor of difference and disciplinary outsiders.) By locating the seeds of decline inside "critical theory" itself, in pathologies of exhaustion or inner conflict, these historical narratives of internal decay elide the conflicts of power and struggles for institutional control that increasingly engulfed the post-structuralist project in architecture.[26]

A history of the attack on post-structuralist theory cannot be accommodated within a traditional history of ideas narrative or within an older historical paradigm of evolutionary development, where the seeds of destruction are located in an internal *telos*. Was theory responsible for its own demise, or was theory's own historical trajectory shaped by conflicts over "the institutional control of the debate about architecture"?[27] Theorists had been breaking away from a service role for theory and refused, as Mark Wigley declared, to observe "the traditional and instrumental relationship between theory and practice."[28] Perhaps theory (and its theorists) was exhausted, but one could argue, they were exhausted from being relentlessly "attacked" rather than by theory's own internal pathologies.[29] A history of theory in architecture is a history of institutions, networks, and places of knowledge formation, not just the peaking and succession of ideas.[30]

1998 Archiving

The anthology archives have preserved few documents of architecture's experimental post-structuralist writing genre and, as we will see, when experimental texts were included, the genre itself was frequently ignored or minimized. My brief essay does not review all of the anthologies as I have done elsewhere;[31] instead I focus here on two anthologies, namely, K. Michael Hays's *Architecture Theory since 1968* (1998) and Charles Jencks and Karl Kropf's *Theories and Manifestoes* (1997, 2nd edition 2006) to understand how pieces were archived and framed by editorial gender practices. To understand how gender inflects editorial description and taxonomy we can compare two essays of experimental post-structuralist writing that were included in the *Architecture Theory since 1968* anthology, Robert Segrest's previously mentioned "The Perimeter Projects: Notes for Design" and Jennifer Bloomer's "Abodes of Theory and Flesh: Tabbles of Bower." The two essays share many features of content and form and could be considered companion pieces, although the anthology's chronological ordering system files them at 1984 and 1992 respectively.

Like many examples of post-structuralist écriture, the Segrest and Bloomer essays are difficult to classify under topic labels. They run wildly across multiple authorial names and ideas. Both incorporate the architectural everyday: he the suburbs, she the vernacular balloon frame. Both use Walter Benjamin and classical myth and deal with the place of writing in architecture. Importantly, both address gender, with a particular interest in the gendering of binary conceptual organizing categories; Bloomer overtly in her study of the structure/ornament pair, and Segrest more covertly in his metaphorisation of transgressive tactics in the city as a "witches' brew" contesting relations, between the gendered binary opposition of the criminal/prostitute/transgressor and the magistrate/authority/orderer [sic].[32] A close reading of Segrest's text reveals gender tropes and analyses threading through his text, in references to suburbia, Greek myths, and criminal/magistrate characters. The framing editorial glosses contain faint traces of the gendered thinking that shaped taxonomies for archiving and labeling these comparable essays. The editorial commentary on Segrest neglects to mention the gender frames in his essay and instead foregrounds Benjaminian elements, as the editor observes that Segrest works with the quotidian – "the trivia and trash of everyday life" – and other surrealist strategies such as "heretofore unintentional and irrational activities" and "a geography of incidents and necessarily decentered subjects," thus considering "architecture as the *writing* of events." The essay is "a phantasmagoria of fragments no less somber than the anomie typically reserved for the damaged modernists from Piranesi to James Joyce. It is here that Segrest registers an ambiguity characteristic of architecture theory in the mid-1980s, a skeptical, transgressive kind of writing whose convulsions somehow resemble laughter."[33] Segrest is placed within an avant-garde modernist lineage and the writing mode is interpreted as an intellectually skeptical position. He is a stand-in for transgressive writing.

In the anthology archive the longest analysis of the formal practices of l'écriture emerges in the *Architecture Theory* anthologization of Bloomer. In his framing remarks the editor identifies an oppositional feminist practice he calls "*architecture feminine*," a practice that recuperates the "marginalized feminine condition" by addressing the "reduction and distortion of women's work by 'phallocentric codes of rationality, objectivity and hierarchy.'" The editor describes this break away from the "masculine economy" as a minor architecture, as Hays picks up on Bloomer's appropriation of a Deleuzian term to denote the critical function of writing and thought generated by cultural insiders within a majority culture. The language becomes tangled when he attempts to explain the architectural component of this term, as he argues that *l'architecture féminine* is the inscription of the "'marked' sexual-textual body." Leaving aside the problem of what that statement might mean as description of gender analysis (for it conflates gender with sex), the gloss then draws on one of Bloomer's own references to her pregnancy. In the editor's words her pregnancy is an inviolable feminine space that the editor claims "cannot be presided over by the male gaze." However, Bloomer's own textual addendum to her piece rejects the metaphor of pregnancy as a description of creativity as "inappropriate" and unequal to the task of describing the collaborative nature of the installation and textual work explored in her essay. She lists her three male and one female collaborators by name. The editor then draws the reader's attention to the centrality of experimental writing strategy in Bloomer's work and positions the genre in this way:

> her deconstruction of boundaries between those texts and her architectural object ("theory and flesh"), refuse traditional modes of presentation and exegesis even at a stylistic level. In fact, Bloomer's texts achieve another level of emotional and epistemological significance when she performs them in public, using different accents, even different voices (…).[34]

In the editor's thematic and metaphorical pairings Bloomer is aligned with emotions, the body, sex, and performance. Robert Segrest's body remains "unmarked" in the editor's gloss and although Segrest explores and deconstructs gender norms, his own gendered subjectivity is not the subject of the editor's gaze. One (male) essayist's writing is aligned to transgression, Piranesi and Joyce, the other (female) essayist is linked to feminist theory, the body, women's reproduction, and emotion. This focus on the woman writer's "personal" motivation can have quite problematic effects for women by suggesting a personal "and therefore partial and non-objective analysis."[35]

The editor's introduction to the anthology *Architecture Theory since 1968* alludes to a larger theoretical project of rehabilitating theory according to a rationalist agenda, as Hays writes, "I have rationally reconstructed the history of architecture theory in an attempt to produce (as Louis Althusser recommended) the *concept* of that history."[36] Elsewhere, towards the end of the introduction, Hays notes that since 1993 there are "important developments in architecture theory not covered by this anthology" and the most important of these advances are defined in the footnote as "Feminism and identity politics."[37] Nevertheless he then declares that "I still believe, however, that the texts included here will then constitute the necessary history on which those new theories will be built." In the footnote Hays explains that these post-1993 developments are not concerned with reification, although a feminist would argue that reification as a form of abstraction governs the production of stereotypes of gender, sexuality, race, etc. Hays goes on to declare: "Theory is a practice explicitly ready to undertake its self-critique and effect its own transformation." These strictures make it more difficult to absorb the lessons of post-structuralist écriture; a writing mode that undermines the theorist's claim to self-mastery, punctures the dominance of the "rationalist" intellect with the creative and disruptive mimicry of the subconscious, and presents ongoing challenges to the authority claims of the theorist. The open questioning of authorship and authority would have complicated the anthology's claim for the continuing viability of theory in a historical moment dominated by a backlash against theory. Post-structuralism's multi-voiced mode contains challenges to theory's claim to rationalism; by feminising it and aligning it with tropes of the body, sex, and the feminine, theory sidetracked and marginalised these challenges.

L'écriture was not expunged entirely from the broader architectural anthology system, however, although its critical and political significance was frequently overlooked or disguised.[38] In Charles Jencks and Karl Kropf's *Theories and Manifestoes of Contemporary Architecture* anthology (1997/2006), John Hejduk's fictionalizing *Victims* text (1986) is positioned within an individualist frame rather than noted as an intellectual movement. For example, Jencks and Kropf observe, "Hejduk nevertheless showed an idiosyncrasy." The extract's title, borrowed from Hejduk's book, is "Thoughts of an Architect." Its meaning is double-edged, referring to the subject as a generator of ideas and rationalizing the fragmentary, poetic, figurative text as a series of thoughts. Here's Hejduk: "Drawings and tracings are like the hands of the blind/touching the surfaces of the face in order to understand/a sense of volume, depth and penetration."[39] An extract from Daniel Libeskind's *Chamber Works* (1983) was glossed in individual terms, as the editors observe: "At times gnomic in his writing, Libeskind uses juxtaposition, oxymoron and paradox as heuristic devices to reach beyond the limits of the verbal."[40] In Jencks and Kropf's anthology, l'écriture becomes a sign of individual expression. This individualizing of the theoretical and political aims of experimental writing was consistent with the anthology commentary on Bloomer cited earlier. When individual texts are described as personal expressions, theory veils over the historical turn to experimental writing. A focus on the personal ignores the shared protocols of new writing methods that excavate the politics of subjectivity and the political structures of the discipline.

L'écriture and its many women exponents were further marginalized in secondary histories due to methods that focus 1980s and 1990s theory through the prism of the practicing architect. A prominent theory book looking backwards at post-structuralism in architecture was titled *Derrida for Architects*. As the title suggests, the book was dominated by the assumption that the function of theory in architecture is to be of use to practicing architects (i.e., those who build). This focus excluded all of the North American women theorists Mark Wigley had noted in 1995, when he observed, "the majority of writers in this quasi-generation of architectural theorists are women." Wigley was included in *Derrida for Architects* but not his fellow *Assemblage* comrades: Bloomer, Bergren, Beatriz Colomina, Diana Agrest, or Catherine Ingraham.[41]

Conclusion

This chapter has traced post-structuralist experimental writing in order to investigate gender and subjectivity as key topics in 1980s and 1990s architectural theory. The genre's formal experiments focused on the function of writing in architecture, the role of writing as experiment rather than communication, problems of authority and mastery, and the privilege accorded to rationalism and buildings in definitions of architecture. Post-structuralist experimental writing was an experiment in form. It was sometimes accompanied by new work in architectural drawing, installations, and studio practice, and opened new areas for speculation. Post-structuralist experimental writing and its key ideas became increasingly contentious during the escalating architecture theory wars, and some of its central topics were subsequently minimized through being feminized or individualized in the theory anthology archive.

By briefly summarizing the afterlife of experimental post-structuralist writing in the anthology archival turn and in subsequent secondary histories, this chapter argues that post-structuralism's critical account of subjectivity has not yet significantly affected the historical methods applied to the period of theory's ascendancy. The positioning of architecture écriture in the anthology system reflects the gendering and marginalizing of l'écriture. By leaving its many practitioners out, or by transforming serious inquiry and formal experiment into a question of subjectivity as individual expression, we lose the sense of the systematic use of the writing genre to contest metaphysical models of subjectivity. Transgressive laughter and punning might be the spoken registers of this writerly mode, but it was a serious intellectual project aimed at probing architecture's foundational paradigms. Discussions of theory's demise are still governed by long-standing historical models focused on decline and more specifically on *internal* decline. These stubborn historical archetypes need to be addressed if we are to write histories that understand post-1968 architectural theory within a complex of sociopolitical forces. Although some cast these inquiries within the terms of disciplinary insiders and outsiders (theory as "an invading force from outside"), theory's inquiry into architecture's identity and the construction of its subjects raised questions about theory's capacity for mastery, authority, and self-knowledge. These issues remain gravely pertinent.

Notes

1. Mark Wigley, "Story-Time," *Assemblage*, 27 (August 1995): 91.
2. Antoinette Burton, *Dwelling in the Archive* (New York: Oxford University Press, 2003), 31.
3. See Karen Burns, "EX LIBRIS: Archaeologies of Feminism, Architecture and Deconstruction," *Architectural Theory Review* 15, no. 3 (December 2010): 242-65 and Karen Burns, "A Girl's Own Adventure: Gender in the Contemporary Architectural Theory Anthology," *Journal of Architectural Education* 65 (March 2012): 125-34.
4. K. Michael Hays and Catherine Ingraham, "Editorial: On Turning 30," *Assemblage*, no. 30 (August 1996): 7 and K. Michael Hays and Alicia Kennedy, "Editorial," *Assemblage*, no. 37 (December 1998): 7.
5. The term is accepted in literary theory and its confusions and problems duly noted. See Benoit Dillet, Robert Porter, and Iain Mackenzie, eds., *The Edinburgh Companion to Poststructuralism* (Edinburgh: Edinburgh University Press, 2013), 12.
6. Daniel Libeskind, "Notes for a Lecture: Nouvelles Impressions d'Architecture," *AA Files*, no. 6 (May 1994): 3-13.
7. The mirroring of composition and authorial identity is found in Romantic period writing. See Andrew Bennett, *Romantic Poets and the Culture of Posterity* (Cambridge: Cambridge University Press, 1999).
8. See the work of Julieanna Preston and Taking Place.
9. *AA Project Reviews 1976-1977* (London: AA Publishing, 1977), n.p.
10. Jennifer Bloomer and Robert Segrest, eds., *Art Papers* 8, no. 4 (July-August 1984) and *Assemblage*, no. 1, "Without Architecture" special issue (October 1986): 24-35.
11. Writers in this vein include the ones already mentioned, as well as Diller and Scofidio, Mark C. Taylor, Jeffrey Kipnis, Ann Bergren, Thomas Leeser, Harris Dimitropolous and LIQUID Architecture, Mark Rakatansky, bell hooks, Heidi J. Nast and Mabel O. Wilson, Silvia Kolbowski, and Judy Berland.

12. Jennifer Bloomer and Robert Segrest, "Iowa/Australia/Georgia," *Assemblage*, no. 41 (April 2000): 14. Their final *Assemblage* contribution used an interwoven set of memories rather than collage techniques. For writers associated with the technique who were writing in more conventional ways by 1998 see Jennifer Bloomer, "Pale Houses, Silenced Shadows," *Assemblage*, no. 37 (December 1998): 46-47; and Ann Bergren, "Jon Jerde and the Architecture of Pleasure," *Assemblage*, no. 37 (December 1998): 8-35.
13. Michael Speaks, "Writing in Architecture," *Any*, no. 1 (May/June 1993): 6.
14. Andrea Kahn, "Representations and Misrepresentations: On Architectural Theory," *Journal of Architectural Education* 47, no. 3 (February 1994): 162-68. See p. 166 for the terrorist reference.
15. See also Libero Andreotti, "The ANYWAY Conference, Barcelona, June 4-7 1993," *Journal of Architectural Education* 47, no. 3 (February 1994): 184. A description of the Vittorio Gregotti editorial in *Casabella* is included in Wigley, "Story-Time," 91.
16. Wigley, "Story-Time," 89.
17. See A. Krista Sykes, ed., *Constructing a New Agenda: Architectural Theory 1993-2009* (New York: Princeton Architectural Press, 2010), 16, for her account of Michael Speaks and Robert Somol/Sarah Whiting's criticisms of 1990s "critical theory," in which she notes, "While the attitudes of their authors differ, both of these writings characterize the critical project as exhausted."
18. Robert E. Somol, "*Les liaisons dangereuses*, or My Mother the House," *Fetish. Princeton School of Architecture Journal* no. 4 (1992): 65.
19. In September 1993 *Harper's Magazine* published an excerpt from an academic essay, Todd Gitlins, "The Left Lost in the Politics of Identity," http://harpers.org/archive/1993/09/the-left-lost-in-the-politics-of-identity/2/.
20. Vanessa Faye Johnson, "Difference as Identity in 'The Other Story' and the 1993 Whitney Biennial" (PhD diss, University of Louisville, 2010), http://dx.doi.org/10.18297/etd/697, 32; 36.
21. Richard Jensen, "The Culture Wars 1965-195: A Historian's Map," *Journal of Social History* 29 (October 1995): 26; James Davison Hunter, *Culture Wars: The Struggle to Define America* (New York: Basic Books, 1991); Andrew Hartman, *A War For the Soul of America: A History of the Culture Wars* (Chicago: University of Chicago Press, 2015); Roger Chapman and James Ciment, eds., *Culture Wars: An Encyclopedia of Issues, Viewpoints and Voices* (New York: Routledge, 2015); and Gregory S. Jay, *American Literature and the Culture Wars* (Ithaca: Cornell University Press, 1997).
22. See Johnson, "Difference as Identity."
23. Susan Bickford, "Anti-Identity Politics: Feminism, Democracy, and the Complexities of Citizenship," *Hypatia* 12, no. 4 (1997): 111-31.
24. K. Michael Hays, ed., *Architecture Theory since 1968* (Cambridge, Massachusetts: The MIT Press, 1998), xiv, xv, footnote 8.

25. Call for Papers, for "Theory's History, 196X-199X. Challenges in the Historiography of Architectural Knowledge" (Brussels: KU Leuven, February 6-8, 2017), 1. https://architectuur.kuleuven.be/theoryshistory/.
26. Wigley, "Story-Time," 85. On p. 89 he writes, "The battle over contemporary theory is really being waged in corridors, in letters and telephone calls, rather than in the classroom or the press."
27. Ibid.
28. Ibid., 88.
29. Ibid., 89. Here Wigley describes the events as "the attack on theory."
30. For an exemplary instance of this kind of historical analysis see Arindam Dutta, ed., *A Second Modernism: MIT, Architecture, and the "Techno-Social" Moment* (Cambridge, MA: The MIT Press, 2013).
31. See the essays referenced in footnote 3.
32. Segrest, "The Perimeter Projects," in Hays, *Architecture Theory since 1968*, 561 (the witches' brew); 562 (the gendered binary).
33. All quotations in this paragraph are from Hays, *Architecture Theory since 1968*, 552.
34. Ibid., 758.
35. A feminist analysis by Suvendrini Perera and Sherene H. Razack transforms subjective experience into an intellectual mode of inquiry. See: Suvendrini Perera and Sherene H. Razack, "Introduction. At the Limits of Justice: Women of Colour Theorize Terror" in *At the Limits of Justice: Women of Colour on Terror*, ed. Suvendrini Perera and Sherene H. Razack (Toronto: University of Toronto Press, 2014), 6. Kate Nesbitt's editorial gloss on Diana Agrest, as a theorist who has personally experienced discrimination as a woman, also transforms the structural experience into a personal one. Kate Nesbitt, ed., *Theorizing a New Agenda for Architecture: An Anthology of Architectural Theory, 1965-1995* (New York: Princeton Architectural Press, 1996). See Burns, "A Girl's Own Adventure": 128-29.
36. Hays, *Architecture Theory since 1968*, xii.
37. Ibid., xiv.
38. An exception is the feminist anthology of Jane Rendell, Barbara Penner, and Iain Borden, eds., *Gender Space Architecture: An Interdisciplinary Introduction* (London: Routledge, 2000), but the book is explicitly interdisciplinary, concerned with space rather than architecture. It is not an historical anthology of architecture.
39. Charles Jencks and Karl Kropf, eds., *Theories and Manifestoes of Contemporary Architecture*, 2nd ed. (Chichester, UK: Wiley-Academy, 2006), 285.
40. Jencks and Kropf, *Theories and Manifestoes*, 281.
41. Richard Coyne, *Derrida for Architects* (Oxon, England & New York: Routledge, 2011). Two English theorists from a later generation (Peg Rawes and Jane Rendell) are included.

CHAPTER 14

Consequences of Pragmatism: A Retrospect on "The Pragmatist Imagination"

Joan Ockman

By way of introduction

The following essay centers around a project – a deliberate intervention into "theory's history" – that I undertook as director of the Temple Hoyne Buell Center for the Study of American Architecture, a semi-independent unit within the Graduate School of Architecture, Planning, and Preservation at Columbia University. I ask the reader's indulgence if I write this account partly in the first person as I think it will be the simplest and most honest way to tell the story.[1]

My tenure began in 1994. Not having previously identified myself as an Americanist, I felt obliged to think through the name of the institution I was now heading. What, if anything, was distinctively "American" about American architecture? What were the implications for formulating an intellectual project at the Buell Center in the mid–1990s? Soon after my appointment, I also began working on a long essay on Alexander Dorner, a German museum director and art historian who, during the Weimar Republic, transformed a provincial museum in the city of Hannover into a contemporary art institution. Convinced that "anyone wishing to construct a new esthetics, art history, or philosophy of the museum must first expose himself to the impact of practical life," Dorner enthusiastically embraced the new contents of modernity. To him this also entailed discarding the metaphysical foundations of Western thought (Fig. 1).[2] Forced to flee Nazi Germany in the 1930s, he emigrated to the United States, where he discovered the Pragmatist philosophy of John Dewey. What Dorner found most revelatory in American Pragmatism was the critique of metaphysics implicit in Dewey's conception of art as experience and the path this opened beyond traditional aesthetics. In 1947 Dorner published a book entitled *The Way Beyond "Art."* He dedicated it to Dewey, and Dewey wrote an introduction for it.

Fig. 1. Alexander Dorner, *The Way Beyond "Art,"* Wittenborn, Schulz, 1947.

Dorner's embrace of Dewey proved a little belated, as it turned out. In the two decades after World War II, Dewey's democratic-reformist brand of Pragmatism suffered a decline, eclipsed by the politics of the Cold War and the harder-nosed logic of Analytic Philosophy, many of whose representatives had, like Dorner, been forced to flee European fascism for the United States. Yet starting in the 1960s, in another pendulum swing, the fortunes of Pragmatism began to revive again. Recuperated by Richard Rorty and other philosophers, Neopragmatism became an instrument with which to challenge the positivism of the Analytic school. The revival of Pragmatism also coincided with the assault on metaphysics that French post-structuralists were then carrying out (Fig. 2).

This history, about which we shall shortly dilate further, led me to consider whether American Pragmatism, widely credited as the only philosophy in the Western canon fledged in the United States rather than imported from abroad, might offer a fresh point of departure for thinking about the history and theory of modern architecture and, more ambitiously, whether it might offer a way to bridge the schism that had opened in recent decades between architectural theory and practice. Most simply defined, Pragmatism is a theory of practice. It also anticipates postmodernism in its anti-foundationalism. This led me to wonder whether Neopragmatism might provide some new insight into the relationship between modernism and postmodernism in architecture. I didn't know the answer to these questions, especially since in its undermining of foundational truths and its emphasis on practice, Neopragmatism also seemed to cast doubt on the inherent value of theoretical speculation. This was clearly a slippery slope. But as W. J. T. Mitchell pointed out in the mid-1980s in response to a diatribe by two Pragmatist literary critics, "the antitheoretical polemic is one of the characteristic genres of theoretical discourse."[3]

In any event, to assess Pragmatism's potential for architecture, it seemed essential to gain a better understanding of what this "American philosophy" was about historically, and why and how it was being refunctioned for use in the late 20th century.

Pragmatism after postmodernism?

With a similar aim here, let us venture a little further into the history of Pragmatism. As Dewey insisted, it is necessary to grasp our time in thought.[4] From the outset, Pragmatist philosophy affirmatively and unapologetically presented itself as a modern way of thinking. Emerging in the decades around the turn of the 20th century in the writings of three father figures, Charles Sanders Peirce, William James, and Dewey, as well as other leading thinkers, it was anything but a monolithic corpus

Fig. 2. *New York Review of Books*, May 9, 1996, review by Michael J. Sandel of Alan Ryan's *John Dewey and the High Tide of American Liberalism*.

of ideas. Already in 1908, one intellectual historian pointed out its contradictions in an essay titled "Thirteen Pragmatisms."[5] But what constituted its shared core was, first, a belief that truth was constructed, not given; and second, a preference for action over reflection. Theory, as the word's etymology from the Greek *theoria* implies, is by definition contemplative, a spectator sport. Practice, or *praxis*, on the other hand, involves participation. Against other philosophies' armchair engagement with reality, Pragmatism came down on the side of hands-on experience, trial-and-error experimentation, innovation, and an open-ended future.

It occurred to me that the advent of Pragmatism not only coincided with the rise of industrial capitalism but also with the emergence of modern architecture and urbanism. This contemporaneity – including a common location in Chicago in the 1890s – had largely been ignored by historians of architecture.[6] Yet in stating in 1928 that "America" was the oldest country in the world because "it is she who is the mother of the twentieth-century civilisation," Gertrude Stein, a student of William James, clearly perceived that the course on which the United States had embarked was also destined to transform the rest of the world.[7] The firsthand reports of European architects like Hendrik Petrus Berlage, Erich Mendelsohn, and Richard Neutra seemed to confirm her intuition.

To other European intellectuals, however, Pragmatism appeared then and later as little more than a craven celebration of the machine age and the dollar – "a Ford efficiency engineer bent on the mass production of philosophical tin lizzies."[8] Its stress on ends over means – on "cash-value," as James put it, using an intentionally crass metaphor[9] – made it suspect to European thinkers of various stripes, from Heideggerians to Marxists. Ernst Bloch, whose "principle of hope" might have found some sympathy with Dewey's "social hope," denounced Pragmatism as a theory in which truth was synonymous with the "utility of ideas for business."[10] Those who were hostile to mass culture, including the critical theorists of the Frankfurt School, remained especially hostile to a Pragmatist ethos.

Yet in its initial phase of development, Pragmatism was part of a wider social, educational, and political reform movement in the United States known as Progressivism. It had close ties with endeavors like Jane Addam's Hull House, with the first wave of American feminism, and with Dewey's own Laboratory School in Chicago. As explicit in the thought of Dewey, its most socially and politically minded exponent, Pragmatism was not a triumphalist philosophy of laissez-faire capitalism but rather a theory that commented on and criticized capitalism from within. Dewey had few illusions about the dangers inherent in a system driven by the profit motive, but he believed they could be mitigated through organized and creative intelligence. If his writings lacked the tragic coloration of his Continental counterparts, he would remain a crusader against social injustice throughout his life and a public intellectual who spoke out on subjects from war to racism to educational reform. Against the arguments of some of his contemporaries that an advanced industrial society could only be governed efficiently by a cadre of technocrats, Dewey wagered in *The Public and Its Problems* (1927) that modern communications technologies like radio and the syndicated press would bring citizens together and facilitate the construction of a "Great Community."[11] Were he alive today, he would surely look to social media as a vehicle for new kinds of political agency and civic culture.

Dewey was no Pollyanna, however. Witnessing the crises of the 1930s, he decried the gross disparities of wealth in the United States and the venality of the banking system. Once a moral philosophy based on belief in equality and toleration of differences, the liberal worldview had become an alibi and ideological prop for the powerful, he feared. In calling for a "renascent" and "radical" liberalism, he envisioned something remote from what goes under that name today. "Liberalism must now become radical," he stated, "meaning by 'radical' perception of the necessity of thoroughgoing changes in the setup of institutions and corresponding activity to bring the changes to pass."[12]

But if Dewey's faith was shaken by historical events, especially during the Depression, he refused to abandon the "party of hope." Some considered his politics naive. But hope over truth was among the legacies he would bequeath to Richard Rorty a generation later. When asked in 1917 whether he was an optimist or a pessimist, Dewey replied, "I am a tremendous optimist about things in general, but a pessimist about everything in particular."[13] He was, in fact, influenced by the writings of both the young Marx and Antonio Gramsci. Like Rorty after him, he would have subscribed to Marx's eleventh thesis on Feuerbach.[14] Like Gramsci, who counseled "optimism of the will" in the face of "pessimism of the mind," he believed in institutional reform, including (and especially) educational reform. But unlike his Marxist counterparts, he did not see class conflict as inevitable, and his vision of social change was incremental and meliorist rather than revolutionary.

After World War II, with the influence of Peirce, James, and Dewey on the wane and an imported-from-Vienna Logical Empiricism – now renamed Analytic Philosophy – in the catbird seat in American philosophy departments, Pragmatism was not so much rejected as selectively adapted by Analytic philosophers like Rudolf Carnap, W. V. O. Quine, and Hillary Putnam. According to historians Robert Hollinger and David Depew, the midcentury period was a second or interim stage in Pragmatism's evolution, that of a "positivized and scientized pragmatism."[15] Yet in 1962 Thomas Kuhn's book *The Structure of Scientific Revolutions* signaled the emergence of a more skeptical attitude towards the truths of empirical science, suggesting – especially in Rorty's tendentious reading – that scientific conclusions had no more validity than interpretations in other fields of knowledge and human experience.

Fig. 3a. Richard Rorty, *Philosophy and Social Hope*, Penguin Books, 1999.

Fig. 3b. Richard Rorty, *Achieving Our Country: Leftist Thought in Twentieth-Century America*, Harvard University Press, 1998.

In the wake of Kuhn's questioning of scientific truth claims, Rorty's edited volume *The Linguistic Turn*, which appeared in 1967, represented a repudiation of his own Analytic training. With subsequent books like *Philosophy and the Mirror of Nature* (1979) and *Consequences of Pragmatism* (1982), Rorty initiated a third stage of Pragmatism, or Neopragmatism, which he framed not just as post–Empiricist but also as post-philosophical and postmodernist. Rorty now demoted philosophy to "theory," describing it as a subjective discourse and, most provocatively, "a matter of telling stories."[16] The similarities to the ideas of Jacques Derrida were evident; the French philosopher of Deconstruction and the American philosopher of Neopragmatism were "natural allies," as Rorty himself put it.[17]

Yet for Rorty, as for his younger colleague Cornel West, Neopragmatism was not just a matter of demolition work at the level of philosophy and textual criticism. It was also an effort to sustain Dewey's "social hope" at the level of politics (Figs. 3a, 3b). Politics was a different form of practice from professional philosophy, Rorty insisted. It took place not in the ivory tower but at the ballot box and on the picket line, at the union meeting and in the front of the bus. "Disengagement from practice," he stated, "produces theoretical hallucinations."[18] Increasingly impatient with his academic colleagues on the left who were "haunted by ubiquitous specters

[of] 'power'" *à la* Foucault,[19] he denounced their "cultural politics" as cynical and nihilistic. Nothing short of a "moratorium on theory" was required.[20] Not quite a ban, Rorty's call for a moratorium on theory recalls (in an altogether different context) Louis Sullivan's call a century earlier for a moratorium on ornament. Like architectural ornament for Sullivan, philosophy – or theory – was a desirable, even essential, form of cultural production for Rorty. But in its current state of abusiveness ("Hopelessness has become fashionable on the Left – principled, theorized, philosophical hopelessness"[21]) it had ceased to be a social good. In his late book *Achieving Our Country*, his most explicit stand on behalf of American exceptionalism, he endorsed Dewey's belief that "the only point of society is to construct subjects capable of ever more novel, ever richer, forms of human happiness."[22]

From the theory-death of architecture to the death of architectural theory

The preceding excursus is intended not only to give a sense of Pragmatism's historical and political complexities but also to clarify the thinking behind my recourse to this philosophy as I set out to formulate a program at the Buell Center. Rorty's unabashedly patriotic liberalism was by no means unproblematic, but I felt that the question of American national identity, and of identity politics in general, begged to be addressed specifically in relation to American architecture (Fig. 4).[23] Even more pressingly, new architectural currents were surfacing in the U.S. in the mid-1990s that demanded attention. While the "theory frenzy" of the preceding two decades was beginning to abate somewhat,[24] it had produced a backlash, with an increasing number of American architects shunning hyper-intellectualization and impatient to plunge back into the business of building (Fig. 5). In this conjuncture, Pragmatism appeared to me not just a useful interlocutor, as already suggested, but also a way to challenge the unthinking and largely depoliticized culture that prevailed in architecture at this moment. Might it be possible to smuggle some of Dewey and Rorty's social ideas back into architectural discourse? This was the gambit of the "Pragmatist Imagination" project, which would come to fruition in 2000.

I am not going to claim that it was a success.

Before turning to this project, however, it is necessary to say something more about the state of architecture culture in the last three decades of the last century. While the inflation of theory was in synch with what was going on across academia in the 1970s and '80s, the architectural manifestations had their own special features and flavor and their own cast of celebrities, epigones, and naysayers. What was striking was how quickly architectural theory in the United States blossomed into a full-blown, marketable commodity from what had been little more than a

CHAPTER 14. CONSEQUENCES OF PRAGMATISM   277

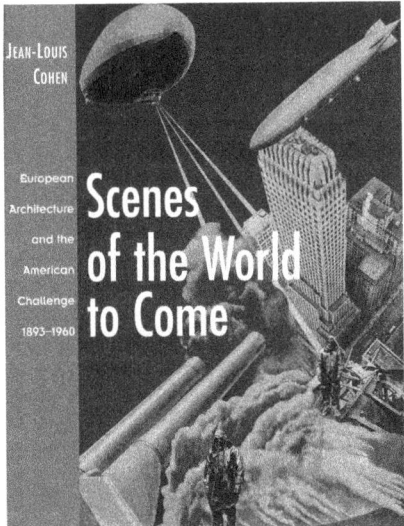

Fig. 4. Jean-Louis Cohen, *Scenes of the World to Come: European Architecture and the American Challenge, 1893–1960,* catalog of exhibition at Canadian Centre for Architecture in Montreal, Flammarion, 1995.

Fig. 5. First issue of the journal *Praxis*, "Architecture & the University," 1999, edited by Amanda Reeser Lawrence and Ashley Schaefer.

cottage production after World War II. It is not possible to rehearse that whole story here.[25] Yet it is important to touch on a handful of flashpoints, ones that loomed especially large from my particular vantage point in New York City.

The journal *Oppositions*, a product of the Institute for Architecture and Urban Studies (IAUS), an architectural "think tank" founded in midtown Manhattan in 1967 by Peter Eisenman with support from his mentor Colin Rowe and the backing of the Museum of Modern Art, heralded things to come. Some of the institute's initial energies were directed towards urbanism, as its name implies, reflecting the engagement with the city that characterized progressive-liberal architectural practice in the United States in the 1960s. Yet by the early 1970s, when the IAUS began publishing its journal, attention shifted to more purely intellectual concerns. From the first issue, the rubrics "History," "Theory," "Oppositions" (later changed to "Criticism"), and "Documents" structured *Oppositions*'s editorial content. Frankfurt School theory and neo-Marxian interpretations, especially as represented by the writings solicited from the circle around Manfredo Tafuri at the Istituto Universitario di Architettura in Venice, were among the new and formidable currents of thought that *Oppositions* imported into a still sparse American theoretical discourse and deployed, at least at first, to counteract the juggernaut of postmodernism.

By the mid-1970s, however, and most vividly with the staging of the exhibition *The Architecture of the École des Beaux-Arts* at MoMA in 1975, postmodernism had

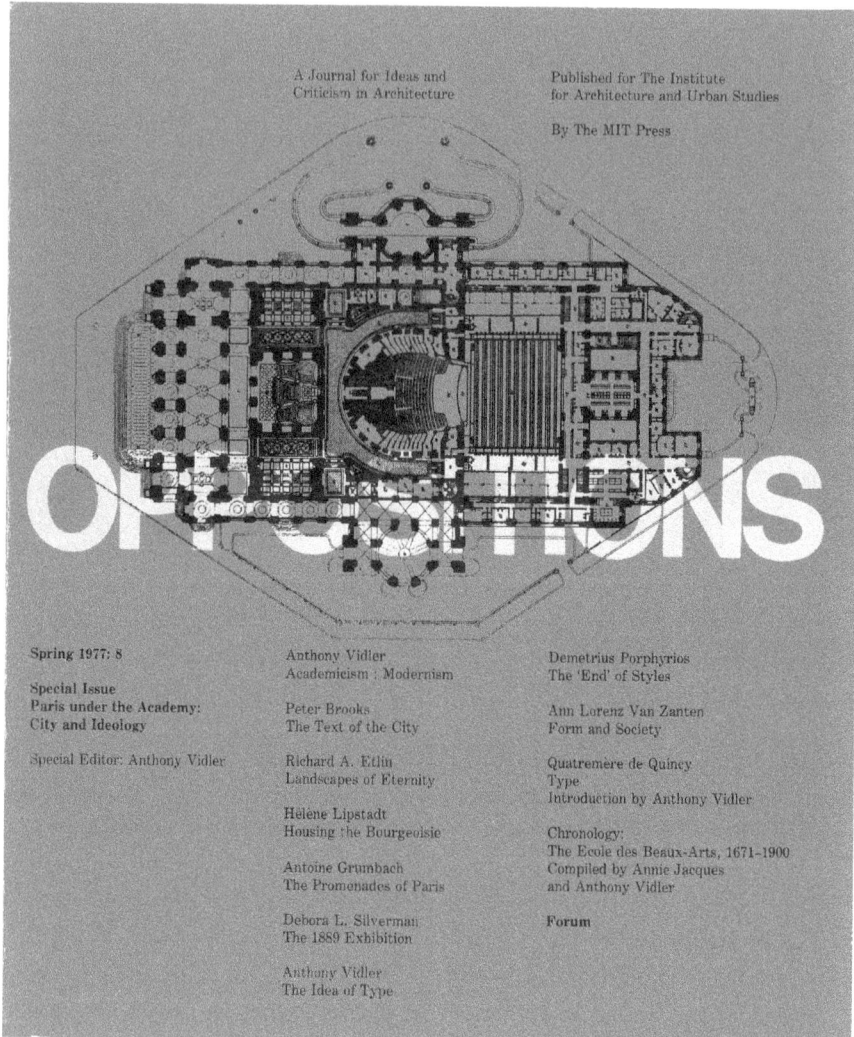

Fig. 6. *Oppositions* 8, Spring 1977. Special issue on "Paris under the Academy," edited by Anthony Vidler.

become an accomplished fact. The editors at *Oppositions* put their own gloss on the incursion of the Académie into the erstwhile bastion of high modernism while acknowledging the reality (Fig. 6). Concurrently, professional architecture schools in the United States began reorganizing their academic courses, inventing the hybrid "history/theory" or "history/theory/criticism." Over time these backslash-linked offerings tended to coalesce into a separate program in the curriculum, and specialized instructors were hired. The model of the studio critic tasked with teaching a theory or history seminar from time to time did not altogether disappear, but as history/theory increasingly became semi-autonomous from instruction in design, technology, and professional practice, its faculty were expected to have an academic degree in addition to a professional one, or at least a record of scholarly publication. The first doctoral program in an American architecture school, MIT's History, Theory, and Criticism of Architecture and Art, launched by Stanford Anderson and Henry Millon, opened in 1974, and others followed in quick succession.

By the early 1980s, postmodernism in architecture was an established international style with local variations, as well as being a media phenomenon. Instrumental in its success was the hugely expanded machinery of theoretical production. "Theory" became a new career path in architecture education and took on a life of its own in conferences, lectures, and exhibitions. *Oppositions* published its final issue in 1984, already in slightly modified and reduced format, coinciding with the closure of the IAUS in its original setup. Two years later the journal *Assemblage* began a run out of Cambridge, Massachusetts, under the direction of K. Michael Hays. It would last until 2000. While maintaining *Oppositions*'s attention to architectural history, it underwent a shift from the earlier journal's Italian inflection to French-oriented post-structuralism. A meeting and subsequent collaboration between Eisenman and Derrida, brokered in 1985 by Bernard Tschumi in the context of Tschumi's winning competition project for the park of La Villette in Paris, turned into an emblematic encounter between architecture and philosophy. The subject of a long essay by Jeffrey Kipnis in *Assemblage* 14 titled "/Twisting the Separatrix/," the Eisenman/Derrida dalliance – figured by the backslash, gendered feminine for arcane Derridean reasons – was traced in a series of oppositions that Kipnis proceeded, in virtuoso fashion, to deconstruct, with the master binary architecture/philosophy playing its reversible game.[26]

That Eisenman's architecture should excite the attentions of a French philosopher of the aura and stature of Derrida was naturally a compliment to Peter and very thrilling to avant-garde architectural culture in the mid-to-late 1980s. Though relatively short-lived, at least from the philosopher's side, the bromance provided ballast for the mixed metaphor that soon underwrote a new architectural -ism, Deconstructivism, which became the subject of another blockbuster show at MoMA in 1988 (Fig. 7). There the most politically committed of twentieth-century avant-gardes, Russian Constructivism, underwent its ultimate depoliticization, staged as antechamber to the work of seven international architects who, taken collectively, had built little to date and whose affinities were less a matter of shared ideas than personal ties and tactical public relations. The metaphor of construction/destruction was further stirred and shaken in the main catalog essay, where it was overlaid with a pseudo-Freudian narrative of "violated perfection."[27] All of this was backed by the full publicity apparatus and prestige of MoMA, resulting in an event comparable in notoriety to the International Style show five and a

Fig. 7. Philip Johnson and Mark Wigley, eds., *Deconstructivist Architecture*, exhibition catalog, Museum of Modern Art, 1988.

half decades earlier. If in the earlier exhibition European modern architecture was stripped of its social concerns and repackaged for capitalist consumption, in the later one "Decon" was offered up as materialized theory and aestheticized politics.

Much of the new theory-driven work, both textual and architectural, was marked by intense intellectual ambition as well as dense jargon. Strands of other fashionable theories, from psychoanalysis to postcolonialism to feminism, were woven in, mixed and matched according to the author's predilections, and stars from other disciplinary galaxies entered the architectural firmament. Among them was Fredric Jameson, who made an initial appearance in architectural circles at a symposium held at the IAUS in its waning days. This event was sponsored by Revisions, a group of younger architects mainly based in New York, of which I was a member. The neo-Marxist literary critic and theorist delivered a brilliant reading of Tafuri, calling, if somewhat vaguely, for a "Gramscian alternative" to the Venice historian's intransigent negativity, and we included it along with a chapter from Tafuri's book *The Sphere and the Labyrinth* (as yet unpublished) in a volume titled *Architecture Criticism Ideology* (Fig. 8).[28] The third term in our title was meant to drive home the point that theory was a form of ideology. If, as I realize now, we had chosen *Theory* instead of *Ideology*, we would have had the acronym *ACT*. But activism wasn't so much on our agenda at the time.

A year after the *Deconstructivist Architecture* show, the fall of the Berlin Wall occurred, a world-shattering event. On the exhilarating global horizon that was opening up, the theory wars and paper architecture of the 1970s and 1980s appeared increasingly irrelevant and provincial, and the raging American debates on postmodernism began to look like a tempest in an East Coast teapot. Soon enough, the avant-garde's death-by-theory was being widely autopsied across the disciplinary spectrum.[29] Excitement in architecture was also mounting over the increasing availability of powerful new computer technology.[30] Not that the obsession with theory dissipated overnight. The infatuation with Derrida and Foucault soon gave way to one with Deleuze, whose thinking architects now found more attuned to a global-digital age and dynamic, future-oriented form of practice. *Assemblage* continued to publish, but ANY (an acronym for Architecture New York) made the bigger splash, appearing belatedly in 1991. The series of ten conferences it staged, cleverly organized around the prefix "any," were studded with celebrity architects and theorists, who trotted the globe in a movable talkfest. Like *Assemblage*, the ANY publications, under Cynthia Davidson's skilled editorial direction, came to an end in 2000. A newcomer, *Grey Room*, picked up the relay, making its debut the same year and broadening its purview beyond architecture to encompass art, media, and politics. Persisting to the present day, *Grey Room* has had the longest run in the lineage of publications just described. But by the turn of the millennium the "golden age" of theory was "long past."[31]

One more event needs to be registered in concluding this highly compressed and admittedly selective history. The opening of Frank Gehry's Guggenheim Museum in Bilbao in 1997 not only astounded the cultural world with its titanium-clad bravura but also served notice that theory, if not dead, was largely superfluous. "Bilbao" was built fact, and Gehry could justify its existence simply by proclaiming it to be art.

Fig. 8. Revisions (Joan Ockman et al., eds.), *Architecture Criticism Ideology*, Princeton Architectural Press, 1985.

The Pragmatist Imagination project

In 1998 the Skidmore Owings & Merrill Foundation unexpectedly approached me and asked if I would be interested in proposing a "millennium project" that they might underwrite. As the reader may now comprehend, "Pragmatism" came tripping off my tongue. It did not prove difficult to interest SOM in the idea. Pragmatism seemed to have something to do with the firm's early history, the mid-century period when it made its reputation designing office buildings like Lever House in New York and other corporate headquarters. These edifices were hailed in their day not only as expressions of a benevolent business capitalism but also as products of rational problem-solving, teamwork, and innovative technology; their values chimed with those of Pragmatism. Or so the case was made.

After extensive discussions, SOM generously agreed to fund not one but two events, the first a workshop organized by the Buell Center and held in the spring at Columbia, the second a symposium the following autumn at the Museum of Modern Art, a higher-profile event, as the foundation desired. The workshop was to be speculative and framed around a series of "Pragmatist questions." It would engage leading thinkers from around the world and across a range of disciplines. The symposium would focus more explicitly on architecture. Publications were to come out of both events; if possible, the one from the workshop was to be out prior to the symposium so as to "educate" architects in advance about was at stake.[32]

In starting now to think in earnest about staging a pair of public events around Pragmatism, I saw the problem as twofold: first, how to inform architects about the history and significance of this philosophy; and second (and essential from a more political standpoint), how to salvage the term *pragmatist* from its more familiar and generic associations with practicality and, more pejoratively, expediency and opportunism. I wanted to draw a clear distinction between what I began calling capital–P Pragmatism and lowercase–p pragmatism. Pragmatism not only had to be introduced into architectural discourse as a theory of practice and, as such, a potential means of suturing the rift between academia and the profession, but also as a socially engaged theory of practice, one that drew on the philosophy's progressive background more than its positivistic one. The relationship between Neopragmatism and postmodernism also had to be central.

First, of course, I needed to educate myself. I had already taught a seminar at Columbia in 1996 entitled "American Architecture and American Pragmatism"; I repeated it in 1999. I also sought out the collaboration of two scholars on the wider university faculty who were knowledgeable about architecture, John Rajchman, a philosopher teaching in the art history department, and Casey Nelson Blake, a historian who headed the program in American Studies. Rajchman had written extensively on French post-structuralism. He had also coedited an anthology titled

Fig. 9. "The Pragmatist Imagination: Thinking about 'Things in the Making,'" Buell Hall, Columbia University, May 2, 2000. Video still. Courtesy of the Temple Hoyne Buell Center for the Study of American Architecture.

Post-Analytic Philosophy (1985) with the African American philosopher and activist Cornel West, who had been a student of Rorty's at Princeton. Rajchman was interested not only in the link between Derridean deconstruction and Rortyan Neopragmatism but especially in the Deleuzian connection, which went by way of Henri Bergson, whose ideas had had a powerful impact on William James early on and who would be crucial to Deleuze later. Rajchman proposed the passage from James's most Bergsonian book, *A Pluralistic Universe* (1909), that gave the Pragmatist Imagination project its subtitle, "Thinking about Things in the Making." Stating in 1909 that "what really exists is not things made but things in the making," James made clear Pragmatism's fundamental concern with temporality, growth, and creative evolution and with processes rather than objects.[33] Blake, for his part, was interested in public art and democratic space and had extensively explored the ideas of Randolph Bourne, Lewis Mumford, and other leading Progressive Era intellectuals who belonged to early American Pragmatist circles.

In preparation for the two-day workshop, we put together a reader of over five hundred pages and distributed it to the thirty-three invited presenters and moderators. Among them were philosophers, sociologists, cultural theorists, historians from several fields, a legal scholar, an activist artist, and a hip hop musician, along with a sprinkling of architects and architectural theorists.[34] Some had previously engaged with aspects of Pragmatist philosophy either directly or tangentially, but only one or two would have identified themselves as a Pragmatist or a Neopragmatist. Our

Fig. 10. Joan Ockman, ed., *The Pragmatist Imagination: Thinking about "Things in the Making,"* Princeton Architectural Press, 2000. Publication of the workshop proceedings. Graphic design by Brett Snyder.

intent was to foster unscripted exchanges and possibly to forge unorthodox connections – the event was, in short, to be a thought experiment. But in framing the half-dozen sessions around specific questions, we also wanted to zero in on matters that went to the heart of Pragmatist thinking: how to imagine the future in light of the past? How to construct democratic public space? How to understand technology's social impacts? How to relate aesthetic experience to ordinary experience? How to reconnect philosophy to everyday life? How to approach issues of citizenship and place making in an increasingly globalized world?

After the workshop, Blake expressed reservations about the event. Not unjustifiably, he was wary that architects would consume Pragmatism like one more intellectual fashion. He also felt that the presentations by a number of the speakers, which ranged from Marxian critiques to reflections on economic globalism, had stretched the meaning of Pragmatism too far, maintaining only a tenuous connection to it as "a historically coherent intellectual tradition."[35] By most of those who participated or were in the audience, however, the workshop was received with considerable interest, and I believe it is fair to say that the discussions and the subsequent publication succeeded in opening up some new avenues of thought (Figs. 9, 10).

On the heels of this experience, Rajchman and I went to work on the symposium, collaborating on the planning with Terence Riley, MoMA's chief architecture curator (Fig. 11).[36] It was now the turn of architects turn to fathom what consequences, if any, Pragmatism had for them. The individual talks and panel discussions at the symposium were, it may be stated frankly, uneven. Of the two

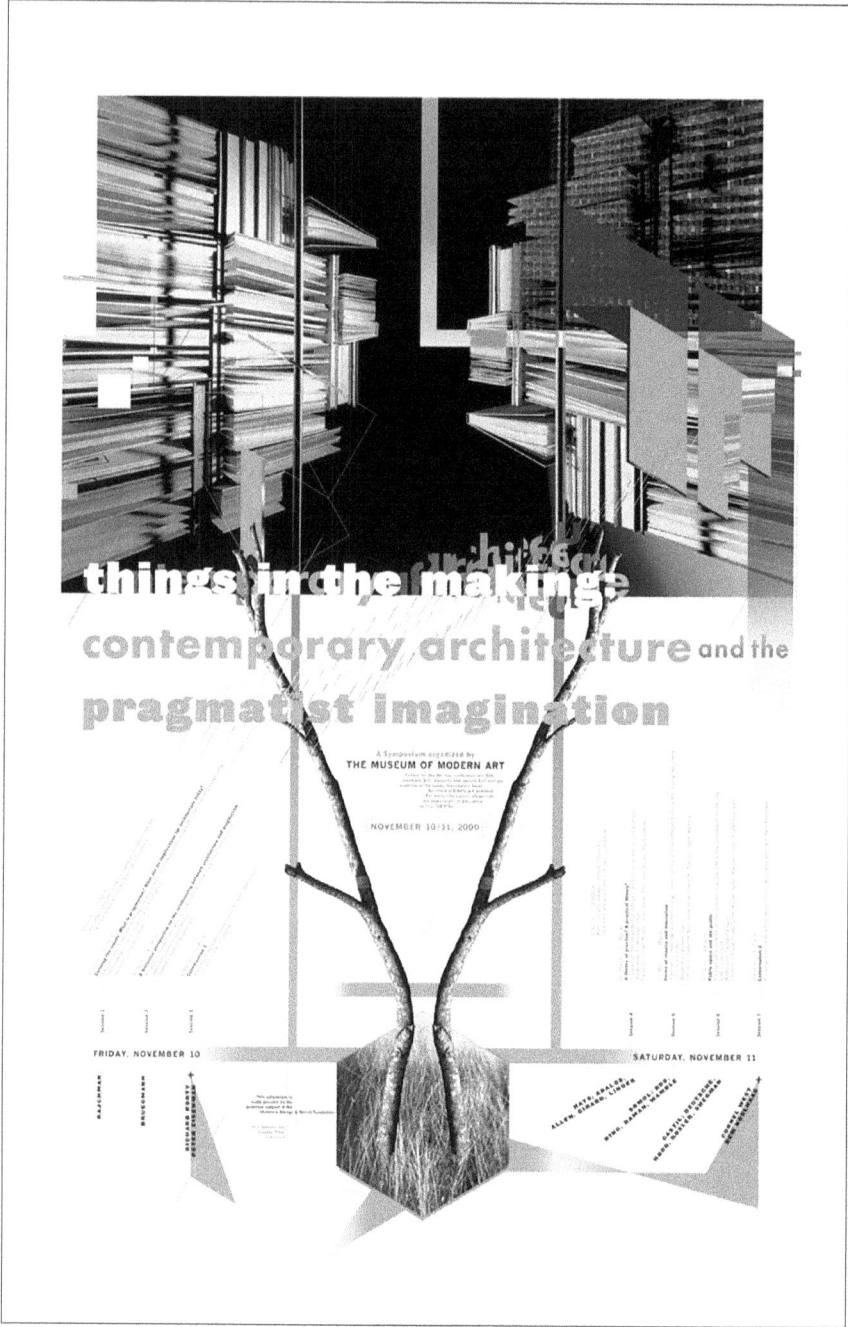

Fig. 11. "Things in the Making: Contemporary Architecture and the Pragmatist Imagination." Poster for Museum of Modern Art symposium, November 10-11, 2000. Graphic design by Bates, Hori. Courtesy of Allen Hori.

Fig. 12. Peter Eisenman, Terence Riley, and Richard Rorty at Museum of Modern Art symposium. Photo by Laura Lewis.

dozen participants, many of the practitioners reverted to lowercase–p interpretations, endeavoring to find visual equivalents for a set of ideas that resisted easy translation into architectural imagery. This resistance seemed to me not necessarily a bad thing, especially given the "slash and crash" literalism of Deconstructivism.

Of the theorists who took part, Michael Hays, having gamely agreed to moderate the first session, took a dissenting position, issuing a polemical statement in advance of the symposium entitled "Against Pragmatism." While stating that he welcomed an open-minded revisiting of the legacy of Dewey, James, and Peirce, he defended "the rich legacy of architecture theory since 1968" and assailed Neopragmatism, especially in its Rortyan version, as "ideological smoothing" – uncritical compliance with, and legitimation of, the status quo.[37] The most cogent and philosophically informed of those who undertook to refute him was Stan Allen. Stating that he had "no feelings of nostalgia for the theory-driven practices of the past decades," Allen disputed Hays's claim that a Pragmatist conception of architecture was synonymous with "generic instrumentalism." Citing the American poet William Carlos Williams's dictum "no ideas but in things," he called for a form of practice that operated "in and on the world" and was tough-minded but also generous, thoughtful but also optimistic. Another presentation that was likewise bent on moving beyond the theory/practice impasse came from Robert Somol. Entitled "Performing with a Vengeance," it put forward the alternative of "design as research." The issue, Somol asserted in a lively presentation, was "to provide trajectories for a design-research agenda that positions the discipline as a projective operation." Advocating Deleuzian diagrammatics as one such trajectory, Somol's talk would serve as a first draft for a widely read essay on which he would collaborate two years later with Sarah Whiting.[38] The latter would, in turn, become Exhibit A in the case for the "postcritical," or (as Somol prefers) the "projective."

But undoubtedly the most provocative moments at the symposium came in two keynote conversations that framed it, each involving a leading architect and a leading philosopher. The opening conversation was between Peter Eisenman and Richard Rorty (Fig. 12), the closing one between Rem Koolhaas and Cornel West.[39] In his preliminary remarks, entitled "The Artist's Use of Philosophy," Rorty, mounting a characteristic attack on metaphysical truth claims, expressed the view that philosophy had nothing more valuable than any other field to impart to creative artists and architects:

> Do not think that making past ideas coherent with one another will ever enable you to find a substitute for imagination. Do not think that philosophy will ever succeed in its attempt to trump poetry and the arts. Do not look to philosophers for anything different than the sort of inspiration that you get from poets, painters, musicians, and architects. For the ability to find coherence will never give you more than a perspicuous archival arrangement of the imaginative products of the past. It will never provide authoritative guidance for the imagination of the present.

If this disavowal of philosophy's efficacy proved slightly confounding to the assembled architects, Eisenman, in turn, upheld the need for "doubt" – for an ongoing critical-theoretical discourse within architecture that unsettled the discipline's "certainties." Their ensuing dialogue revolved around the difference between what Eisenman called "criticality" and Rorty called "novelty," with the philosopher making the case that the latter, if it was effective (that is, genuinely inventive and not just frivolous), posed the greater challenge to architecture's established practices as it did not rely on *a priori* assumptions.

The conversation between Koolhaas and West proved more contentious (Fig. 13).[40] Koolhaas began by stating that he was disturbed by the "almost nationalistic" claims that had been made for Pragmatism as an American philosophy by participants in the symposium. He pointed out that in *Delirious New York* he had argued that architects in the United States had historically been unconscious of, or impervious to, the ideological implications of their work; hence his "retroactive manifesto" had been a necessary act of revisionism – a "mopping up" operation, as he put it – to defend the virtues of a pragmatic architecture that lacked the wherewithal, or at least the desire, to produce a manifesto for itself. Ironically, in imputing an unconscious ideology of (lowercase–p) pragmatism to American architecture, Koolhaas offered a generalization no less sweeping than the chauvinist agenda of

Fig. 13. Cornel West and Rem Koolhaas at Museum of Modern Art symposium. Photo by Rainer Ganahl. Courtesy of the photographer.

which he accused the symposium. This led to West to demur. While he agreed that jingoism was always to be avoided, to deny that ideas and practices belonged to particular contexts was to be dishonest "about where you are." In his view it was better to ask, "How do we accent historical specificity, distinctiveness, without falling into chauvinist, nativistic traps?" Conversation then turned to the politics of architectural theory and practice, and more specifically to the nature of Koolhaas's own practice. In the question-and-answer period a member of the audience posed the following to Koolhaas:

> Research is clearly a very important part of the practice of your office and your intellectual life. Although I'm captivated by this research, I don't get a sense of whether there is any progressive incentive or motivation to it.

Allowing that it was an important question, Koolhaas responded:

> I would say [we use] research to transform these brutal demands that come to us into forms or operations that in themselves have a progressive component.... I think you would have to look at our work as ... a radical reading of the current conditions.

Which led West to observe:

> The word "research" is, of course, used in a number of ways. But I like the word "inquiry" better.... Judgment is always a question of some evaluation. And inquiry is much more open about that. Research has such a positivistic, scientistic history that you might begin to think the facts are talking to you as opposed to you [talking] to them.... Design as inquiry strikes me as a little more intellectually honest than design as research.

More than a semantic quibble, West's distinction between inquiry and research effectively summed up the difference between Pragmatism and pragmatism.

(Unintended) consequences

Following the symposium, reviews in the *New York Times* and elsewhere expressed equal parts interest and incomprehension (Fig. 14).[41] For my own part, and in hindsight, it increasingly appeared that the project had served to open Pandora's box. This isn't to say that the postcritical position wasn't already in the making, so to speak, before the MoMA symposium. But it now had a philosophical rationale, or at least an articulated discourse.[42] The discourse of the postcritical would unfold over the next several years, producing a certain amount of heat and light before itself running up against the accelerating cycle of intellectual consumption.

Among the things that put the brakes on the postcritical, at least temporarily, were the shock of September 11, 2001, and subsequently the recession of 2008. The first triggered an outpouring of grief and empathy, with architects in New York and elsewhere sharing in an idealistic moment of solidarity with their fellow citizens and feeling a renewed sense of social responsibility. Soon after 9/11 Koolhaas received the commission for the CCTV headquarters from the government of China – a lucky break, as he himself acknowledged, as it enabled him to escape the smoking ruins in Manhattan for Beijing. Empathy has never been his strong suit.[43] Meanwhile, the protracted rebuilding of Ground Zero devolved into business as usual. While the beginning of the Obama presidency inspired a newly hopeful political climate, recovery from the worst of the economic crisis soon permitted a resumption of pragmatist (lowercase–p) agendas, in both the United States and, for aggressive global architects, around the world. This retrenchment may continue to serve them well in the age of Trump and Brexit; as the Trump administration prepared to take office in late 2016, the prospect of bountiful infrastructure projects had some American architects licking their chops.[44] On the intellectual side, it is noteworthy that many of those who allied themselves with the postcritical a decade

Arts & Ideas
The New York Times

The New Face Of Architecture

It's about rolling with the punches, and it's called pragmatism. It's defined more by what it's not than what it is.

By SARAH BOXER

You may remember the romantic hero of Ayn Rand's novel "The Fountainhead." He is Howard Roark, an uncompromising Modernist who blows up his own building when he sees that someone has altered it. Chances are, though, that you have no recollection whatsoever of Roark's foil, Peter Keating. He is a compliant and pragmatic fellow who will do anything to keep developers and the public happy. He is the architect no one remembers.

Yet these days Keating is in the limelight. If Roark was the caricature of independent-minded Modernism, Keating has become the caricature of architecture's latest trend: its embrace of pragmatism, the century-old American philosophy of Charles Peirce, John Dewey and William James.

For a few years now, pragmatism has been enjoying a little revival. Pragmatist anthologies have been published. There is a group of prominent philosophers, including Richard Rorty, Cornel West and Hilary Putnam, who are identified as neo-pragmatists. And now there is a budding architectural movement. Last spring Columbia University was the host of an architecture conference on the subject, and its proceedings are being published by Princeton Architectural Press. This month architects, philosophers, engineers and critics gathered at the Museum of Modern Art for "Things in the Making," another conference on the marriage of architecture and pragmatism.

Just what does the marriage mean? Are architects becoming more like Peter Keating and less like Howard Roark, more business oriented and less visionary? Is this the end of grand modern architectural theories and the beginning of cost-driven practicality? Or is this an attempt to ground architecture in a philosophy that is all-American rather than European?

The answers are not all that clear, even to pragmatism's advocates. Pragmatist architecture is defined mostly by what it is not. It has no fixed notions of truth or beauty. It does not advocate one artistic style over another. It does not link a particular style with a particular meaning or form with function. It is not Modernist, postmodernist or deconstructionist. In fact, it doesn't really even have practitioners.

It is, as John Rajchman, a philosopher, said, focused on things we can't quite pin down, on "unformed things" and "interstitial spaces," in things that are not yet made. The pet phrase of pragmatist architecture, "things in the making," comes from a quote from William James: "What really exists is not things made but things in the making. Once made, they are dead."

Pragmatism is first and foremost a philosophy with a nonabsolutist idea of truth. A hundred years ago, James wrote that a belief is true if it benefits us to think so. You decide that God exists or that the sky is blue simply because you like the practical consequences of thinking them true. James asked: "What difference would it practically make to anyone if this notion rather than that notion were true?" Or, as he once put it, "What is its cash value in terms of practical experience?"

One of the main ideas that architects have taken from pragmatism is that truth and beauty are all tied up, as Dewey said, with the rest of human experience. They are organic, they constantly shift, they evolve.

Robert Bruegmann, an architectural historian, offered the shifting history of the Marquette Building of 1893 in Chicago as an

Continued on Page B11

From Modernist to "pragmatic": top, Lever House, the 1952 icon on Park Avenue; middle, Frank O. Gehry's Guggenheim Museum, in Bilbao, Spain, a vehicle for critical thinking; bottom, a "pragmatic" television studio in Taiwan, where buildings are expected to have happy decoration.

Fig. 14. Review of Museum of Modern Art symposium by Sarah Boxer, *New York Times*, November 25, 2000.

ago now occupy leading posts in academia, and the managerial jargon of neoliberalism – performativity, implementation, risk analysis, deliverables, big data, design intelligence, et al. – has thoroughly permeated the design studio. The theory fetish of the late 20th century has yielded to the research project of the twenty-first.

One of the lessons that may be taken away from a project like the Pragmatist Imagination is that history has its own agendas, despite carefully laid plans to hijack them. Ironically, the operational-affirmative position has always been closer to the critical-negative one than their respective progenitors would care to admit. While Rem Koolhaas and Manfredo Tafuri might initially appear strange bedfellows, both emerged out of the political disillusionment of the 1960s, and early in their careers both expressed scorn for any would-be redemptive form of architectural practice. Much as Tafuri attacked architects in *Architecture and Utopia* for naively harboring "hopes in design,"[45] Koolhaas has denounced architecture as a trivial pursuit in an apocalyptic world of junkspace (even as he himself continues to produce major buildings all over the world).

From a philosophical perspective, it may be that Neopragmatism stands in the same relation to neoliberalism and postmodernism as early Pragmatism did to classical liberalism and modernism. In precisely this respect, however, Rorty's relationship to Dewey is paradoxical. His attempt to partition politics off from philosophy and aesthetics remains impossible in a world in which cultural practices are inseparable from other forms of social and environmental production. No field demonstrates this more dramatically than architecture. Likewise, his assault on the traditional truths claimed by philosophy has an insidious affinity with the relativism of the alternative-fact, fake-news, reality-show universe in which we currently find ourselves.

Still, Rorty's Deweyan project of sustaining a narrative of "social hope" with respect to the democratic and egalitarian reconstruction of civic institutions and public discourse may yet be among the best strategies – at once radical and reformist, quixotic and pragmatic – available to progressive-minded people right now.[46] As a final commentary, not just related to architecture, it is noteworthy that a decade after Rorty's death in 2007, his book *Achieving Our Country* has suddenly been rediscovered and is being read alongside George Orwell's *1984*. One dystopian passage in particular has gone viral. In it Rorty warns that a sense of hopelessness among a large and disempowered group of voters will inevitably lead to the election of a strongman who purports to speak in their name. The strongman will "assure them that, once elected, the smug bureaucrats, tricky lawyers, overpaid bond salesmen, and postmodernist professors will no longer be calling the shots." After the new leader has taken office, he will turn his back on his populist promises; he will likely "worsen economic conditions" and "make his peace with the international super-rich." While his specific abuses of power will be unpredictable, "One thing that is very likely to happen is that the gains made in the past forty years by black and brown Americans, and by homosexuals, will be wiped out." Others too will suffer: "Jocular contempt for women will come back into fashion"; "a renewal of sadism" on the part of those who resent being dictated to by academics with elite credentials "will come flooding back."[47] These are the perils, Rorty admonishes, of intellectual condescension and political indifference.

One last reflection on the other half of the title of the Pragmatist project. Concerning the question of imagination, on which we have only touched in passing, the last words will be Dewey's:

> [Imagination] designates a quality that animates and pervades all processes of making and observation. It is a *way* of seeing and feeling things as they compose an integral whole. It is the large and generous blending of interests at the point where the mind comes in contact with the world. When old and familiar things are made new in experience, there is imagination. When the new is created, the far and strange become the most natural inevitable things in the world. There is always some measure of adventure in the meeting of mind and universe, and this adventure is, in its measure, imagination.[48]

Notes

1. I wish to express my gratitude to Hilde Heynen for her thoughtful comments on this paper.
2. Alexander Dorner, *The Way Beyond "Art"–The Work of Herbert Bayer* (New York: Wittenborn, Schultz, 1947), 18. See Joan Ockman, "The Road Not Taken: Alexander Dorner's Way Beyond Art," in *Autonomy and Ideology: Positioning an Avant-Garde in America*, ed. Robert Somol (New York: Monacelli Press, 1997), 80-120.
3. W. J. T. Mitchell, ed., *Against Theory: Literary Studies and the New Pragmatism* (Chicago: University of Chicago Press, 1985), 2.
4. Paraphrased from Isaac Joseph, "Reconsidering Pragmatism and the Chicago School," in *The Pragmatist Imagination: Thinking about "Things in the Making,"* ed. Joan Ockman (New York: Princeton Architectural Press, 2000), 187.
5. Arthur O. Lovejoy, "The Thirteen Pragmatisms," *Journal of Philosophy, Psychology and Scientific Methods* 5, no. 1 (January 2, 1908): 5-12.
6. With very few exceptions. For one, see Hugh Dalziel Duncan, *Culture and Democracy: The Struggle for Form in Society and Architecture in Chicago and the Middle West during the Life and Times of Louis H. Sullivan* (Totowa, NJ: Bedminster Press, 1965).
7. Gertrude Stein, "Why Do Americans Live in Europe?" *transition* 14 (Fall 1928): 97.

8. The American Pragmatist George Herbert Mead thus sarcastically summarized the philosophy's hostile reception in Europe. Cited in Hans Joas, *Pragmatism and Social Theory* (Chicago: University of Chicago Press, 1993), 98-99.
9. James first used this phrase, which he would repeat, in a lecture of 1898 entitled "Philosophical Conceptions and Practical Results," in *Pragmatism: The Works of William James* (Cambridge, MA: Harvard University Press, 1975), 268.
10. Joas, *Pragmatism and Social Theory*, 112.
11. See John Dewey, *The Public and Its Problems* (New York: Henry Holt, 1927), 157. This book by Dewey was an answer to the journalist Walter Lippmann, who had put forward the technocratic thesis in *The Phantom Public* (1925).
12. John Dewey, "Renascent Liberalism," in *Liberalism and Social Action* (New York: G. P. Putnam's Sons, 1935), 62. Cited by Richard Bernstein in "Dewey's Encounter with Trotsky," *Inter-American Journal of Philosophy* 3, no. 2 (December 2012): 7.
13. Alan Ryan, "Pragmatism Rides Again," *New York Review of Books* (February 16, 1995), 30, n. 1.
14. "Philosophers have only *interpreted* the world, in various ways; the point is to *change* it." Karl Marx, "Theses on Feuerbach," in Karl Marx and Frederick Engels, *The German Ideology, Part One*, ed. C. J. Arthur (New York: International Publishers, 1970), 123.
15. Robert Hollinger and David Depew, *Pragmatism: From Progressivism to Postmodernism* (Westport, CT: Praeger, 1995), xvi.
16. Richard Rorty, "Philosophy without Principles," in Mitchell, *Against Theory*, 134-35.
17. Ibid., 135.
18. Richard Rorty, *Achieving Our Country: Leftist Thought in Twentieth-Century America* (Cambridge, MA: Harvard University Press, 1998), 94.
19. Ibid.
20. Ibid., 91.
21. Ibid., 37.
22. Ibid., 31.
23. A major exhibition curated by Jean-Louis Cohen at the Canadian Centre for Architecture also had a strong influence on my thinking at this time; see Jean-Louis Cohen, *Scenes of the World to Come: European Architecture and the American Challenge, 1893–1960* (Paris: Flammarion, 1995).
24. The phrase "theory frenzy" is Sylvia Lavin's; see her essay "The Uses and Abuses of Theory," *Progressive Architecture* 71, no. 8 (August 1990): 113.
25. On the situation of theory in the United States after World War II, see my essay "Looking Back at the 1960s Looking Back: History and Historiography at the Modern Architectural Symposia," in *MAS: The Modern Architecture Symposia, 1962–1966*, ed. Rosemarie Haag Bletter and Joan Ockman with Nancy Eklund Later (New Haven: Yale University Press, 2014), 17-42.
26. Jeffrey Kipnis, "/Twisting the Separatrix/," *Assemblage* 14 (April 1991): 31-61.

27. Mark Wigley, "Deconstructivist Architecture," in *Deconstructivist Architecture,* ed. Philip Johnson and Mark Wigley (New York: Museum of Modern Art, 1988), 10-20.
28. Fredric Jameson, "Architecture and the Critique of Ideology," in Revisions (Joan Ockman et al., eds.), *Architecture Criticism Ideology* (New York: Princeton Architectural Press, 1985), 69.
29. See, among others, Paul Mann, *The Theory-Death of the Avant-Garde* (Bloomington: Indiana University Press, 1991).
30. Stan Allen has effectively captured these phenomena, at least as they played out in one sector of the American architecture scene, in "The Future That Is Now," in *Architecture School: Three Centuries of Educating Architects in North America*, ed. Joan Ockman (Cambridge, Mass.: MIT Press, 2012), 202-29.
31. Terry Eagleton, *After Theory* (New York: Basic Books, 2003), 1. For a more monumental (over 700-page) postmortem on literary theory, with a title somewhat similar to that of the conference that gave rise to the present publication, see Daphne Patai and Will H. Corral, eds., *Theory's Empire: An Anthology of Dissent* (New York: Columbia University Press, 2005).
32. The workshop publication actually came out a month after the symposium. A symposium volume never appeared.
33. The passage from James continues: "Once made, [things] are dead, and an infinite number of alternative conceptual decompositions can be used in defining them. But put yourself in the making by a stroke of intuitive sympathy with the thing and, the whole range of possible decompositions coming at once into your possession, you are no longer troubled by the question of which of them is the more absolutely true. Reality falls in passing into conceptual analysis; it mounts in living its own undivided life—it buds and burgeons, changes and creates. Once adopt the movement of this life in any given instance and you know what Bergson calls the *devenir réel*, by which the thing evolves and grows. Philosophy should seek this kind of living understanding of the movement of reality—not follow science in vainly patching together fragments of its dead results." William James, *A Pluralistic Universe* (New York: Longmans, Green, 1909), 264.
34. The participants included Stanley Aronowitz, Marshall Berman, Casey Blake, Sandra Buckley, Teresa Caldeira, Jean-Louis Cohen, Jonathan Crary, Rosalyn Deutsche, Kenneth Frampton, Gerald Frug, Peter Galison, Elizabeth Grosz, Andreas Huyssen, Isaac Joseph, David Lapoujade, Reinhold Martin, Brian Massumi, Mary McLeod, Paul Miller a.k.a. DJ Spooky, Chantal Mouffe, Joan Ockman, John Rajchman, Martha Rosler, Hashim Sarkis, Saskia Sassen, Sandhya Shukla, Richard Shusterman, Abdoumaliq Simone, Anders Stephanson, Bernard Tschumi, Nadia Urbinati, Mabel Wilson, and Gwendolyn Wright.
35. Casey Blake, "Afterword: What's Pragmatism Got to Do with It?" *Pragmatist Imagination*, 270.

36. The symposium took place at MoMA on November 10–11, 2000. We modified the title from that of the workshop in order to make the architectural focus clear: "Things in the Making: Contemporary Architecture and the Pragmatist Imagination." The participants included Iñaki Abalos, Stan Allen, Caroline Bos, Robert Bruegmann, Rosalyn Deutsche, Peter Eisenman, Raymond Gastil, Christian Girard, K. Michael Hays, Walter Hood, Gene King, Rem Koolhaas, Mark Linder, Joan Ockman, Mahadev Raman, John Rajchman, Terence Riley, Richard Rorty, Martha Rosler, Roger Sherman, Robert Somol, Mark Wamble, and Cornel West.
37. All quotations from the symposium come from an unpaginated transcript of the recorded proceedings.
38. See Robert Somol and Sarah Whiting, "Notes around the Doppler Effect and Other Moods of Modernism," *Perspecta* 33 (2002): 72-77. For initial efforts to put the postcritical debate into context, see George Baird, "'Criticality' and Its Discontents," *Harvard Design Magazine* (Fall 2004/Winter 2005): 16-21; and Reinhold Martin, "Critical of What? Toward a Utopian Realism," *Harvard Design Magazine* 22 (Spring/Summer 2005): 104-9. Another early polemicist of postcritical pragmatics was Michael Speaks, ironically a former doctoral student of Jameson, and among the most unabashed of the academic apologists for a neoliberal agenda; see, among other writings, Michael Speaks, "Design and the New Economy," *Architectural Record*, January 2002, 72-79.
39. Eisenman and Koolhaas were chosen as keynote speakers not only because of their reputations as two of the most theoretically inclined practitioners in the field. Eisenman had been at Princeton in the 1960s when Rorty was teaching there and had admired him from afar. Koolhaas has implicitly and explicitly endorsed a form of practice that he himself has characterized as "pragmatic." In *Delirious New York*, for example, he presents Raymond Hood – approvingly – as a "specialist in pragmatic sophistry at the service of pure creation"; see *Delirious New York: A Retrospective Manifesto for Manhattan* (New York: Monacelli Press, 1994), 195. Like Eisenman and Rorty, Koolhaas and West had never met, although both were teaching at Harvard at the time of the symposium. Interestingly, while Harvard had no problem putting its imprimatur on Koolhaas's *Harvard Design School Guide to Shopping*, published by Taschen in 2000, West's scholarship and his recording of a rap CD were deemed to undermine the values of the university, leading to a widely publicized feud with the university president, Larry Summers, that caused West to leave the faculty two years later.
40. The conversation between Koolhaas and West was moderated by Rajchman and included interventions by Rorty and others. It is published in Spanish and English in *AV Monographs* 91 (2001): 14-33, as part of a special issue titled "Pragmatism and Landscape."

41. See Sarah Boxer, "The New Face of Architecture," *New York Times*, November 25, 2000, B9, B11; and Philip Nobel, "What Pragmatism Ain't: Architectural Theorists Do a Number on William James's All-American Philosophy," *Metropolis* (July 2001): 84-85.
42. For a comprehensive account of the Pragmatist Imagination project that delves more deeply into both individual contributions and surrounding debates, see a recently completed dissertation: Pauline Lefebvre, "Tracer des reprises du pragmatisme en architecture (1990-2010): Penser l'engagement des architectes avec le réel" (PhD diss., Université Libre de Bruxelles, 2016).
43. See Rem Koolhaas, "Delirious No More," *Wired*, June 1, 2003, https://www.wired.com/2003/06/i-ny/.
44. On the reaction of the leadership of the American Institute of Architects immediately after Donald Trump's election, see "AIA Pledges to Work with Donald Trump, Membership Recoils," *Architect's Newspaper*, November 11, 2016, https://archpaper.com/2016/11/aia-pledges-work-donald-trump-membership-recoils/.
45. Manfredo Tafuri, *Architecture and Utopia: Design and Capitalist Development*, trans. Barbara Luigia La Penta (Cambridge, MA: MIT Press, 1976 [orig. ed., 1973]), 182: "Today, indeed, the principal task of ideological criticism is to do away with impotent and ineffectual myths, which so often serve as illusions that permit the survival of anachronistic 'hopes in design.'" This statement, with which Tafuri concludes his book, was a direct slap at Tomás Maldonado's recently published *La speranza progettuale* (1970), among other things.
46. For a deeper understanding of the relationship between Rorty's philosophy and politics, see various essays in his *Philosophy and Social Hope* (London: Penguin, 1999).
47. Rorty, *Achieving Our Country*, 90-91.
48. John Dewey, *Art as Experience* (New York: Minton, Balch, 1934), 267.

CODA

A Discipline in the Making

Hilde Heynen

We started this book by wondering about the historiography of recent architectural theory, questioning the process of canonization, and suggesting that the act of history writing itself tends to obscure some of the factors that play a role in the actual unfolding of this field. Architectural theory, like other scholarly and scientific disciplines, is not a totally autonomous intellectual endeavor. It is conditioned by academic institutions, funding opportunities, publication channels, relations with the profession, and geopolitical constraints – to name just the most obvious elements. Historiography all too easily overlooks such factors, giving priority to narratives that focus on the most famous names and the most obvious movements and tendencies, making these ever more famous and obvious while unintentionally oppressing the many other strands and authors that might also merit attention. The factors guiding this narrowing-down process are rarely scrutinized, because they seem to be accidental rather than constitutive for the field. Post-structuralist, feminist, and postcolonial criticisms have nevertheless pointed out that these seemingly unimportant conditioning patterns contribute to the reproduction of a very specific figure of knowledge – a figure that is intimately entangled with a hegemonic, white, patriarchal, and commodified culture. Architectural theory, as represented in historiography, thus often falls short of what we might hope and expect it to be.

We are indeed witnessing a situation in which architectural theory, which supposedly thrived on post-structuralist, feminist, and postcolonial critiques, did not fully process these inputs in a thorough self-reflection. Late twentieth-century architectural theory, as it was canonized in the 1990s,[1] was thus mostly described as a field dominated by American EastCoast intellectuals, whose concerns rarely had to do with actual problems faced by architects in real-world situations. Mary McLeod pointed out this situation in her seminal 1996 paper on "'Other' Spaces and 'Others'":

> What is disturbing is the link between theory and the architectural culture surrounding this theory. In the United States the focus on transgression in contemporary architecture circles seems to have contributed to a whole atmosphere of machismo and exclusion. One is reminded of how often avant-gardism is

a more polite label for the concerns of angry young men, sometimes graying young men. (…) These blatant social exclusions, under the mantle of a discourse that celebrates the "other" and "difference", raise the issue of whether contemporary theorists and deconstructivist architects have focused too exclusively on formal subversion and negation as a mode of practice.[2]

The setup of the 2017 conference that generated many of the essays for this book explicitly addressed these issues. It asked contributors to "screen the unspoken rules of engagement" and focus on "singular and 'minor' expressions of theory" that might harbor in "local discourses."[3] Many contributors took up the challenge. Hence a reflection on the chapters that made it into this volume allows to identify some of the conditioning patterns that shaped the figure of late twentieth-century architectural theory (although I certainly cannot claim to be exhaustive in this analysis).

The modifying factors that stand out most clearly can be ordered under three headings. The first pattern has to do with the question of *what kind of knowledge* architectural theory strives towards, or, put differently: what other discipline(s) are considered to offer guidance and a model to aspire to? The second pattern relates to the question of *what is at stake* in architectural theory: how do architectural theorists see the added value of their work? What battles are they fighting and why? These questions are entangled with the third set of considerations, which focus on *positionality*. Here the questions are about geographical, institutional, and temporal factors that favor some voices, in some languages, while disadvantaging others.

What kind of knowledge?

In the time period after 1968, architectural theory changed gears, so it seems. There is a telling difference between Joan Ockman's *Architecture Culture 1943-1968* and Michael Hays's *Architectural Theory since 1968* – two volumes that were meant to work as a tandem.[4] Ockman's title did not highlight "theory" as a key word, which suggests that it was not yet configured as a separate discipline. Moreover, her set of authors comprised many more practicing architects than Hays's did, and the texts she anthologized were much shorter. She thus selected from other *kinds* of text than Hays did. Generally, the texts that she chose were primarily oriented towards either a general public or practicing architects. Hays, on the other hand, selected more sophisticated, philosophically complex, and intellectually challenging texts for a readership composed of other theorists or mature students.

The authors in *The Figure of Knowledge* identify different frames of reference, according to which architectural theory is modeled on the basis of different scholarly disciplines. In many chapters the pilot discipline is philosophy — as it was for Michael Hays. This is related to the urge of several architectural theorists to upgrade their discipline into a recognizable scholarly field that is part of the humanities. In contrast to this ambition, other authors continue to situate architectural discourse as more closely aligned with architectural and art criticism. Lastly there is a chapter that discusses architectural theories as implicit rather than explicit bodies of thought, underlying a series of practices that rarely are perceived as "architectural theory."

1. Pilot discipline: philosophy

In both the opening and concluding chapters of this book, the main frame of reference is philosophy. André Loeckx's chapter, which I coauthored [CHAPTER 1], deals with the vicissitudes of semiotics in architecture. Semiotics is the study of signs, originating from linguistics, but gaining increasing importance in the 1960s and 1970s as an instigator of seminal changes in philosophy. The French version of semiotics — semiology, based on the works of Ferdinand de Saussure — was implicated in the shift from structuralism to post-structuralism in that period. The Anglo-Saxon version — building upon the works of Charles Sanders Peirce and Charles W. Morris — became a reference point for aesthetics. The exciting insights into processes of signification and coding emerging from both these strands, generated an increasing interest in the philosophy of culture. Semiotics also inspired many developments in related fields such as literary theory, art theory, and cultural studies. No wonder that architectural critics and historians, interested in finding a solid basis for their understanding of architecture, turned to semiotics as a promising field that could foster a theory of architecture worthy of the name. Conversely, some semioticians — most notably Umberto Eco — turned to architecture as a complex field allowing them to test the productivity of their concepts. Loeckx and Heynen discuss the work of a plethora of architectural writers — including Geoffrey Broadbent, Charles Jencks, Philippe Panerai, Aldo Rossi, and Peter Eisenman — tracing how the philosophical changes induced by semiotics and semiology registered in architectural discourse. They critically engage with the difficult issue of how post-structuralist architectural discourse relates to everyday social reality, questioning the role of the architectural theorist as somebody potentially far removed from the concerns of practicing architects and the challenges implied by transforming cities. Their conclusion reconfirms, however, the necessity for architectural theory to fundamentally engage with philosophical discourses, in order to deepen its own knowledge basis and to strengthen its argumentative power.

Joan Ockman, in the final chapter of this volume [CHAPTER 14], likewise focuses on an important philosophical movement, namely Pragmatism. Pragmatism is a specifically *American* intellectual tradition, going back to the work of William James and John Dewey. In her semi-autobiographical reflection, Ockman ponders on the project she devised, together with philosopher John Rajchman and historian Casey Blake, to launch Pragmatism as an American answer to the disturbing effects of the reliance upon "French Theory" (read: semiotics and post-structuralism) that was prevalent in architectural theory up till the 1990s. Regretfully admitting that her Pragmatist project was not a success, she also ends her essay, like Loeckx and Heynen, by pointing to the inevitable entanglements between architecture and its sociopolitical condition – entanglements that can only be unraveled by further theoretical reflections that build upon these philosophical traditions.

Like Ockman, Paul Holmquist [CHAPTER 9] turns to an American imprint of philosophy in the meanderings of architectural theory in the late twentieth century, the central figure in his essay being Hannah Arendt. Positioning Arendt's philosophy as a "phenomenological account of human politics intrinsically related to a fabricated common world," Holmquist discusses how both Kenneth Frampton and George Baird took up elements from her thinking to construct their own theoretical approach – Frampton by elaborating on the "resistive political capacity of architectural construction," Baird by envisioning "how architecture can accommodate (...) a passionate, symbolic public realm." Both architectural theorists thus take their clues from philosophical discourse in order to formulate their thoughts on architecture.

Lastly, Karen Burns [CHAPTER 13] also departs from philosophical musings by putting the post-structuralist topic of gender and subjectivity center stage. For her, the experimental writing initiated by French philosophers such as Hélène Cixous or Luce Irigaray was highly significant for the production of architectural theory in the 1980s and 1990s. Authors such as Daniel Libeskind, Robert Segrest, Jennifer Bloomer, and Ann Bergren published writings that explored the borderland between fiction, rational analysis, and designerly ways of thinking, emulating the experimental prose of the so-called *écriture féminine*. According to Burns, later historiography cleansed architectural theory from this once important genre, revealing the backlash of neo-conservative and anti-feminist forces.

2. Architectural theory as part of the humanities

Closely related to the positioning of philosophical traditions as pilot disciplines was the desire to construct architectural theory as a fully academic scholarly field that could hold its own among other humanities. This part of the story has to do with the status of architectural history. Whereas architectural history was generally seen, up till the 1960s, as part of the more general field of art history, this began to change in the later years of the decade. It was no longer obvious that architectural history would be taught by art historians, since architects themselves began to claim expertise and to develop relevant scholarship.[5] Among the emerging new generation of architectural historians there were a lot of architects: Manfredo Tafuri, Christian Norberg-Schulz, Kenneth Frampton, Charles Jencks, and Alan Colquhoun; all had degrees in architecture before they turned to architectural history. Late twentieth-century architectural theory, one could claim, is to a certain extent the offspring of this academic battle for hegemony in the teaching of architectural history, since it was through elaborating theoretical discourses that these newly minted scholars began to differentiate themselves from their old-fashioned rivals, who were art historians without the benefit of an architectural education.[6]

This new situation also relates to the establishment of doctoral programs in architectural schools in North America as well as in Europe, as Ole W. Fischer argues in the present volume [CHAPTER 6]. Fischer narrates how prestigious architectural schools such as MIT in Cambridge (Massachusetts) and ETH in Zürich (Switzerland) responded to the crisis of modernism by institutionalizing programs in history and theory of architecture that educated students towards a PhD. What was at stake in these programs, according to Fischer, was no less than "a revision of modernity as a scientific project." By awarding doctoral degrees in "History, Theory, and Criticism of Architecture" (MIT) or "Geschichte und Theorie der Architektur" (ETH), these schools ostensibly displaced the discourse about architecture from the field of art towards the broader humanities, claiming for architectural history and theory a position as a scholarly discipline. Through the very existence of these doctoral programs, architectural theory moreover became more academic and sophisticated in its exchange with other fields of knowledge.

A similar background story can be traced in the contribution by André Loeckx and myself on semiotics in architecture [CHAPTER 1]. The semiotic turn we discuss was motivated by a desire to find a well-structured and scientifically valid discourse that might be transposed to architecture. Architectural theory in a sense relied upon semiotics to reinvent itself as a scholarly valid discourse. This endeavor also contributed to the academization of architectural discourse, because it generated an exchange with a long-established field in the humanities such as linguistics.

Sebastiaan Loosen [CHAPTER 5] likewise points to epistemological questions as important drivers of the interest in architectural theory. According to him, the 1970s in Belgium was a time where architects were at a loss to answer basic questions about what values they should adhere to and why. He argues that "the intellectual malaise was so profound" that different voices "might even be found to differ on the fundamental level as to *what* knowledge about architecture actually *is or should be*" (p. 127). Within this diverging field, some protagonists indeed turned to science and the humanities to find foundations on which to build architectural knowledge.

These three chapters thus highlight how architectural theory in the late 20th century not only based itself upon philosophy as the discipline to be emulated but also claimed for itself a place among other humanities. By establishing doctoral programs, fostering scholarly publications such as *Assemblage* (US) or *Archis* (the Netherlands), and seeking to publish with university presses, architectural theory aimed for a position within the university. By becoming more academically savvy, it also drifted away from its previous, free floating status as an activity indulged in by architects who were first of all practitioners and only afterwards teachers and writers, to now become a full-time occupation for academics.

3. Art criticism

Architectural theory nevertheless did not fully divorce itself from art and architectural criticism as practiced in the broader field of culture. As the name of the doctoral program in MIT – HTC (History, Theory, Criticism) – already indicated, architectural theory's alliance with history *and* with criticism remained operational. Some of the chapters in this book thus point towards figures and situations where architectural theory manifested itself in and through art (or architectural) criticism.

We see this phenomenon most clearly at work in the figure of Lara-Vinca Masini, discussed by Peter Lang [CHAPTER 3]. Masini was a critic, curator, editor, publisher, and writer who, according to Lang, "played a pivotal role from the outset in the emergence of the *Superarchitecture* movement that would spawn radical groups like Superstudio, Archizoom, and successively, UFO, 9999, Zziggurat and others" (p. 81). Her appearance in a book on architectural theory might be surprising because she is not internationally well known and there is not one key text that would summarize her ideas and that could act as vehicle to spread her fame. Indeed, the relevance of her work in architectural theory does not solely reside in her writings. What Lang makes clear is that it is in the *practice of curating* that she acts out her ideas on art, architecture, history, and the city. Through her installations and exhibitions, through her selection of specific works of specific artists for specific places in the city, she shaped new relations between private and public, between architecture and art, between history and the present, and between the city's morphology and its historical legacy. Her exhibitions questioned the received image of Florence as the Renaissance capital, veering away from the ever-repeated celebration of its fifteenth-century heritage and opening it up for more disturbing questions about its recent past and its position in the present. Masini's work, one can claim, *enacts* a theoretical position and is thus valid as another possible "figure of knowledge" for architectural theory – alongside its well-rehearsed manifestation in seminal texts and academic disputes.

Robin Boyd, as presented by Philip Goad [CHAPTER 2], can be compared to Lara-Vinca Masini in certain respects. As an Australian architect and critic with a wide international network, he played some role in international exchanges, but his main impact – like that of Masini – was local and strongly connected to his own personality. Whereas he wrote many articles and books that were well received at the time, his lack of a clear theoretical or aesthetic allegiance, according to Goad, played a role in the withering away of his visibility after his early death. Boyd always wrote from the point of view of the practicing architect that he also was. Hence his work aimed more for the astute formulation of specific criticism, rather than for the abstract formulations of a more generally valid theory. In the few cases that his work came close to a theoretical position – like in his 1965 *Puzzle of Architecture* – his relaxed journalistic writing style, which avoided reaching firm conclusions, made it eminently readable but less apt as a theoretical manifesto with retaining value as an anchoring point for future discussions.

Sebastiaan Loosen's chapter [CHAPTER 5] also points towards art and architectural criticism as an important face of architectural theory. Whereas some of his protagonists turned to science and the humanities to find a stable footing for architectural discourse, there were others (such as Mil De Kooning, Geert Bekaert, and bOb Van Reeth) who advocated an architectural intellectuality that was permanently engaged with the real. This "realist" position was in a certain sense mistrusting words and discourse, since the ideal situation would be that "the real" would speak for itself. Hence these critics saw their own writings as a labor that came close to a notion of *poiesis*, the Greek word for "making": in their eyes, the work of the critic resembles that of the poet more closely than that of the philosopher. Their theoretical utterances were thus deeply entrenched with a literary and poetical vocabulary and writing style that steered away from generalizations and often emulated the practice of criticism in its focus on specific works and phenomena.

4. "Theory" versus "theories"

A last frame of reference is the one invoked by Matthew Allen in his discussion of programming in the 1960s [CHAPTER 4]. His starting point is the "premise that it is worth questioning the distinction whereby *Theory* upholds standards of critique while (minor, ad hoc) *theories* are tied down to contingencies of practice" (p. 102). He thus suggests that the genre of Theory canonized in the well-known anthologies superseded another competing genre – that of "theories" embedded in practices and techniques. His argument is made clear by delving into the recent history of "programming" in architecture. In the 1960s "programming" was gaining momentum as a more advanced formulation of the main idea of functionalism ("form follows function" became "form follows program"). In the ideological battle of the early 1980s, the centrality of the idea of "programming" was repudiated – to be replaced by the "negation of functionalism" as formulated by Peter Eisenman and others. Programming however did not disappear from architecture, but went as it were underground: it continued to be the driving force behind the elaboration of computer programs for architecture – very clumsy and laborious ones at first, more smooth and effective ones later. Allen thus argues that the victory of "Theory" writ large is somewhat of a mirage: underneath this seemingly dominant "Theory" there are many other "theories," based on a very different set of assumptions and methods, that continue to be operational and influential without being recognized or articulated on the explicit level of "Theory." He illustrates this view through an analysis of printouts from early computer programs, which he sees in terms of aesthetic schemata illustrating different "figures of knowledge' at work in architectural computation.

This chapter is a particularly salient one in this volume, because it shows that architectural theory as a body of ideas is not confined to the ones that are made explicit in philosophical or critical texts. Indeed, architectural theory might be *embodied* in architectural practices such as computational design, as argued by Allen, or *enacted* rather than articulated, as in the work of Lara-Vinca Masini. We can go even further and argue that implicit theories of architecture could be recognized, e.g., in the study curriculum of architects, in the way architectural offices are organized, or in the way competition briefs are formulated. All these instances have, as a backdrop, ideas and convictions on what architecture is or should be – that are made operational in the practice of teaching, managing an office, or organizing a competition. These ideas are not always explicitly elaborated in long texts, but careful analysis – like the one proposed here by Allen – allows to recognize, discuss, and criticize them – which is the work of (the history of) theory.

What is at stake?

Another way of looking at these essays has to do with the question of how they identify what is at stake in architectural theory. Here I recognize two lines of engagement. The first one deals with the issue of autonomy: is architecture (or architectural theory) an autonomous field developing according to its own logic or is architecture a field that is in constant interaction with other domains that influence its configurations? The second line of engagement maps the ideological battles between different approaches that strive for dominance or criticize existing hegemonic patterns.

1. Autonomy versus heteronomy

Louis Martin [CHAPTER 7] refers to Stanford Anderson's distinction between an *internal* and *external* history of architecture. An internal history focuses on what is unique to architecture, while an external one highlights the social conditions that constrain and enable the developments in architecture. Martin uses this distinction to claim that in the case of Melvin Charney, the Montreal architect and artist, architectural theory is enriched and enabled by concepts drawn from external disciplines (notably semiotics), while its internal structure nevertheless remains remarkably stable. This stable structure has to do with a way of thinking that relies upon dualities ("architecture and engineering" [Le Corbusier], "feeling and thinking" [Giedion], "twin-phenomena" [Van Eyck]). In the case of Charney, such dualities were framed as oppositions: "design versus architecture," "image versus Process," and so on. Charney thus exemplifies – at least in the eyes of Martin – how the paradigmatic shift in architectural theory from a biological to a linguistic analogy did not structurally change the dualistic way of thinking inherited from the Modern Movement. Inserting external references (theories of the sign a.o.) in this case only reinforced the internal logic of the field. It is Martin's contention that this process illustrates what he calls, following Anderson, the "semi-autonomy" of architecture and architectural knowledge.

Martin concludes his chapter with a series of exploratory considerations that challenge the starting points of this book and of this coda. For him, the theoretical frameworks that waxed and waned in architectural theory – critical theory, postmodernism, critical regionalism, deconstructivism, or pragmatism – are more than surface phenomena and cannot be explained away as the result of external influences. In his view, the paramount objective of historiography is therefore to "uncover the latent logic of the field in mapping the relationship between these concepts and explaining their role in the development of architectural 'knowledge'" (p. 175). He likewise underscores that the configuration of architectural knowledge remains relatively stable in the long run, although its thematic contents change. With these statements Martin clearly endorses a viewpoint that favors an internal rather than an external history of architecture and its theory, because he sees external factors as influencing but not determining.

In contrast with Martin, Andrew Toland [CHAPTER 8] sees "an evolution of architecture's intellectual culture away from internal disciplinary questions" (p. 182) since the 1990s. He interprets the "dirty realism" that is the topic of his chapter as the harbinger of this very evolution. Mapping the discourse of dirty realism as proposed by Liane Lefaivre in her interpretation of the work of a group of architects figure headed by Rem Koolhaas, Toland compares this new discourse with earlier versions of realism and with the attempts of historians like Manfredo Tafuri or Fredric Jameson to interconnect architectural developments with processes of globalization. The main question addressed by this discourse is that of the agency of architecture and urbanism: is it possible for architects and urban designers to not only take into account the "real" environment of a globalizing world but to design, in the words of Lefaivre, "lyrical objects that provoke reflection and action in connection with a world that reflects the social and ecological realities of our cities – realities that are becoming ever 'dirtier'" (p. 186)? This rapprochement between internal and external factors led, according to Toland, to an ambivalent aesthetic mode of response, in which intellectual and affective dimensions were interwoven – an aesthetic mode that recognized the totality of the globalized world as a construct, in the face of which however the design disciplines were all but powerless.

Sebastiaan Loosen [CHAPTER 5] likewise recognizes a moment of impotency in the confrontation between an architectural culture that was used to looking inwards and one that needed to look outwards to address a societal condition. In the moment of crisis provoked by the demise of modernism, architectural culture in Belgium apparently was at a loss, unable to determine what exactly the criteria should be with which to assess architectural projects. The internal logic provided by modernist discourse apparently no longer sufficed, but neither was there a common understanding of what other logic could replace the modernist one. Loosen interprets this situation as a genuine confusion as to the epistemological status of architectural knowledge: the protagonists in the debates that he maps had very different ideas about how architecture related to (or should relate to) social reality. It is apparently in such moments of crisis that an internal history of architecture, which would stress its autonomy, no longer suffices, since the historical actors themselves struggle with how to understand architecture's relation to external realities.

2. Ideological battles

As stated above, architectural theory did not always put into practice a self-reflection, applying the critical insights it imported from other disciplines on its own configuration. Hence the sometimes angry and disappointed tone of later reflections looking back at key moments that seemed promising from a feminist or postcolonial perspective but that were not carried through.

One can recognize this disappointment in Karen Burns's contribution to this volume [CHAPTER 13]. She traces how a particular strand of architectural theory that experimented with modes of writing and that was seen as a central concern of theory in the first half of the 1990s was sidelined in the anthologies that were produced in the second half of that decade. Her interpretation is that this strand fell victim to the "Culture Wars" that were waged against critical theory generally and its feminist overtones specifically. These "Culture Wars" were part of a largely successful neo-conservative project that managed to discredit architectural theory as a feminized and futile practice of endless arguments that led nowhere. And the architectural theory that was passed on to the next generation was one that did not recognize its own feminist genealogy. Whereas one could have expected that the feminist experimental *écriture* would have been honored in subsequent historiography, this did not happen, due to gendered editorial practices. The end result is a marginalization of *l'écriture* and its many women exponents, who disappeared from view in the folds of the dominant narrative.

One aspect of Burns's diagnosis is further analyzed by Sandra Kaji-O'Grady in her chapter on the feminization of architectural theory [CHAPTER 12]. She zooms in on the metaphors that were used in the early 2000s when architectural theory was repudiated for its supposed ineffectiveness and when the "critical project" came to be seen as "exhausted." She writes:

> The figure that was conjured [in this battle] was a male architect-writer whose impotency was exposed by the action-oriented pragmatism of the architect-builder. These attacks used the very same gendered dichotomies that feminist theorists had sought to expose at the heart of the architectural discourse (p. 243).

For Kaji-O'Grady this attack on theory had severe consequences, since careers were forged or faltered and many theorists shifted their work more towards history or towards the newly minted "architectural humanities." She observes that the year 1996, which could be framed as a moment of "triumph of feminist theory in architecture" given the many topical publications that came out that year, also might be seen as the beginning of the end. The outsider status, which had briefly allowed women in architecture to engage in a critical dialogue fueled by their marginality, did not protect them against the backlash unleashed by anti-theory and anti-feminist forces. Historiography moreover added insult to injury by minimalizing the import of this whole episode.

Both Burns and Kaji-O'Grady write from a position of close alignment with the feminist and women authors of the 1990s – Burns as part of that cohort, Kaji-O'Grady as a slightly younger sympathizer. They are both also rather explicit about this alliance and about the perspective from which they write. This is not always the case. Many historiographic endeavors tend to present themselves as "neutral" and "objective," not by stating this explicitly but rather by keeping silent about their perspective. According to Ricardo Ruivo [CHAPTER 11], this attitude has generated a questionable historiography of the Soviet avant-garde, which, to his mind, was an "invention" of Western scholars rather than an adequate narration of what actually unfolded in the early years of the USSR. He claims that "this historiography of Soviet architecture became a tool for the consolidation of a specific, today dominant architectural ideology, which is linked to the ascension of a liberal alternative to the left" (p. 227). Referring to Tafuri and Anatole Kopp, Ruivo insists that the continental narratives describing constructivism from the viewpoint of "operative criticism" were more true to the original discourse and intentions of their protagonists, since they explicitly recognized the political motivation of the Russian avant-garde of the 1920s. Anglo-American historiography, which later came to dominate, was, on the other hand, inclined to overlook this political dimension, focusing on aesthetic categories instead. It is this historiography that is now mainstream and that, unwittingly perhaps, reproduces a neo-liberal ideology by looking away from the intense political battles about the right way for communism that were so important to the Russian architects and artists from the 1920s. This type of historiography flattens out what was an intensive intellectual and cultural struggle and thus silently reinforces Western, mainstream ideological concepts that are not spelled out but assumed.

Carmen Popescu [CHAPTER 10] revisits the discourse of "critical regionalism," which was meant to offer a valid alternative to modernism without succumbing to the seduction of historicism and formalism, as practiced by the postmodernists of the Strada Novissima in Venice's first architectural biennale of 1980. She also frames the intellectual pursuit of a solid theoretical foundation for critical regionalism – the motivation behind the work on critical regionalism of Tzonis and Lefaivre on the one hand and Frampton on the other – by pointing towards the battle lines between those who wanted to continue in the line of modernism and those who embraced historical formal languages. To her mind, the battle was inconclusive – or at least the intellectual superiority of the "critical regionalism" project could not be established since the movement suffered a "loss of criticality" – because it didn't recognize that it was on the one hand constructing a historiography while simultaneously being considered to be helpful as a guideline for the contemporary production of architecture. Popescu doesn't use the term here, but her contention seems to be that critical regionalism didn't really work out because operative criticism doesn't remain credible in the long run. If my interpretation is correct, this would mean that Popescu takes a different position from Ruivo. Whereas Ruivo seems to advocate that operative criticism is the best approach, since it at least allows readers to understand where the historian is coming from, Popescu rather points to the incommensurability between history and criticism. Her concluding remarks moreover suggest that critical regionalism entailed a veiled attempt to prolong the hegemony of a specifically *Western* discourse, and that its loss of criticality had to do with its insufficient processing of postcolonial and subaltern critiques.

Positionality

Since the 1980s, post-structuralist, feminist, and postcolonial criticisms have made us aware of the importance of situated and embodied knowledge.[7] The identity of the researcher or scholar in terms of class, age, gender, nationality, ethnicity, etc. is not merely external to the construction of knowledge but impacts and conditions research questions, methodologies, funding opportunities and so on. Hence it is not superfluous to question the position from which architectural theorists in the recent past were writing, nor is it futile to ask the same question regarding the contributors to this volume.

In pondering these questions, it becomes very clear that the Anglo-Saxon discourse has been the central point of reference for architectural theory since roughly 1968. Although there existed and exist lively and interesting platforms of exchange in French, Italian, Spanish, German, Dutch, and other languages, their impact was and remains limited by their language. Whereas the avant-garde in the 1920s relied upon German, French, and Russian (see, e.g., the journals *Vetsj, Gegenstand, Objet*), the postwar world indeed witnessed a growing dominance of English. In this "American century", English became virtually hegemonic. This can be deducted from the fact that ambitious editors of periodicals in other languages thought that they should at least provide abstracts in English; or from the circumstance that the import of many theorists based outside of the English-speaking world is often assessed in terms of whether or not translations of their work are available in English. Since English became our lingua franca, it is by being translated in English that writers have access to a globalized audience.

The editors of *The SAGE Handbook of Architectural Theory* (2012) indeed stated that "the best known centres of architectural theory are located within the Anglo-Saxon cultural sphere – London, the American East and West Coasts, one or two centres in Australia. Paris, Venice and Berlin, like Barcelona and Rotterdam, are on the map, but they do not have the same force of gravity. Other parts of the world – the whole of Asia, Africa and Latin America – do not really play along."[8] This academic hegemony is not just a product of American soft power or of economic dominance. It also directly relates to funding opportunities, for it is only in these places of centrality that one finds professors of architectural history and theory who are expected to do research and to publish internationally.

This situation gives rise to a complex dynamic of center and periphery. In North America – and especially at the East Coast – 'French theory' was of utmost importance in the last decades of the 20th century.[9] This discourse also had a large impact on architectural theory, as can be seen from the contributions of Ockman [CHAPTER 14], Fischer [CHAPTER 6], Martin [CHAPTER 7], Kaji-O'Grady [CHAPTER 12] and Burns [CHAPTER 13]. Arguably, the 'French theory' version of the ideas and works of continental philosophers such as Michel Foucault, Jean-François Lyotard, Pierre Bourdieu, Jean Baudrillard, Henri Lefebvre, or Jacques Derrida differed from the original version – if only because the work often was only partially translated. The intellectual context and the rich interaction with other thinkers was also obscured from view, resulting in a "French theory" that current French intellectuals barely recognize as such (a recent PhD dissertation thematizes, e.g., how in the 1990s Jacques Derrida was a big shot in Anglo-Saxon architectural theory whereas he barely registered on the French architectural scene).[10]

Philip Goad [CHAPTER 2] analyses an interesting example of this center-periphery dynamic by discussing the work of Robin Boyd. As an Australian and a regular visitor to North America and the UK, Boyd had easy access to publication channels such as periodicals. When it came to books, however, his publishing house was an Australian one, which meant that his books were not readily available on the American market. Hence the impact of his work is less than it could have been. Peter Lang points to the fact that his protagonist – Lara-Vinca Masini – published only in Italian and that her work was never translated into English. This, he thinks, was one of the reasons why she never became internationally significant, although she was quite well known in Italy.

The figure of knowledge for architectural theory is thus partially shaped by these geographical and institutional factors. They also contribute to what one could call a different sensibility on both sides of the Atlantic. It seems to me that architects and teachers in Europe have more of a direct line with planning administrations and government bodies. There is also a stronger tradition of architectural competitions and there are thus more entanglements between public bodies and architectural intellectuality. Hence in Europe the impact of architectural theorists, however indirect, on what actually gets built, seems to be more important than in the United States. This might be one of the reasons why the criticality debate, which was so pertinent in North America, seemed to be far less relevant from a European point of view.[11] This different sensibility might also be the reason for which the dividing lines between history, theory, criticism, and practice might be more permeable on this side of the ocean, as one might deduce from, e.g., the contributions by Loosen [CHAPTER 5], Lang [CHAPTER 3] and Toland [CHAPTER 8] – although Martin's chapter about the Canadian architect Charney [CHAPTER 7] presents us with a counterexample (but then again, Canada is in many respects more European than American).

This volume of course does not escape the logic of academic hegemony either, certainly not when one looks at the geographic location of the authors of the different chapters. The book simply confirms that architectural theory and its historiography is firmly based in North America (six authors) and Europe (seven authors), with quite some inputs from Australia (four authors). Masculine dominance likewise is confirmed (twelve male versus five female authors). Thematically only Ricardo Ruivo [CHAPTER 11] and Carmen Popescu [CHAPTER 13] deal with topics that escape this geographic confinement – the Russian avant-garde on the one hand, critical regionalism on the other. (It should be mentioned though that this outcome is partially an artefact: some of the most engaging contributions to the 2017 conference dealt with architectural theories that were developed in the communist world. For editorial reasons, however, these papers were developed into a theme issue of the periodical *Architectural Histories*.)[12]

All in all the contributions in this book clearly show that many different factors and circumstances play a role in the evolution of a discipline of architectural theory in the late twentieth century. Without being exhaustive in its analysis, this volume nevertheless makes clear that the discourse of the period was much richer, much more complicated, and much more entangled than we are led to believe through the process of canonization. If we want to foster an architectural culture that embraces this critical legacy, it is important that we continue to have an open mind for trajectories and ideas that do not belong to the mainstream but that are inspirational and instructive, maybe not in spite of, but rather because of their marginality.

Notes

1. Kate Nesbitt, ed., *Theorizing a New Agenda for Architecture: An Anthology of Architectural Theory, 1965-1995* (New York: Princeton Architectural Press, 1996); Neil Leach, ed., *Rethinking Architecture: A Reader in Cultural Theory* (New York: Routledge, 1997); K. Michael Hays, ed., *Architecture Theory since 1968* (Cambridge, MA: The MIT Press, 1998).
2. Mary McLeod, "'Other' Spaces and 'Others'," in *The Sex of Architecture*, ed. Diana Agrest, Patricia Conway, and Leslie Kanes Weisman (New York: Harry N. Abrams, 1996), 21-22.
3. The Call for Papers for "Theory's History, 196X-199X. Challenges in the Historiography of Architectural Knowledge" can be consulted at https://architectuur.kuleuven.be/theoryshistory/.
4. Joan Ockman, ed., *Architecture Culture, 1943-1968: A Documentary Anthology* (New York: Columbia University GSAPP/Rizzoli, 1993); Hays, *Architecture Theory since 1968*.
5. Jorge Otero-Pailos, *Architecture's Historical Turn: Phenomenology and the Rise of the Postmodern* (Minneapolis: University of Minnesota Press, 2010).
6. Stanford Anderson, "Architectural History in Schools of Architecture," *Journal of the Society of Architectural Historians* 58, no. 3 (1999): 282-90. DOI: https://doi.org/10.2307/991520.

7. Donna Haraway, "Situated Knowledges: The Science Question in Feminism and the Privilege of Partial Perspective," *Feminist Studies* 14, no. 3 (1988): 575-99. DOI: https://doi.org/10.2307/3178066; Hilde Heynen and Gwendolyn Wright, "Introduction: Shifting Paradigms and Concerns," in *The SAGE Handbook of Architectural Theory*, ed. C. Greig Crysler, Stephen Cairns, and Hilde Heynen (London: SAGE, 2012), 41-55.
8. C. Greig Crysler, Stephen Cairns, and Hilde Heynen, eds., *The SAGE Handbook of Architectural Theory* (London: SAGE, 2012), 7.
9. Sylvère Lotringer and Sande Cohen, eds., *French Theory in America* (New York: Routledge, 2001).
10. Céline Bodart, "Architecture et déconstruction, remises en jeu d'une rencontre: Raconter, traduire, hériter" (PhD diss., Université Paris 8/Université de Liège, 2018).
11. Jane Rendell, *Critical Architecture* (New York: Routledge, 2007); Ole W. Fischer, "Architecture, Capitalism and Criticality," in Crysler, Cairns, and Heynen, *The SAGE Handbook*, 56-70.
12. Hilde Heynen and Sebastiaan Loosen, eds., "Marxism and Architectural Theory across the East-West Divide," Special Collection of *Architectural Histories* 6-7 (2018-2019). DOI: http://doi.org/10.5334/ah.401.

About the Authors

Matthew Allen has a PhD in the History and Theory of Architecture from Harvard University. Currently a Lecturer at the University of Toronto, Allen is trained as an architect and has completed degrees and worked in comparative history, physics, and computer programming. He previously worked for MOS, Preston Scott Cohen, UrbanData, and other firms at the leading edge of contemporary practice. Allen has written peer-reviewed historical and theoretical papers on computation, art, and architecture, as well as numerous critical essays in venues such as *Log*, *e-flux*, *Domus*, *Perspectives on Science,* and the *Journal of the Society of Architectural Historians*. His research has been supported by the Social Sciences and Humanities Research Council of Canada, the Jackman Humanities Institute, the Canadian Centre for Architecture, Gehry Technologies, and other institutions.

Karen Burns is an architectural theorist and historian based at the University of Melbourne. Her research focuses on feminist and design histories of architecture. She was a founding member of Parlour: Women, Architecture, Equity (2012-2018). Her forthcoming coauthored books include *The Bloomsbury Global Encyclopedia of Women in Architecture, 1960-2015* (Bloomsbury, 2021) and *Parlour, Women, Architecture, Activism* (MIT Press, forthcoming 2020/2021). Her essays have been included in *Desiring Practices* (Black Dog), *Post-Colonial Space(s)* (Princeton UP), *The Josephine Baker Reader* (McFarland & Co), *A Gendered Profession* (Routledge), *AA Women in Architecture* (AA Publications), *Architecture and Feminisms* (Routledge), *Women, Practice, Architecture* (Routledge), *Industries of Architecture* (Routledge), *Speaking of Buildings* (Princeton UP), and *Production Sites* (Routledge). She has published journal essays in *Assemblage*, *19*, *Footprint*, *JAE*, *Architectural Theory Review*, and *Fabrications*.

Ole W. Fischer is an architectural theoretician, historian, critic, and curator; he teaches as Associate Professor at the University of Utah School of Architecture. Before his appointment in 2010, he taught at the ETH Zurich, Harvard GSD, MIT, and RISD. He has been appointed as visiting professor of architectural theory at the TU Vienna and the TU Graz. He lectured and published internationally on history, theory, and criticism of architecture, among other subjects in: *Archithese, Werk, JSAH, MIT Thresholds, Arch+, AnArchitektur, GAM, Umeni, Beyond, West 86th, Framework*, and *log*. He contributed chapters to various books, such as *The SAGE Handbook of Architectural Theory* (London: 2012) and *This Thing Called Theory* (London: 2016). He is the author of *Nietzsches Schatten* (Berlin: 2012) and coeditor of the peer-reviewed architecture journal *Dialectic* (since 2011/12).

Philip Goad is Chair of Architecture and Redmond Barry Distinguished Professor at the University of Melbourne and the Gough Whitlam Malcolm Fraser Chair of Australian Studies at Harvard University for 2019-2020. He is the coauthor of *Architecture and the Modern Hospital: Nosokomeion to Hygeia* (Routledge, 2019) and coeditor of *Bauhaus Diaspora and Beyond: Transforming Education through Art, Design, and Architecture* (Miegunyah Press/Power Publishing, 2019) and *Australia Modern: Architecture, Landscape, and Design* (Thames & Hudson, 2019). He was co-curator of the exhibit *Augmented Australia* at the Australian Pavilion at the Venice International Architecture Biennale in 2014, Visiting Professor at the Bengal Institute of Design in Dhaka in 2016, and Visiting Patrick Geddes Fellow at the University of Edinburgh in 2016. He is currently researching his next books, one on post–World War II Australian-US architectural relations, the other on Australian architect and critic Robin Boyd.

Hilde Heynen is a Professor of Architectural Theory at the University of Leuven, Belgium. Her research focuses on issues of modernity, modernism, and gender in architecture. In *Architecture and Modernity: A Critique* (MIT Press, 1999) she investigated the relationship between architecture, modernity, and dwelling. She also engaged with the intersection between architecture and gender studies, resulting in the volume *Negotiating Domesticity* (coedited with Gulsum Baydar, Routledge, 2005). She coedited the 2012 *SAGE Handbook of Architectural Theory* (with Greig C. Crysler and Stephen Cairns). More recently she published an intellectual biography of Sibyl Moholy-Nagy (Bloomsbury, 2019; Sandstein, 2019). She was president of the European Architectural History Network between 2016 and 2018.

Rajesh Heynickx is a Professor in Architectural Theory and Intellectual History at the University of Leuven, Belgium. He has published articles in *Modern Intellectual History, Modernist Cultures, Environment, and History* and *Architectural Theory Review*, among many others. In 2018, together with Stéphane Symons he acted as coeditor of *So What's New About Scholasticism? How Neo-Thomism Helped Shape the Twentieth Century* (De Gruyter, Berlin). At the University of Leuven's Department of Architecture, he is spokesman of the FWO-Scientific Research Network "Texts ≈ Buildings: Dissecting Transpositions in Architectural Knowledge (1880-1980)."

Paul Holmquist is an Assistant Professor of Architecture at Louisiana State University; his research and teaching focus on the interrelationship of architecture, political theory, and theory of technology, particularly in terms of conceptions and experience of the public realm. He holds a Doctor of Philosophy in Architectural History and Theory from McGill University, where his doctoral dissertation examined Claude-Nicolas Ledoux's architectural theory in relation to the moral and political philosophy of Jean-Jacques Rousseau. Holmquist has taught architectural history, theory, and design at universities in the United States and Canada, and his research has recently been published in *THE PLAN Journal*, *Chora 7: Intervals in the Philosophy of Architecture*, and *Reading Architecture: Literary Imagination and Architectural Experience*.

Sandra Kaji-O'Grady is Professor of Architecture at the University of Queensland. Between 2005 and 2018 she held successive leadership roles at the University of Technology, Sydney, the University of Sydney and the University of Queensland. Concurrently she conducted research in contemporary architecture, theory, and politics and was actively engaged in architectural criticism for professional journals. Her recent publications include two books coauthored with Chris L. Smith, *LabOratory: Speaking of Science and its Architecture* (MITP, 2019) and the anthology *Laboratory Lifestyles: The Construction of Scientific Fictions* (MITP, 2018). Her current research explores the ways in which animals, and pets especially, are brought into human societies as co-consumers and coworkers through architecture. She is also undertaking a collaborative project on the architecture of biocontainment.

Peter Lang is a former Professor of Architectural Theory and History at the Royal Institute of Art, Stockholm (2013-2019). While at the Royal Institute of Art, he founded R-lab, a research platform investigating a range of subjects from social conflict and symbolic spaces to material culture and environmental crises. R-lab, now based in Rome, continues to run independent research initiatives. Peter Lang earned a PhD in Italian history and urbanism at New York University in 2000 and works on the history and theory of postwar Italian architecture and design, with a focus on nineteen-sixties Italian experimental design, media, and environments. He has written on and curated a number of projects on the Italian Radical Design and on contemporary urban culture. He is a member of the Rome-based urban arts research group Stalker since 1997.

André Loeckx is Emeritus Professor of Architectural Theory at the University of Leuven, Belgium. He is the coeditor, with Hilde Heynen, Lieven De Cauter, and Karina Van Herck, of the volume *"Dat is Architectuur": Sleutelteksten uit de 20ste* *eeuw* (010, 2001). His research and teaching focused on the role of architecture and urban design in human settlements in a context of development, culminating in the volume *Urban Trialogues: Visions, Projects, Co-productions: Localising Agenda 21* (UN, 2005, coedited with Kelly Shannon, Raf Tuts, and Han Verschure). He also became involved with urban renewal in Flanders, Belgium, as an expert, a critic, and a motivator. These experiences are documented in volumes such as *Framing Urban Renewal in Flanders* (SUN, 2009) and *Urban Renewal in Flanders 2002-2011* (coedited with Els Vervloesem and Bruno De Meulder, ASP, 2012).

Sebastiaan Loosen is a scholar based at the University of Leuven, Belgium. After obtaining degrees in architectural engineering and in philosophy at the same university, he recently completed his doctoral dissertation, *Shaping Social Commitment: Architecture and Intellectuality in the 1970s and '80s* (2019), on the formative years of architectural theory in Belgium, more specifically on the various vantage points from which "the social" was addressed in architectural thought. The key themes that permeate his work are historiographical challenges, social commitment, and the intricacies of a globalizing architectural culture. On these themes, in addition to the current volume, he recently coedited, with Hilde Heynen, for EAHN's open access journal *Architectural Histories* a Special Collection on "Marxism and Architectural Theory across the East-West Divide." His current work aims to chart the role of architectural schools, centers, and institutes in contributing to the 1960-80s "development" agenda by offering "South-oriented" training programs in architecture, urbanism, and spatial planning.

Louis Martin is a Full Professor in Art History at the Université du Québec à Montréal. A nonpracticing architect, he holds a PhD in the History, Theory, and Criticism of Architecture from Princeton University. During the 1990s, he was curator of the Contemporary Architecture Collection at the Canadian Centre for Architecture. His research program aims at establishing a cartography of architectural theory, tracing its links with external fields since the 1960s with a focus on the thematic shifts of the internal dialectic of the discipline revealed by the historical transformation of its terminology. He is editor of *On Architecture: Melvin Charney, A Critical Anthology* (2013). He taught at the Université de Montréal, McGill University and University of Toronto. He published several essays in edited books and periodicals such as *Log*, *Assemblage*, *Future Anterior*, *Les Cahiers de la recherche architecturale et urbaine*, *JSAH*, *Exposé*, and *Casabella*, among others.

Joan Ockman is an architectural historian, critic, and educator. Currently the Vincent Scully Visiting Professor of Architectural History at Yale School of Architecture, she also holds appointments at the University of Pennsylvania and

Cooper Union. She previously taught at Columbia University's Graduate School of Architecture, Planning, and Preservation, where she served from 1994 to 2008 as director of the Buell Center for the Study of American Architecture. She began her career in the mid-1970s at the Institute for Architecture and Urban Studies in New York, where she was an editor of the *Oppositions* journal and the Oppositions Books series. Among her book publications are *Architecture School: Three Centuries of Educating Architects in North America* (2012), *The Pragmatist Imagination: Thinking about Things in the Making* (2000), and the award-winning *Architecture Culture 1943-1968: A Documentary Anthology* (1993). She was named a Fellow of the Society of Architectural Historians in 2017.

Carmen Popescu is an art and architectural historian, trained in Bucharest and in Paris, and currently Professor PhD Hab. of Architectural History at the Ecole Nationale Supérieure de Bretagne (Rennes, France). Her main research explores politics and ideology in their interaction with architecture, analyzing these connections from different points of view and projecting them on a historiographic background. She worked lengthily on the (tensed) rapport between centers and periphery. She published extensively on all these topics, organized several international conferences and took part in numerous such events. Recently, she started to examine the notion of transgression, that she addresses both as a reaction against the normativity of the era of modernity and as a new paradigm in the making. She is at the origin of the international research project TRANSGRESSING THE NORMED SPACE, which gathers scholars from different countries.

Ricardo Ruivo is a Portuguese architect, researcher, and teacher at the AA School of Architecture. He graduated in architecture at the Faculty of Architecture of the University of Porto in 2009, and holds a Master in architectural history. He finished his PhD, on the contradictions between architectural ideologies and political engagement around the Soviet avant-garde, at the Architectural Association in 2018. He has been tutor in History and Theory Studies at the AA since 2014, and currently teaches a diploma course on the history and Western historiography of Soviet architecture. Ruivo's research work mainly addresses the relationship between architectural form and political content in architectural discourse and in historiography, seen as ideological production. He gives particular importance to the problems surrounding architectures' own efforts at self-politicisation, with emphasis on how the writing of history influences and is influenced by the contemporary agendas.

Andrew Toland is a Lecturer in the School of Architecture at the University of Technology Sydney. He was previously an Assistant Professor of Landscape

Architecture at the University of Hong Kong. He holds degrees in architecture, law and economics. Current research work covers "realism" discourses in recent architectural culture; the political ecology and political economy of large scale infrastructure projects in Asia; and the historical and current intersections of landscape phenomena and evolving legal categories encompassing the non-human realm.

www.ingramcontent.com/pod-product-compliance
Ingram Content Group UK Ltd.
Pitfield, Milton Keynes, MK11 3LW, UK
UKHW021847140426
5217IPUK00022B/1636